/12

Responding
to
New
Realities

Responding to New Realities

Edited by Gilbert A. Jarvis

In conjunction with the American Council on the Teaching of Foreign Languages

National Textbook Company, *Skokie, Illinois 60076*

Foreword

The *ACTFL Review of Foreign Language Education, Volume 5* continues a series (initially the *Britannica Review of Foreign Language Education*) that is an annual attempt to collect, analyze, synthesize, and interpret the work of the profession.

The very demanding timetable for an annual review requires considerable cooperation among many persons. First and foremost, the work of the chapter authors, who had to meet very difficult deadlines, is acknowledged.

I also wish to thank C. Edward Scebold, Executive Secretary of ACTFL, for his splendid leadership and facilitation of the entire process. Likewise, thanks are due to the staff of National Textbook Company, in particular to Leonard Fiddle, Executive Vice President and Editorial Director; Carol Ann Goode, Managing Editor; and Karla Heuer, who skillfully edited the final manuscript.

The Advisory Committee—John L. D. Clark, Charles Hancock, Thomas Kelly, and Stephen Levy—is to be credited with planning the volume's structure. They also provided considerable advice and consultation, for which I am grateful.

Special thanks are due to Carol Hosenfeld, who in the role of Assistant to the Editor contributed greatly to all phases of the volume's preparation—from initial planning, through many hours of editing, to final preparation of the index. Finally, I want to thank Ronna Turner, Cathy Kaiser, and especially Mary LaBelle for their conscientious performance of the hundreds of clerical tasks involved.

Contents

1

Introduction

Gilbert A. Jarvis
The Ohio State University

During the past few years many pessimists within the profession have wanted the name "foreign language teacher" added to the list of endangered species. Not all had the same motivation. For some this perception was their most honest appraisal of what they saw happening to foreign language education. Many others broadcast the message of doom in the hope that the warning would arouse colleagues to action, for it is well known that extreme threats often provoke equally intense affirmative action that has far-ranging remedial effects. Others were motivated by the notion that they could elicit sympathy from outside the language teaching establishment. The status of the profession became a plight where foreign language educators were reduced to the appeal of the "underdog."

But foreign language education is a very heterogeneous collection of approximately 80,000 people. It encompasses many who have chosen not to expend their energies in a collective wringing of hands. They have chosen an affirmative route. Each in his own way has elected to *respond to the realities* around him. Not all the responses have been glamorous or dramatic. In some instances teachers have thought, have questioned, and have read; and in this inquiry they have had insights that were new to them—and often to the profession. Some have disseminated their insights for the benefit of others by writing in the professional literature. Others have simply walked into their class-rooms, offices, or research laboratories and have done something they had never done before. Still others have discussed with colleagues for

---

Gilbert A. Jarvis (Ph.D., Purdue University) is Associate Professor of Foreign Language Education at The Ohio State University, where he teaches graduate courses in second-language learning, research, and measurement. He has also taught courses in the undergraduate teacher-education program. Dr. Jarvis has taught French at the elementary, secondary, and college levels. He is Head of the Physiology and Psychology of Language Learning Section of the *ACTFL Annual Bibliography*. His articles have appeared in publications such as *Foreign Language Annals*, *The Modern Language Journal*, *The NALLD Journal* and *The Britannica Review of Foreign Language Education*. He has directed teacher workshops and spoken to teacher groups in many parts of the country.

the first time questions that for more than a decade had seemed to be answered. In many corners of the profession a teacher has talked with a student—and has learned. Researchers have begun to look intensively at "student factors" or "individual differences."

Those who have responded to the realities elude a single label, but they all have in common one characteristic. They share a trait with Mrs. Wendy Perkins, former Spanish teacher in Worthington (Ohio) High School, who provides a vivid, concrete example of one person's response. During the summer of 1972 she worked more than 300 hours in preparation for individualizing her third-year class. Working with only a typical selection of textbooks, materials, and equipment, she created a continuous-progress program. She recalls how on the first day of classes she heard her own voice tremble as she was saying things to her students that she had never said before. She felt sensations of uncertainty and even loneliness. But by the end of the year Mrs. Perkins was communicating more than the usual demographic data (such as the year's having been her first in which not a single student dropped the course). She was also poignantly recounting how she could never again stand before a full-class group without reading the messages in their eyes: "Please say that again." "Oh, you're not going to say that again, are you?" "Could you say that in a different way?"

Wendy Perkins' response was individualized instruction. The responses of others in the profession range as far as creative imagination has carried them. But they all share a zeal, a commitment to action, that involves the expending of more energy than the norm. Furthermore, their work involves efforts to help people—to benefit society. Implicitly they embody a belief that the kinds of learning subsumed under what we know as foreign language education are indeed worthwhile. Our frequent verbalizations of such beliefs have made them trite, but too often the verbalizations have not been translated into committed behavior. So many of us have been able to "talk the talk," but so few of us have been able to "walk the walk."

The work of many who have "walked the walk" is described in this volume. Ironically, sharing information about innovation is dangerous. The more innovative the work, the greater the likelihood that some segments of the profession will reject it. The foreign language teacher whose work resembles his work of five, ten, or 15 years ago will find relatively few of his thoughts or practices described in these chapters. In experiencing this mild form of future shock he may reject the unfamiliar as unrealistic, irrelevant, or impractical for his unique situation. (It is ironic that this same concept of "uniqueness," which we so often ignore in the day-to-day interaction with our students, becomes one of the first we invoke when we need a self-serving argument.)

Too many of us have grown comfortable in repeating ourselves and may even have come to accept the repetition as inevitable. Within this frame of reference, change is dismissed under a rubric such as "new jargon for old ideas." "There is nothing new under the sun," they chant. Yet one can say with an equal amount of truth that there is little "*unchanging* under the sun." In foreign language education all the components of the educational process have changed. The goals are now different; the strategies and arrangements for attaining the goals are different. Perhaps most drastically, learners with different experiences and attitudes populate today's classes. Thus, in some domains the change is real and extreme. The pluralistic concept, for example, is radically different from the profession's former self-righteous prescription. In other domains the change is of lesser magnitude but is nonetheless real. A learning resource center for tape-guided practice is clearly not a language laboratory, but the same equipment may be used. In still other domains the change is no more than new nomenclature for existing phenomena. One sees repeated changes in grammatical terminology, when the underlying conceptualization remains unchanged.

One can argue that all these kinds of change—from profound to superficial—are in fact healthy and necessary. Change seems to be an inherent part of the educational system. Thus, to spurn change merely because some of the change is superficial is to ignore the expectations of society. When change is absent within a segment of education, that segment is inevitably faulted. The status quo may have advantages, but the segment is out of step with the parade.

Foreign language education must continue to respond to the realities that surround the profession. Change must be continual and vigorous, irrespective of the extent to which it is subsequently shown to be substantive or superficial. The voice crying "nothing new" does the profession a genuine disservice—*even* in those rare correct instances. Some of the responses described in this volume will remain forever a part of the educational process; others will be forgotten in five years. This is not a flaw but a sign of vitality.

The reading of this volume is facilitated by an awareness of its thematic structure. The four divisions (Realities, Reflections, Responses, and Responsibilities) are interrelated.

In the first division Stephen L. Levy has vividly delineated the realities we face. Many represent the legacy of past errors made by the

3

profession, but others are simply factors in society that require accommodation or modification within foreign language education. Some of the realities become *opportunities*, if the profession responds appropriately.

In the Reflections division Wahneta M. Mullen has looked at change and innovation with two purposes. She has reflectively surveyed the general direction of change and has analytically identified contributing factors and consequences. Her extensive research is subsumed under the revealing chapter title "Many Learners, Many Goals, Many Curricula."

The third division of the volume, Responses, is comprised of a series of chapters that describe in significant detail the responses made by various segments of the profession to the realities. The detail provided should facilitate the reader's evaluation of the material as well as permitting its utilization when he sees it as applicable to his work.

In the first Response chapter María M. Swanson writes a powerful justification for bilingual education and a careful evaluation of the directions of extant programs. She describes flourishing programs and extrapolates principles for establishing successful curricula.

Thomas E. Kelly provides a rationale for interdisciplinary studies as well as an up-to-date summary of programs. He comprehensively considers the relationship of institutional structures to the teaching-learning process. Kenneth A. Lester and Toby Tamarkin provide the reader with the theoretical and historical background of "career education," a concept that has already permeated many other areas of education. They see a potential relationship with foreign language education and effectively describe programs where this potential has already been realized.

O. R. Dathorne sees literature from "outside the metropolis" as a response to a felt need of many students. Rather than merely reviewing pedagogical techniques, Dathorne chooses to identify and describe significant twentieth-century literature that has particular meaning for today's students. He further provides very pertinent analytic and background information for the teacher (who until now has had little access to this literature).

June K. Phillip's chapter may well be the first document in which the profession is clearly perceived as being within an era of individualized instruction rather than merely looking forward to it (or wondering whether it is a valid direction). She provides descriptions of programs of varying scope and a useful synthesis of the views and research of those who have already had several years of experience with such curricula.

Howard L. Nostrand in "Empathy for a Second Culture: Motivations and Techniques" has taken a large step toward providing the profession with a theoretical framework for the culture component of foreign language teaching. He describes classroom strategies and devices that are organized into a practicable pattern.

Progress in foreign language education depends upon much more than what happens in classrooms. Classroom practice is optimal when it is based upon theory that explains seemingly diverse phenomena and therefore helps us to understand the behavior encountered. Terence J. Quinn thoughtfully and lucidly documents the current status of our "Theoretical Foundations," with particular emphasis upon the evolution of the role of linguistics. He also describes exciting directions in several emerging disciplines.

In the final division, Responsibilities, two leaders in foreign language education look carefully upon the implications of today's changing status. William E. De Lorenzo considers aspects of teacher education as they impact upon future directions of the profession and identifies several specific areas of responsibility. C. Edward Scebold focuses upon the changing role of professional associations. He considers what is required of both the individual and the organization if we are to mobilize a strong profession.

In a scholarly and creative way the authors have documented transition in foreign language education during 1972. They have collected, analyzed, synthesized, and interpreted information with a particular goal in mind. Their aim has been not merely to inform but to provide the reader with information in a form that will permit him to make use of it in responding to his own realities.

Realities

2

The realities facing the profession

Introduction

Stephen L. Levy

John Dewey High School
Brooklyn, New York

Volume 4 of the ACTFL *Review of Foreign Language Education* had as its theme "a reappraisal." Its mission was twofold: to appraise the part in foreign language education and to make projections into the future. The theme of this present volume of the *Review*, "responding to new realities," has a close affinity to that of its predecessor. Volume 5 examines the initial steps being taken to cope with and to direct the phenomena now surrounding the profession. In essence, this volume is an examination of the "now."

At a time when there is rapid and dramatic change within the profession, it behooves us to stop and examine the realities that exist in our operation. The current picture of foreign language education can be described as a collage of contradictions: There is innovation as well as stagnation within the profession; there is excitement as well as apathy; there is optimism as well as pessimism; and there is courage as well as fear.

A collage of contradictions

The student activism of the 1960s made us cognizant of the discontent felt by American youth toward our educational system. This activism, coupled with the declining enrollments and the abolition or easing of foreign language requirements by colleges and universities, has made us take a closer look at *what* we are doing, *how* we are doing it, *with whom* we are doing it, and *why* we are doing it. Charles E. Silberman (33) points out in his book *Crisis in the Classroom* that

the need of the moment, clearly, is not to celebrate our successes but to locate and remedy the weaknesses and failures. The test of a society, as of an institution, is not whether it is improving, although

Stephen L. Levy (M.A., Middlebury College) is the Assistant Principal (Supervision) of the Foreign Language Department at John Dewey High School, Brooklyn, New York. He studied at the Universidad Nacional Autónoma de México and attended NDEA Institutes in the United States and Spain. He is a member of ACTFL, AATSP, AATF, and NYSAFLT. He has served as a consultant at workshops on the individualization of instruction in foreign languages sponsored by West Chester State College, ACTFL, NYSAFLT, and the Northeast Conference on the Teaching of Foreign Languages. His articles have appeared in *Foreign Language Annals, Bulletin of the NYSAFLT* and *Individualization of Instruction in Foreign Languages: A Practical Guide*, published by The Center for Curriculum Development.

certainly such a test is relevant, but whether it is adequate to the needs of the present and of the foreseeable future (p. 29). *Adequate to today's needs?*
This is indeed what Volume 5 has set out to do.

Goals and objectives of foreign language education

A perusal of the foreign language curriculum manuals that have appeared during the past two decades indicates three primary goals of foreign language instruction: language competence, an insight into culture, and an acquaintance with literature. Within these broad goals the communication aspect of language has received the greatest emphasis. Formal analysis of language, acquaintance with literature, and translation have received less attention until after communication skills have been developed (Lawson, 22; 28; Powers, 29). *Recent goals*

The primary objective of foreign language instruction prior to 1959 had been reading, with emphasis on analysis of grammatical rules and translation. High school students who sat in foreign language class-rooms of that era were the intellectually elite or college-bound students. In 1959, however, objectives and methodology changed so that the primary objective of foreign language instruction became communication, with emphasis on the listening and speaking skills. The decade of the 1960s saw the shift from grammar-translation to audiolingual to an eclectic approach that harmonizes the four language skills (Lipton and Mirsky, 26).

The Sputnik era in American education and its effect on foreign language instruction in particular resulted in the primacy of the communicative skill. The skills of reading and writing the foreign language were relegated to positions of lesser importance in the time hierarchy of instructional programs. Students and parents alike, caught up by the claims of the "new key" in foreign language instruction and its consequent "near-native proficiency," anticipated levels of achievement similar to those advertised by commercial language schools. "Instant language" became the desired goal of the students, but when they found that they could not "rap" on a topic of interest to them in the foreign language, as they were able to do in their other language course (namely, English), their interest and motivation waned, and as a result, the numbers of students who chose to continue their foreign language sequence declined. *Disillusioned students*

Teachers were equally guilty in the proliferation of these widely acclaimed but unrealistic goals and objectives. Strasheim (38), in her *Unrealistic teachers* discussion of the inability of teachers to "tell it as it is" when talking about their own teaching prowess, states that ". . . this inability 'to tell it as it is'—instead of 'like we'd like it to be' has led to some of the loftiest objectives and most incredible curriculum guides in the annals of printing" (p. 339).

While we implemented these unrealistic goals, we were insensitive to the students who sat before us in our classes. An unfortunate common denominator of the grammar-translation and audiolingual methodologies is that each method had the *same goal* for *all* students enrolled in the foreign language program. Individual differences and interests had not been considered when the underpinnings of these methods were established; yet, while we were changing our goals and objectives to what we believed to be more realistic and relevant within a closer world community, the attitudes, goals, objectives, and basic values of our students were also undergoing rapid and drastic changes. *Monolithic thinking* *Changing students*

The 1970 Northeast Conference Report (27) pointed out that students often enter the study of a foreign language with high aspirations and expect to be able to use the foreign language as they do their native tongue. Students, and their parents as well, have *unrealistic goals* when we consider the training the school can offer and the time period available. School administrators, moreover, often oversell foreign language programs in order to obtain adequate enrollments in the courses. Thus there is an inherent potential for disappointment and loss of motivation. *Motives of administrators*

Ironically, the statement on objectives made by the Modern Language Association in 1953 still has validity today. Modern language study was viewed as a progressive, never complete experience. Learning should have positive value at any point in the process. Language study, in a skillfully taught program, provides a new experience that broadens the student's horizon. The student's language experience involves understanding the spoken language, speaking, reading, gaining a new understanding of language and its structure, and deepening and expanding the knowledge of another people's culture as well as his own. The emphasis given these areas and the interests and aptitude of the learner affect his progress. Language skills may never be perfected, but the result of the student's contact with the language and its culture should enrich him throughout his life. The language experience benefits the slow student as well as the gifted student (Birkmaier, 3). Although these are the underlying rubrics of the present curriculum manuals, have we implemented each of the pronouncements made by

11

the Modern Language Association within the democratic bases of the American educational system?

Rivers (31) points out that over the years the foreign language profession has vigorously structured and shaped its learning experiences (which inevitably became inflexible) and has eliminated all but those students whom teachers deemed most likely to adapt to the pattern of the often-stereotyped advanced courses. The quixotic search for the ideal, a vestige of the restrictive and selective policy of higher education, where all enrolled students are to achieve "near-native mastery of the language in all skills" has caused us to create a vicious cycle of frustrated and hostile foreign language dropouts who go on to become parents and community leaders who do not want a replication of these experiences for their children. *An elitist profession*

A cycle that haunts us

Rivers draws from the views of Keniston (20) when she points out that the present generation is born with affluence and is also bored with it. Today's students are the first to have an extended and leisured youth with opportunities for intellectual, emotional, and moral development without the basic demands previous generations have felt in meeting their societal responsibilities. The students of this generation are advocates of a flexible, unstructured, qualitative, and experiential education. Nevertheless, efforts to democratize foreign language education by involving a broader segment of the American student population have met with minimal success. There remains a dramatic difference between the foreign language enrollments in inner-city schools and well-to-do suburban schools as well as among various geographic regions. In some communities progress is being made. In more and more instances students enrolled in foreign language courses are not solely representative of the intellectually elite students of previous decades. The door has been opened to foreign language instruction for *all* students. In presenting the case for foreign languages for all students, Sandstrom and Pimsleur (32) present such arguments as "We do not know whom to exclude," "We cannot predict who will need foreign language in later life," "Foreign lands are more accessible," "Foreign language study is educationally beneficial," "There are new educational and career opportunities that require foreign language expertise," and "Exclusion may be damaging" (pp. 110–12). *FL for all*

The goals of foreign language programs have too often been stated in broad and sweeping terms. The generalizations expressed in the statements of goals led the student to formulate his own erroneous and unrealistic goals with respect to what he would achieve in the program in which he was enrolled during the time he spent in the program. *Difficulties in stating goals*

12

Within this context, both the teacher and the student were unaware of the achievable behavior that would result after the student's participation in that language program. The present goals of foreign language programs are being founded on behavioral objectives that leave no doubt in the mind of the learner and the teacher about the realistic expectations of the program. Valette and Disick (41, pp. 4–5) indicate the multiple values of performance objectives in foreign language education today. Yet Rivers (31) cautions us not to focus too much attention on the formal structure of our programs while implementing such innovations as behavioral objectives for the same content as always.

In reestablishing and redesigning our goals and objectives for foreign language education in the 1970s, the profession must learn from its experiences in the past. Any lock step philosophy that is further bound by restrictive procedures in the selection of students and involves a futile search for a nonexistent panacea in methodology will only breed apathy, disinterest, and the eventual alienation of students from our programs in even greater numbers. We have recognized a diversity and pluralism in the languages of the world and in their speakers, and we must build diversity and pluralism into our programs if we are to be a valid part of the educational system.

Student and community attitudes

Society is never static. Education has always been viewed as man's preparation for his role in society. Thus the school is the microcosm of that larger society into which each human being must pass. The effects of international, national, and local catastrophes are felt within the microcosm of the school. Today, however, changes in the larger society have been occurring at so rapid a pace that the schools are caught in a time lag. The changing role of man in society is also causing havoc in the schools, for the traditional role played by man is being replaced by his own genius, technology. Therefore, the school, if it is to remain a true reflection of the greater society, must constantly reexamine and reevaluate its programs and its policies to prepare the youth of today for a meaningful and active role in the society of their tomorrow.

Reality: the rate of change in society

Foreign language instruction has been affected by this change in the present educational milieu. Technology and our nation's involvement in an easily accessible and closer world community have given greater justification for the study of foreign languages by all members of the school community. Yet the students in our secondary schools

13

and colleges are not rushing to register for our courses. In large numbers they are conspicuously avoiding enrollment in foreign language curricula.

The United States is one of the few countries where a monolingual person can be considered an educated man. This country has never placed importance on the study and mastery of languages as have other countries. Immigrants to the United States at the end of the 19th century and at the beginning of the 20th century sought to assimilate themselves and their offspring as quickly as possible into the dominant culture by learning English. The common bond of the "melting pot" of various ethnic heritages was the abandonment of the mother tongue.

The study of a foreign language has traditionally been limited to those students who aspire to college entrance, and it has consequently come to be regarded as an "elitist" subject. It was elitist because the children of the socially elite broadened their cultural background, and elitist in the middle class home because language study was a status symbol and was usually indicative of the child's intellectual ability in other areas (Sandstrom and Pimsleur, 32).

The student of the 1970s is more aware, more active, more articulate, and more open in his challenge to the status quo than his predecessors. The effect of student involvement and leadership exemplified by the activism on the college campuses during the last years of the 1960s was felt in the secondary schools as well. Since the secondary school is the avenue for entrance into a college or university, it is only natural that the effects of the changes in the entrance and degree requirements, as well as changes in the attitudes of the students, would be replicated on the secondary school level.

Attitude toward foreign language study plays a significant role in a student's decision to begin, to continue, or to terminate his language study. Dernorsek (8) suggests that the most frequent causes of attrition in foreign language enrollments, as evidenced by attitudinal studies conducted in various parts of the United States, are loss of interest, poor grades, a feeling that no additional study would be required for college preparation, completion of the requirement, fear that the next level would be too hard, preference for another subject, scheduling difficulties, and the advice by the student's counselor to take a different subject because his language grades were not very good.

The youth of the 1970s are not *goal* oriented; they are *role* oriented, and they want to be active participants in everything they do. They are not willing to put in countless hours to achieve a goal that is nebulous

14

and irrelevant to their present lifestyles. They do not have the same long-range goals that the generations of the 1950s and 1960s had. They are no longer a captive audience; and school, as a reflection of society, has changed to meet these youngsters on a more equal footing. The easing or abolition of the language requirement for admission to a college or university and the concept of "open enrollment" that is practiced in many colleges now provides easy accessibility to a higher education for students of all academic backgrounds. Thus, the rapid change in the student population is a reality that the profession dare not overlook.

Foreign language requirements in colleges

Toffler in *Future Shock* (39) doubts that today's curriculum "makes sense," and to make his point he invites the reader "to explain to an intelligent fourteen-year-old why algebra or French or any other subject is essential for him" (p. 410). He sees adult answers as usually evasive for the simple reason that "the present curriculum is a mindless holdover from the past."

An inspection of the foreign language entrance and degree requirements provides an explanation for foreign language attrition. The MLA's Fall 1970 survey of foreign language entrance and degree requirements showed a significant decline in the prevalence of foreign language requirements in United States colleges (Brod, 4). In 1965–66, 33.6 percent of the colleges surveyed reported an entrance requirement in foreign languages. In 1970–71, only 27.4 percent reported the continuance of the entrance requirement. Degree requirements have also changed. In 1965–66 88.9 percent reported a requirement in foreign languages for the B.A. degree; in 1970–71 the percentage dropped to 76.7 percent. Brod also indicates that the effect of changes in requirements upon enrollment trends is complicated by the fact that not all institutions abolish the foreign language requirements outright; many colleges decrease the number of required semesters or expand the number of options available to the student.

Entrance requirements

Degree requirements

This inference of decreased enrollments as a result of the trend toward the abolition or reduction of foreign language requirements is based on the results of the MLA's 1970 Survey of Foreign Language Entrance and Degree Requirements. This survey was conducted concurrently with the enrollment survey, but the questionnaires from which it drew its data were addressed to foreign language department chairmen rather than to registrars. A consistent pattern of declining enrollments in those institutions in which there was some easing of the foreign language requirements was noted.

The enrollment statistics in foreign languages (which will be examined in the next section of this chapter) also indicate an increase in enrollment in the category of "less commonly taught" languages such as Chinese, Hebrew, Japanese, and Portuguese. These figures can also point out a new trend in foreign language study: a resurgence of ethnic pride in one's heritage as motivation for studying a particular language.

Enrollments

Enrollment statistics over the past few years were the first indicators that problems existed in foreign language education in the United States. Throughout the 1960s the statistics indicated a rosy upward trend in foreign language enrollments. Suddenly, the trend was reversed, and enrollments began to decline. Reasons offered have been quaint. Was this decline in enrollments the result of the "pill" (a factor that may diminish the school-age population), or was it that the students were heeding the advice of the Surgeon General (. . . is harmful to your health)? It was not the former because in 1970 there were 13,301,883 students enrolled in the public secondary schools, Grades 9 to 12, as opposed to 12,721,352 in 1968 (12). The same holds true for enrollments in higher education: total college enrollments in the United States in 1970 were 8,484,026 as compared to 7,513,091 in 1968 (Brod, 4). Thus, the latter, albeit a facetious response, may be a more valid response in explaining the decline in foreign language enrollments. An examination of the current context in which we operate will probably indicate the varied reasons for the decline in foreign language enrollments.

Causes of the decline
A simplistic cause?

A facetious cause?

The Fall 1970 Survey of Foreign Language Enrollments in Public Secondary Schools (12), conducted by the staff of the American Council on the Teaching of Foreign Languages under contract with the United States Office of Education, confirms the widespread suspicion within the profession that the growth trend of the 1960s has been reversed. In 1968, 27.7 percent of the public secondary school enrollment was registered in modern foreign language study. In 1970 this enrollment declined to 26.4 percent. On the college level the picture is similar. Brod (4) states that since the last report in 1968 the overall decline in foreign language enrollments has been about 1.4 percent. The 1970 survey is the first in the series of college enrollment surveys that showed

Losing ground in the total curriculum

16

this decline. This is an alarming figure because there is a continued, steady growth of college enrollments in general, yet foreign languages are not playing the role in the college curriculum that they once did.

The MLA's foreign language research staff is completing its Fall 1972 survey of enrollments in foreign languages in United States colleges and universities. In a report comparing registration figures for Fall 1972 with those for Fall 1970 for a representative sample of 1,312 colleges (about 55 percent of the total number of colleges offering foreign languages), we see a decline of 8.7 percent. The data require careful interpretation, however. For example, a decrease of 10.6 percent was indicated for four-year institutions, but the junior colleges included in the sample showed an increase of 3.8 percent (Brod, 5). *Junior colleges: an exception*

The latest data: disconcerting

Enrollment by language

Spanish continues to be the language with the largest enrollments. In the public secondary schools, the enrollment grew from 1,698,034 in 1968 to 1,810,775 in 1970. On the college level, Spanish enrollments rose from 364,870 in 1968 to 389,150 in 1970. French followed Spanish in total enrollment of students in the public secondary schools. However, a downward trend in the enrollment is noticed: 1,328,100 in 1968 as compared with 1,230,686 in 1970. On the college level in 1968 388,096 students were enrolled, while in 1970 the enrollment decreased to 359,313. In the public secondary schools, German had an enrollment of 423,196 in 1968. This number decreased to 410,535 in 1970. In higher education, the figures for German went from 216,263 in 1968 to 202,569 in 1970. Enrollment in Russian has also decreased: 24,318 students enrolled in 1968 as compared with 20,162 students in 1970. The college enrollments follow the same pattern: 40,696 in 1968 as compared with 36,189 in 1970. Italian is the language that has shown the most growth between the two surveys. In the public secondary schools in 1968 26,920 students were enrolled. In 1970 there were 27,321 students. On the college level in 1968 there were 30,359 students enrolled in Italian courses, while in 1970 the number jumped to 34,244. *Italian: the largest increase*

French: the largest decline

Enrollments in other languages such as Hebrew, Japanese, Chinese, and Swahili continued to grow. Brod (4) also reports that "while registrations in four-year colleges and universities declined by 3.9 percent, registrations in the junior colleges continued to grow unimpeded, although not at the spectacular rate prevalent in the early- and mid-1960s (18.0 percent between 1968 and 1970, compared with 47.2 percent between 1960 and 1963)" (p. 46). *Other languages*

The sample from the Fall 1972 survey of foreign language enroll- ments in U.S. colleges and universities referred to earlier indicates the following downward trends in languages: French enrollments dropped 16.7 percent, German 12.5 percent, Italian 5.9 percent, Spanish 5.4 percent, and Latin 7.7 percent. It also shows a slight increase for Russian—0.6 percent—and Ancient Greek—24.4 percent. The aggre- gate increase between 1970 and 1972 was 20.3 percent for the category of "less commonly taught" languages. Chinese, Hebrew, Japanese, and Portuguese continue to be the fastest growing languages in this category.

Most recent data: pessimistic

Where does the attrition take place?

Dernorsek (8) points out that the effect of the general loosening of the high school graduation language requirement or the college entrance requirement may be reflected in the decline in enrollment in beginning language classes in 1970 when compared to the 1968 figures. The percent of beginning-course students in French, German, and Spanish who elected a second-level course remained about the same between 1968 and 1970—47.6 percent. Despite the reduction trend in requirements, third-course enrollments in the three languages rose approximately 3 percent over their 1968 levels. In 1970, 39.7 percent of the students enrolled in second-level courses elected third- level courses as opposed to 36.8 percent in 1968. Attrition is usually greater after second-level courses than after first-level courses because many students discontinue their foreign language study after they have fulfilled a two-year requirement. The length of sequence for foreign languages is only two years or less in 44 percent of public secondary schools. An examination of the 1970 third-level course enrollment from the standpoint of beginning-level enrollments indicates that 18.9 of an initial 100 students who enrolled in Course I continued into Course III.

Attrition after the second level

Why are we losing or leaving behind more than 80 percent of the students who begin Course I in our foreign language programs? The reports of Hancock (15) and Dernorsek (8) identify many of the reasons students give for terminating their study of a foreign language when they do. Moreover, we cannot ignore the role of attitude as a factor that contributes to a student's successful mastery of a second language. Nor can we bury our heads hoping that when we look up, the realities of current foreign language enrollment patterns will have disappeared. We must learn to translate student attitudes into programs that will sell readily on the current educational market. Dernorsek

18

(8) puts it succinctly: "As language study becomes more and more a "free market" commodity, it becomes subject to the laws of supply and demand. And in any market, the vendor's survival depends both on the quality of his product and his ability to create and interpret the demand" (p. 4).

Language study and the free market

If enrollment statistics and statistics dealing with college entrance and degree requirements in foreign languages do accurately predict a trend for the future, the reality of our situation is fraught with negativism, apathy, pessimism, and fear. Yet this need not be a negative factor. We have long had a captive audience of students in our foreign language classes who were there because the study of a foreign language was a requirement for admission to the college of their choice. These students were also joined by others who had a genuine interest in learning and mastering another tongue. But the former group of students was usually in the majority, and too often they went through the motions of foreign language learning but never felt that they had really learned the language. Perhaps this abolition or lessening of the language requirement will help us to formulate a curriculum that has realistic and achievable goals in consonance with the needs and interests of our students in their present and foreseeable future. As reflected in the "responses" in this volume, this fear of extinction is serving as a catalyst for change—positive change—that will make foreign languages a vital and meaningful and achievable subject area for *all* students. Individualization of instruction, personalization, interdisciplinary courses, bilingual education, and the concept of career education within foreign languages are responses that will strengthen our position in the total curriculum. Foreign languages will no longer be "harmful to their health" because the students will find success, satisfaction, and relevancy in our courses.

Abolition of requirements

Financial allocations

The bubble has burst! During the latter part of the 1950s and well into the decade of the 1960s the new goals of foreign language education received the financial support of the federal government through the National Defense Education Act (NDEA). This federal program provided funds for the establishment of summer institute programs for teachers, at which the nation's teachers could be retrained in the latest methodologies and could work with the newest materials that had been developed in foreign language education. NDEA funds were also provided to school districts for the purchase of audiovisual aids and the

The dollar crisis

19

installation of language laboratories. These were expected to reinforce the philosophy of the audiolingual method and the emphasis on foreign language teaching for the goal of communication. It was hoped that teacher-training programs would adopt the philosophy, spirit, and curriculum ideas engendered in these institutes and thereby improve foreign language teaching in the United States. The allocation of these funds did accelerate inquiry into foreign language learning and teaching, but the desired effect on the college teacher-training programs was not achieved.

Only partial success

When the federal funding was exhausted, the foreign language teachers looked to their local school districts for the same commitment that the federal government had offered. School boards and taxpayers, overburdened by the increasing per pupil cost of education, were not receptive to increasing school taxes in order to meet the rising costs of education. As funds decreased, administrators were forced to spend their monies cautiously and judiciously. Invariably, "the pinch of funds" was felt in foreign language programs across the country because administrators were not willing to allocate excessive amounts of money to programs that reached only 26.4 percent of the total public secondary school enrollment (12). The reality is that FLES (Foreign Language in the Elementary School) programs have been eliminated from many school systems across the country, and in-service training programs for teachers have been cut. Federally funded programs are virtually nonexistent at this time.

Local monies not forthcoming

Hopefully, as our programs change to meet the needs and interests of our students, local school districts will become more receptive to assuming much of the financial burden that had previously been assumed by the federal government.

Professional insularity

Articulation

Ironically, a profession whose primary objective is "communication" has not succeeded in achieving this goal within its own ranks.

Communication: an ironic failure

Many foreign language educators are in agreement about the value of an extended sequence in foreign language learning for many of our youngsters. To provide for this extended sequence and to capitalize on the physiological elements that seem to enhance achievement in the development of language skills, FLES programs were initiated. FLES is also an invaluable tool in the inculcation of attitudes that are needed if the student is to live in a culturally pluralistic world.

Despite the proclaimed value of FLES and the evidence that successful programs exist, many programs have not achieved satisfactory results. The reality of FLES today is that although there are successful on-going programs, many FLES programs are being erased from the elementary school curriculum because of tighter and tighter budgets. Lipton (25) tells us that, in addition to budgets, other factors account for elimination of FLES programs, in particular the attitudes expressed by community leaders and administrators who question what the students learn. They believe that only a limited amount of language can be acquired in a FLES program, and that therefore it is a waste of time and money. The availability of qualified personnel can also be a factor that leads to the elimination of FLES programs. Very rarely is there specific certification for FLES teachers. Yet parents are consistently in favor of a FLES program for their children because it creates an aura of prestige. Moreover, parents are able to see tangible evidence that young children learn the language very well when they compare their own level of success in learning a foreign language in high school or college.

Lipton believes that even if you cannot have a well articulated program from elementary to junior high school, the FLES experience is invaluable in and of itself because it reaches children at a point in their lives that can never again be duplicated. Their minds and their hearts can be opened at an early age to other peoples of the world and other styles of living.

One of the reasons for the lack of articulation between school levels and programs (even where goals are supposedly constant) is that each of us on each level has a strong sense of self-preservation, and consequently, we sometimes tend to negate the accomplishments of other levels or programs. The junior high school does not provide for students who have had a FLES background, and they must start at the beginning once again. The secondary school negates the FLES and junior high school programs and is critical of the role they have played in the student's foreign language experience. The college questions what the student has learned in his secondary school language class and often maintains a philosophy that is similar to that of the secondary school toward the junior high school. An example of this juxtaposition is grammar-translation versus the goal of communication in the four skills of language learning. The college also frequently assigns the "required" or lower level courses to the round-robin of graduate assistants, while those instructors with greater skill and awareness of the goals of the program are given the upper level and more esoteric courses that are usually taken by the language major.

This lack of articulation and the lack of concern and provision for dealing with what the student brings to his language class from his previous language experience causes the student to "turn off" to foreign language study. Articulation between school levels and programs need not be an impossible dream but rather a vital requirement if foreign language instruction is to flourish. The individualization of instruction is a process that can be an effective tool in bridging the articulation gap because it can concern itself with each student and give merit and integrity to his previous language experience (Levy, 23).

Just as we compartmentalize ourselves by level—FLES, junior high school, secondary school, and college—so do we isolate ourselves from the remainder of the student's educational curriculum. Warriner (42) tells us that the Northeast Conference Report in 1966 (Corrin, 7) prepared one of the earliest articles dealing with an interdisciplinary approach in foreign languages. Hocking (16) states that the obsolete assumption under which foreign language programs have progressed over the years (that foreign language study is directed ultimately toward literature), coupled with the assumption that foreign language study was solely for college preparation, has shackled the development of a foreign language program that looks beyond its own limits of language study. Over the years general curriculum projects have not benefited from the participation of foreign language teachers, and language study has become an area unique unto itself. Changes in the ability and interests of students enrolled in foreign language programs, the more active and participatory role of students in designing curriculum, the option of a longer language sequence, and individualized instruction are all factors that are finally leading foreign language instruction out of a primarily unidirectional path and are giving it a new direction and a new role in educational programs (Warriner, 42).

Isolation from other curricular areas

Professional organizations

Another type of compartmentalization that has fostered professional insularity is that of the professional organizations that exist in the various languages on the national, state, and local levels. This plethora of organizations, each with its own dues, publications, and annual meetings, has weakened the position of the foreign language profession on the national level. Teachers have been asked to choose which organization they will support, and this division of loyalty has impeded the

Isolation within professional organizations

true cohesive spirit of a foreign language profession. Traditionally, teachers have affiliated themselves with the AAT (American Association of Teachers) of their major language on the national and local chapter levels. They may also be members of a regional or state organization that includes all foreign language teachers. Some teachers do not belong to any type of professional organization. The profession has been divided into teachers of French, Spanish, German, etc., and teachers of a particular level, for example, high school or college. The proliferation of organizations has thereby thwarted any potential clout that a strong national organization of foreign language teachers of all languages at all levels could have in improving the image and resuscitating the interest in foreign language study. Unity of action can only be achieved by a unified profession. Until this becomes a true reality, the present reality of duplication of effort and expense with only minimal gain and success will continue to detract from the individual and collective effort of language teachers.

No powerful voice

Unity

Methodology

Throughout the history of foreign language teaching in the United States there have been periods of boom and bust in enrollments. Events have had both positive and negative effects on foreign language programs. However, a pervading pedagogical dogmatism in teaching and learning strategies has risen over the years. The "traditional," or grammar-translation method of teaching, was carried over into the modern languages from the language programs in Latin and Ancient Greek that dominated the secondary school and college curricula. Reading comprehension was viewed as the only valid goal of these programs. The needs of the nation during World War II changed, and communication by means of the aural-oral skills became the focal point of the Army training schools. It was not until the latter part of the 1950s that the primary objectives of language study became listening comprehension and speaking, in addition to reading and writing. Federal support by means of the National Defense Education Act (NDEA), and Title VI in particular, helped to reshape and redirect foreign language instruction.

Pedogogical dogmatism

Throughout the history of foreign language instruction in the United States, teachers have sought *the* method of teaching, be it grammar-translation or the audiolingual method. We have been an "all-or-nothing" profession; the retraining of teachers in the audiolingual method that was incorporated under Title VI confirms this position.

An all-or-nothing profession

Moreover, the profession believed that it had found the panacea that would answer the needs of the students who now lived in a shrinking world community and that all would be well with foreign languages because our students would be able to "communicate" in the language they were studying. Technological advances (such as the language laboratory) were being used as an adjunct to the classroom situation in the audiolingual method. We *seemed* in truth to be part of the contemporary scene.

Our success was short-lived. The parrot-like responses of our students as a result of the audiolingual method and the tiresome and tedious repetition of dialogue lines in the classroom and again in the language laboratory were not what our students considered their goals in language study. Declining enrollments, campus unrest, and the changing interests and role of students have made the teachers look for another solution to right the "artificial boom" that had had undesirable consequences. A humanistic approach to foreign language teaching in which foreign language teaching would be placed in an appropriate cultural context became the theme of the 1972 Northeast Conference on the Teaching of Foreign Languages (Dodge, 10). Language learning and understanding of the cultural system complement each other, and each facilitates the learning of the other.

The recognition of individual differences and individual interests of our students has created another bandwagon: individualized instruction. In the past few years no foreign language conference has overlooked having individualization of instruction somewhere on its program. This topic was also the theme of Volume 2 of the ACTFL Review of Foreign Language Education (Lange, 21). However, the proponents of individualized instruction take great care to point out that the individualization of instruction is *not* a panacea, nor is it a teaching method *per se*. It is a process that does away with a lock step approach to foreign language learning with narrowly conceived objectives and a single goal for all students.

Individualization in perspective

An eclectic approach to the teaching of foreign languages has emerged. Teachers are no longer advocates of a single philosophy of foreign language teaching. They have learned of the dangers that such a commitment brings with it, and they have begun to implement the best features of each of the methodologies, thereby creating a functional eclecticism in which they feel comfortable and can meet the needs of all the students in their classes. Answers to teacher queries and problems are no longer dogmatic and simple. Teachers cannot turn to authority for answers; instead, teachers themselves must possess

Healthy eclecticism

Problem-solving ability

24

problem-solving skills. The transition from parroting doctrine to making sound decisions about instruction is not only difficult but also uncomfortable. This uneasiness is a reality to which all in the profession must adapt.

Materials and technology

Textbooks

Pedagogical dogmatism has also created a dogmatism in the types of materials that we have traditionally used in our classes. The publisher who must sell his product to stay in business typically has been receptive to the needs of his customers. Over the years textbooks that have appeared on the market have reflected the rigid, dictatorial philosophy *Publishers* that the profession had assumed in its methodology. Textbooks have been one-method oriented; they scarcely provided for alternatives within the class or for individual differences. Interests of the students and teachers who used these materials were likewise ignored. When the market flourished at the beginning of the 1960s, the publishers all climbed aboard the bandwagon and either commissioned new texts that reflected *the* method of that decade or revised already existing texts to conform with the methodology in vogue. The result of this movement has been a plethora of textbooks, each proclaiming its "super ability" to meet the needs of the profession by audio tapes of the drills in the accompanying book as well as by complete testing programs. With each revision or commission, the price per text soared. Teachers became advocates of a specific textbook series just as they did of a methodology or a learning strategy. Now we again see the beginnings of a similar movement in promising textbooks that are "the be *History repeats itself?* all and end all" for individualized programs.

In a paper presented at the 1972 Annual Meeting of the American Council on the Teaching of Foreign Languages, Steiner (37) spoke about "Sense and Nonsense in Foreign Language Textbooks." She *Sense and nonsense in texts* spoke of her projections regarding the textbooks of the future and indicated that they would be characterized by flexibility, adaptability (to ability levels and pacing), diversity and variety (of reading passages, conversational topics, vocabulary items, cultural materials, etc.), learning activity packets, accompanying audio visual aids, greater emphasis on history and culture, and areas such as career education in foreign languages. Accountability will also be a factor as publishers will be asked to prove how their materials help teachers and students reach

25

the desired objectives. Yet the textbooks of the future are completely contingent upon the profession. They are "designed by" the profession in the sense that publishers will produce only materials that will be selected and used by teachers. Simple concern for profit will preclude the publication of materials that will not be marketable because of changing methodologies and enrollment statistics.

Frequently teachers have kept their programs within the confines of textbooks, and the success of a foreign language program was the result of the versatility or lack of versatility of the materials. The time lag that exists in the school's ability to adapt to the needs of our ever-changing society is also an important factor in textbook materials. Timeliness is as important in the educational world as it is in the fashion world. It is for this reason that textbook series cannot and should not be the sole determinant in our curriculum. Magazines and newspapers are important additions to our daily classroom activities if we are to maintain and sustain a vital and contemporary program.

Audiovisual aids and the language laboratory

Traditionally the volume and diversity of hardware that exists for use in foreign language classes has always surpassed the volume, diversity, and quality of software. Smith (36) tells us that educational technology has failed to keep its promise for instruction because it has provided more potential capabilities than teachers could use. *Technology and teachers*

The traditional audio aid in the foreign language classroom has been the tape recorder. When language laboratories were installed by the thousands in schools during the 1960s, there was a dearth of taped material available. By providing tapes and records of the drills in their textbooks, publishers came to the rescue of teachers, who had been spending countless hours preparing their own tapes. Thus the creative spirit that could have encouraged foreign language study through imaginative materials was squelched by tapes that invariably mono- *Unimaginative tapes* toned the same unimaginative drills. For the teacher to find the specific drill he wanted at a particular time, he had to search through the tape to find the appropriate place, or he had to spend additional time breaking down the unit or lesson into smaller segments on other reels.

The roles of the language laboratory in the high school and in the *The language laboratory* college were different. In the high school the time spent in the laboratory usually replaced a class period. In the college the language laboratory was often used as an adjunct to the class, and students frequented the laboratory in their free time. In many secondary schools the language laboratory did not fulfill its promise. Consequently it soon fell into disuse and often became a storage room in the school.

Individualized instruction is resuscitating the role of the language laboratory in the foreign language program. It provides for additional practice in the aural-oral skills and can also be the setting for individual testing of these skills. Administrators today are often very cost conscious because of stringent budgetary allotments. Therefore, we have seen the entrance of another portable, compact, and reliable teaching and learning aid—the cassette recorder. Language laboratories are being replaced with media centers that have greater flexibility and adaptability within the new approaches being implemented in foreign language instruction today. Teachers, however, live with a legacy of unpleasant memories of the substantial sums of money spent on little-used language laboratories. These negative attitudes are a distinctly unfortunate reality of foreign language education today.

Language lab equipment: a new role

Smith also tells us that programmed instruction is another unful-filled dream because the materials have never fulfilled their potential. Good results and boredom are both characteristic of programmed materials. He adds that many quality programs that were produced at great expense continue to go unknown and unnoticed.

Programmed instruction

Computer-assisted instruction (CAI) is a system in which an instructional program is stored in a computer. It provides information and guidance to the student, along with control and evaluation, until a predetermined level of proficiency has been reached. There has been a great deal of writing on CAI in the previous volumes of the *ACTFL Review of Foreign Language Education* Series (Arendt, 1; Asher, 2; Clark, 6; Dodge, 9; Erickson, 11; Gougher, 13; Green, 14; Hoye, 17; Lipton, 24; Richardson, 30; Smith, 34; Smith, 35). Computer-assisted instruction is costly and time consuming to program, but it may well be worth the investment. It is becoming more common each year at all school levels, although there are few foreign language materials yet available.

CAI

Teacher-prepared materials

As more and more teachers become involved in the process of individualized instruction, more and more teacher-prepared materials are appearing in classrooms. They serve either to supplement or eliminate the traditional textbook. These materials appear as worksheets or learning activity packets. Many foreign language conferences now have exhibits of teacher-prepared materials (Keaton, 19) to provide other teachers with the opportunity to see what their colleagues are doing. Jenks (18) warns teachers to be careful when reviewing this

Teacher-prepared materials and individualization

type of material because of the inferior quality of teacher-prepared materials he has seen.

The reality of materials and technology in the foreign language classroom is now one of diversity and pluralism. No longer is the textbook or the basic series the sole instrument used in the learning process. The textbook does remain, but it is hoped that within this decade we shall see textbooks on the market that do not limit and "fence in" the innovative spirit of the teacher and the creative spirit of the student. Hopefully, in the field of technology the software will catch up with the advances made in the hardware so that quality materials will be prepared. CAI will expand and serve a vital function in the instructional program, especially in individualized programs. Teacher-prepared materials must always be a vital part of every type of class and language program that serves to meet the personalized needs of the students.

Testing

According to Clark (6), recent trends in foreign language teaching have direct and far-reaching implications in the area of testing. Variety in course goals makes the administration of uniform tests to measure course achievement a less feasible and less valid procedure than it once was.

In many communities throughout the nation aptitude tests have been administered to students to determine their suitability for foreign language study. Valette (40) states that the aptitude test should not be used to exclude students from language classes at any school level because other factors contribute to a student's success, including motivation, general intelligence, the effectiveness of the teacher and of the materials employed, and the time allowed for learning. Consequently, the present trend is to use the data provided by an aptitude test to help define and design the best type of course that is suited to the learning style of individual students (Clark, 6).

Aptitude: one factor in success

Many language tests attempt to measure the student's performance in the language. This trend is consonant with the emphasis on and the popularity of behavioral objectives in foreign language teaching today. Testing serves as a diagnostic indicator that carries with it a prescriptive factor that can lead the student to mastery. In criterion-referenced testing the criterion has been preestablished, and both the teacher and the students know what the expectancies are. Because this concept differs significantly from traditional testing, few teachers

Criterion-referenced evaluation

understand well the new rationale and procedures. Lack of widespread understanding of these procedures that suit new curricula is a reality the profession must soon remedy.

If the goal of foreign language instruction today is "communication," how is this goal tested and how is the student evaluated? Heretofore, student achievement and proficiency in a foreign language was measured by test items that stressed linguistic competence. Communicative competence has received less emphasis. We have been a profession that has stressed linguistic accuracy and has measured discrete-point items in our testing programs. This obsession (which is not even a reality in our native language) has thwarted the learner's desire to jump into a conversation, to try to express his ideas. He must cope with the fear of penalty for any linguistic errors he might make. Yet genuine language ability is the important factor in a communication-oriented program. However, the testing of real-life communication is a difficult feat to achieve within the constraints of the school setting, and this difficulty remains a reality with which the test makers must come to grips.

Evaluating communicative competence

Staffing the foreign language classroom

Recruitment

The reality of the job market today for foreign language teachers at all school levels is that the employer has a larger population from which to choose and can therefore exercise great selectivity.

A buyer's market

Teacher certification is usually granted by each state; no national norms guide the states in establishing their criteria for certification. Usually state certification is granted to prospective teachers on the basis of their having satisfactorily completed specific courses. This system is known as experience-based teacher education. Some states are now moving in the direction of performance-based teacher programs that appear more effective in assessing the competency of the prospective teachers in the teaching milieu.

The Report of the Working Committee of the 1971 Northeast Conference (Powers, 29, p. 29) questioned the actual existence of a "foreign language teaching profession" (which could influence certification). They concluded that the foreign language teaching profession is an "amateur profession" because (a) it has not yet found a stable and enduring place in the educational community; (b) it has not reached

Input from the profession

substantial agreement on purposes and goals; (c) it has not yet been able to systematize its specialized knowledge and transmit this new knowledge rapidly; (d) it has not set standards for membership; (e) it has not eliminated incompetents from its ranks; (f) it has not commanded full-time activity on the part of its members as well as a commitment to continuing self-renewal and improvement; (g) it has not devised a plan for recognizing and rewarding various levels of attainment; and (h) it has not achieved a functional and unified organization. Until the "foreign language teaching profession" comes to grips with these discrepancies, it will remain an amateur profession, and the certification of teachers will remain within the autonomous and often ill-informed aegis of the state education departments and local agencies.

Teacher training

Examination of the current educational scene has indicated that schools are far from static. Student attitudes and increased student involvement in decision making at all levels have created an ever-changing school scene. If the students change, so must the teachers; thus, we are witnessing the emergence of the teacher in a new role in today's educational process. College-based teacher-education programs must be aware of and receptive to the changes that are taking place. Their courses and programs must reflect these changes and prepare the prospective teachers for new and diversified roles in the nation's schools. *Need for teachers to change*

In the 1960s the National Defense Education Act (NDEA) provided for the retraining of language teachers within the new goals of foreign language education. Wolfe and Smith (43, p. 102) state that while the Institute and Fellowship programs had a meaningful impact upon the profession, the regular undergraduate curriculum in teacher education did not capture the spirit, the philosophy, and the competencies of the funded NDEA Institutes.

The new student in today's educational scene has redirected the teacher's role in this process. Consequently, teachers feel the need for reaffirmation of the goals of foreign language education and of their function in this process. They feel the need to be exposed to the new directions that are being taken within foreign language education today. The NDEA Institutes of the previous decade fulfilled this need. Today, however, with the absence of federally funded programs such as those sponsored by NDEA and EPDA, the various national, state, regional, and local organizations are attempting to meet these needs by means of various kinds of workshops. "Pre-conference workshops" *Workshops*

30

are held prior to their annual meetings. These workshops meet the voiced needs of their constituencies in such areas as individualized instruction and the teaching of culture. Summer workshops on the individualization of instruction are sponsored by colleges and universities and offer college credits to the teachers who enroll in them.

Teaching, like the learning process, is as much a continuum of development for the neophyte as it is for the experienced teacher. Teachers must recognize this when they enter the profession. A strong and effective profession is one that is committed to active participation in this continuum and believes that to retain its strength and viability *Constant regeneration needed* it must constantly regenerate itself through introspection, reading, and in-service study programs.

Differentiated staffing

In a foreign language program that emphasizes learning for mastery, the concept of differentiated staffing is based on the contribution of *Matching personnel to functions* three categories of personnel whose activities are carefully coordinated and blended into a meaningful program of learning activities. The three categories of personnel include the certified teacher, paraprofessional personnel (native aides, teacher aides, instructional aides, language laboratory technicians, and language secretaries), and the pre-service category that includes the student teacher and the teaching intern. While differentiated staffing may be a budgetary expedient in many communities (increased number of "staff" members for the same budget allowance), the educational underpinnings intend more time for the certified teacher to interact with the students in his charge by creating a smaller pupil/teacher ratio and thereby affording the student more individual attention. Differentiated staffing creates a "team approach" to foreign language learning and in essence can be highly effective when the division of responsibilities is so arranged that it capitalizes on the talents, abilities, and interests of all members of the differentiated staff in meeting the needs and interests of all the students enrolled in the program.

Summary

1 An examination of the "realities" of foreign language education today points out that the profession is passing through an exciting period of transition or renaissance. The stagnation, apathy, pessimism, and fear that were brought about by declining enrollments, the abolition or easing of the language requirement

in colleges, and the "new" student have created an emerging and blossoming multi-directional foreign language program in education today.

2 Our goals have been redesigned to meet the needs of the new students in our classes. We have also reassessed the reality of what can actually be achieved within the time the student spends learning the foreign language.

3 Students of all academic backgrounds have been welcomed into our classes, and our language programs are being designed around the needs and interests of these students. This has broadened the base and role of foreign language instruction in our schools to include interdisciplinary courses, bilingual programs, and career education that includes foreign language study.

4 While we have not yet done all that needs to be done to unify the profession, we have begun to take the steps that are necessary to reaffirm and reinforce our position in the present educational curriculum. The focus on the student through individualized instruction and personalization will strengthen our position in the curriculum and will help the students to enjoy and succeed in our classes. We are now aware that inertia as well as the search for a single panacea can only lead to self-destruction. We are looking to our students, and their success will be our success.

5 Foreign language education *will* thrive because in a culturally pluralistic world, harmony and peace are the direct result of "communication," which is the basic objective of foreign language study.

References, The realities facing the profession

1 Arendt, Jermaine D. "Media in Foreign Language Teaching," 157–89 in Dale L. Lange,ed., *Individualization of Instruction.* ACTFL Review of Foreign Language Education, Volume 2. Skokie, Illinois: National Textbook Company, 1972.

2 Asher, James J. "Implications of Psychological Research for Second Language Learning," 157–86 in Dale L. Lange and Charles J. James,eds., *Foreign Language Education:A Reappraisal.* ACTFL Review of Foreign Language Education, Volume 4.

Skokie, Illinois: National Textbook Company, 1972.

3 Birkmaier, Emma M. "Modern Languages," 861–88 in Chester W. Harris,ed., *Encyclopedia of Educational Research*. New York: Macmillan, 1960.

4 Brod, Richard I. "Foreign Language Enrollments in U.S. Colleges." *Bulletin of the Association of Departments of Foreign Languages* 3, ii(1971):46–50.

5 ——— *Interim Report*, 1972 [of foreign language enrollments in U.S. Colleges] [Mimeo.]

6 Clark, John L.D. "Measurement Implications of Recent Trends in Foreign Language Teaching," 219–57 in Dale L. Lange and Charles J. James,eds., *Foreign Language Education:A Reappraisal*. ACTFL Review of Foreign Language Education, Volume 4. Skokie, Illinois: National Textbook Company, 1972.

7 Corrin, Brownlee Sands,ed., "Content and Crossroads:Wider Uses for Foreign Languages," 59–81 in Robert G. Mead,ed., *Language Teaching:Broader Contexts*. [Reports of the Working Committees of the Northeast Conference on the Teaching of Foreign Languages.] New York: MLA Materials Center, 1966.

8 Dernorsek, Cheryl. *Attrition in Foreign Language Instruction*. [Mimeo.]

9 Dodge, James W. "Machine-Aided Language Learning," 311–41 in Emma M. Birkmaier,ed., *Foreign Language Education:An Overview*. ACTFL Review of Foreign Language Education, Volume 1. Skokie, Illinois: National Textbook Company, 1972.

10 ———ed., *Other Words, Other Worlds:Language-in-Culture*. [Reports of the Working Committees of the Northeast Conference on the Teaching of Foreign Languages.] New York: MLA Materials Center, 1972.

11 Erickson, Gerald M. "Classics:The Teaching of Latin and Greek and Classical Humanities," 275–322 in Dale L. Lange,ed., *Individualization of Instruction*. ACTFL Review of Foreign Language Education, Volume 2. Skokie, Illinois: National Textbook Company, 1972.

12 "Foreign Language Enrollments in Public Secondary Schools. Fall 1970." *Bulletin of the Association of Departments of Foreign Languages* 4,ii(1972):20–21.

13 Gougher, Ronald L. "Individualization of Foreign Language Learning:What Is Being Done," 221–45 in Dale L. Lange,ed., *Pluralism in Foreign Language Education*. ACTFL Review of Foreign Language Education, Volume 3. Skokie, Illinois: National Textbook Company, 1972.

14 Green, Jerald R. "Purposes and Goals in Foreign Language Education:A Look to the Future," 1–33 in Dale L. Lange and Charles J. James,eds., *Foreign Language Education:A Reappraisal*. ACTFL Review of Foreign Language Education, Volume 4. Skokie, Illinois: National Textbook Company, 1972.

15 Hancock, Charles. "Student Aptitude, Attitude and Motivation," 127–55 in Dale L. Lange and Charles J. James,eds., *Foreign Language Education:*

A Reappraisal. ACTFL Review of Foreign Language Education, Volume 4. Skokie, Illinois: National Textbook Company, 1972.

16 Hocking, Elton. "The Schools Take Over Foreign Languages," *Journal of Secondary Education* 39(1964): 243–50.

17 Hoye, Almon G. "Interaction of Student and Teacher with the Learning Environment," 259–94 in Dale L. Lange and Charles J. James,eds., *Foreign Language Education:A Reappraisal*. ACTFL Review of Foreign Language Education, Volume 4. Skokie, Illinois: National Textbook Company, 1972.

18 Jenks, Frederick L. "What's This I Smell?. . . What's This I Taste?. . ." *American Foreign Language Teacher* 3,ii(1972):2.

19 Keaton, Ruth. "Teachers Provide Program Highlight." *Accent on ACTFL* 3,iii(1973):12–13,28.

20 Keniston, Kenneth. "You Have to Grow Up in Scarsdale to Know How Bad Things Really Are." *New York Times Magazine*. (27 April 1969):27–29.

21 Lange, Dale L.,ed., *Individualization of Instruction*. ACTFL Review of Foreign Language Education, Volume 2. Skokie, Illinois: National Textbook Company ,1972.

22 Lawson, John H. *Should Foreign Language Courses Be Eliminated? No! But Modifications Are Needed*. [EDRS: ED 039 823].

23 Levy, Stephen L. *Student-Centered Learning: At What Level or Levels Is It Most Effective?* [Paper presented at the Third International Conference of the New York State Association of Foreign Language Teachers and the Ontario Modern Language Teachers' Association, Rochester, New York, March 1973.]

24 Lipton, Gladys C. "Curricula for New Goals," 187–218 in Dale L. Lange and Charles J. James,eds., *Foreign Language Education:A Reappraisal*. ACTFL Review of Foreign Language Education, Volume 4. Skokie, Illinois: National Textbook Company, 1972.

25 ——— Personal communication, 1973. [Interview.]

26 ——— and Jerome G. Mirsky. "Foreign Language Education," 127–55 in William J. Ellena,ed., *Curriculum Handbook for School Executives*. Arlington, Virginia: American Association of School Administrators, 1973.

27 Nelson, Robert J. and Leon A. Jakobovits,eds., "Motivation in Foreign Language Learning," 31–104 in Joseph A. Tursi,ed., *Foreign Languages and the "New" Student*. [Reports of the Working Committees of the Northeast Conference on the Teaching of Foreign Languages.] New York: MLA Materials Center, 1970.

28 New York City Foreign Language Program for Secondary Schools: French, Levels 1–5. New York: New York City Board of Education, 1966.

29 Powers, James R.,ed., "Professional Responsibili-

ties," 15–50 in James W. Dodge,ed., *Leadership for Continuing Development*. [Reports of the Working Committees of the Northeast Conference on the Teaching of Foreign Languages.] New York: MLA Materials Center, 1971.

30 Richardson, Charles P. "Teachers, Students, and Media as Co-agents in Learning," 295–320 in Dale L. Lange and Charles J. James,eds., *Foreign Language Education: A Reappraisal*. ACTFL Review of Foreign Language Education, Volume 4. Skokie, Illinois: National Textbook Company, 1972.

31 Rivers, Wilga M. "Foreign Languages in a Time of Change," 108–19 in *Speaking in Many Tongues: Essays in Foreign Language Teaching*. Rowley, Massachusetts: Newbury House, 1972.

32 Sandstrom, Eleanor L., and Paul Pimsleur, "Foreign Languages for All Students?" 105–33 in Joseph A. Tursi,ed., *Foreign Languages and the "New" Student*. [Reports of the Working Committees of the Northeast Conference on the Teaching of Foreign Languages.] New York: MLA Materials Center, 1970.

33 Silberman, Charles E. *Crisis in the Classroom*. New York: Viking, 1971.

34 Smith, Alfred N. "Strategies of Instruction for Speaking and Writing," 113–31 in Dale L. Lange, ed., *Individualization of Instruction*. ACTFL Review of Foreign Language Education, Volume 2. Skokie, Illinois: National Textbook Company, 1972.

35 Smith, W. Flint. "Language Learning Laboratory," 191–237 in Dale L. Lange,ed., *Individualization of Instruction*. ACTFL Review of Foreign Language Education, Volume 2. Skokie, Illinois: National Textbook Company, 1972.

36 Smith, Philip D., Jr. "Media in Individualized Instruction: A Look at Today and Thoughts Toward the Future," 108–12 in James W. Dodge,ed., *Sensitivity in the Foreign Language Classroom*. [Reports of the Working Committees of the Northeast Conference on the Teaching of Foreign Languages.] New York: MLA Materials Center, 1973.

37 Steiner, Florence. *Sense and Nonsense in Foreign Language Textbooks*. [Paper presented at the Annual Meeting of the American Council on the Teaching of Foreign Languages. Atlanta, Georgia, 1972.]

38 Strasheim, Lorraine A. " 'Creativity' Lies Trippingly on the Tongue." *The Modern Language Journal* 55(1971):339–45.

39 Toffler, Alvin. *Future Shock*. New York: Random House, 1970.

40 Valette, Rebecca M. "Testing," 343–74 in Emma M. Birkmaier,ed., *Foreign Language Education: An Overview*. ACTFL Review of Foreign Language Education, Volume 1. Skokie, Illinois: National Textbook Company, 1972.

41 Valette, Rebecca M. and Renee S. Disick. *Modern Language Performance Objectives and Individualization: A Handbook*. New York: Harcourt, Brace, Jovanovich, 1972.

42 Warriner, Helen P. "Foreign Language Interdisciplinary Programs and Activities," 125–62 in Dale L. Lange,ed., *Pluralism in Foreign Language Education*. ACTFL Review of Foreign Language Education, Volume 3. Skokie, Illinois: National Textbook Company, 1972.

43 Wolfe, David E., and Philip D. Smith, Jr. "Teacher Education for New Goals," 97–126 in Dale L. Lange and Charles J. James,eds., *Foreign Language Education: A Reappraisal*. ACTFL Review of Foreign Language Education, Volume 4. Skokie, Illinois: National Textbook Company, 1972.

Reflections

3

Many learners, many goals, many curricula

Many learners

Compared to your other classes, how do you feel about Spanish class?

HEATHER: I like learning about South American kids, but my stomach gets all tight when the teacher drills us with lots of questions.

BOB: The best thing is that I sit next to my pal.

JOSÉ: I failed last year, but I know by her eyes and her gentle voice that this teacher understands me.

If you were the teacher, how would you change this course?

HEATHER: I could go twice as fast if I could keep my book open and figure things out myself.

BOB: I'd let us speak Spanish by going to teach the Puerto Rican kids how to play basketball.

JOSÉ: I'd have us work together more, rather than alone.

Are you going to study Spanish next year?

HEATHER: Oh yes, I want to learn as much as I can; I'll need it, because I'm going to be a social worker.

BOB: Well, I'll wait and see if there are some good mini-courses; I'm in Spanish mostly for fun.

JOSÉ: I guess so. I gotta have two years to get into ———— U.

How do you feel when the teacher looks out the window while asking you a question?

HEATHER: It doesn't bother me. She doesn't do it with me. Besides, everybody knows I'll answer it right.

BOB: Well, she does that sometimes; I wonder if she cares what I say.

JOSÉ: I feel real awful, and it makes me miss the question when a

Wahneta M. Mullen

The University of Iowa

Photograph of students of Steuben Junior High courtesy of Anthony Gradisnik and the Milwaukee Public Schools.

Interests

The affective domain

Wahneta M. Mullen (Ph.D., Indiana University) is Assistant Professor of French and Education at the University of Iowa. She has taught French and Spanish at the secondary level and in college and was a state foreign language consultant for three years. She is presently serving as recording secretary of the Central States Conference on the Teaching of Foreign Languages and is a member of ACTFL and AATF.

37

teacher does that. I do a lot better when we work in groups and my pals can help me.

What do you do when you are learning a line of a dialogue?   *The cognitive domain*

HEATHER: I think of the English meaning for it.

BOB: I repeat the sounds to myself because we don't really need to know the meaning.

JOSÉ: I try to remember the picture we had with it.

Few terms are used more frequently by educators than *individual*   *An overwhelming sense of*
differences. Most teachers probably first encountered it in a beginning   *diversity*
undergraduate education course. It is a phrase uttered frequently at curriculum meetings and written repeatedly on the pages of our professional journals. These noble-sounding words are regularly bantered about at PTA meetings. Tragically, these words have too often remained mere verbalizations.

But now, the times make it imperative that education be concerned   *Learner-centered education*
directly with the individual. The entire educational process is, in a sense, regulated by the learner. "He controls an input into curriculum objectives, and his nature further dictates characteristics of the instructional process" (Jarvis, 52, p. 202). Learning any skill or subject matter is an individual, personal process dependent upon what the learner brings to the task in talent, experiential background, and interest (Dodge, 28). Today's students are not only different from one another; they are different as a group from those of preceding generations. Above all, they are more aware and more active; they are bold in challenging current practices and values. In recent years foreign language educators have been making a greater effort to study the characteristics of the total personality of this "new" learner in order to design curricula that he will perceive as worthwhile.

The profession has traditionally catered to a very small group of   *College-bound elite*
social and intellectual elite, frequently stereotyped as the docile female who was college bound. Green (38) points out that countless students have been denied language study because they did not meet the criteria for admission to foreign language classes. He further observes that the elite student population has created a false sense of accomplishment in language teaching. Foreign language teachers have often talked about their classes as being very heterogeneous, while in reality they were quite homogeneous; they included only a very small segment of the total school population. But in recent years there has been a growing recognition that *all* students can benefit from foreign language study.   *Foreign language study for all*
Many writers (Green, 38; Grittner, 41; Rivers, 81; Strasheim, 92)

38

have therefore interpreted the vanishing foreign language requirement as a powerful catalyst for including the entire population. Language teachers are making increasing efforts to appeal to a broader clientele through more varied and meaningful curricula.

Who, then, might be the potential foreign language learners? Grittner (41) is committed to the view that all can profit from the right kind of exposure to a second language and culture. In reflecting on the narrow selection and high attrition in foreign language study, he asks whether the experience of learning a foreign language is so unimportant that we can afford to eliminate almost everyone from serious contact with it. The new California curriculum guide (33) would provide the opportunity for foreign language instruction from kindergarten to 12th grade for all, with programs designed to meet diverse needs, interests, and motivations of students. The 1970 Northeast Conference Report (Sandstrom and Pimsleur, 84) recommends foreign language for all children as an integral part of their basic education. Sandstrom and Pimsleur see this as a realistic and legitimate goal of the profession and *Success for all* further maintain that all can learn a foreign language if given adequate time and the appropriate environment. The stipulation is added that the learner must be in a class where he can succeed. Under these conditions, Gahala (35) sees hope for a place for the nontalented in foreign language study. Polinsky (75) makes a plea for including the educable and emotionally disturbed. Green (38), however, is cynical *Teacher attitudes: the great* about the implementation of a program of foreign language study for *obstacle* all; he recognizes the great effort that will be required to reorient teacher attitudes to the value of foreign language study for a total population. Lip service to foreign language for all is not sufficient. Language teachers must design courses and provide learning experiences that will be interpreted by students as worthy of their time and effort. Mead (67) adheres to the position that all students who wish to study foreign language and culture, whether in academic or vocational programs, should have the opportunity to do so, but should not be forced. Nelson and Jakobovits (69) would include as learners only those who are motivated to learn. Thus, in the potential clientele a full range of heterogeneity must be expected and respected (Rivers, 81). The learner now is any person—a thinking, feeling human being. In a sense, he is everyman. And strangely enough, that is new in foreign language education.

As teachers acknowledge that language learning involves the whole person and personality of the learner, concern about his pre-instructional characteristics is greater than ever before (Green, 38). We must dis-

39

cover more about the constellation of previous experiences and innate abilities that he brings to the learning task. In the past teachers largely ignored as a factor the uniqueness of the individual learner. Indeed, they considered that the function of education was to smooth out differences between individuals—to make a common product of every student. Students were interchangeable in terms of what they learned in school. Now these differences are being acknowledged and described so that instructional activities can be geared towards accommodating the needs and interests of the individual. Smith (88) emphasizes that our schools consist of people with widely differing needs, talents, and backgrounds; he urges recognition of the need to extend the range of human variability and to understand that being different does not mean being inferior. The learner is a human being with huge potential for development regardless of his origin or race: "He is an active and inter-active organism with his own unique mental make-up and with an innate desire to put purpose and meaning into the environment as he interacts with it" (Grittner, 45, p. 8).

Uniqueness of individual

Just as there are tremendous differences among individuals in foreign language classes today, these individuals, in turn, differ from those of a former generation. Students of the present generation are inter-nationalists and interculturalists (Rivers, 81) as well as idealists (Potter, 77). In contrast to the established culture, which is money and thing oriented, the emerging culture is person and people oriented (Sobol, 89). This is manifested by student involvement in social action and concern for equality and fairness for others. In their commitment to brotherhood they want all races to have the same opportunities. They do not want the handicapped excluded. They insist that those who are not so able as they be given a chance. All this is in marked contrast with the earlier emphasis on competition, on being the best, on making the most money. Increasingly, the question among the young is not, "What can I accomplish?" but "What can I become?" not "What prize can I win?" but "What will make me feel and be better?" (Sobol, 89, p. 28). They are fulfillment oriented rather than achievement oriented; personal and subjective rather than impersonal and objective. Among the problems of articulation Sobol sees for the schools are those of school and life, head and heart, have's and have not's, and old values versus new values. The students of this generation are now oriented rather than future oriented; they find long-range goals uninteresting or boring. They are not satisfied to study a foreign language only to meet a future requirement; they also seek immediate relevance to contemporary life (Dodge, 28). The emerging generation

Today's students

Fulfillment orientation

40

is confused and concerned in a world with cities in disorder, racial tensions, pollution, a drug culture, and a new morality (Keller, 57). Young people today are more mature—biologically, socially, and psychologically—than Americans have ever been (Gorman, 37). In spite of greater capability, however, they are more often and more completely excluded from the mainstream of the life in the home, in the world of work, and in the school than ever before. It should not be surprising that they vigorously and frequently insist on a "piece of the action."

Modern technology may be a factor affecting today's youth as it never has in the past. It has broadened the student's experiences, outlook, and expectations. Coleman (25) explains that the children who came of age during the 1960s, the postmodern generations, developed a cognitive style that was different from previous generations in quite fundamental ways. The main difference is an alteration in the *Processing knowledge* very way knowledge is processed. The generations born after Gutenberg and before 1950 assimilated most knowledge in a linear fashion, by reading; the postmodern generation, however, accentuates different senses, especially the tactile and auditory. Young people today process knowledge much more globally, and a communications system has resulted that is different from those of other generations.

Today's students have modified the central purpose of education; *Student demand for changes* today they demand that education contribute to self-fulfillment, that it help deepen their humanity. Achievement is not enough. Foshay (34) maintains that the strictly intellectual approach, which in the past characterized most of our thinking, was never adequate for actual problem solving. Today's student is increasingly vocal in his demands for a more personalized and relevant curriculum. Baughman (10) identifies what the student wants from school: enhanced choice making, an opportunity for self-identity, self-expression, trust, demanding and understanding teachers, and a cooperative approach. Fearing and Arendt (32) advise that students want fewer requirements in their courses of study; they "will enroll in language courses if they have a personal interest or need for them, but they resent being required to take them" (p. 6).

Learner needs have long been considered in the curriculum building *Needs of the young* process. They have usually been divided into needs the learner perceives and those that, in effect, society imposes upon him. Only recently have we been willing to consider seriously the needs coming *from* the learners as well as those we impose as eminently good for him. As special needs of today's student Foshay (34) and Van Til (101) emphasize the need *Learning how to learn*

41

to learn how to learn. They emphasize that the development of learning skills should become the focus of deliberate attention in the schools of the 1970s. Steiner (91) says, "the greatest good we could do our students is to teach them to structure their own learning objectives, to decide in advance what they want to do, to decide what the assessment tool will be, to list the activities and the resources that will, they believe, lead them to the fulfillment of their goal" (p. 273).

The humanistic view of learner needs is emphasized repeatedly in the literature. For example, Smith (88) places first priority on the need to grow to full stature as a human being. Grittner (41) advises that the learner must learn to live with diversity at home and abroad. Bennis (11) focuses on affective needs; the individual needs to feel useful, potent, and good. High priority needs, according to Glasser (36), are concerns with problems of identity and search for mutual love, respect, and fulfillment. The learner needs sympathetic guidance to look at life, to look at himself, and to make value decisions (Wilhelms, 106). The need for success is underscored by Gahala (35) and by Birkmaier (12), who contends that the student needs a stimulating and enriched learning environment and freedom to learn. A chance to explore and experiment is cited by Van Til (101). Glasser (36) insists the student needs some degree of structure. Feedback about progress and remedial work as required are stressed by Altman (5). The individual needs social involvement in which he can express his ideas (Grittner, 44). According to Kalivoda and Elkins (55), the needs of the learner must be considered from the point of view of the student himself rather than from that of the teacher. Grittner (43), however, cautions that the needs of the student tend to be capricious. The learner is perpetually in the dilemma of not knowing what he himself will have wanted from his education 20 years from now.

"Humanistic" needs

Can the learner identify his needs?

The great heterogeneity of today's clientele results in a great diversity of needs, and it demands that teachers make concentrated efforts to know their students. Bourque (15) admonishes that teachers listen to the student to learn of his wants, needs, interests, aspirations, and fears. In a more formal "listening," questionnaires, interviews, conferences (93), and essays (61) are being utilized more frequently for this purpose. Lipton (63) recommends that teachers ask three questions periodically to learn more about the student's point of view:

Knowing student sentiments

1   What do you like most in our foreign language class?
2   What don't you like about our foreign language class?
3   If you were the foreign language teacher, how would you teach the class (p. 189)?

Student feedback suggests that interest-centered curricula may be desirable. At the high school in Waukesha, Wisconsin, teachers study information on student interests and attitudes obtained through an extensive survey in order to make language learning more enjoyable and worthwhile for all students. An assessment of student interests provides a basis for structuring a series of mini-courses offered to third-, fourth-, and fifth-year students of French and Spanish.

Survey of student interests

An investigation in 1973 at the University of Illinois by Rivers (80) reveals that students in requirement courses want more listening and speaking practice; they want more reading, not only of literature, but also of newspapers and magazines through which they can keep abreast of current affairs. About 20 percent (higher in German and Russian) indicate an interest in scientific and technical writing. Students also express an interest in learning more about the people who speak the language, perhaps through films. No one wants more grammar, nor do they indicate an interest in more writing. This extensive survey merits further study by foreign language educators. Little is known about variations in interest from institution to institution and among various age levels. While many students are voicing an interest in more language for communication and more culture, Hutchinson (50) and Gahala (35) stress that many young people who do not fit the academic stereotype may be interested in finding out about another culture through the foreign language.

The cultural background of the learner is a significant factor in determining his frame of reference and in assessing his needs in order to design a curriculum tailored to those needs and interests. Badillo (9) reminds the profession that language is more than simply a way of communicating: It is a link to a whole culture and many rich heritages. "Thus, by stifling a student's self-expression in his own native tongue, you are also destroying his sense of identity and self-esteem" (p. 297). Many Mexican-Americans, Puerto Ricans, Orientals, American Indians, and other foreign language speaking children, who have been short-changed and neglected by the typical American educational process, now seek identity and relevance to their concerns in their school experiences. Children who have limited English-speaking ability and who come from environments where the dominant language is other than English have special and unique educational needs. In addition to a need to learn English, they need a knowledge of and pride in their culture and heritage.

Cultural background to determine needs

The preoccupations, value systems, and characteristic approaches of the disadvantaged learner must be taken into consideration. With an

Disadvantaged learners

43

understanding of his preferred modes of learning, the teacher can choose materials and design lessons that will utilize them to the fullest. The learner from a disadvantaged background typically prefers the concrete to the abstract; he responds to concrete material for which he sees an immediate application; therefore, he enjoys learning foreign words and phrases he can employ immediately in the context of his class or neighborhood. He learns through activity, through seeing, hearing, touching, role playing; thus the use of visual presentations—flash cards, drawings, films, music, songs, and practical vocabulary—is particularly appropriate. He appreciates firm leadership from the teacher; he is not eager to work in small groups in which he will need to make group decisions. Since he is accustomed to learning orally rather than through the written word, reading the foreign language may not appear to be of vital importance to him (Rivers, 81).

Many black students desire a clear and unambiguous identity; they are seeking this identity more and more through the exploration of their lost African heritage. Rivers (81) sees this as a case for the teaching of Swahili, or other African languages in high schools, as many black groups have been seeking.

Correlations have been high between foreign language enrollments and various socioeconomic factors (Dodge, 28), and the contrast between enrollments in inner-city schools and suburban schools has been marked. Landor (59), however, brings to our attention the fact that the mind is not cultivated any differently on one side of the railroad tracks than on the other or differently among the dark-skinned than among the light, or differently among the "bright" than among those apparently endowed with only "ordinary" talents.

Language learning and socioeconomic factors

Individual differences extend beyond socioeconomic factors, ethnic background, and interests. Numerous relevant variables—many of which have not yet been identified—exist within the learner. Birkmaier (12) sees students as differentially successful when they are involved in reading, listening, various sensory approaches (e.g., role playing); under pressure of deadlines and tests; operating at varying rates; or motivated by competition or peer teaching. Teachers who have moved into individualized programs have quickly observed that some students work well without guidance, while others need careful supervision. While the academically talented is generally comfortable with abstractions, Birkmaier stresses that the slow learner is usually characterized by his physical approach to learning. Hancock (47) and Nelson and Jakobovits (69) have discussed at length aptitude, attitude, and motivation in the learner. Motivation is probably receiving the most attention

Motivation

in the recent literature. Allen (2) emphasizes that students are motivated by what gives pleasure and success; he believes that curriculum organization makes little real difference in motivation. Experience has shown that motivation is a more important factor than intellectual ability for success in foreign language study.

Jakobovits (51) states that there is no adequate research to prove any relationship between age and success in foreign language learning; but interest and learning style do vary according to age. Grittner (41) suggests that the optimum time for introduction to the spoken language is between Grades 4 and 7. The 1972 Northeast Conference Report (29) recommends that cultural and linguistic training should begin early, preferably by the age of ten. The fact is that the majority of young people begin language study in the secondary schools, and today many are beginning their experience with a foreign language in the junior and community colleges. Cordes (26) reports enthusiastic junior college classes composed of housewives and retired people in a healthy admixture with younger students. Marottoli (65) and Brown (18) report dramatic increases in the numbers of adults in commercial language schools. Too often this large potential clientele has been ignored by the profession.

Optimal age for language learning

Ages of learners

Cloos (24) found that sex differences in foreign language learning are most significant at the senior high school and beginning college levels, with female students exhibiting a higher ability than males in both foreign language aptitude and achievement. A study by Smith (87) corroborated the findings of Cloos, yet Politzer and Weiss (76) found no significant difference in achievement in relation to sex composition of the classes in their limited study. Allen (2) notes that girls are more motivated academically. Certainly, differences in interests of boys and girls must be considered (Lipton, 63).

Sex differences

Van Til (101) urges a concern for economy in learning. Shepherd (86) recognizes the limited learning time available and suggests that one aim should be efficient use of classroom time. Fearing and Arendt (32) note that various foreign language offerings as well as a number of new and interesting courses in the curriculum compete for the student's time.

Inadequate learning time

A most important aspect in today's educational scene is that of the changing student-teacher relations. The young people are highly vocal in demanding the rationale of what we are doing and what we are asking them to do. They want to be involved in decision making. The new student wants to do what he perceives as important. Thus he may react negatively to the traditional teacher-directed situation that dic-

A new teacher-learner relationship

45

tates what he is going to learn, how he is going to learn it and when (Arendt, 8). The teacher is responsible for identifying the needs and wants of the individual student. The teacher must also make the student aware of the purposes for learning. A proper balance of these factors is essential for motivation. Grittner (45) urges us to accept the student as he is and to develop the interests and talents that he has. The message is simple but eloquent.

Many goals

I do my thing,
and you do
your thing.

I am not in
this world
to live up
to your
expectations.

And you are
not in this
world to live
up to mine.

You are you
and I am I.

And if by
chance
we find
each other,

it's beautiful—Perls (74)

Flow charts and diagrams are often deceivingly simple when they are used to represent the curriculum building process. Indeed, statements such as "learner characteristics and societal needs determine instructional goals" are usually accepted as simple truisms. Few would quarrel with them. Yet, the establishment of curricular goals may well be the most demanding task of educators in terms of time, energy, and frustration. Learner needs and characteristics are not readily identifiable—neither to the professional nor to the learner himself. Societal needs are equally nebulous and highly elusive to consensual

Establishing goals: education's most difficult value judgement

46

agreement. Perhaps, this great difficulty in establishing goals is what has resulted in the delegation of responsibility for goal formulation to various agencies and status groups.

Mackey (64) points out that the federal government influences language policy both directly and indirectly. Well known examples of the impact of government on language policy are the National Defense Education Act of 1958 and the current sponsorship of career education programs. Mandates from state legislatures also affect decisions concerning educational goals. Some state legislatures, for example, are already requiring the implementation of career education. As a further specific example of the influence of a state legisalture, the Stull Bill in California affects teachers in all subject areas by requiring that goals be stated in terms of specific performance objectives. Similar mandates are likely in other states. California, New Mexico, and Massachusetts are among states that have formalized requirements for bilingual education. *Federal government influence* *State legislature influence*

Goal formulation is sometimes influenced by state departments of education, especially in states that provide considerable guidance through that agency. *Wholeness in Learning* (105), for example, relates foreign language learning to the educational policy of the State of Maryland. The Michigan Department of Education sponsored committees of teachers from all levels of instruction who have outlined performance objectives in the cognitive and affective domains at four "stages" in foreign language learning (73). *State departments of education*

The Association for Supervision and Curriculum Development, as well as similar agencies, likewise affect decisions concerning goals. Through different periods these groups have directed general educational policy toward educating the individual to meet societal needs or toward the development of the individual human being. ASCD has promoted humanistic education for a number of years, and currently it is endorsing the career education movement. *Professional organizations*

Through the years subject-matter experts have had a voice in curricular goals, to the degree that curricula were built upon an "organized-body-of-knowledge" approach. Brooks (17), for example, uses the totality of language as a basis for organizing the curriculum. He represents the view that language learning is a sequential series of steps. However, as the learner becomes the center of attention for curriculum planning, the importance of the subject-matter expert is considerably diminished. *Subject-matter experts*

Textbook authors have also exerted influence upon our choice of goals. Many teachers have followed without question the goals of a *Textbook authors*

47

given text. Sometimes the goals are merely implicit, but at other times they are stated explicitly, as in *Jeunes Voix, Jeunes Visages* (62).

Finally, the local community affects decisions regarding goals in foreign language study (Fearing and Arendt, 32; Rivers, 81; 103). Goals are established, taking into consideration the school board, parents, administrators, teachers, and students. The school philosophy states the rationale for the total curriculum and determines goals for particular subject-matter areas. It would seem that activity at this level is most pertinent to meeting local needs. At this local level the learner becomes the center of concern. As the classroom teacher studies the individual, his learning style, his personal needs and interests, he must relate these learner factors to the goals emanating from the various status groups and agencies. Because the learner today is eager to state his own goals and interests, the teacher must further integrate these student goals into the curricular building process.

Local community

Teacher as synthesizer and interpreter of goals

Students are willing to indicate curricular goals that they perceive as important. Communication, perhaps for travel, is a goal identified by great numbers of students (Arendt, 8; 61; Potter, 77; Rivers, 81). Understanding other peoples and their cultures through language is another high priority goal (Cavanaugh, 20; Fearing and Arendt, 32; Rivers, 81; Tursi, 98). Studies by Archer and O'Rourke (7) and Rivers (80) reveal interest in reading newspapers, magazines, and literature in translation as well as literature in the target language. An increasing number of students want to use the foreign language in their vocation (Tamarkin, 95; Rivers, 80). Many vocational students prefer courses with limited goals that will enable them to operate on a basic functional level with a given clientele (Dodge, 28). Personal interests, exploration, self-identity, and leisure, as well as intellectual challenge (Rich, 79) also have been identified as goals of learners. According to Fearing and Arendt (32), Grittner (45), and Gahala (35), it is imperative that teachers use student interests as a focal point in planning content and activities if the student is to be motivated to use the foreign language for his own purposes. If foreign language programs are going to attract and retain a broader population, personal and curricular goals must be congruent.

Student-indicated goal areas

Personal and curricular goals

In recent years the traditional goals of foreign language were principally concerned with development of competency in the four skills in their natural sequence, insight into the culture, and acquaintance with the literature. All learners, regardless of ability, were expected to follow a set sequence in a lock step pace to achieve the same goals—goals that were largely dictated by the college requirement.

Traditional goals: a study in rigidity

These rigid traditional goals no longer fulfill the needs and desires of many present day students.

To what degree have goals stated in the past been realized? The 1971 Northeast Conference Report (Dodge, 28) notes that in spite of announced goals, the communication aspects of language, specifically listening, speaking, and reading, are at present receiving the greatest emphasis. Acquaintance with literature is being given somewhat less attention until the communication skills have been developed. Culture, while not neglected, has generally been looked upon as supplementary information to be added to foreign language courses occasionally, rather than the natural framework in which language takes place and has meaning. Rivers (81) notes that there is not much evidence of cultural enrichment in language classes, though teachers have paid lip service to this objective for a number of years. Many students have likewise not achieved fluency and competency; these goals Hanzeli and Love (48) now see as unrealistic. Strasheim (92) observes that the values of foreign language study have, in fact, accrued only to the foreign language major. An elimination of foreign language requirements, therefore, will likely force teachers to examine the objectives set out in syllabi and in the literature in order to ascertain whether they relate to what actually goes on in their classrooms (Rivers, 81).

Part of the problems of the past resulted from unrealistic goals; students and parents as well as teachers had unreasonable expectations of the foreign language program. Many have recently been advocating changes in goals. Glasser (36) urges a more realistic statement of goals that are sensible objectives that help students. Allen (2) recommends setting achievable goals within a given lesson, unit, or course. Student motivation is encouraged not by the setting out of reasonable and relevant objectives that salve the instructor's conscience, but by student perception of the attainment and attainability of those objectives (Rivers, 81). The purpose of many innovations today is to reach beyond the limitations of lock step and the implicit unrealistic assumption that all high school students are preparing for college (Dodge, 28). The high attrition rate, which is well known to all, has resulted from traditional language programs that have not been designed for the majority of students (Cavanaugh, 20). The goals were appropriate for an elite few—a clientele that does not itself approve of any form of elitism.

Lipton (63) observes that the newer goals of language teaching today have developed essentially along two principal lines:

1 Preparation for living in today's culturally diverse society so that foreign languages are tools for implementing a total education

Growing emphasis on communication

Lack of realism

Elimination of requirements

Traditional goals made attainable

Characteristics of newer goals

49

program of goals, content, and procedure for learning for each individual.

2 Preparation for living in the world of the future so that "copability" is not just an invention of the mind but is an essential part of an education package that is responsive to individual needs (p. 190).

Foreign language study is no longer limited to the goals directed toward skill training but is concerned with the formative education of a human being. To survive in this changing world, language teaching must demonstrate the value of its contribution to the quality of life (Rivers, 81). This is a task the profession has long talked about but which has seen little fruition. According to Strassheim (92) our purpose is:

> To contribute to the student's intellectual, social, aesthetic, and emotional growth through foreign language study in an effort to assist the student toward a more positive approach to other peoples through in-depth experiences with the thought processes and social behavior of native speakers and thus help him to interpret and cope with the societies he will encounter in life (p. 24).

Comprehensive goal formulation

Understanding other people

Grittner (44) sees the all-encompassing goal of the foreign language program as that of developing all individuals into more fulfilled human beings; teaching students through language to think, to feel, to understand, to perceive—and doing these things increasingly on their own. The new Maryland curriculum guide (105) for the middle grades, which focuses on *Wholeness in Learning*, outlines in detail general educational goals and student objectives in foreign languages in the areas of civic responsibility, positive self-image, career education, empathic and human relationships. To these Glasser (36) would add the goal of success and satisfaction with what the student is doing, making learning a pleasurable and lasting experience.

Foreign language study to enhance all human capacities

It should be noted that one of the unique characteristics of foreign language learning within the curriculum is that there are relatively few prerequisites to the study of a foreign language. The student begins his study closer to a zero point than he does in most subject areas, where there are typically many explicit or implicit prerequisites. With *appropriate instruction* the learner has a high probability of success.

Unique chance for success

In discussions of goals one often finds distinctions made between terms such as *humanistic goals* and *pragmatic goals*, *goals* and *objectives*, as well as between *goals* and *purposes*. Some uniformity seems to be emerging. The term *goals* seems to be applied frequently to more general and abstract statements. *Objectives* usually implies greater specificity and

Terminology

Goals versus *Objectives*

the use of behavioral terminology. A *purpose*, particularly as used by Valette and Disick (100), seems to be a very general statement of a reason for the objective or goal. It often relates the objective to a larger context (e.g. to develop attitudes of interest in and enjoyment of foreign language learning). It is one component in the process of stating performance objectives.

Purposes

The manner in which goals and objectives are described has received considerable attention recently (Grittner, 40; Steiner, 90; Valette and Disick, 100). If one accepts education as an inherently purposeful activity, much of the discussion is reduced to debate over the form in which objectives or goals are stated. When a learner and a teacher come together, both have purposes (which are hopefully congruent). Those purposes can be described in general and abstract terms, or they can be stated in very specific behavioral terms. Both have advantages and disadvantages. The global statements (such as often appear in department or school philosophies) subsume many aims in a relatively brief goal statement but are not sufficiently specific to guide day-to-day instructional decisions. Behavioral objectives, however, do facilitate instructional decisions but become quantitatively unmanageable where summary statements of goals are needed. Thus, it seems practical to view the various kinds of statements as aspects of one total goal-refinement process, where the kinds of statements differ only in levels of generality (27).

Understanding the debate about objectives

Travel, use of foreign language in a career, or national defense would be broad purposes for various goals. Potter (77) notes that travel has motivated greater interest in speaking the foreign language. National defense has been a reason for development of native-like fluency in the four skills; use in a career would be a purpose for limited goals focusing on specific vocabulary. Development of cross-cultural understanding is cited repeatedly as a means for attaining most of these purposes. According to Brooks (16), this is one of the best possible end products of our language courses, and it can be a part of the learner's experience from the beginning. Cavanaugh (20) similarly calls for a change in the basic philosophy that governs most high school programs. He would subordinate grammar to developing an understanding of and interest in foreign peoples. He recommends a shift in which language becomes an adjunct—though an important one— to culture, not the reverse. At all levels "teach something" the student will retain and which will be beneficial to him after he ceases to study the foreign language. By linking the culture and language the student would gain a broadened awareness of life in the foreign country without the drudgery of an all-

Cultural goals

51

language approach. Seelye (85) and Morain (68) have discussed in detail the goals and procedures for teaching culture.

In all areas of education a main focus today is on career goals. *Career goals*
River's study (80) reveals that students who are studying foreign language as an elective at advanced levels at the university often do want to use it in their vocations. Rivers (81), however, insists that vocational *Objections to career orientation* goals in foreign language are not convincing reasons for continuing a foreign language program. Grittner (44) holds emphatically to the position that "it is both illogical and dysfunctional to make education an instrument of career and earning power" (p. 16). He explains that almost none of the students in *any* specific high school class will ever make direct use of the subject matter of the class in a future occupation. Career goals and curricula are discussed in detail by Lester and Tamarkin in Chapter 6.

Affective goals would meet the wants and needs of students in *Affective goals* developing a positive self-image, in providing a feeling of success regardless of the student's rate of achievement, and in helping him to recognize and deal with his feelings. Valette and Disick (100) have given examples of five stages of behavior in the affective taxonomy. Objectives for the affective domain are also stated rather specifically in *Performance Objectives for Foreign Languages in Michigan Schools* (73).

Papalia and Zampogna (71) urge that teachers must be aware of the learner's feelings. In an experimental group where the stress changed from subject matter to emphasis on both the cognitive and affective domains, results suggest that the students in the experimental group were challenged, cared about each other, worked according to their ability, were more satisfied with the work in the class, and scored higher in the four skills on achievement examinations.

To shape the curriculum closer to the needs and potentials of the learner and to help him move toward free and responsible maturity, *Student involvement in setting goals* he must be progressively involved in making decisions about his educational program (Keller, 57; Van Til, 101). Grittner (45) cautions against excessive freedom for the student; we "cannot base our curriculum on the confused and transitory gropings of youth" (p. 11). He would concur with Sobol's (89) view of the teacher's role, as one of guiding, but not dominating nor abdicating.

The learner wants and needs to know what is expected of him and why he is engaged in an activity. The teacher who understands the "personal character of motivation can help individual students to set themselves attainable goals, no matter what their degree of aptitude, thus building up their self-confidence and increasing their motivation" (Rivers, 81, p. 64).

Although community college students generally want a practical approach to language study, they are also interested in the study of foreign literature, especially in translation in the first- and second-year courses (Archer and O'Rourke, 7). Marottoli (65) and Brown (18) report on the increasingly large number of adults in commercial language schools for personal interest or for business. A multinational company headquartered in St. Paul sponsors a club with 700 employee members who meet for language lessons and practice and who travel together all over the world (Arendt, 8).

Diverse clientele/diverse goals

An interest-centered curriculum could well be a matter of survival for a number of secondary language programs by the end of this decade (Grittner, 45). The learner-centered program would recognize the importance of student initiative and participation in planning what is to be studied and ways in which classes are to be run. It would allow more scope and choice and independence to the learner. The learning method would also be put in the hands of the learner (Fantini, 31). According to Trump (97), it would reduce required learning and respond to students' demands for options. Bourque (15) and Potter (77) report that student involvement in planning leads to greater motivation and greater depth in learning. Most teachers seem to agree that the student needs guidance; perhaps the teacher's responsibility would focus on preparing a framework with options. The contract is seen by many educators as a satisfactory vehicle for cooperative teacher-student program planning (Bockman and Bockman, 13; Bornscheuer, 14; Karrasch, 56).

Learner-established goals: the future in FL Education?

Cooperative planning would take on different dimensions at elementary, secondary, and college levels. The profession is just beginning to learn how much students at the different age levels can contribute to the planning process. When teacher and learner agree on goals, variability of achievement and motivation are taken into account.

Many curricula

Curriculum, in a general sense, refers to the various operations and materials that will lead to the attainment of the goals. Obviously these operations and materials must be considered in the full complexity of resources available; learner needs, backgrounds, abilities, and learning styles; and teacher abilities and traits. One way of approaching this mass of factors is to consider the preeminence given to the learner.

"Curriculum" as the arrangements for attaining goals

A shift toward a more humanized curriculum reflects a basic shift in the relationship between cognition and affect (Fantini, 31). In the traditional institution, affect was viewed only in terms of motivation as the means for connecting the learner with the institutional content—academic knowledge as determined by the need of the discipline. The reformed institution reverses the flow by linking knowledge to the learner's intrinsic concerns. It is person rather than subject oriented.

Degree of emphasis upon learner

Allen (2) asks that teachers attempt to tailor a program to meet the needs and interests of each member of the class and that time and opportunities should be provided for each student to progress at his own will and pace. While initial capabilities of the learner play an important part in determining the conditions required for subsequent learning, some decisions of great importance to education cannot be made by applying a knowledge of the principles of learning. These decisions are clearly humanistic. For instance, many aspects of personal interaction between a teacher and his students do not pertain in a strict sense to the acquisition of skills and knowledges that typically form the content of the curriculum; among these, motivation, attitudes, and values are tremendously important. Focus on the unique characteristics of the learner requires highly diversified curricula and what has come to be known as individualized learning (Dodge, 28).

While most educators would agree that individual student-prescribed programs would be desirable for accommodating learning factors, they recognize the problems of implementation of an ideal program. Pointing out the difficulty in reconciling the idealized and the feasible, Jarvis (53) acknowledges that compromise is necessary, inevitable. Warriner (103) stresses that there are many interpretations of individualizing learning and many ways to individualize. She sees individualizing instruction as a matter of degree rather than an absolute. It is not exclusively continuous progress in which each student moves at his own pace; this is one of the more advanced stages of the concept that might serve as a goal for all educators. For many reasons the extreme of individualizing learning may be beyond the reach of the majority of teachers in the forseeable future. She, too, calls for compromise. Individualizing instruction must be seen as a goal that can be sought in varying degrees; every foreign language teacher can, if he tries, take at least one or even a few steps along the way. It is an attitude directed toward helping each student maximize his ability and opportunities for learning to whatever degree this can be done.

Individualized learning: the ideal and the feasible

Individualization seen as a continuum

It thus becomes a continuum which includes the entire range of

54

approaches, even in the conventional classroom, from the use of eye contact between teacher and student to personalizing the dialogue to use of group instruction within the class to differentiated assignments to mini-courses to the continuous progress approach (p. 6).

Individualizing learning thus comes within the reach of every teacher.

All components of the curriculum need to be reconsidered and their relationships altered toward achievement of the goal of success for every individual learner. Changes in format, scope, and content are required. There is a need to distinguish between what is being taught and how it is being taught. The process of acquiring knowledge must be recognized as more important than any specific content of the curriculum (Grittner, 40). The typical teaching of foreign language has been too technical, not sufficiently human. Van Til (101) would have any discipline teach less in order to teach more.

Success as a goal

Although the 1970 Northeast Conference Report (Tursi, 98) stressed the importance of a long sequential study of a second language to attain mastery, that Conference in 1971 (Dodge, 28) recognized the need for an open-ended sequence. Interestingly, the 1972 Northeast Conference (29) recommends that cultural and linguistic training should begin early, preferably by the age of ten. The long sequence is challenged, however, by Green (38) because it has generally failed to hold students. Lafayette (58) sees the long sequence as good, but not necessary. Altman (4) urges recognition of the notion that foreign language study can be meaningful in any amount, and that "meaningfulness can only be made by the learner, not by the teacher" (p. 11). The length of study required would depend upon the personal goals of the individual. Hanzeli and Love (48) feel that the current definition of mastery must be deflated, and attention should be focused on the learning process rather than the length of study. They urge, first, a change in teacher attitudes.

Length of the FL sequence

The selection of content has long been one of the most neglected areas of curriculum planning. It has been frequently acknowledged that changes in our formal programs have left the content generally unaffected (Lafayette, 58; Rivers, 81; Strasheim, 92). Yet supplying and organizing lesson content to fit the existing needs and desires of the students may be the best way for the teacher to manipulate motivation (Tursi, 98). The amount of material to be studied would vary according to the needs and abilities and interests of the individual learner. Although content should vary in order to reflect local conditions, espec-

Selection of content

ially the preoccupations and interests of the community (Rivers, 81), the description of what is to be learned at any moment must be primarily dictated by the scope of the whole language and the use to be made of it (Tursi, 98). A new kind of content would have both intellectual and practical thrust; it would overcome knowledge for the sake of knowledge Grittner (45) would select content in response to three questions:

1 Is it a genuine sample of cultural or linguistic material?

2 Does it fit the student's level of maturity and intellectual development?

3 Is it appealing to the student: Does he perceive it to be interesting or worthwhile (p. 16)?

The focus must be on eclecticism when designing curricula for a plurality of student needs and a diversification of content. Instead of prescribing content and methodology, teachers must provide a myriad of approaches, content, materials, organizational patterns, techniques, and pacing to meet needs of a particular individual in a specific situation (Grittner, 45). The curriculum must be less tied to the text, the teacher, the period, or the classroom. There is a need for an expanded view of the learning environment. Lipton (63) reviews a number of programs in which foreign language education is brought out into the world beyond the boundaries of the school building. When language is recognized as a vehicle of expression, not an end in itself, a multiplicity of opportunities is open to the teacher. Language will be learned as it is used purposefully. Since there is a great variety of content and of activities from which to choose, suitable approaches and pace of learning can be as varied as the personalities and temperaments of the students (Grittner, 45).

Wholeness in Learning (105) illustrates such a flexible approach. It presents a framework for a unit of study that has as its component parts: key ideas, concepts, performance objectives with assessment tests, and tasks. No attempt is made to develop each component, but rather to give a number of specific examples within each one to guide a teacher desiring to follow this procedure. It provides for the teacher structure to organize the whole unit in advance so that he can devote more of his energies to guiding student learning.

Rivers (81) would encourage teachers to think through the implications of each situation as it arises and to develop their programs as they and the students see them. Educators must gather all that is good from past methods and entertain the possibility of providing more than one curriculum using more than one approach at more than one time to more than one group of students (Lafayette, 58). This might well

Complexity of curricular decisions

A sample structure

56

imply, for example, a restructuring of the program to allow for two groups, one working alone and one following the traditional teacher-directed classroom. It also implies a need for further research on modes of learning.

While the recommendation is made that organization and scheduling *Scheduling* be flexible to accommodate the various rates at which students learn, Arendt (8) notes that in many places flexible scheduling has been scrapped. Papalia and Zampogna (71) feel no special school schedule is required to meet individual needs. Viable solutions to problems of organization and scheduling are still being sought.

What then are the options on curricula? Looking first at beginning foreign language study, one notes that there are fewer FLES programs today, a situation that is likely to continue, given budgetary crises of most school systems. The focus in existing programs, however, is on a broader view of language study. There is much attention to the foreign culture as well as to interdisciplinary approaches. The Latin FLES *Latin FLES program in* program in Philadelphia is an excellent example of a meaningful curri- *Philadelphia* culum successfully reaching a broader population. Teachers emphasize oral Latin, English vocabulary study through Latin roots, and the influence of ancient Greece and Rome on our own culture and civilization. Reports show that 5th-grade Latin pupils performed one full year higher than other pupils on the Iowa Vocabulary Test. Multisensory instructional materials are an essential part of the program (30). Another FLES model that is being effectively related to *FLES in Washington, D.C.* thousands of children of varying abilities and cultural backgrounds is the program in French, Spanish, and Latin in Washington, D.C. (Dodge, 28).

Wherever foreign language study is begun, Rivers (81) proposes a *A two-stage design* two-stage program. Its purpose would be to provide an opportunity for more students to develop an openness to new ideas and new ways of expression and a tolerance of difference. Stage 1 would be designed as terminal; it would be planned in such a way that whoever passed through it would have acquired something of educational and humanistic value, even if this were his only contact with a foreign language in his lifetime. The teacher would be challenged to make the stage interesting in order to recruit for Stage 2 students who really wanted to master the language. She envisions Stage 1 as an end in itself and not merely a prerequisite for the next level. An outline of goals for Stage 1 follows: *Goals for Stage 1*

1 An introduction to language itself through a specific foreign language, to the way language operations express meanings, and

to the way the native language and the foreign language interpret reality

2   An introduction to the way another people thinks, feels, values, and acts

3   An experience of being another people, where the language knowledge acquired would be immediately acted out

4   An experience of communicating with another people.

Included in the program aims would be "involvement of all students in planning, in group research and interaction, in interdisciplinary exploration, and in human contacts in nearby communities or through correspondence" (p. 117). Stage 2 students would have elected to strive for mastery of the foreign language. In trying to reach a broader population on a Stage 1-Stage 2 approach, it would be reasonable to expect a large dropout rate. *Stage 2*

Alternative approaches would provide for various terminal courses with goals related to the interests and needs of the students in any specific course. The goal would be achieved regardless of the length of the course. Some goals would take longer to achieve than others, but this is understood by the students. Courses might last from one semester to four or more, each of which should give the student a complete experience (Rivers, 81). Lafayette (58) urges colleges and universities to reconsider their entire structure of lower-level language courses to see whether it might be possible to offer a variety of terminal courses aimed at a much broader population.

An exploratory program would allow a way to make language learning accessible to all students and to offer it at the right age, according to Grittner (41). In this program the highly motivated student who has a particular aptitude for language study would be able to go on to rather high levels of achievement. An exploratory concept outlined for Grades 5 to 8 would provide, for all students, a foreign language learning experience that is worthwhile for its own sake. Each student could judge from this introduction whether he wanted to continue the study of a foreign language. The unique aspects of the exploratory program are: *Exploratory programs*

Characteristics of exploratory programs

1   The program is self-sufficient; there is no attempt to make it fit sequentially with subsequent foreign language instruction in the senior high school.

2   The emphasis is on breadth; that is, the program offers a bona fide sampling of many aspects of foreign language learning.

3   The program is nonselective; its purpose is to provide a language learning experience for *all* students, regardless of grade point

average or vocational aspirations, or other alleged predictors of success.

4 The atmosphere in the class is "low pressure"; emphasis is on covering a limited amount of material thoroughly.

5 Homework is minimal. The basic idea of the exploratory curriculum is to do a few things that represent foreign language learning and do them well. Content would include certain key cultural concepts using the foreign language wherever possible as well as some limited work in the four skills and pronunciation of sounds of the new language.

Most teachers tend to agree that there is a need for a solid core of basic language to be controlled before the student can benefit from a highly diversified program (Grittner, 45; Rivers, 81). This level seems to allow the least flexibility; it presents the greatest challenge to wrap the essentials in a new package and to provide creative involvement when the student's control of language is minimal. The 1971 Northeast Conference (Dodge, 28) presented a model of an undifferentiated core of instruction. The initial course, which would emphasize the sound system, basic grammar, and simple vocabulary, would be open to all students. Then they would pursue studies of their choice, following vocational or personal objectives or academic interests leading to college objectives.

Core before diversification

The primary task of the beginning level in most programs continues to be skill development. Although a program may be designed around a common core of content, both pace and skill emphasis may well vary. Hanzeli and Love (48) ask whether the core of the foreign language program can be altered. This appears to be a question where consensual agreement within the profession would be highly desirable.

Grittner (45) makes a convincing argument for attention to the interests of students; he sees the interest-centered curriculum as the implementation of humanistic education. Whatever the student is interested in doing would become the starting point; there would always be a direct, perceptible line between student practice and where that practice leads, including a visible personal outcome for each practice session; the content would be oriented to outcomes the learner perceives to be relevant; satisfaction would not be postponed until the advanced levels. The student would also be involved in decisions about how he could best attain those outcomes. Rivers (81), recognizing the need to relate to student concerns, suggests that one may need to resort to discussion in English to achieve vigorous discussion of questions that are of deep concern to the students. She recommends the use of

Day-to-day relevance in the curriculum

A legitimate use of native language

59

research projects to pursue interests. Gahala (35) outlines program activities and values for the nontalented in foreign language.

"Tracking," "practical" or "conversational" language courses are increasing as alternatives to the "normal" course, which has generally been designed for the college-preparatory student. Junior and community college enrollments continue to grow rapidly with a majority of their population coming from the lowest socioeconomic level. Allen (3) stresses that a central question is "How do we get the 'non-academic' student interested in foreign language study and how do we keep him interested?"

Beyond the introductory level, teachers have provided a great variety of diversified program offerings. Lipton (63) thoroughly describes innovative curricula. Although she reports mainly the metropolitan scene on the East Coast, most of the programs could be adapted to any school. Many programs are also described in other chapters of this volume.

Mini-course concept

There is a proliferation of specialized courses, especially mini-courses, as programs are attempted that accommodate the needs and interests of a heterogeneous population. Agatstein (1) uses topics suggested by students and ties them in with literary pieces. Courses have been designed for students who wish to focus on listening, speaking, or specialized reading.

Relating to the entire curriculum

The foreign language program must relate to all aspects of the curriculum (Rivers, 81). *Wholeness in Learning* (105) outlines a program in which students in the middle grades experience another culture through its language; an interdisciplinary approach relates geography, art, music, folklore, dances, etc., to each unit theme. Interdisciplinary approaches have been discussed at length by Warriner (102). She adds that the concept of interdisciplinary programs is more securely, if less obviously, rooted in the foreign language curriculum today (103). See also chapter 5 in this volume.

Curricular arrangement for career goals

As indicated earlier, interest in career-oriented language programs is growing rapidly. Tamarkin (95) developed a program in Career Spanish to fill a basic need in the community college two-year sequence. All students begin with one semester of basic Spanish. In the second semester they may choose to continue with the traditional sequence or to study Spanish for Career Preparation. Lipton (63) reports on new programs in which students have opportunities for work/study experiences using the foreign language; she predicts for the future more career-communication courses, with major stress on utility, and opportunities for work/study and on-the-job practice. Lester and

Tamarkin discuss in detail curricula for careers using foreign language in Chapter 6.

The College of San Mateo is enjoying considerable success by responding to needs and interests of people in the community; conversation classes and mini-courses have attracted younger and older people (Cordes, 26). In response to requests, it is offering Spanish for Police Officers, for Social Workers, and for Nurses; German for Travelers and Business People; and French for Airline Personnel. The college also has experimented with half-speed traditional first-semester courses to accommodate students who have difficulty learning language. Courses for native speakers only have been structured to give the native the special training he needs. A topical survey of foreign literature in translation is being planned. In addition to offering a number of career training courses, Loop Junior College in Chicago has provided courses in The Sounds of English specifically for native speakers of Spanish and Swahili, Spanish for Hispano-americanos, Modern Hebrew, Japanese, and Italian (Quiros de Haggard, 78). They are exploring the possibility of offering Polish for Americans of Polish descent and programs for bilingual secretaries. English as a second language is an important program in community colleges in areas where large migrant or immigrant populations are served. Hussey (49) stresses the urgency for these students to learn English well enough, within a relatively short time, to pursue academic courses in their curricula or to get and hold jobs. She reports a need for TESL-trained teachers, materials and tests.

Gregory (39) believes that the student's "feelings, motives, aspirations, and values become valid subject matter as the learning process forces them into his and his teacher's consciousness" (p. 87). As the teacher takes advantage of those situations in which feelings and emotions, both his and his students', become prime concerns; affect becomes content. As the teacher provides information that will help his students achieve a better understanding of their own feelings and as he continually strives to improve human relationships in his classroom, education becomes personal growth. Teaching becomes helping a student go where *he* wants to go. Gregory outlines and demonstrates procedures for helping preservice and in-service teachers learn how to deal with affect as content. Keller (57), too, would place emphasis on feelings as a means to humanize education. The way to a man's mind is through his feelings. He would include development of inner resources and feeling of identification with the past and with one's neighbors. Thus he suggests that students can be encouraged to

One college's diversification

A course about English

Language study as a course in affect

61

express their feelings in journals in which they put down their thoughts, questions, reactions to what they read, hear, and experience.

There are scattered reports from colleges and universities of program modifications directed toward meeting student needs based on individual aptitudes and interests (Clausing, Mueller, and Voge, 23; Jian, 54; Marti, 66; Teichert, 96). Curricular offerings at the University of Illinois include general courses, accelerated courses, intensive courses, independent study, and proficiency tests for faster advancement. The student has a choice of the following modalities: modified audiolingual, eclectic, reading approach, conversational, and computer-assisted instruction. Intermediate courses provide a variety of content: literature (including black literature), civilization and culture, contrastive French and American culture, scientific material, newspapers and magazines, and individually selected content (Rivers, 80). Rich (79) reports on self-instructional programs in critical languages. Students have given as reasons for taking the courses: cultural interest, desire to travel, intellectual challenge, career goals, and belief in the growing importance of the non-western world. Self-instruction gives a chance to test student interest; if enough students are attracted, a full-time teacher and schedule can be provided. The strategy also serves the student interested in an uncommonly taught language for which demand is limited.

Bilingual-bicultural curricula

A variety of approaches to curricula for bilingual-bicultural education exist. The structure of these programs depends to a great extent upon the ethnic organization of the local community. The program of the Milwaukee Public Schools (6), for example, is structured to develop reading skills in the dominant language and comprehension of basic concepts of space, time, and quantity in the primary grades. Oral comprehension and reading skills in English and in Spanish and studies in mathematics receive most attention in the intermediate grades. The program at the secondary level, which welcomes non-hispano students, focuses on content learning in the areas of history, sociology, economics, and geography. An aspect of the Milwaukee program that is particularly noteworthy is the active involvement of community members in program planning.

Bilingual-bicultural curriculum arrangements

Courses in Chippewa language, developed by the Minnesota Department of Education (21), have been implemented in elementary schools in Minnesota, Wisconsin, and Canada. The program, which is bicultural rather than bilingual, correlates language activities with

Chippewa language courses

62

other subjects. Established in response to requests from the Indian community for teaching of the native language so that it will not be lost, the program has resulted in greater interest of parents in the schools. North Dakota, too, has begun implementation of an Indian studies curriculum, with the goal of reaching all schools in the state by the fall of 1974 (Whitman, 104). The program is planned to include all areas pertaining to Indian experience—culture, history, language, tribal government, literature, ecology, science, arts and crafts, recreation, and music and dance. All of the project workers are fluent in the tribal language. Emphasizing this vital part of culture, one of the staff workers says, "The language—that's ours; that's us." Hopefully the Indian studies curriculum will lessen considerably the huge dropout rate, which is blamed on the "lack of relevant education materials and of teachers sensitive to the needs of Indian children" (p. 58).

Sample curricula in New Mexico

New Mexico, where 41 percent of the school population is of Spanish-speaking background, was the first state in the nation to issue a statement of policy on bilingual education. Bilingual programs there, mostly in Grades 1 to 4 at this time, adhere to one of two basic curricular plans. The Armijo Bilingual Demonstration Center, for example, has structured studies in language arts, social studies (with heavy orientation toward the value system of hispanic culture), mathematics, and fine arts in Spanish for a half day. The English component is designed with complementary classes in social studies, mathematics, music, and art. Most programs follow the plan of Las Cruces where a dual language approach is organized to study the same content in two languages. Pascual (72) emphasizes that the values of the culture are stressed, not to make the child more Mexican or Indian than American, but to make the children aware of their culture's own contributions and values. Aspects of the bilingual-bicultural curriculum are discussed in detail in Chapter 4 of this volume.

Goals and not curricula

It is interesting to note that the concept of diversity has not yet had much impact upon "curriculum"—as opposed to "curricular goals." There is widespread acceptance of varying goals for different students, but for any given goal there is much less discussion of multiple curricula—or multiple routes for attaining the goal. Discussion of diversity has not yet come to grips with individual differences in learning style, modes, or strategies. This concern may indeed dominate future attention of the profession.

Implications

As multiple goals and diverse curricula for a wide range of learners are defined and described, it becomes necessary to consider implications for the teacher. With the trend toward emphasizing the needs of the learner, it may seem that the importance of the teacher is diminished. Yet the student is emphasized only when the teacher is willing and able to do it. "The teacher remains the primary mover, the primary motivator, the primary agent relating the learner to the subject matter to be learned" (Hammerly, 46, p. 504). The teacher must first be thoroughly committed to the belief that all children can learn a foreign language, although they may vary in learning rates and ability (Tursi, 98). The responsibility of helping students both to establish suitable goals and to achieve them lies with the teacher (Sutton, 94). He must be attentive to the learner, for his role is to be responsive rather than prescriptive (Jarvis, 52). Allen (2) perceives the teacher as a co-learner and a catalyst. According to Warriner (103), he is the source of quality control. He must make available to the student his expertise and his experience so that the cooperative decisions of student and teacher result in efficient learning. He is challenged to establish interpersonal relationships which cause the student to want to do things on his own (Grittner, 45). Flexibility is thus the most important requirement for teachers at all levels today; they need the ability and the courage to experiment with reshuffling of all components of the curriculum, absorbing the best from various past methods into the context of present and future programs. Still, teachers are perplexed and threatened by the constant demands for change and innovation (Rivers, 82). Obviously, not all of them are ready for change.

Importance of teacher

Teacher anxiety

The greatest concern of many teachers is that of adjusting to new routines and practices required to achieve the diverse goals of heterogeneous classes. The teacher can gain useful ideas from articles in journals, but he urgently needs to observe and experience new approaches before making a decision whether to change to a more flexible program that would respond to the needs of individual students. Lipton (63) says, "to coerce any teacher to do anything without his understanding and commitment is an exercise in unreality" (p. 202).

Innovative curricula

It is not essential that the teacher's information, skills, and learning styles be perfectly matched with those of a student (Lange and James, 60). Teacher individuality is a trait to be respected too, as much as student individuality. Just as there is no single best way for all children to learn, there is no one magical formula that all teachers must adopt. Wolfe and Smith (107) and Kalivoda and Elkins (55) have discussed in detail the role of the teacher in relation to new goals.

No single best way to teach

Materials

The role of materials becomes more important in a program that proposes to accommodate learners from a wide range of backgrounds, rather than just the traditional middle-class, college-oriented student. Grittner (45) believes the textbook is still needed to introduce the student in an orderly progression to the structural concepts of the language. The teacher must, however, expand and reinforce the text with a great variety of supplementary materials and activities. An extensive collection of books and audiovisual resources must be easily accessible for student use and reference. Learning activities that involve students in full participation would require production supplies that would enable students to produce their own films, slides, sound tracks, tapes, and foreign language publications. Green (38) predicts that the text will give way to packets, packages, and learning kits, each of which can be easily and inexpensively replaced, revised, or updated as necessary.

A lesser role for published textbooks

The trend is toward more teacher involvement in developing or adapting materials, as evidenced by the extensive display of teacher-prepared materials at the 1972 ACTFL Conference. Numerous approaches have been developed at the local level to allow greater freedom to the learner through using a variety of materials. Rosenthal (83) outlines procedures for developing learning activity packages to provide alternative objectives, media, methodologies, resources, and follow-up activities that would be suitable for varied student learning patterns. Acknowledging the amount of time required for writing learning activity packages, she calls for colleges to coordinate the efforts of groups of teachers in developing these materials. The University of Minnesota (99) has taken an initial step in this direction. Rosenthal (83) recommends the use of LAPs developed by other teachers and further urges the establishment of clearing house centers to facilitate the exchange of learning packages.

Thus, it appears that we have finally begun to put materials, whether they be published textbooks, films, or teacher handouts, into the proper perspective. They are resources—resources to be used in attaining the goals established—nothing more, nothing less.

Materials in perspective

Evaluation

A diversity of goals and efforts toward personalized curricula requires profound changes in evaluation. First, it becomes evident that large-scale programs of achievement testing may not be desirable (Green, 38). Clark (22) sees increasing importance for the role of formative evaluation for guiding individual student progress. In this view much

Formative evaluation

65

more emphasis would be placed upon evaluation of the student to help him learn rather than evaluation to label him. Tests would be used to indicate mastery of material in small increments at each level before continuing; they would give important feedback to show how much students have learned (Sandstrom and Pimsleur, 84). The learner-centered curriculum would utilize criterion-referenced measures of performance rather than norm-referenced measures (Trump, 97). Student progress would be evaluated on the basis of individual past record rather than on a comparison with others in the same group; at the same time data might be provided that would allow each person to know what others are accomplishing.

There is an obvious need to develop achievement tests for measuring student acquisition of specific language-use goals that have been discussed in this chapter. To allow even the least able students greater opportunity to experience some degree of success, there is a need to test "passive" knowledge as well as "active" knowledge (Sandstrom and Pimsleur, 84). Clark (22) views self-testing as a means to increase student motivation through closer personal involvement in the measurement process.

The problems for teachers in developing a large number of tests with alternate forms must be acknowledged. Even though some teachers might have the time and energy to devote to this task, they may *Can teachers create good tests?* lack knowledge and skill in test development to produce test items that would yield reliable evaluation of desired student behaviors. Clark suggests that an independent organization might develop a pool of test items from which schools could choose items that would be appropriate to their local situations.

If the needs of a broader population of learners are to be met, there must be continuing attention to the measurement of student-related learning variables. More reliable information is needed about aptitude, individual learning styles, student attitudes, and motivation (Clark, 22). Sutton (94) suggests that the affective domain could and should be considered in evaluating the success of a student or program. She posits that it would be as "logical to administer an attitude survey as a standardized achievement test to students in individualized study programs" (p. 110).

Summary

1 The change in many foreign language classrooms during the past few years has been both rapid and dramatic. Consider, for

example, the perception of a prospective teacher who during the late 1960s studied a foreign language in an average high school, who pursued a typical teacher-education program (which reflected the earlier experience as a student), and who then interviewed for a teaching position in one of the more innovative programs described in this volume! *One* curriculum, *one* set of goals, and a *single* type of learner have not only become plural, but the order has been reversed; hence, the full meaning of "many learners, many goals, many curricula" continues to become a reality of foreign language education during the early 1970s.

2 The learner—his time, his wants, his needs—is now given much more attention. Today's foreign language teacher is more aware than ever before of the great variation within any given class of interests, aptitudes, motivations, aspirations, experiences, ages, and sex. He sees that these variables do have a real impact on learning. Today's clientele also differs from that of the previous generation, especially in its values and approaches to learning. Students identify a multiplicity of goals, both humanistic and utilitarian. These goals do not seem strikingly different from those stated by the profession. There are, however, indications that the profession is merely beginning to achieve the proposed goals. Students need to be involved in cooperative planning in order to reconcile personal goals with instructional goals.

3 With an understanding of the types of abilities the students want to develop and the kinds of interests they have, many curricula can be designed. A diversity of programs must be implemented in which any student can really learn something he believes in and can feel that he is doing it successfully.

4 Diversification of goals implies a new attitude toward materials for the foreign language program as well as toward evaluation strategies. New and diverse goals that entail further teacher preparation in in-service programs, the writing of additional materials, experimentation with new ideas, and the new attitudes about the teacher role may make teachers' lives more difficult. But the result will be fuller lives.

5 It seems reasonable to conclude that the trends of recent years toward diversification and pluralism, toward greater autonomy for the learner, and away from prescription seem to be continuing —and there is no indication in the work of 1972 that a change from this direction is imminent.

References, Many learners, many goals, many curricula

1 Agatstein, Michael. "La révolte des jeunes or an Experiment in Relevancy," *French Review* 43(1970): 637–40.

2 Allen, Edward D. *The Teacher as Catalyst: Motivation in the Classroom*, [Paper presented at the Central States Conference on the Teaching of Foreign Languages, April, 1973.] [Mimeo.]

3 Allen, Louise H. "The College of the 80's—Or Where the Action Is," 14–25 in Wilga M. Rivers, Louise H. Allen, Sandra Savignon, and Richard Scanlan,eds., *Changing Patterns in Foreign Language Programs: Report of the Illinois Conference on Foreign Languages in Junior and Community Colleges, 1972*, Rowley, Massachusetts: Newbury House, 1972.

4 Altman, Howard B. "Foreign Language Instruction: A Mandate for Pluralism," 3–13 in Wilga M. Rivers, Louise H. Allen, Sandra Savignon, and Richard Scanlan,eds., *Changing Patterns in Foreign Language Programs: Report of the Illinois Conference on Foreign Languages in Junior and Community Colleges, 1972*. Rowley, Massachusetts: Newbury House, 1972.

5 —— "The Three R's of Individualization: Reeducation, Responsibility, and Relevance." *Foreign Language Annals* 6(1972):206–13.

6 *Application for Continuation of the Milwaukee Bilingual Education Program*, Title VII, Title I, ESEA Milwaukee Public Schools, 1973.

7 Archer, Raymond, and Daniel O'Rourke. "Student Interests in Foreign Language Programs," 186–91 in Wilga M. Rivers, Louise Allen, Sandra Savignon, and Richard Scanlan,eds., *Changing Patterns in Foreign Language Programs: Report of the Illinois Conference on Foreign Languages in Junior and Community Colleges, 1972*, Rowley, Massachusetts: Newbury House, 1972.

8 Arendt, Jermaine D. *Where from Here?* [Paper presented at the Iowa Foreign Language Workshop, Iowa City, March 1973.]

9 Badillo, Herman. "The Politics and Realities of Bilingual Education." *Foreign Language Annals* 5(1972):297–301.

10 Baughman, M. Dale. *What Do Students Really Want?* Bloomington, Indiana: Phi Delta Kappa Educational Foundation, 1972.

11 Bennis, Warren. "The University Leader." *Saturday Review: Education* 55(1973):43–44,49–50.

12 Birkmaier, Emma M. "The Meaning of Creativity in Foreign Language Teaching." *Modern Language Journal* 50(1971):345–53.

13 Bockman, John F., and Valerie M. Bockman. "Contracts Versus the Commitment Process." *Foreign Language Annals* 6(1973):359–66.

14 Bornscheuer, Joan H. "The Grade Contract and the Language Class." *Foreign Language Annals* 6(1973):367–70.

15 Bourque, Jane. "Voice of the Student." *American Foreign Language Teacher* 1,i (1970)3–5,42.

16 Brooks, Nelson. "Culture—A New Frontier." *Foreign Language Annals* 5(1971):54–61.

17 —— "The Rung and the Ladder," 135–47 in Joseph A. Tursi,ed., *Foreign Languages and the "New" Student*. [Reports of the Working Committees of the Northeast Conference on the Teaching of Foreign Languages.] New York: Modern Language Association Materials Center, 1970.

18 Brown, Vivian. "Spanish Is Becoming America's Second Language." *Des Moines Tribune* (31 January 1973):13.

19 Bruner, Jerome S. "The Process of Education Revisited." *Phi Delta Kappan* 53(1971):18–21.

20 Cavanaugh, Neal F. "Should There be Foreign 'Language' Courses?" *The Bulletin of the National Association of Secondary School Principals* 56(1972): 91–95.

21 *Chippewa Indian Language Project*. St. Paul, Minnesota: Department of Education, 1969.

22 Clark, John L.D. "Measurement Implications of Recent Trends in Foreign Language Teaching," 219–58 in Dale L. Lange and Charles J. James, eds., *Foreign Language Education: A Reappraisal*. ACTFL Review of Foreign Language Education, Volume 4. Skokie, Illinois: National Textbook Company, 1972.

23 Clausing, Gerhard, Klaus A. Mueller, and Wilfried M. Voge. "Individualized German Instruction at the College Level—A First Appraisal." *Foreign Language Annals* 6(1972):73–87.

24 Cloos, Robert I. "A Four-Year Study of Foreign Language Aptitude at the High School Level" *Foreign Language Annals* 4(1971):411–19.

25 Coleman, James. "The Children Have Outgrown the Schools." *Psychology Today* 5,ix(1972):72–76,82.

26 Cordes, Henry M. "Keeping the Door to the Future Open Through Imaginative Course Development," 209–13 in Wilga M. Rivers, Louise H. Allen, Sandra Savignon, and Richard T. Scanlan,eds., *Changing Patterns in Foreign Language Programs: Report of the Illinois Conference on Foreign Languages in Junior and Community Colleges, 1972*. Rowley, Massachusetts: Newbury House, 1972.

27 *Deriving Curricular Objectives Training Unit*. Berkeley, California: Far West Laboratory for Educational Research and Development, 1971.

28 Dodge, James W.,ed., *Leadership for Continuing Development*. [Reports of the Working Committees of the Northeast Conference on the Teaching of Foreign Languages.] New York: Modern Language Association Materials Center, 1971.

29 —— *Other Words, Other Worlds: Language-in-Culture*. [Reports of the Working Committees of the Northeast Conference on the Teaching of

Foreign Languages.] New York: Modern Language Association Materials Center, 1972.

30 "Dramatic Results Achieved in Philadelphia School District's Elementary School Latin Program." *Accent on ACTFL* 2,iii(1972):22.

31 Fantini, Mario D. *The Reform of Urban Schools.* Washington: National Education Association, Center for the Study of Instruction, 1970.

32 Fearing, Percy, and Jermaine D. Arendt. *The Extended Foreign Language Sequence: With Emphasis on New Courses for Levels IV and V.* St. Paul: Minnesota Department of Education, 1971.

33 *Foreign Language Framework for the California Public Schools.* Sacramento: California State Department of Education, 1972.

34 Foshay, Arthur W. *Curricula for the 70's: An Agenda for Invention.* Washington, D.C.: National Education Association, 1970.

35 Gahala, John W. "Me? Study a Language? I Don't Know No English." *Accent on ACTFL* 2,iii(1972):12–13.

36 Glasser, William. "The Identity Society." *Learning* 1,ii(1972):28–29.

37 Gorman, Burton W. "Change in the Secondary School:Why and How?" *Phi Delta Kappan* 53(1972): 565–68.

38 Green, Jerald R. "Purposes and Goals in Foreign Language Education:A Look to the Future," 1–34 in Dale L. Lange and Charles J. James,eds., *Foreign Language Education:A Reappraisal.* ACTFL Review of Foreign Language Education, Volume 4. Skokie, Illinois: National Textbook Company, 1972.

39 Gregory, Thomas B. *Encounters With Teaching: A Microteaching Manual.* Englewood Cliffs, New Jersey: Prentice-Hall, 1972.

40 Grittner, Frank M. "Behavioral Objectives, Skinnerian Rats, and Trojan Horses." *Foreign Language Annals* 6(1972):52–60.

41 —— "Foreign Languages and the Changing Curriculum." *Newsletter*, Wisconsin Department of Public Instruction 24,ix(1971):6–13.

42 —— "Individualized Foreign Language Instruction:New Myths and Old Realities." *Canadian Modern Language Review* 25,i(1972):8–14.

43 —— "Pluralism in Foreign Language Education:A Reason for Being," 9–58 in Dale L. Lange, ed., *Pluralism in Foreign Language Education*, ACTFL Review of Foreign Language Education, Volume 3. Skokie, Illinois: National Textbook Company, 1973.

44 —— *Training Foreign Language Teachers in an Age of Pluralism.* [Paper presented at Indiana University, Bloomington, Indiana, Spring 1972.]

45 —— *The Teacher as Co-Learner:Interest-Centered Materials*, [Paper presented at the Central States Conference on the Teaching of Foreign Language, April 1973.] [Mimeo.]

46 Hammerly, Hector. "Recent Methods and Trends in Second Language Teaching." *Modern Language Journal* 55(1971):499–505.

47 Hancock, Charles R. "Student Aptitude, Attitude, and Motivation," 127–56 in Dale L. Lange and Charles J. James,eds., *Foreign Language Education: A Reappraisal.* ACTFL Review of Foreign Language Education, Volume 4. Skokie, Illinois: National Textbook Company, 1972.

48 Hanzeli, Victor E., and F. William D. Love. "From Individualized Instruction to Individualized Learning." *Foreign Language Annals* 5(1972):321–30.

49 Hussey, Marie. "English as a Second Language in Illinois Junior and Community Colleges," 177–85 in Wilga M. Rivers, Louise H. Allen, Sandra Savignon, and Richard Scanlan,eds., *Changing Patterns in Foreign Language Programs:Report of the Illinois Conference on Foreign Languages in Junior and Community Colleges, 1972.* Rowley, Massachusetts: Newbury House, 1972.

50 Hutchinson, Gail. Interview in *Accent on ACTFL*, 3,i(1972):22–23.

51 Jakobovits, Leon A. *The New Linguistics and Foreign Language Teaching.* Rowley, Massachusetts: Newbury House, 1972.

52 Jarvis, Gilbert A. "Teacher Education Goals: They're Tearing Up the Street Where I Was Born." *Foreign Language Annals* 6(1972):198–205.

53 —— "Individualized Learning—Where Can We Risk Compromise?" *Modern Language Journal* 55(1971):375–78.

54 Jian, Gerard. "Le Programme de première année à Berkeley," *French Review* 45(1972):846–49.

55 Kalivoda, Theodore B., and Robert J. Elkins. "Teaching as Facilitation and Management of Learning," 61–98 in Dale L. Lange and Charles J. James,eds., *Foreign Language Education:A Reappraisal.* ACTFL Review of Foreign Language Education, Volume 4. Skokie, Illinois: National Textbook Company, 1972.

56 Karrasch, Ada. "Contracts Cure," *Accent on ACTFL* 3,iii(1973):10.

57 Keller, Charles R. "Humanizing Education," *The Bulletin of the National Association of Secondary School Principals* 56(1972):9–16.

58 Lafayette, Robert C. "Diversification:The Key to Student-Centered Programs." *Modern Language Journal* 56(1972):349–54.

59 Landor, R.A. "Foreign Language in Elementary Liberal Education." *Modern Language Journal* 55(1971):508–10.

60 Lange, Dale L., and Charles J. James. "Foreign Language Education:A Reappraisal" 377–91 in Dale L. Lange and Charles J. James,eds., *Foreign Language Education:A Reappraisal.* ACTFL Review of Foreign Language Education, Volume 4. Skokie, Illinois: National Textbook Company, 1972.

61 *Language:Missouri Youth Speak Out*, Jefferson City: State Department of Education, 1972.

62 Lenard, Yvonne. *Jeunes Voix, Jeunes Visages*. New York: Harper & Row, 1970.

63 Lipton, Gladys. "Curricula for New Goals," 187–218 in Dale L. Lange and Charles J. James, eds., *Foreign Language Education:A Reappraisal*. ACTFL Review of Foreign Language Education, Volume 4. Skokie, Illinois: National Textbook Company, 1972.

64 Mackey, William F. "Foreword," vii–xiii in Leon A. Jakobovits, *Foreign Language Learning*, Rowley, Massachusetts: Newbury House, 1970.

65 Marottoli, Vincent. "The Success of the Private Language Schools:A Lesson to Be Learned." *Foreign Language Annals* 6(1973):354–58.

66 Marti, Gertrude. "An Intensive French Experience: Some Observations and Results." *French Review* 45(1972):1145–51.

67 Mead, Robert G.,Jr. "Teaching Foreign Languages:A Brief Retrospect and Prospect," 124–37 in James W. Dodge,ed., *Other Words, Other Worlds: Language-in-Culture*. [Reports of the Working Committees of the Northeast Conference on the Teaching of Foreign Languages.] New York: Modern Language Association Materials Center, 1972.

68 Morain, Genelle G. "Cultural Pluralism," 59–98 in Dale L. Lange,ed., *Pluralism in Foreign Language Education*. ACTFL Review of Foreign Language Education, Volume 3. Skokie, Illinois: National Textbook Company, 1973.

69 Nelson, Robert J., and Leon A. Jakobovits,eds., "Motivation in Foreign-Language Learning," 31–104 in Joseph A. Tursi,ed., *Foreign Languages and the "New" Student*. [Reports of the Working Committees of the Northeast Conference on the Teaching of Foreign Languages.] New York: Modern Language Association Materials Center, 1970.

70 *A New Rationale for the Teaching of Foreign Languages in Illinois:A Humanistic View*. Springfield: Office of the Superintendent of Public Instruction, 1972.

71 Papalia, Anthony and Jospeh Zampogna. "An Experiment in Individualized Instruction through Small Group Interaction." *Foreign Language Annals* 5(1972):302–06.

72 Pascual, Henry. Personal communication, 1973.

73 *Performance Objectives for Foreign Languages in Michigan Schools*. [Working Draft.] Lansing: Michigan Department of Education, 1973.

74 Perls, F. [Poster.] Interplanetary, P.O. Box 1338, Sausalito, California 94965.

75 Polinsky, Aaron S. "French for the Educable and Emotionally Disturbed." *French Review* 44(1971): 724–29.

76 Politzer, Robert L., and Louis Weiss. *The Successful Foreign-Language Teacher*. Philadelphia: Center for Curriculum Development, 1971.

77 Potter, Edithe J. "French Conversation for Young Adults." *Modern Language Journal* 55(1971):505–08.

78 Quiros de Haggard, Aurora. "The Colleges of the 80's—The Challenge of the 70's," 27–39 in Wilga M. Rivers, Louise H. Allen, Sandra Savignon, and Richard Scanlan,eds., *Changing Patterns in Foreign Language Programs:Report of the Illinois Conference on Foreign Languages in Junior and Community Colleges, 1972*. Rowley, Massachusetts: Newbury House, 1972.

79 Rich, Leslie, "A Bargain in Any Language." *American Education* 8,ix(1972):25–27.

80 Rivers, Wilga M. "The Non-Major:Tailoring the Course to the Person–Not the Image." in K. Jankowsky,ed., *Language and International Studies*, Monograph Series No. 26. Washington, D.C.: Georgetown University Press, 1973.

81 ——— *Speaking in Many Tongues*. Rowley, Massachusetts: Newbury House, 1972.

82 ——— *Students, Teachers, and the Future*. [Working paper for the Steering Committee of the Modern Language Association Foreign Language Program for the Seventies, 1973.] [Mimeo.]

83 Rosenthal, Bianca. "Developing a Foreign Language Learning Activity Package." *Modern Language Journal* 57(1973):195–99.

84 Sandstrom, Eleanor L., and Paul Pimsleur,eds., "Foreign Languages for All Students?" 106–32 in Joseph A. Tursi,ed., *Foreign Languages and the "New" Student*. [Reports of the Working Committees of the Northeast Conference on the Teaching of Foreign Languages.] New York: Modern Language Association Materials Center, 1970.

85 Seelye, H. Ned. "Analysis and Teaching of the Cross-Cultural Context," 37–81 in Emma Birkmaier,ed., *Foreign Language Education: An Overview*. ACTFL Review of Foreign Language Education, Volume 1. Skokie, Illinois: National Textbook Company, 1972.

86 Shepherd, Everitt W. "An Experiment in Individualized Advanced French." *Foreign Language Annals* 3(1970):394–99.

87 Smith, Philip D.,Jr. *A Comparison of the Cognitive and Audiolingual Approaches to Foreign Language Instruction*. Philadelphia: Center for Curriculum Development, 1970.

88 Smith, William L. "Closing the Lid on the Melting Pot." *Phi Delta Kappan* 53(1972):265–84.

89 Sobol, Thomas. "The Broader Meaning of Articulation." *Phi Delta Kappan* 53(1971):25–29.

90 Steiner, Florence. "Behavioral Objectives and Evaluation," 35–78 in Dale L. Lange,ed., *Individualization of Instruction*. ACTFL Review of Foreign Language Education, Volume 2. Skokie, Illinois: National Textbook Company, 1972.

91 ——— "Individualized Instruction." *Modern Language Journal* 55(1971):361–74.

92 Strasheim, Lorraine A. "Foreign Language:Part of a New Apprenticeship for Living," 18–25 in Lorraine Strasheim,ed., *Foreign Language in a New*

Apprenticeship for Living. Bloomington: The Indiana Language Program, 1971.

93 "Student Position Paper." *Michigan Foreign Language Newsletter*, 1,ii(1972):17.

94 Sutton, Donna E. "Problems of Individualized Instruction—How Some Successful Programs Deal with Them," 86–118 in Ronald L. Gougher,ed., *Individualization of Instruction in Foreign Languages:A Practical Guide.* Philadelphia: Center for Curriculum Development, 1972.

95 Tamarkin, Toby, "Career Spanish," 223–27 in Wilga M. Rivers, Louise H. Allen, Sandra J. Savignon, and Richard T. Scanlan,eds., *Changing Patterns in Foreign Language Programs:Report of the Illinois Conference on Foreign Languages in Junior and Community Colleges, 1972.* Rowley, Massachusetts: Newbury House, 1972.

96 Teichert, Herman U. "An Experimental Study Using Learning Packages in Beginning College German." *Modern Language Journal* 56(1972): 488–90.

97 Trump, J. Lloyd. "On Humanizing Schools." *The Bulletin of the National Association of Secondary School Principals* 56(1972):9–16.

98 Tursi, Joseph A.,ed., *Foreign Languages and the New Student.* [Reports of the Working Committees of the Northeast Conference on the Teaching of Foreign Languages.] New York: Modern Language Association Materials Center, 1970.

99 *University of Minnesota Foreign Language Curriculum Units.* Minneapolis: Foreign Language Curriculum Materials Center, 1972.

100 Valette, Rebecca M., and Renée S. Disick. *Modern Language Performance Objectives and Individualization.* New York: Harcourt, Brace, Jovanovich, 1972.

101 Van Til, William S. "One Way of Looking at It: A Fighting Chance." *Phi Delta Kappan* 53(1972): 325.

102 Warriner, Helen P. "Foreign Language Interdisciplinary Programs and Activities," 125–61 in Dale L. Lange,ed., *Pluralism in Foreign Language Education.* ACTFL Review of Foreign Language Education, Volume 3. Skokie, Illinois: National Textbook Company, 1973.

103 ——— *The Teacher as Quality Control:Program Options.* [Paper presented at the Central States Conference on the Teaching of Foreign Languages, April, 1973.] [Mimeo.]

104 Whitman, Carl. "Indian Curricula from Indians: Breakthrough in North Dakota." *Learning* 1,iii (1973):53–58.

105 *Wholeness in Learning:A Curriculum Guide for Foreign Language Programs in the Middle Grades.* [Working draft.] Baltimore: Maryland State Department of Education, 1972.

106 Wilhelms, Fred T. "Multiple Ways to a More Humane School." *The Bulletin of the National Association of Secondary School Principals* 56(1972):1–8.

107 Wolfe, David E. and Philip D. Smith, "Teacher Education for New Goals," 97–126 in Dale L. Lange and Charles J. James,eds., *Foreign Language Education:A Reappraisal.* ACTFL Review of Foreign Language Education, Volume 4. Skokie, Illnois: National Textbook Company, 1972.

Responses

4

Bilingual education: The national perspective

Introduction

"Now the teacher speaks Spanish!" proclaims a headline in a recent national newspaper. The article outlines the problems encountered by young Mexican-Americans entering public schools in the Southwest— problems that in a 1972 report the United States Commission on Civil Rights attributes to "cultural exclusion" in the area of language, heritage, and community involvement in school affairs (34, p. 13). "This situation is beginning to change," continues the reporter as he then proceeds to describe a bilingual education program in Texas, its philosophy, and its accomplishments.

New items featuring bilingualism and bilingual education programs appear daily in newspapers from coast to coast. They all seem to convey the excitement of a great discovery. However, the discovery is not that there are native-born American children for whom the English language and the American way of life are virtually foreign. Neither is the discovery the discernment that these children experience a number of educational and psychological setbacks in our schools, that many never overcome the obstacles and eventually fail or drop out. Nor is it the recognition that this repeated failure has helped to perpetuate among certain ethnic groups a socioeconomic status that is among the lowest in the United States.

The excitement is generated by the realization that children from linguistic and ethnic minorities are not linguistically and culturally deprived, that by age five they too have mastered all the basic phonology and major grammatical structures of their language, that they too have

María Medina
Swanson
*Illinois Bilingual Education
Service Center*

Bilingual education in the news

An exciting discovery

María Medina Swanson (M.A., University of Texas at Austin) is Director of the Illinois Bilingual Education Service Center in Mt. Prospect. A native of Puerto Rico, she attended schools in Puerto Rico and Europe before coming to the United States. After teaching French and Spanish at the college and secondary levels for eight years, she served as State Foreign Language Supervisor in Texas from 1968–71. She was president of the Texas Foreign Language Association and is on the ACTFL Bibliography Committee. She has taken an active part in national conferences and workshops dealing with foreign language instruction and bilingual education. A member of various professional organizations, she also serves on the advisory board of the National Dissemination Center for Bilingual-Bicultural Education and the Illinois Bilingual Advisory Council.

been learning about themselves and the world around them, that when they come to school they too are ready to begin acquiring the various concepts and skills our educational system deems necessary, and that these concepts and skills are being learned in a language other than English—the child's native language.

The discovery is bilingual education.

Bilingual education: Basic information

Bilingualism is the ability to understand and communicate in two languages and to function in each language independently of the other. A child who has two language systems is *bilingual*. He may have equal skills in both but is usually more proficient in one than the other. A *bicultural* child is able to function in either of two cultures and to shift from one to the other as he chooses or as the occasion demands. *Bilingual education* is the use of two languages—one of which is English in the United States—as media of instruction and the incorporation of two cultures—one of which is the culture of the child from non-English background—into the school curriculum. It is *not* merely "foreign language" teaching. It is *not* merely teaching English to children who speak other languages. It is *not* merely "education for bilinguals." *Brief definitions*

Bilingual education is advantageous for several reasons. The use of English as the sole medium of instruction has left thousands of children illiterate in their native languages and has contributed to low-achievement levels in English itself (Andersson and Boyer, 8). A child begins learning long before he comes to school. By the time he is five years old, he has mastered practically the entire sound system and much of the grammatical structure of his native language. His language already reflects a set of values tied to a particular group—to a way of thinking, feeling, and acting (Pacheco, 87). These are strengths to build upon rather than handicaps to successful learning. By using his native language for classroom instruction, the child is allowed to continue uninterrupted from home to school, permitting immediate progress in concept building rather than postponing development until a new language has been acquired (Saville and Troike, 114). *Rationale*

That bilingual education really works and does not hinder progress in English has been shown. As early as 1962 Peal and Lambert compared socioeconomically matched bilingual and monolingual children and found that the bilingual children performed as well on intelligence tests and had the added advantage of knowing a second language (Andersson and Boyer, 8). Recent research studies have shown that an *Some results*

English achievement

76

equal or better command of the second language is achieved if school begins with the native language as the medium of instruction and introduces the second language gradually (Balasubramonian et al., 14; Seelye and Balasubramonian, 115). A recent study in Texas provided evidence that first-grade Spanish-speaking children could learn to read in English better and with greater facility if taught to read in Spanish first (Ramírez, 100). By learning to read in Spanish in kindergarten, they acquired the important concept of sound-symbol correspondence in a language they understood and for which they were ready. The following year they were able to transfer the skills to English reading as a continuation of the Spanish reading course.

Reading in Spanish first

A bilingual education program is a program carefully designed to meet the individual needs of children. It includes the following elements:

Program characteristics

- use of the child's home language to initiate him to the school environment
- development of language skills in the child's home language
- development of language skills in the child's second language
- use of the child's dominant language to teach him subject-matter concepts
- use of the child's second language to teach him subject-matter concepts
- development of the child's self-esteem, positive identity with his cultural heritage, self-assurance and confidence, and a legitimate pride in both cultures
- involvement of parents in all aspects of the program—planning, implementation, evaluation.

It is *not* an ESL program although English as a Second Language instruction is an important component (99, 124). Those who can benefit from bilingual education include children from non-English-speaking backgrounds who may not be able to succeed in traditional educational programs, students who may be able to succeed in a regular school program but who should be provided the opportunity to continue their first language development and to receive affirmation of their cultural identity at school, and children from English-speaking backgrounds who will become fluent in another language and learn to participate in a second culture.

Student characteristics

Bilingual education: Background

Although bilingual schooling is by no means an innovation in the United States (instruction in two languages was fairly common during the 19th century), the current interest in bilingual programs dates back only to 1963 when the Dade County Public Schools, in order to meet the special needs of the increasing number of Cuban children enrolling in the school system, established at the Coral Way School the first bilingual program in the United States since World War I (Andersson and Boyer, 8). Furthermore, it was not until 1967 that Congress acted in favor of bilingual education by passing the Bilingual Education Act, which as Title VII of the Elementary and Secondary Education Act, allocated funds for bilingual programs.

Recent history

The interest of the foreign language profession in bilingual education is evident in the instrumental role that foreign language educators have had in the developmental stages of bilingual programs (Andersson, 6) as well as in the present involvement of many foreign language supervisors at state and local levels in the implementation and evaluation of many programs. Articles on bilingualism and bilingual education frequently appear in the professional literature. Three of the four preceding volumes of the *ACTFL Review of Foreign Language Education* have included bilingual education as a major topic. Since each chapter has provided a unique focus reflecting not only the specific areas the author chose to emphasize but also the particular developments taking place in the bilingual education movement, they provide a good background for this chapter.

Role of foreign language profession

Preceding Review *chapters*

When the first of these chapters appeared (Ulibarrí, 130), there were fewer than two dozen bilingual programs in public schools throughout the country. Congress had passed the Bilingual Education Act, but funds had not yet been appropriated. The implementation of bilingual programs was solely a matter of local initiative, more or less actively encouraged by pressures exerted by minority groups. Accordingly, Ulibarrí devoted a major segment of his chapter to the problems of linguistic minorities, in particular of the Mexican-American population in the Southwest. Limited self-actualization, low socioeconomic status, and forced conformity to the values of the majority culture were identified as major sources of frustration leading to resignation, to second-class citizen status, or to retreat into the anomic world of the barrio. Bilingual education, by helping the minority child develop an integrated personality and a positive self-concept, Ulibarrí concluded, can prepare him to function in two languages and sociologically in two cultures.

Volume 1

By 1971 when Volume 3 of this Series was in preparation, a number of developments had transpired to make the setting more favorable for bilingual education. Federal support for bilingual programs had then

Volume 3

become available through funds appropriated under Title VII of the Elementary and Secondary Education Act. Leading educators had formulated elaborate rationales for bilingual education that took into consideration linguistic, psychological, educational, and economic needs of non-English-speaking ethnic minorities. Various models for bilingual education programs had been proposed to accommodate the specific needs of particular groups of students, school settings, or ethnic communities. The number of bilingual programs was now approaching 200—of which 164 were federally financed. Pacheco (87) *New developments* thus emphasized the developments taking place in bilingual programs. He focused on program activity in the area of teacher training, curriculum development, community involvement, and evaluation, as he identified advances made and existing needs. He observed that bilingual programs have encouraged and enabled children from non-English-speaking backgrounds and economically depressed environments to participate in an open society while preserving and rediscovering their cultural identity. However, Pacheco stressed, eventual expansion to include other heterogenous groups—i.e., monolingual Anglo children— is necessary to assure educational and social benefits for all segments of our multilingual-multicultural society.

In the fourth volume of the Series, Christian and Sharp (33) *Volume 4* examined the variety of cultural factors that have contributed to the present interest in bilingual education. Although the United States has always maintained a variety of languages and cultures, the social and economic status of members of ethnic and linguistic minorities *Desire to maintain cultural* has been directly proportional to their willingness to sacrifice their own *identity* cultural identity in favor of the majority language and culture. In recent years, the authors point out, mounting reactions against absorption into a modern cultural system based on science, technology, urbanization, industry and commerce—a system that ignores personal, emotive, and instinctive dimensions—have helped to create a new interest in cultural pluralism. Ethnic and linguistic minority groups are openly expressing their language and culture. Whether bilingual education as one of the responses to the demands of the minority groups will in fact support maintenance of other languages, thereby promoting pluralism, or whether it will merely be a temporary bridge to linguistic and cultural assimilation remains to be seen. However, bilingualism and bilingual education are indeed relevant to today's realities and thus can provide the foreign language profession with a living rationale that foreign languages are really not so foreign in the United States. Furthermore, as Christian and Sharp emphasize, bilingual education could revolutionize foreign language teaching by presenting foreign language teachers with a new breed of student—fluent and literate native speakers—thus challenging the foreign language teacher to become the connecting link between the cultural values acquired by the child in his home and the great cultural tradition of his ethnic group.

Effect on foreign language classes

Bilingual education today: An overview

In establishing bilingual education programs a great many changes have had to take place, not only in school programs but in state laws, educational philosophies, and cultural values and attitudes. An overview of bilingual education, therefore, cannot limit itself to the development of programs; it must take into account the impact of these programs on the educational process, society, and government.

Bilingual program data

To what extent, then, have bilingual programs been replicated nationally? At present the exact figures are not available because the data are scattered among an assortment of funding agencies. However, in an effort to remedy this situation the Center for Applied Linguistics has recently undertaken the preparation of a directory listing national bilingual programs (Brisk, 26). Although data are still being gathered, Brisk estimates that approximately 450 to 500 bilingual programs are presently operating in the United States. Of these, 216 are supported by Title VII federal funds; between 200 and 250 are financed by state and local funds, special grants, and private endowments.

Number of bilingual programs

The geographical distribution of bilingual programs includes 30 states, Guam, Puerto Rico, the Virgin Islands, and Saipan. The greatest concentration of programs is found in the continental United States— the Southwest, the Northeast, and the Midwest. California and Texas have the largest numbers of Title VII programs, with 62 and 41 respectively. However, the number of programs in Massachusetts and Illinois is even greater due to the allocation of state funds for bilingual education. There are approximately 124 programs in Massachusetts (Mazzone, 77) and 100 in Illinois—of which 95 operate under state funds. Other states with significant numbers of bilingual programs are New York, with 25 Title VII programs and 22 sponsored by the New York City Board of Education (Hernández et al., 59); New Mexico, with 12 Title VII programs and, according to Brisk (26), a considerable

Geographic location

number of locally sponsored projects; and finally, Arizona, with nine, and Colorado, with seven federally funded bilingual programs.

TABLE 1

Distribution of Title VII Bilingual Programs 1972–1973

Alaska 1	Maine 3	Oregon 1
Arizona 9	Mariana Islands 1	Pennsylvania 2
California 62	Massachusetts 7	Puerto Rico 1
Colorado 7	Michigan 4	Rhode Island 2
Connecticut 3	Montana 3	South Dakota 1
Florida 3	New Hampshire 1	Texas 41
Guam 1	New Jersey 4	Utah 1
Idaho 1	New Mexico 12	Vermont 1
Illinois 4	New York 26	Virgin Islands 1
Indiana 2	Ohio 1	Washington 2
Louisiana 4	Oklahoma 3	Wisconsin 1

SOURCE: *Guide to Title VII ESEA Bilingual-Bicultural Projects in the United States: 1972–1973* (57).

The languages involved in the Title VII programs are Spanish, French, Chinese, Portuguese, Japanese, Russian, Italian, Chamorro, and 13 Indian languages—Navajo, Yuk, Pomo, Ute, Passamaquoddy, Crow, Northern Cheyenne, Cree, Zuni, Keresan, Choctaw, and Chero-kee (Peña, 91; Tennant, 126). In addition, the state of Massachusetts (Mazzone, 77) funds programs in Greek, Armenian, and Lithuanian, and Illinois recently initiated a program in Macedonian and a pilot program involving 14 different languages in one elementary school. *Linguistic distribution*

Although in most programs English is the other language (the second or foreign language), in Puerto Rico (20) the situation is reversed. Children of Puerto Rican parents returning to the island after living for prolonged periods in the United States often do not know sufficient Spanish to understand school subjects in that language. Hence, in the Puerto Rican bilingual program English is used as the language of instruction, while Spanish is taught as a second language. *Puerto Rico: a special case*

Spanish programs are by far the most numerous, leading all the other languages combined by a ratio of more than 10 to 1. The Indian languages, headed by Navajo, with 10 projects of its own, form the second largest block. French, originally represented by five programs located in Louisiana, Maine, and New Hampshire is expanding due to the establishment of programs in Haitian French in New York,

81

Massachusetts, and Illinois. Portuguese and Chinese also have multiple projects. The remaining languages are sparsely distributed.

To what extent are bilingual programs meeting needs?

In view of the multiplicity of obstacles that have had to be overcome, the number of programs and the variety of language groups served is noteworthy. However, even the most optimistic among the proponents of bilingual education will readily admit that this effort is meeting but a *A fraction of the need* fraction of the need, that although progress has been made, it has been painfully slow. The discrepancy that exists between the number of children from non-English-speaking backgrounds in our schools, children who lack much more than the linguistic tools to succeed in the middle-class Anglo-oriented curriculum, and the number of ethnic-minority children actually participating in bilingual programs is undoubtedly one of the toughest realities that has to be faced. The magnitude of the need is exemplified in Tables 2 and 3.

TABLE 2
Approximate Number of School-Aged Children in the United States Needing Bilingual Education

Ethnic/Language Group	Approximate Number
Mexican-American	3,100,000
Puerto Rican	800,000
Other Spanish Speaking	380,000
French Speaking	350,000
American Indian (including Eskimo)	180,000
Portuguese	60,000
Chinese	40,000
Japanese	20,000
Russian	8,000
Chamorro	7,500
Other	10,000
Major States	*Approximate Number*
California	800,000
Texas	650,000
New York	350,000
New Mexico	100,000
Illinois	70,000
Colorado	60,000
Arizona	50,000
Total in the United States	5,000,000

SOURCE: Peña (92).

82

TABLE 3

Approximate Number of School-Aged Children in the
United States Enrolled in Title VII Bilingual Programs

Ethnic/Language Group	Apprixomate Number
Mexican-American	70,913
Puerto Rican	14,179
Other Spanish Speaking	6,046
French Speaking	2,095
American Indian (including Eskimo)	2,810
Portuguese	567
Chinese	639
Chamorro	240
Multilingual	2,897
Major States	*Approximate Number*
California	27,184
Texas	34,991
New York	10,238
New Mexico	5,449
Illinois	1,372
Colorado	2,212
Arizona	3,017
Total in the United States	100,391

SOURCE: Compiled from information listed in *Guide to Title VII ESEA Bilingual-Bicultural Projects in the United States* (57).

Yet, as discouraging as these comparisons may be, they provide the motivating force for those committed to the goals of bilingual education—the involved teacher, the concerned administrator, the determined parent, or the dedicated politician—to continue their campaign to inform the public of the educational needs of non-English-speaking children. Their efforts are essential to the future of bilingual education. As Andersson (6) remarks, the greatest task is to convince communities that the maintenance of non-English languages is desirable and that a non-English-speaking child can become literate in English best by first becoming literate in his native language.

Need to inform public

The sociocultural context

Since the term *bilingualism* itself denotes proficiency in two languages and a capacity to function in two cultures, the interaction between the social environment and bilingual education and the influence they

83

exert on each other cannot be overlooked. In this section we examine three areas as they relate to bilingual education—the nonethnic majority, the school, and the ethnic minority—focusing on current developments and how they relate to bilingual education.

The nonethnic majority

Since bilingual programs have been in existence less than four years, it is not surprising that middle-class Anglo America is practically unaware of their existence. The obvious reason for this situation is that since the ethnic majority generally lives in a different neighborhood with children attending different schools, there is virtually no contact *Two different worlds* with representatives of the ethnic minority. Even in areas with sizable representation of the ethnic group, for example the southwestern United States, the spheres of activity for both groups remain quite separate.

In the recent upsurge of ethnic pride and aggressive assertion of personal dignity among long-time oppressed groups such as the Mexican-American, Puerto Rican, American Indian, and Franco-American, the Anglo community has assumed a tolerant but rather superior and *Anglo response* distant attitude. Their response to the current emphasis on cultural diversity and cultural pluralism in general is lack of concern. Only when the "territorial" laws are violated (when the ethnic group "gets out of hand" and demands fair housing, fair employment practices, better school programs for their children) do the ethnocentric qualities of the Anglo majority come to the surface. Kjolseth (65) designates this prevalent attitude as the "law of Anglo love of ethnic irrelevance," or the "Disneyland preference of symbolic ethnicity." In other words, the less locally relevant a language and culture, the higher its social status; the more locally relevant, the lower its social status.

Basic attitudinal changes will have to take place before the nonethnic majority can learn to relate to other ethnic groups without feeling threatened or intimidated by groups whose language, culture, and values differ from its own. The ethnocentric barrier that Anglo- *Ethnocentric barrier* Americans have put between themselves and the linguistic minorities in the United States must be lifted. These changes cannot take place while our schools and other institutions are propagating the myth that the United States is superior to all other countries, that the American way of life is the best in the world, and that the Anglo-American culture is the only valuable culture in the United States. Bilingual-bicultural programs, as they exist today, cannot possibly accomplish this. Their goal is to equip children from non-English-speaking backgrounds with the educational opportunities that are available to children of majority parents. What bilingual programs can do, but hardly any programs are presently doing, is to design a bicultural component that would not be limited to the students in the bilingual program but would extend to all students in the community. Only by exposing children at an early age to another culture, not as a quaint little presentation on Friday afternoons but as an integral part of every activity in the school day, can societal attitudes be ultimately changed (Gardner and Lambert, 55). The only way to dispel ethnocentric notions is not to let them form from the begininng. The majority of Anglo-American children are in need of such programs; they need to learn about other cultures; they need to be brought out of their isolation. If Anglo-American children do not have equal educational opportunities—are they not, then, culturally deprived?

Need for bicultural component

The American school

Unlike the Anglo community whose values and attitudes they harbor, school administrators and teachers in districts with any number of children from non-English-speaking ethnic minorities have had to acknowledge at least that these children experience special problems in American schools. These problems have been traditionally attributed to the child's linguistic and cultural ties. Since the school system has been designed substantially by Anglos for Anglos, it is geared to meet the needs of the ethnic majority. The intrusion of children from homes where a different language is spoken and different attitudes and values are held is viewed as a threat to the attainment of the school's goals. In the past, as Arciniegas (11) points out, the school system has resorted to various mechanisms and devices that encouraged dropouts especially among certain ethnic, social, and economic groups of students. Recent outside pressure from the federal government and from minority groups, however, has caused the schools to look for alternative solutions. In general, Arciniegas comments, schools are simply doing more of what they have always done in the past, which has never worked before. He concludes that the obvious attitude is to change as little as is absolutely necessary in order to maintain the status quo.

Schools' traditional response

More of the same

The antagonism of some school systems toward any efforts to remediate the blatant oppression of children from ethnic minorities is dramatically recounted by Mangers (73). As the new principal of an elementary school in a small community in Southern California, Mangers made repeated attempts to improve the educational program for the Mexican-American children who made up 70 percent of the

A case study of oppression

85

school population. He describes his efforts to eliminate the negative attitudes of the majority of the faculty, his efforts to involve the Mexican-American community in school functions, and the opposition he met in each instance. This was a case of a school board made up entirely of members from the power elite. The children from these families comprised only 3 percent of the total school population, yet the entire school curriculum was geared to their needs. After 16 months of fighting windmills the principal was forced to leave. Hopeless as such conditions may seem, there have been instances such as in Crystal City and Del Rio, Texas, where the community has organized, demanded, and succeeded in bringing about change.

Fortunately, situations like the one depicted by Mangers are diminishing. The majority of schools with ethnic minority representation are attempting to improve the educational opportunities of these children. Regrettably, it is often for the wrong reasons and in the wrong direction. The "bilingual problem" is viewed by school personnel as a *The "bilingual problem"* handicap to be overcome. As members of a subculture, the students are considered "culturally disadvantaged." The values fostered in the child's group are interpreted as detrimental to his success in school and consequently in American society. Arciniegas (11) maintains that present public school efforts reflect a "cultural deficiency" approach based on the false premise that the problem lies primarily within the ethnic minority culture. The schools feel that the best solution is to make over the cultural group in the image of the greater society. He adds, "in order to accept the Mexican-American, society dictates that *A handicap* the youngster must first be 'de-Mexicanized' " (p. 18). ESL programs and transitional bilingual education programs support this stance. The use of the child's home language in most of these programs is temporary, becoming simply a more effective way to accomplish his acculturation.

Another way of responding to the "bilingual problem" is what Arciniegas refers to as "tracking" or "dumping." Minority children *"Tracking" or "dumping"* are pulled out of the regular school curriculum and placed in special programs designed for low-intelligence children. In the elementary schools they are placed in the slow groups, and in the upper grades they are channeled toward the vocational courses. The result, of course, is that the minority children are lock stepped into a program that will prevent them from attaining the educational goals of the Anglo majority. This type of program also leads to isolation of the ethnic minority from the rest of the students within the school (Casso, 29).

Another type of "dumping" that is prevalent in schools is to lower the grade of the child. The rationale behind this action is that since the *Lowering the grade*

86

ethnic student lacks sufficient command of English to perform the required work at his grade level, it would obviously be simpler for him to be placed in a class where at least he would be familiar with the subject matter. The psychological damage this approach engenders in the non-English-speaking minority child is rarely overcome. The students themselves are the first ones to criticize this procedure. Recently I read an article in a small town newspaper featuring interviews with several of the town's Spanish-speaking young people. A recent graduate —the only Mexican-American to graduate from his school that year— remarked that he had seen 12- and 13-year-old Mexican children placed in the first grade because they couldn't understand English. "Don't you think that would hurt a kid psychologically?" he asked. Another student recounts how she was put back to the third grade in three different schools. Her remarks were: "I was so bored because I was learning the same things I had learned before in Mexico." Another consequence of lowering a child's grade, especially if it involves placing older children in the first or second grade, is peer ridicule. The effect on the minority child is that he feels inferior simply because he cannot understand English.

Psychological damage

Peer ridicule

Competence in the English language is not the only criterion school personnel employ in channeling minority students into low-achievement programs. The Anglo orientation of the child is also a determining factor. The I.Q. myth illustrates this. Nothing is as bewildering to a child from a different culture than the battery of tests that are religiously administered in our public schools. The bewilderment does not stem solely from the difficulty the child experiences with the individual test items, which, as many studies have pointed out, are biased in favor of the Anglo-American culture. What really intimidates the student is the total testing procedure: Tests are often administered by strange persons with a strange accent; instructions are read impersonally and without explanation; the timing periods seem short; and finally, the solemn, military-like stance of the proctors is imposing. The child from a different linguistic and cultural background is severely disadvantaged, not only because of his limited competencies in the English language and Anglo culture but also because in the majority of cases minority children have not been exposed to the ceremony of the standardized test. It is not surprising, then, that minority children are often placed in special-education programs because of results in intelligence tests (Casso, 29). Others are channeled into low-aptitude (low-achievement) programs. Feeling

I.Q. myth

inadequate, inferior, and displaced, the minority child may drop out of school.

Many of the responses of the school to the bilingual-bicultural problems are ineffective and even harmful due to unintentional implications arising from lack of knowledge about the ethnic minorities' cultures. Zintz (136) maintains that entirely too many teachers are not prepared to understand, much less to accept, different cultural values. The result is that through lack of sensitivity they can create a feeling of inadequacy and inferiority in the bicultural and bilingual child. Imagine, for instance, a little Mexican-American boy in the first grade. The teacher is presenting a unit on health and nutrition. In front of her is a chart with pictures of various foods that make up a good, nutritious breakfast: fruit juice, eggs, toast, milk, cereal. The Mexican-American child may come to the conclusion that if this is what a good breakfast consists of, then the breakfast that he is served at home is inferior. Aragón (10) illustrates similar situations, common during a given school day, that result in unintentional implications that the child's culture is not so good as the Anglo culture. By failing to incorporate ethnic-related experiences into the classroom, the school is in fact telling the child that his language and his culture are of no concern to them, and hence they have no value. Aragón contends that the self-concept of the minority child becomes progressively more negative the longer he is in school.

Unintentional implications

Lower self-concept

Even in the teaching of English as a second language, the schools often hurt the ethnic child by failing to consider cultural differences as well as linguistic differences. Zintz (136) illustrates this with an anecdote about an Eskimo child reading the Dick and Jane series. He is puzzled by a number of things that have not been explained by the teacher: Dick and Jane play together, yet he knows that boys and girls do not play together; their dog Spot comes indoors and does not work; their father leaves for an "office" each day, yet he never brings food home with him; and so on. In the same article, Zintz includes concepts found in stories in basic readers that conflict with the Navajo child's concept of himself, his family, and his community. For example, to the Anglo-American child, pets have human-like personalities, but to the Navajo, pets are distinct from human personality; in the basic reader, life is pictured as child-centered, whereas in the Navajo community life is adult-centered; the Anglo community views children and parents as masters of their environment, while Navajo children accept their environment and live with it. In the American community children are energetic, outgoing, obviously happy; but in the Navajo

Cultural differences

community children are passive and unexpressive. If the teacher ignores *Teacher attitudes* these cultural differences or, worse, communicates the attitude that the child's way of thinking as well as the beliefs and behavior his mother taught him are wrong because they conflict with Anglo values, the result is damage to the child's self-concept as well as a negative attitude toward learning English. The overall effect of the typical school responses to the bilingual-bicultural problem has been disastrous. "Schools try to brainwash the Chicanos. They try to make us forget our history, to be ashamed of being Mexicans, of speaking Spanish. They succeed in making us feel empty and angry inside," says a student in San Antonio (Kuenster, 66, p. 20). The cultural exclusion in the school has precipitated an identity crisis in the minority child. He is told that he must choose between the Anglo culture or his own culture. But how can he choose, if he is neither but is both. Hence the dilemma: *A dilemma* The minority student wants to be educated, but to achieve education he must reject that which is dearest to him (Ramírez, 101). The lack of success of the various attempts of American schools to eliminate the bilingual-bicultural problem can be attributed to the ethnocentric attitude prevalent in approaching the ethnic minority. As Ballesteros (15) so aptly states:

> The real problem in our society today—and therefore the real problem in education today—is not the "Mexican-American problem," nor the "Puerto Rican problem," nor the "Cuban problem," it is the "Anglo-point-of-view problem." The viewpoint determines *"The Anglo-point-of-view problem"* what happens in the school—what emphasis will be given or denied racial, cultural, and language values. It is this point of view that labels Mexican-American, Puerto Rican and Cuban students "disadvantaged," "handicapped," and "deprived," because the school does not understand their language and culture (p. 26).

If our educational system is truly committed to meeting the needs of ethnic minority children, it must discard the present approaches and seek new alternatives. Arciniegas (11) proposes that the one viable *More humanistic response* alternative is a more humanistic response to the demands and needs of culturally different students. The fundamental features of this approach are:

1 School systems must accept and demonstrate in educational form and practice an authentic commitment to a pluralistic model of society.
2 The school must be organized as a microcosm of the "ideal" society we want to build.

3 Schools must emphasize teacher-student and family-student influences in shaping instructional programs. Student-to-student and intercultural group interactions should be accepted parts of the curriculum.

4 The school must recognize that both low- and high-socioeconomic students will benefit from interethnic experiences as well as from communication across class, racial, and ethnic lines.

5 School systems need to incorporate what the ethnic community has to offer in planned learning experiences for all youngsters.

6 School systems must involve themselves in city, state, and federal plans to improve the opportunity structure of society in general for ethnic minority groups.

Redbird-Selam and Selam (104) propose six realities that the schools should consider when teaching the culturally different:

1 Culture influences every aspect of learning; how an individual feels about himself influences what he learns and how he behaves.

2 Culture influences ways of establishing rapport.

3 Culture influences communication.

4 Culture influences what educational variables are going to be effective.

5 Culture influences value orientation.

6 Culture affects teaching methods.

Teaching the culturally different

Bilingual-bicultural programs that emphasize the maintenance of the ethnic language and the concept of cultural pluralism are making headway in meeting the needs of culturally different students. Since some of these programs have succeeded in incorporating into the curriculum social studies (cultural courses) based on the ethnic minority, perhaps the logical starting point would be to expand courses on the ethnic group culture, presently limited to the bilingual program, into the regular school curriculum. Coordination and communication between the bilingual program and the rest of the school program is a prerequisite to changing attitudes.

Need for coordination and communication

Ballesteros (15) raises another issue dealing with attitudes. He questions the term *language handicap* as presently applied to any child who has a socioeconomic disadvantage and who also lacks a sufficient knowledge of the English language. Angel (9) questions whether the difficulties that minority students experience in school are the result of linguisitic or cultural differences, or social or economic factors. Both Angel and Ballesteros believe that the problem is attributable to a school system that conforms to middle-class values and addresses the learning style of middle-class students. The lower-class children,

Language handicap or socoieconomic disadvantage

whatever their cultural origins, are more likely to become drop-out statistics. This implies that for the school system to reach ethnic and linguistic minorities, its ethnocentric focus must change. Only then can the goals of bilingual programs and other attempts to meet the needs of non-English-speaking children from ethnic minorities be attained.

School focus

The ethnic minority

Chicano, Boricua, Lakota, Acadien, Navajo—these and other ethnic minorities who not long ago were hesitant to call attention to themselves for fear of losing a job or being maligned or even because they were ashamed of their language, their culture, and their people are no longer hiding behind general terms like "Spanish" or "French" or "Indian," but are proudly proclaiming their heritage by using the name that is the very essence of their culture and closest to their heart.

Pride in ethnicity

Rosehill, 18th Street, East Harlem, Oglala, Breaux Bridge, Montopolis, Rough Rock, El Barrio—the neighborhood to which the minority group retreated from the alien world of the Anglo majority now provides the unifying force for an increasingly active, reform-minded ethnic community.

Reform movement

In striving to do away with economic oppression, social prejudice, lack of educational opportunities, the key target of the reform movement is the ethnocentric philosophy of Anglo superiority that dictates that all other cultures are a hindrance to the individuals who cling to them and therefore must be eradicated rather than reinforced. The effect of this philosophy on the minority individual is portrayed in the words of Luis Valdez of El Teatro Campesino:

> They say this is the melting pot. I wonder who invented the melting pot. Horrible term! You melt people down, God! It shouldn't be that way. Our country should be a place where the individual is sacred. We have so many different sorts of people. Every man has his own heart. Who gives you the right to cut out a man's heart and put it in a melting pot (Ramírez, 101, p. 45)?

Dissatisfied with the failure of the present educational system to meet the needs of their children, unwilling to accept the premise that in order to succeed they must betray their cultural and linguistic traditions, ethnic communities throughout the United States are actively supporting bilingual education. Language serves the purpose of establishing a common identity, a unifying factor as well as an issue about which the ethnic community can rally forces, becoming a political voice pressuring for its own rights and interests (Vázquez, 133).

Language: a unifying factor

About two years ago in a South Texas town, the Mexican-American population that historically had been an oppressed, powerless majority (Castañeda-Shular et al., 30, pp. 27, 43) succeeded in organizing to effect major changes in the political structure of the community. The central target was a school system that aggressively opposed the use of Spanish among the ethnic minority that comprised about 90 percent of the student body (Palomares, 88).

The community in action

In recent months I have had the opportunity to observe a community in action. A dedicated, well-organized group of Mexican-American parents in a midwestern community, led by a concerned school janitor, was able to "convince" an insensitive and definitely recalcitrant school administration that Spanish-speaking children in the schools had special needs, that the school system was not meeting these needs, that the solutions the school had proposed to improve the situation were inadequate, that a bilingual-education program would provide the best answer to the needs of Spanish-speaking children, and a proposal for a bilingual program should be submitted to the State Education Department. Unlike the Texas group, the Mexican-American community in this case had the added disadvantage of being a very small minority; yet, due to the personal commitment and determination of each individual, they were successful in accomplishing their goal.

Organizations such as the Mexican-American Council on Education (MACE), the League of United Latin American Citizens (LULAC), the National Educational Council of La Raza, the Association of Mexican-American Educators are all actively engaged in improving the educational conditions of Mexican-Americans throughout the United States. They are enthusiastic supporters of bilingual programs.

Support from organizations

Spolsky and Holm (122) note that for the first time in the history of Indian education, the Navajo community is exerting pressure on the Bureau of Indian Affairs and state school systems to pay more attention to their educational needs and wishes. They want the Navajo language to be used throughout the schools; they want to become literate in their language; they want their language and heritage maintained. Furthermore, the Navajo community through organizations like the Dine ʙi'Olta, is exerting pressure to control its own schools.

Pressure from Navajo community

A recent concern is emerging in the communities for the maintenance of even obsolescing Indian languages such as Shoshoni, languages that throughout the years have lost prestige even among their own peoples. Miller (79) comments on this trend by noting that Shoshoni, which he would have predicted to become obsolete within another generation,

Trend to save Indian languages

is now being taught in various communities. He adds that since the support is coming from "the most acculturated and sophisticated communities, the very places where the language is least used," and since there are isolated communities where Shoshoni is still the vehicle of communication, it is quite possible that the language can be kept alive.

The Puerto Rican community in New York, for years unable to reach New York's mammoth educational system, has been able to bring about significant educational changes through effective organizations such as the Puerto Rican Forum, ASPIRA, the Puerto Rican Educators Association, the United Bronx Parents, and other groups representing the interests of the community. Among their aims are: making the curriculum relevant, the establishment of more bilingual programs, improvement of school-community relations, and increasing community action and political power (Pérez, 93; Vázquez, 133). *New York Puerto Rican efforts*

These efforts to maintain the Spanish language and Puerto Rican culture are not limited to the Puerto Rican communities on the mainland. De Granda (40) notes the progressive devaluation of Spanish and the increasing imposition of the English language in a variety of spheres on the island of Puerto Rico, a situation he finds alarming. Although Spanish remains the major language of communication, English, at least in written form, is clearly becoming the language of industry, commerce, finance, and in general all the major facets of the economy. He admits that the exclusive use of English in the various publications or directives of federal agencies is inevitable; however, the use of English in technological and scientific publications published by Puerto Rican authors in Puerto Rican journals is deplorable in his opinion. Notwithstanding the reality that this is due to the use of texts and scientific journals from the United States within Puerto Rican universities, the implication is that Spanish is not an appropriate vehicle for the technical and scientific theories. *Use of English in Puerto Rico*

Furthermore, De Granda adds, the zeal to identify with American cultural values has led to the devaluation of the Hispanic values of other countries and the rejection of local opinions that do not reflect American values. This process of "transculturation" can only lead to the elimination of the cultural personality of Puerto Rico. *Transculturation*

De Granda overlooks one increasingly significant element that may influence the present course of events: the return of the Neorican, the Puerto Rican who migrated to the United States, or the Puerto Rican who, although born and raised in the United States, was never allowed to participate fully in that society. These Puerto Ricans, *Neoricans* according to García-Passalacqua (54), may constitute the vanguard of the Puerto Ricans of the future. To them, the United States is not the land of promise that the growing middle class in the island believes it to be. To the Neorican, it is a reactionary and oppressive society that demands great social and human sacrifices in exchange for minimal material progress. It is the oppression and prejudice that has led the Neorican to consider himself a Puerto Rican even if he speaks little or no Spanish. Although his aggressiveness, determination, harshness and coolness are in contrast to the warm, suave, hesitant nature of the Puerto Rican, García believes that a true synthesis is far from impossible. Furthermore, the phenomenon is certain to influence the political future of Puerto Rico. As a commonwealth—Estado Libre Asociado— Puerto Rico does not have direct representation in the Congress of the United States. The first Puerto Rican Congressman, Hermán Badillo, was sent to Washington from New York. Thus Badillo, a Neorican, speaks not only for his constituency in New York but indirectly for all Puerto Ricans on the mainland and on the island.

The affirmation of the Puerto Ricans on the mainland is also evidenced in the increasing demand for bilingual education and the enactment of courses in Puerto Rican studies in more than 15 universities throughout the country—courses that are unheard of in Puerto Rican institutions, García adds. The Puerto Rican of the island, conditioned to emphasize *lo pequeño del puertorriqueño*, develops the theory of limitations about the island. He minimizes his own culture in relation to the "great and powerful" culture of the United States (Silen, 117). The Puerto Rican of the United States has emerged as a political ethnic identity. Perhaps together the two and one-half million Puerto Ricans on the island and the one and one-half million Puerto Ricans on the mainland can make a better future for what both groups hold closest to their hearts: *Borinquen*.

Puerto Ricans on the mainland

A political-ethnic identity

The growing self-expression among ethnic groups is evident in the public news media (68). The number of newspapers published in the different languages throughout the country is increasing rapidly. Moreover, English language newspapers are increasingly including articles in the ethnic minority language, and occasionally entire sections are devoted to that language. Radio and television programming likewise is making considerable progress in presenting programs produced by members of the ethnic minority. In Chicago new television programs such as "Ahora," "Ayuda," and "Oiga Amigo" present local, state, and national news from the point of view of the Spanish-speaking community. The ethnic minority is writing about

The minority speaks

94

itself in books (116), in journals (Leal, 69; Muckley, 82; 105), in plays (Valdez, 131) and in poems (Figueroa, 47; Redbird-Selam and Selam, 104).

> I am Joaquín
> Lost in a world of confusion,
> Caught up in a whirl of
>   Anglo society
> Confused by the rules.
> Scorned by the attitudes
> Suppressed by the manipulations,
> And destroyed
>   By modern life
>
>   Rodolfo (Corky) Gonzáles (Kuenster, 66, p. 39)

The politics of bilingual education

As members of the teaching profession—conditioned to disassociating ourselves, at least in the classroom, from the political arena—we tend to overlook the close relationship that exists between education and politics. Yet, not only is education an extremely important issue in local, state, and federal politics, but it is in itself a highly political activity. Nearly every school district has a school board comprised of individuals who must campaign for election and therefore must be responsive and responsible to their electorate—the voters whose children attend schools in that particular community (Cárdenas, 28).

Education and politics

The involvement of the federal government in the establishment of bilingual programs was not an arbitrary decision formulated by top-level officials but the work of dedicated politicians responding to the special needs of their constituents. The Bilingual Education Act of 1967 was a response to the reality that the children of voters from certain ethnic minorities were being short-changed by the typical American education process. The real political power necessary to effect changes in public institutions does not lie within a particular government agency or a powerful figure. The political force behind bilingual education, whether at the local, state, or national level, is the emerging voice of the ethnic community.

The Bilingual Education Act: a response

When Congress passed the Bilingual Education Act in 1967, it also authorized funds of $400 million over a six-year period for the support of bilingual programs. In view of the five million children needing bilingual education this sum was far from excessive. Even so, authorization is not the same thing as appropriation when it comes to

95

Congressional action. Both Andersson (6) and Badillo (13) highlight the discrepancies between the amount authorized and the funds appropriated each year since the passage of the Act. Including the amount appropriated for 1973–74, the sum total of the appropriation for bilingual-bicultural education is $123 million or roughly 30 percent of the authorized $400 million (Peña, 91). The passage of the grossly inadequate sums, Badillo (13) reflects, is an indication of the failure of many senators and representatives in Congress to understand really what bilingual education is all about. If the situation is to be remedied, broad-based political backing for bilingual education must be initiated at the local level to lobby for increased appropriations.

Authorization vs. appropriation

Unfortunately, the outlook for increased appropriations under Title VII ESEA is rather dim. It appears that the amount of funds appropriated for 1973–74 will remain at the current level of $35 million. Since this is the amount necessary to maintain the existing 217 programs in operation, it will be impossible to fund new programs for 1973–74. This is indeed a discouraging picture. Peña (91), nevertheless, expects an extension of Title VII appropriations for three more years. Even if the amount remains at the $35 million level, he indicates that it will be possible to provide funds for new programs in 1974–75 when a number of projects will require fewer funds, thereby freeing some money.

Federal funds on the wane

Although federal support for bilingual education under Title VII ESEA is definitely on the wane, alternate consolidated funding sources have been established. Unfortunately, as Badillo (13) points out, these may prove detrimental to bilingual education by spreading out funds over various programs and diminishing the importance of bilingual-bicultural programs. Furthermore, they may place a new set of constraints on eligibility. For instance, the new Emergency School Aid Act (ESAA) under the Bureau of Equal Educational Opportunity provides money for implementing bilingual programs. However, to qualify for a bilingual program, the school district must be undergoing desegregation. Thus, actual need for bilingual education ceases to be the major criterion for selection.

Alternate funding sources

Regardless of future Congressional appropriations, the Bilingual Education Act, Title VII ESEA, has made a significant impact on the American educational system. This was a milestone in the area of educational policy alone. The reversal of the "English only" doctrine that dominated our public school system was a major breakthrough. As a result of the Bilingual Education Act, many state laws were changed to allow public instruction in a language other than English. Even the

Title VII: a change agent

federal schools of the Bureau of Indian Affairs, which tenaciously adhered to the "English only" policy in the education of Indian children on the reservation, were able to change (Leibowitz, 70; Tennant, 126).

The Title VII office has provided excellent guidelines that explain the philosophy of bilingual education as well as the policies and requirements of bilingual education programs (99). It has also provided necessary leadership in important areas. One of the greatest contributions of bilingual programs to the educational system, as well as one of the wisest political moves, has been the involvement of the community in all aspects of the bilingual projects, including the planning, implementation, and evaluation.

Perhaps the greatest accomplishment of Title VII has been the leadership that it has provided in encouraging state and local governments to move in the direction of bilingual education. As a result, the political activity in bilingual education is now shifting from the national to the state level. The volume of legislation that is currently going through 17 separate state legislatures is indeed impressive. There are bills to allow bilingual instruction, bills to make bilingual education mandatory, and appropriation bills requesting state funds for bilingual programs. *Shift from national to state level*

In Massachusetts compulsory bilingual education has been in effect since 1972. Any school district in the state having 20 or more children from the same non-English-speaking background is required by law to provide bilingual education. Assistance and reimbursement are provided by the State Bilingual Office (Mazzone, 77). Bills mandating bilingual education have recently passed in Texas and New Mexico; others are pending in Colorado, Illinois, and New York. A number of states have appropriated funds for bilingual education: Illinois, one of the first states to provide funds for bilingual programs (over $3 million within the past two years) is spending $6 million for 1973–74. Texas recently appropriated $6,500,000 for a two-year period; in California the sum of $5 million was also approved for a two-year period; and Alaska has appropriated $200,000 for bilingual education. The Virgin Islands and Pennsylvania have likewise set aside funds for bilingual programs. Other states involved in legislation for bilingual education are Connecticut, Louisiana, Maine, Nevada, Oregon, Washington, and New Hampshire (Peña, 91). *Compulsory bilingual education* *State appropriations*

Although the active support of bilingual education at the state level is heartening, a great deal of ground work still needs to be done to insure passage of legislation. García and Truán (53), both authors of bills for bilingual education in New York and Texas respectively, stress the need for a strong lobby to make each state aware of the needs of bilingual education in that particular state. Even a short report from a bilingual program (Barrera, 16) can do wonders, especially if many such accounts are forwarded to legislative committees. By outlining the special educational needs of non-English-speaking children, two publications of the Office of Public Instruction in Illinois (2; 124) have facilitated passage of appropriation bills for bilingual education. *Need for strong lobby*

In discussing the politics of bilingual education at the state level, special mention must be made of the unique situation in Louisiana. A statewide effort to preserve the cultural and linguistic heritage of the French-speaking people in Louisiana resulted in the appropriation of $500,000 for the establishment of the Council for the Development of French in Louisiana (CODOFIL). One of the major goals of CODOFIL was to provide instruction in French throughout the public schools in Louisiana—an ambitious if not altogether impossible task, in view of the scarcity of qualified teachers. CODOFIL thus turned to the most logical source of French-speaking teachers—France. As a result, a most innovative program of international dimensions is now in effect in that state. There are presently 160 certified teachers from France working throughout the public schools in Louisiana. These French *coopérants*—young men and women who have volunteered two years of their services to the French government (for many this fulfills military requirements)—have been sent to Louisiana at the expense of the French government. While in Louisiana, they continue to receive monthly salary supplements and full insurance benefits from the French government. Local districts provide them with a small monthly salary. Bradley (22) considers the program a complete success. The *coopérants* are utilized by all three Title VII bilingual programs, either as full-time teachers, as resource persons, or as curriculum developers. Furthermore, this program has made the establishment of bilingual programs possible for many more school districts without the aid of federal or state funds. *International cooperation*

Teachers from France

Attempts to replicate the program in the New England area have not been successful due to the absence of a local organization such as CODOFIL. However, a movement has begun to create the Council for the Development of French in New England (CODOFINE), with the hope that through such an organization a similar program of *coopérants* can be obtained for the French-speaking population in those states.

Support for bilingual education programs at the local level is also *Local support* picking up momentum. Individual school districts in New York, Illinois, Texas, Louisiana, Florida, New Mexico—indeed throughout the entire country—are initiating bilingual programs on their own.

The fate of bilingual education ultimately depends on the will of the individuals for whom it is intended. Whenever people get together and decide they want to do things, work gets done, and it does not matter whether it is at the local level, at the state level, or at the national level.

The bilingual program: A closer look

Getting started

Regardless of the funding source, the implementation of a bilingual program remains a local responsibility involving the mobilization not only of a school district but of the local community.

The procedure usually begins with a detailed needs assessment (99; 124). The school district must:

Needs assessment

Provide evidence that it has numbers of children from non-English-speaking environments

Provide information about the linguistic competence of the children

Provide evidence that the educational needs of the children are not currently being met

Include socioeconomic information showing a high concentration of children from low-income families if federal assistance is being sought.

Furthermore, a total commitment to the philosophy of bilingual-bicultural education on the part of administrators, teachers, parents, and community representatives is necessary. Since they are to take part in the planning, development, and implementation of the program, they must all reach a consensus that instruction should be provided in both languages, including instruction in subject areas other than language itself.

Commitment to bilingual-education philosophy

Conducting the needs assessment is only the first phase in the implementation of a bilingual program. This is followed by extensive program planning involving the development of goals and objectives and program models; determining grade levels and schedules; planning for acquisition and development of materials, teacher in-service training, staff development, and community involvement, among other things. It soon becomes apparent that starting a bilingual program involves considerably more than adding a foreign language to the school curriculum. In fact, in many ways it can be simpler to individualize the entire curriculum for 500 students in an elementary school than it is to start a bilingual program for 60 children in the same school.

The following timeline provides an example of some of the various *Timeline*
steps taken by a school district in Illinois towards establishing a
bilingual program.

December, 1972. A superintendent contacts the Bilingual Section at
the Office of the Superintendent of Public Instruction, requesting
information about bilingual education. A copy of the State Guidelines
is mailed to the district; the superintendent is referred to the author
of the Bilingual Education Service Center for assistance with needs
assessment.

January 15, 1973. The BESC staff meets with the superintendent to
discuss the needs of the school district. A tour is made of the schools
with high concentrations of Spanish-speaking children.

January 24, 1973. The State Director of Bilingual Education and the
BESC staff meet with the target school faculty to present an overview of
bilingual education.

February 20, 1973. The author attends a meeting with the Spanish-
speaking parents, other representatives of the community, the school
principal, and selected teachers. The purpose of the meeting is to
discuss the need for bilingual education.

February 27, 1973. A group of parents and teachers meet to set up an
advisory council to study the need for bilingual education.

February 28, 1973. A faculty meeting is held at the target school to
discuss the need for bilingual education.

March 12, 1973. The principal and language arts director meet with
the Bilingual Service Center staff to determine a suitable program
model for the district.

March 16, 1973. The target school principal and language arts
director attend a workshop conducted by the Bilingual Education
Service Center on developing objectives for bilingual programs.

March 20, 1973. The parent-teacher Latino-Americano Club meets
to discuss progress made.

March 27, 1973. The PTA formally endorses the bilingual education
effort.

April, 1973. The Bilingual Education Service Center provides
assistance in proposal development.

April 16, 1973. Proposal is submitted to the State Bilingual Office.

April–May, 1973. The State Bilingual Office studies, evaluates and
negotiates the proposal with the district.

June, 1973. The district receives notification that the program is
tentatively approved pending authorization of funds.

100

July, 1973. Once the funds are authorized, the district is notified to begin actual planning for the implementation of the program in the forthcoming school year.

The timeline for submitting proposals to the Office of Education varies somewhat, but in general, the pattern is the same.

Even if all the necessary steps have been taken and procedures meticulously followed, the school district must face the reality that the program may very well not be funded because the funds available are so limited and the need is so great. If a district is not selected as a project site and the proposed program is too costly for the district to implement on its own, many schools do put into effect an alternate program that is more realistic in terms of the district's own resources. Thus, the commitment to bilingual education generated during the planning stages is perhaps one of the greatest contributing factors to the increasing numbers of bilingual programs or "Title VII spin-offs" (Peña, 91) at the local level. Federal and state funding sources hope this commitment to bilingual education will motivate school districts to continue in their bilingual efforts, even after financial assistance is no longer available.

No guarantees

The bilingual program in practice

Throughout its developmental stages, bilingual education progresses from a vague concept to a rather concrete program that specifies goals and objectives, outlines instructional strategies, and even provides classroom schedules by grade. But, however exemplary, it remains a paper program until it is transposed from the printed page to the classroom, the school, and the community.

True test in the classroom

In this section we examine the bilingual program in practice by presenting the activities of a number of bilingual projects in the areas of program design and instruction, selection and development of materials, teacher training, community involvement, and evaluation. Examples are drawn from other projects, but four programs are used as models: the Region XIII Bilingual Education Program, Austin, Texas in Spanish (Barrera, 17), the Milwaukee Public Schools Bilingual Program in Spanish (80); the Rough Rock Demonstration School, Chinle, Arizona in Navajo (110), and the Bilingual Education Program in St. Martin Parish, Breaux Bridge, Louisiana in French (Delahoussaye, 41).

Although each program is different, they share the basic goals of providing children in the programs with increased educational opportunity and an appreciation of and pride in their cultural heritage.

101

Region XIII Bilingual Education Program
Language: Spanish (Mexican-American)
Grades: 1–4
Classes: 19
Students: 520
Staff: 19 professionals, 9½ paraprofessionals
Schools: 3
Year: 4th

Milwaukee Bilingual Education Program
Language: Spanish (Multi-ethnic)
Grades: K–4, 7–12
Classes: 23
Students: 395
Staff: 14 professionals, 14 paraprofessionals
Schools: 3
Year: 4th

Rough Rock Demonstration School
Language: Navajo
Grades: 1–12, Adult Education
Classes: 30
Students: 480
Staff: 26 professionals, 44 paraprofessionals
Schools: 2
Year: 3rd

St. Martin Parish Bilingual Education Program
Language: French (Creole and Cajun)
Grades: K–3
Classes: 12
Students: 311
Staff: 18 professionals, 8 paraprofessionals
Schools: 2
Year: 3rd

Program design

Objectives for the Region XIII Bilingual Education Program, *Program objectives*
Austin, Texas include the following:
Develop communicative skills in two languages.
Develop math skills in two languages.
Create acceptance and appreciation of the child's cultural heritage
and of the dominant culture.

102

Develop a positive classroom environment in which the child can feel good about himself and his surroundings.

Create acceptance of the value of being bicultural and bilingual.

Help teachers become aware of teaching behavior that has a positive effect on children.

Identify instructional materials and equipment that make a difference in the teaching-learning process.

Involve parents in school activities that will help their children become enthusiastic learners.

Learning activities are carried out in a balanced combination of English and Spanish. Students are initially taught in their dominant language—whether Spanish or English—while receiving instruction in the second language. They are gradually introduced to instruction in the second language so that eventually 50 percent of their school day is devoted to activities in each language. A unique feature of the program is the use of the Montessori instructional system in a bilingual setting at one of the program schools. *Bilingual Montessori School*

Although the program objectives for the Milwaukee Bilingual Program are very similar to those of Region XIII, the program's major goal is to develop a bilingual-bicultural program extending from Kindergarten through Grade 8 at the Vieau Elementary School and to provide bilingual courses at the junior and senior high schools that receive students from Vieau. During the past five years a number of courses at the high-school level have been offered. These are: Spanish *Bilingual high school courses* for Spanish Speakers, Hispano-American Culture, Language and History, Bilingual Reading, Personal Economics, The Hispano in an Urban Setting, and Bilingual Sociology. Students needing assistance with regular academic courses at the high school report to the Bilingual Reading Center to receive individualized instruction from bilingual teachers and paraprofessional aides. At the elementary level primary students attend a nongraded bilingual program including *Nongraded program* English communication skills; Spanish communication skills; bilingual instruction in mathematics, social studies, science, art, and music. Individual pupil achievement records are kept in Spanish language arts and reading. The following schedule for Grades 3 and 4 will give an idea of how a student in the bilingual program spends his day (80).

Daily schedule

9:00–9:10   Routine duties

9:10–10:15   English reading for four groups (Monday, Tuesday, Wednesday, Thursday) Science (Friday)

10:15–10:30 Recess

10:30–11:30 Spanish reading for four groups (Monday, Tuesday, Wednesday, Thursday)
Social Studies (Friday)

11:30–12:00 Mathematics for two groups (slow and advanced)
Both groups taught bilingually—Spanish for Spanish-dominant, English for English-dominant

12:00–1:00 Lunch

1:00–1:30 Language Skills—Spanish and English (Monday, Tuesday, Wednesday, Thursday)
Spanish terms for mathematics (Friday)

1:30–2:00 Spelling and writing (Monday, Tuesday, Wednesday)
Science (Thursday, Friday)

2:00–2:30 Social Studies (Monday, Tuesday, Wednesday)
Art (Thursday, Friday)

2:30–3:00 Music (Monday, Wednesday, Friday)
Gym (Tuesday, Thursday)

3:00–3:15 Special help

The primary aims of the St. Martin Parish Bilingual Program are the development of greater competence in English for the children with limited English-speaking ability and the development of literacy in French for the French- and English-speaking child. These goals are accomplished by the implementation of an activity-centered English curriculum; a strong French program in which each child receives basic French instruction each day; and instruction in French in language arts, mathematics, physical education, music, art, and social science to develop the fluency of students who can already speak French and also to develop appreciation and pride in their cultural heritage. To meet the special needs of the children, individualization and grouping techniques are used extensively in teaching French, language development, and reading. Group compositions vary from unit to unit with the specialized needs of the children as the basis for grouping. Some learning experiences lend themselves to interest grouping while others require need or ability grouping. Peer-learning activities have been carried out with a high degree of success. When several groups are functioning simultaneously, a student group leader is especially effective in reinforcement activities. A strong component of the program in St. Martin's parish is the utilization of the Creole and the Cajun dialects as well as the implementation of a French heritage curriculum. The program has the added advantage of employing the services of

French bilingual program goals

Individualization, grouping, peer-teaching

Use of Creole and Cajun

104

assistant teachers from France participating in the *coopérants* program sponsored by the Council for the Development of French in Louisiana (Delahoussaye, 41).

At the Rough Rock Demonstration School a continuous-progress program emphasizing the development of sequential strands is in effect. English as a second language, math, Navajo language, reading, business English, social studies, and science objectives are being formulated to facilitate the reporting of individual student achievement. Although Rough Rock has a very diverse staff consisting of experienced white teachers, eager beginners, teachers from the Peace Corps, seasoned Navajo teachers, Navajo teacher aides, and adults from the community, they are staunch supporters of the stated goal of the school —to provide an educational experience that will stimulate the total personality development of the Navajo child so that he may stay on the reservation or go forth into the dominant society with a secure foundation of self and culture (110).

Navajo program

Even though bilingual programs have similar goals and objectives, no two programs are exactly alike. Each program bears the unique trademark of the school district and community representatives who, in planning the program, took into account the special needs of the students involved, the nature of the language and the ethnic group, the geographic location, and the available resources. As a result, the Mascenic bilingual program (75) and the St. John Valley program (113), although designed for French-speaking students, are quite different from the St. Martin Parish bilingual program (Delahoussaye, 41). The same can be said for the 143 Spanish-language bilingual programs described in the *Guide to Title VII Bilingual-Bicultural Programs* (57), or the Indian Language Programs highlighted in Bauer (19), Slager and Madsen (118, 119) and Spolsky (121).

Uniqueness of each program

Curriculum materials

The difference in program design may have fostered an attitude that was prevalent among bilingual personnel not too long ago and in some cases still persists today—that to be effective, curriculum materials for bilingual programs must be tailor-made for each particular program. Although the need to develop materials in different languages was legitimate initially because of the scarcity of identified subject-matter materials available in the different languages within the United States, the situation has improved considerably in recent years. Comprehensive lists of curriculum materials that are available commercially have been compiled by the Materials Acquisition Project in San Diego (Peña, 91)

Lists of curriculum materials

105

as well as a number of projects at the state and local level (Alvarado, 5; Rebert, 103). The Dissemination Center for Bilingual-Bicultural Education is a national project established to select, reproduce, and distribute project-developed materials according to the needs of bilingual programs throughout the United States. Annotated listings of suitable project-developed and commercial materials are published in a monthly pamphlet *Cartel*. A project inventory list describing all the project-developed materials on hand can be obtained from the Dissemination Center (61). Any item on the list that has not been selected for mass duplication and distribution will be copied and sent to any project director upon request.

Dissemination Center for Bilingual-Bicultural Education

In the area of curriculum materials, both the Region XIII Bilingual Program and the Wisconsin Bilingual Program stress the identification and acquisition of suitable materials rather than actual development. In the Texas program teachers use the materials in the classroom and are required to evaluate them twice a year. Parents also express their concern about the materials used. Through this process a resource guide is printed with a list of materials evaluated as adequate to meet the needs of Central Texas children.

Acquisition vs. development

The Milwaukee program maintains a Bilingual Resource Center at the Vieau Elementary School to provide staff and persons from other schools who are interested in bilingual education with a convenient reference center to preview bilingual books and materials. Milwaukee is also a field-trial center for the interdisciplinary curriculum materials developed by the Spanish Curricula Development Center, a Title VII-funded program (Robinett, 106). In evaluating these materials, the Milwaukee program works closely with the midwest office of the Curriculum Adaptation Network for Bilingual-Bicultural Education to ensure that the materials are suitable for the various ethnic groups in the midwest region (Armand, 12).

Bilingual Resource Center

Both the Region XIII Bilingual Education Program and the Milwaukee Bilingual Program exemplify the trend that is evident among Spanish bilingual programs throughout the United States. Local projects are placing more emphasis on identifying existing curriculum materials and adapting them to their special needs. Even in the area of local heritage of the various Spanish-speaking groups—a common deficiency of materials developed abroad—availability is increasing rapidly. Books, pamphlets, and resource guides on the cultural heritage of the Mexican-American (Martínez and Edwards, 74; Gorena, 56) and on the Puerto Rican experience in the United States (Batllé et al., 18; Santiago et al., 112) as well as those featuring the culture, history, and

Availability of cultural materials

geography of the island of Puerto Rico (Del Rosario, 42; Pérez Martínez and Diaz de Villar, 94) are now listed along with films and other relevant materials in nationally disseminated curriculum lists (Alvarado, 5; 61). Of course, curriculum development is still needed at the local level in some areas, notably in school districts in which a nongraded continuous program approach to instruction is in effect (Roscoe, 109). But even in such situations, the emphasis is on structuring the learning sequence rather than on actual development of learning materials.

The French bilingual programs, along with other bilingual programs for the less populous linguistic groups, are still very much involved in writing and developing curriculum materials. In the St. Martin Parish Bilingual Program the language arts curriculum developed by the local French curriculum specialists integrates other areas such as music, art, social living, science, culture, and heritage (Comeaux, 36). Bilingual mathematics and physical education curriculum units have also been developed. Local culture and heritage are an integral part of materials developed. Included in some units are topics such as *La Boucherie, La Toussaint, Mardi Gras,* Acadian Heritage, Local Customs, and so forth. Industries that are typical of the area have also been researched for inclusion in the unit. Examples of these are *La Roulaison* and *Les Ecrevisses.* Other efforts to include the local heritage of French-speaking people in the United States are evident in curriculum guides developed in the Lafayette Bilingual Program (Bradley and Coussan, 23, 24; Bradley et al., 25) and in social studies units developed in the French bilingual program in St. John Valley, Maine (Dubé and Paradis, 43; Picard, 95).

Curriculum development in French

Perhaps in the near future the efforts of the *Service de Liaison des Projets Bilingues Français-Anglais* (a coordinating unit for all French-English bilingual programs in the United States presently funded as a component of the Title VII Mascenic Bilingual Program in New Hampshire) (75) will diminish the need to invest so much local effort in curriculum development. The *Service de Liaison* is very active in the areas of needs assessment, curriculum and materials development, staff development, and national distribution. It provides a link between the French bilingual programs in the United States and similar programs in Canada, France, and other countries and has been helpful in sponsoring exchanges of materials among the programs in the United States as well as abroad.

Service de Liaison

The development of curriculum materials is crucial in the bilingual programs for American Indians. Although Indian languages are being used for instruction in the bilingual program, the production of

Lack of Indian-language materials

107

curriculum materials has been very difficult for certain Indian languages due to the lack of standardized orthographies (Slager and Madsen, 118).

Even in the case of Navajo, in which the preparation and publication of reading materials has been a high priority, the need is just beginning to be met. According to Spolsky (121), not enough is published in Navajo to provide a complete reading program for the first grade, not to mention an entire kindergarten through 12th grade bilingual program. Yet Spolsky is optimistic because of the serious attempts that are being made to meet the critical need for Navajo bilingual education.

One of the major producers of Navajo materials is the Navajo Curriculum Center, a component of the Rough Rock Demonstration School. A number of stories, plays, and legends that reflect the cultural heritage of the Navajo have been published within the past year. The Navajo Reading Study at the University of New Mexico has stepped up the production of reading materials in the Navajo language. Periodic listings of these newly developed materials are a regular feature of the various publications sponsored by the Bureau of Indian Affairs (Slager and Madsen, 118, 119; Tennant, 126). Special publications such as the *Kindergarten Curriculum Guide for Indian Children* (Jessen, 63) and bibliographies such as *Young People's Books on American Indians* (Rebert, 103) are very helpful in assisting projects to locate available materials.

Navajo Curriculum Center

Navajo Reading Study

Teacher training

Most bilingual programs are quite active in the area of teacher education. This is an important part of the program because the majority of teachers have not had the opportunity to take special courses on bilingual education at the college level. Even the relatively small number of colleges and universities throughout the country that have provided bilingual education courses within the past few years have really structured courses for graduate students rather than prospective teachers in bilingual programs (Andersson, 7).

The teacher education component of the Region XIII Bilingual Program includes preservice and in-service education components (Barrera, 17). During the summer, courses are offered through the extension division of local universities. These courses are planned to meet the needs of program teachers, but regular classroom teachers and graduate students attend as well. The majority of the courses offered thus far have stressed the areas of reading, individualization of

Preservice, in-service, and extension courses

instruction, and the cultural heritage. Other summer courses are designed for teachers, administrators, and aides who are interested in initiating bilingual programs in their school districts.

Toward the end of the summer a week-long orientation session is held as a preservice workshop for bilingual personnel. In-service workshops are held at least once a month throughout the rest of the year. Most of these sessions deal with the refinement of skills and problem solving. In the meantime, the Central Office staff visits the bilingual teachers to provide assistance when needed.

The Region XIII bilingual staff also provides consultant help to other teachers and schools throughout the region. This includes helping teachers with methods, techniques, and materials that will help them perform more effectively with non-English-speaking children. The bilingual staff also acquaints them with special techniques that will assist them in working with the parents of Spanish-speaking children.

The staff development activities in the Milwaukee Bilingual Program are very similar to those in the Austin program. A week-long preservice training session is held in August, followed by six afternoon in-service sessions throughout the school year. The topics and activities at both the preservice and in-service sessions stress the practical needs of bilingual teachers and supportive staff. The bilingual teaching staff also provides instruction on a daily basis to the teacher aides during the school year. Special workshops and courses are available through *Workshops for college credit* the University of Wisconsin-Milwaukee, which now offers subjects leading to a bilingual education major. Bilingual teachers, as well as the teacher aides in the program who register for courses at the university can apply for tuition and book reimbursement (80).

In the St. Martin's Parish Bilingual Program, teacher training is an on-going program involving not only the bilingual teachers and aides but also regular classroom teachers and other school personnel. This type of coordination is necessary since the English arts component and certain subject areas are taught by the regular personnel of the school, not the bilingual teacher. The utilization of assistant teachers from France in instruction and in the development of curriculum materials also requires special coordination to insure the compatibility of educational philosophies and instructional procedures (Delahoussaye, 41).

At the Rough Rock Demonstration School a Multicultural Teacher *Multicultural Teacher* Education Center has been established to assist classroom teachers and *Education Center: Rough Rock* supportive personnel in meeting the educational and cultural needs of Navajo children (110). This is accomplished through a six-week

109

preservice teacher education program and weekly in-service training sessions during the entire school year. The objectives of the staff development component are to assist teachers with identification of economic, social, religious, cultural, and academic influences on the growth, development, and learning of Navajo children; identification of teaching styles and approaches that are effective educational vehicles in working with Navajo children; and development of the necessary skills to design bilingual-bicultural materials for Navajo children. Specific topics include early childhood education; Navajo language and culture; teaching-learning methods via micro-teaching, music, arts and crafts; and the preparation of visual aids.

As other bilingual programs have done, the Teacher Education Center at the Rough Rock Demonstration School has assumed the initiative of convincing institutions of higher learning to grant credit for some of the workshops conducted at the Center. It has also been instrumental in the establishment of courses designed to train Navajo bilingual teachers at the University of New Mexico and Northern Arizona State University.

Although many individual bilingual projects are doing a commendable job in providing comprehensive in-service training programs for their teachers, resource and specialized staff limitations in the smaller projects can seriously hamper staff-development activities. In the Illinois bilingual program, a special supportive service component has been established to meet this particular need. The Bilingual Education Service Center coordinates the in-service training for all bilingual teachers in the geographically scattered "downstate" bilingual projects funded by the State of Illinois. The Center not only conducts statewide, regional, and local workshops for bilingual personnel, advisory councils, and regular school personnel, but also maintains an extensive bilingual curriculum materials library from which teachers can check out a variety of materials for use in their classroom. The Service Center staff also provides consultative help to individual school districts, community groups, and teachers and coordinates the evaluation program for the "downstate" projects (Swanson, 125).

Bilingual Education Service Center: Illinois

Community involvement

Bilingual education programs must include plans for parents and community involvement in all aspects of the project, including planning, implementation, and evaluation. By interacting with the parents of the children in the bilingual programs, the staff can be more sensitive and more responsive to the needs of the parents and the community. The parents can be a tremendous help to the program by providing support and taking a more active role in determining the nature of the children's education.

In the Region XIII Bilingual Education Programs there are three staff members whose major responsibility is to work in the area of community involvement. A parental involvement specialist and two paraprofessional home visitors keep the bilingual program and the community in constant communication. The home visitation program and the parent advisory board contribute to strengthening the bilingual program by making it more responsive and relevant to the needs of the community.

Home visitation

The community is also involved through special parent-participation and parent-education programs. Parent participation includes a tutor-training program in which parents are trained to work with children in the classroom. They also participate as aides and chaperones, assisting at parties and field trips and in many other activities that enhance and expand school-community relations. In the parent-education program parents are given instruction on the use of educational toys they can use at home with their preschool or school-age children. These toys and other instructional materials such as puzzles, records, tapes, and cassette players are checked out to parents on a regular basis (Barrera, 17).

Parent participation and parent education

In the Milwaukee program the Community Liaison maintains contact between the school, the parents, and the community. Although the Title VII Program has a Bilingual Advisory Committee, a movement has been made toward having the individual schools that are participating in the bilingual program form their own local advisory committees. In this way more parent involvement and input is encouraged, and parents can become better informed about their children's instructional program.

In conjunction with the Equal Educational Opportunity for Spanish-Background Students (a committee established by the school board) meetings of parents and students in 16 different schools with large Latin enrollments have been held. At the Vieau elementary school and South Division High School, a joint ethnic folk fair is planned. Students, parents, and community are involved in the preparation of activities such as booths, food, decorations, talent shows (80).

Whether in Rough Rock or in Breaux Bridge, whether in the role of a resource person for a social studies class or as a member of the bilingual advisory committee, whether a team member evaluating the bilingual program or a room mother helping the teacher with a field trip—the

111

involvement of the parents of children in the bilingual program has succeeded in opening the lines of communication between the ethnic community and the school. Schools, in turn, are more sensitive to the needs of the community and are responding in a variety of meaningful ways as evidenced by such a simple thing as the publication of school notices, bulletins, and even report cards in two languages (80; 110; Leavitt, 71).

School-community relations

Evaluation

As with any instructional program based on goals and objectives, evaluation is an integral part of every bilingual project. Its purpose is to have the project continuously assess to what extent the objectives are being met, to identify the factors that may be facilitating or obstructing the attainment of the objectives, and to allow for periodic revision of the program plan. Therefore, the evaluation plan must provide for the assessment of progress made in the areas of instruction, staff development, acquisition and development of curriculum materials, and community involvement—all of which have a bearing on student performance.

Measuring progress in all components

The Region XIII Bilingual Program, like the majority of Title VII programs, has a full-time evaluator on its staff. An extensive evaluation program is in effect in the three project schools. Testing is done in Spanish and English reading, mathematics, cultural attitudes, oral language proficiency in English and in Spanish, and self-concept. Further evaluation is done for the reading programs. Informal reading inventories are administered twice a year to determine adequate placement of students in particular reading levels.

Program teachers are also evaluated to determine the teacher's competence in individualizing instruction, the style and usage of both languages in the classroom, the effectiveness of aide utilization, and the bicultural aspects of the classroom activities. This helps teachers and program staff to determine needs for further program development.

The evaluation component of the St. Martin Parish Bilingual Program has focused the activities on the development of a French achievement test designed on the local level. The test is criterion referenced and has been field tested on area children; it is being utilized to measure achievement in French during the 1972–73 school year. Consideration is being given to the development of a parent and pupil attitudinal scale geared to the St. Martin Parish project for possible use as an instrument to measure gains in the affective domain.

French achievement test

The evaluation design at the Rough Rock Demonstration School is based on criterion-referenced assessment of the students' progress. Instead of designing a special instrument, student achievement is measured in terms of the number of objectives (from a sequential list) that each individual has completed. The evaluation report includes the number of sequenced objectives that should be completed in the course of a year, the entry date for each student, and the date each student completed each objective. The data processing office then generates a quarterly report containing basic summary information on each student and each class. Since objectives are grouped in levels of increasing difficulty, the reports provide a profile showing the continuous progress of each child and of the class as a whole. In addition to the checklist of individual objectives achieved, pre- and posttests given at the beginning and at the end of a sequence of objectives provide another means of evaluating student progress.

Objectives-based evaluation

Evaluation of the effect of teacher attitudes and behavior on the emotional and psychological well being of the Navajo children in the project is accomplished through regular classroom visitation (110). However, lack of structure and feedback procedures in these observations limit their effectivenesss for evaluative purposes.

In conducting the process evaluation of state-funded bilingual programs in Illinois, Garcelon (52) provides an effective approach. The salient features of these on-site evaluations are:

Process evaluation

- visiting teams that must include a bilingual teacher, a parent, and an administrator from outside the district;
- probes to assess attainment of Illinois bilingual goals as outlined in the district proposal;
- a maximum of two days time;
- immediate feedback—both oral and written including commendations, recommendations, and a program profile—prior to the team's departure

The Milwaukee Bilingual Program evaluation during the past three years has focused on the teaching process, pupil outcomes, community involvement, management, and attitudes. Under the directive of new Title VII guidelines, the evaluation plan during the following two years is limited to the assessment of pupil achievement as measured by performance on standardized tests (80). The areas to be tested at the kindergarten level are language arts and mathematics. At the primary-intermediate level, English language skills (oral comprehension and reading), Spanish language arts (oral comprehension and reading), and mathematics are tested. Some testing will be done at the high school

Measuring performance on standardized tests

level. In all of these areas students in the bilingual program are expected to score as well or better than a comparison group in English language tests and mathematics. On the Spanish language tests their scores should be equal to or higher than in previous years. Test administration, including training of bilingual testers, data collection, and data analysis are the responsibility of the project evaluator.

Reliability and validity

The use of standardized tests raises a number of questions as to the reliability and validity of the instruments available. Do these tests really measure the content and skills achieved by children? Kennedy (64) provides a detailed analysis of the unsuitability of many test items for nonnative speakers of English.

Seelye and Balasubramanian (115) outline steps taken in Illinois to determine the relevancy and cultural-linguistic biases of standardized tests. While determining test suitability, a summative evaluation of the bilingual-education program is being conducted in Illinois using a combination of different evaluation designs. Unlike evaluative activities elsewhere that have focused almost exclusively on the attainment of program objectives, the Illinois evaluation program seeks to provide data on the cognitive growth of Spanish-speaking students in the bilingual program as compared to Spanish-speaking students enrolled in the regular school program.

Preliminary findings

Preliminary analyses of data in ESL achievement indicate no statistically significant difference between the two groups, yet the experimental group received less exposure to English (Balasubramonian et al., 14). Findings in language arts and mathematics indicate that children in bilingual programs made greater mean achievement than their counterparts in the regular school program (97).

Cognitive growth data on a nationwide basis may be available within the next two years. Title VII programs entering the fourth year of funding (80) are now conducting similar evaluations as a result of the new federal guidelines.

Oral language assessment

Another area of evaluation of great concern to teachers and bilingual program planners is oral language assessment. Is the child English-dominant, or other-language-dominant? How proficient is he in each language? How much does he use each language? Since the purpose of bilingual education is to use the child's dominant language as a vehicle of instruction, these are all vital questions. In too many bilingual programs, however, language dominance assessment has been a trial-and-error process with the teacher gasping upon discovering that the linguistic ability of the students in a bilingual class ranges from complete monolingualism in one or the other language.

To get some indication of the language dominance of children entering the bilingual program, some schools have developed questionnaires in the two languages for parents and other community representatives (48). Typical questions regard the use of the different languages in the home, in the community, at work, during recreational activities, and so forth. Although questionnaires can provide valuable information (Mackey, 72), there is a need for instruments that will actually measure the communicative competence of the children themselves.

Language-dominance questionnaires

Fortunately the efforts in this area are increasing. Spolsky et al. (123) report on a validating study of three tests of oral proficiency: the Spanish-English Dominance Assessment Test, developed in New Mexico to place six- and seven-year-old children in appropriate streams in a bilingual school; the Navajo-English Dominance Interview, another placement instrument for six-year-olds; and the Oral Placement Test for Adults designed to place adults in appropriate levels of an ESL program. Results indicate that these instruments are satisfactory for classification and placement of students. In Illinois a procedure for analyzing the Spanish-language development of preschool Spanish-speaking children has recently been standardized with Mexican-American and Puerto Rican preschool children in Chicago (Toronto, 128, 129). The instrument developed will be published by the Northwestern University Press.

New efforts

Bilingual education: Studies and implications

The growing interest in bilingualism and bilingual education among educators, linguists, anthropologists, and social psychologists is evident in the number of studies, reports, articles, and books that have recently appeared on the subject.

Beginning with the all-encompassing work of Andersson and Boyer (8) (a key publication in the field of bilingual education) and the concise, practical handbook prepared by Saville and Troike (114), several important books are now available to persons wishing to know more about bilingualism and bilingual education. Spolsky (120) draws attention to the language barrier created by the language-education policy in schools and presents a picture of contemporary concerns in the language education of minority children in the United States. Fishman (49) places bilingualism in its sociological context and presents enlightening chapters on the stability of societal bilingualism, language maintenance, and language shift. In a detailed account of

Books on bilingualism

115

the bilingual program at the John F. Kennedy School in Berlin, Mackey (72) presents a "free-alternation" program at work. Lambert and Tucker (67) describe an experiment during which English-Canadian children were taught exclusively in French from kindergarten to the 4th grade—except for daily English language arts lessons in Grades 2 to 4. The research plan and procedures are outlined and the impact of the six-year program on the cognitive and attitudinal development of the children participating is discussed. Abrahams and Troike (1) present an excellent collection of essays designed to enable teachers to recognize the linguistic and cultural differences in their students and to put this awareness to work in the classroom. Proceedings from recent national conferences (Mazon, 76; 98) and special issues of journals (84) are excellent sources of both scholarly and practical articles.

In the field of linguistics, an increasing number of articles are appearing that deal with the language characteristics of Spanish speakers in the Southwest. Cárdenas (27) discusses the differences between compound and coordinate bilingualism when the dimension of culture is added. In discussing the major features of Spanish as spoken in the Southwest, Bowen (21) believes that the schools' effort to change the dialect of speakers of Southwest Spanish have been as unreasonable as trying to Briticize the speech of Anglos. He stresses that the school's role should be merely to equip students with an alternate, more standard Spanish dialect without belittling the students' language as substandard or inferior. Christian (32) shows how the socioeconomic hierarchies in the Southwest are formed and maintained by complex social relations and how these social relations are determined and sustained through language.

Bilingualism in the Southwest

In another article Christian (31) observes that the various criteria for cultural-linguistic subdivision of Mexican-Americans in the Southwest determined by the in-group itself are more realistic than the imposed label "Spanish-surnamed," which lumps together all subgroups. The need for culturally democratic learning environments—a setting where a child learns about his own and the dominant culture through cognitive styles that are culturally appropriate for the child— is proposed by Ramírez (101). He includes strategies for parent involvement, teacher training, curriculum development and assessment, which are deemed necessary to obtain the goal of biculturalism. A manual to train teachers (38) and a special questionnaire for home interviews (96) have been developed.

Culturally democratic learning environments

The 44 readings that Allen and Campbell (4) include in their text

Teaching English

116

on teaching English as a second language cover a broad range of topics from linguistic theories to practical classroom approaches, methods, and techniques useful to the bilingual teacher. Davis (39) presents excellent articles that deal with the problems encountered by different linguistic groups in learning English. Dulay and Burt (44) report on a study comparing the errors or "goofs" in English made by young Anglo children with those made by children learning English as a second language. After analyzing 400 utterances made by 145 children, they found that the type of "goofs" were similar for both first- and second-language learners. Robinett (107) outlines the differences that characterize "other-language" speakers and the various programs designed to teach them English. Huntsman (60) provides several strategies for teaching high school students for whom English is a second language to recognize language attitudes and their role in society.

Implications for the foreign language profession

Five years ago, in a statement to a Special Senate Sub-Committee on Bilingual Education, Bruce Gaarder pointed out the discrepancy between the billions of dollars spent in the United States to teach languages and the lack of effort being expended to maintain and develop the competence of American children who already speak those same languages (Andersson and Boyer, 8).

Although the disparity is not so great today and considerable progress has been made toward maintaining the linguistic and cultural heritage of thousands of children, very little actual effort has come from foreign language departments. Obviously, if there is one group of teachers who should be working toward making the United States a multilingual society, it is the foreign language profession. Yet foreign language teachers have been as insensitive to the needs of native speakers of the language they teach as have been subject-matter teachers who strive to teach them concepts in a language they do not understand. Furthermore, foreign language teachers have also contributed to the minority child's feeling of inferiority about his language and his culture. They have failed to recognize the linguistic and cultural heritage the child brings to the foreign language class as strength to build upon. Instead, they have viewed the child's skills and knowledge as handicaps to be overcome (Ward, 134).

Insensitivity of foreign language teachers

History, civilization, and culture courses in foreign language departments at the college level have yet to include the various ethnic groups

117

within the United States. High school and college foreign language teachers list foreign travel, government jobs abroad, and appreciation of a foreign culture as some of the reasons for foreign language study. Very seldom is reference made to the need for foreign languages in American stores, American hospitals, American social agencies, and even in American schools. Similarly, the need to better understand the cultural heritage of Spanish-Americans, French-Americans, Italian-Americans, American-Indians, and the many diverse cultures existing within our boundaries is rarely emphasized. In view of the great need for foreign language that prevails right here in our country, dwindling foreign language enrollments are inexcusable.

Need for foreign language

The above discussion is not intended to admonish the foreign language profession, but merely to point out the important role that foreign language departments must play if the goals of bilingual education are to be attained. Foreign language educators have been instrumental in the establishment of bilingual programs. The interest and support bilingual programs have received from the foreign language profession has been invaluable. But now that the path has been opened for bilingual programs, it is imperative that foreign language teachers go beyond the supportive role. They must become actively involved in the move toward making the United States a truly multilingual-multicultural society.

During its 1972 Annual Meeting, the American Association of Teachers of Spanish and Portuguese formally endorsed the bilingual-bicultural movement in education (Pasquariello, 89, 90; Teschner, 127). Spanish, it was stressed, can no longer be considered a "foreign" language in the United States.

AATSP endorses bilingual education

. . . *Debemos llevar el mensaje a donde vale* (Pasquariello, 90, p. 32). Members were urged to take the message to superintendents, to school boards, to the general public, and to support actively the passage of legislation for bilingual programs. Spanish professors were encouraged to convince the Colleges of Education that foreign languages are essential to the preparation of elementary and secondary teachers today. Spanish Departments were advised to reorient the focus of Spanish programs to include special courses for those students who already speak the language and to structure practical programs designed to teach Spanish needed by students in areas such as law, social work, medicine, psychology, and agriculture. Such efforts would not only help the cause of Spanish speakers in the United States but also benefit the foreign language profession by making the study of Spanish a vital part of life and education in the United States.

Need for practical Spanish

118

An illustration of the enthusiastic response of high school students to a Spanish program that allows them to put into practice what they have learned is reported by Hall and Sturm (58). To help a handful of Spanish-speaking elementary students who were having difficulty with the regular subjects, high school students in their fifth year of Spanish were invited to serve as special tutors. Not only did the "cadet teachers" succeed in helping the Spanish-speaking children, but the English-speaking students and the teachers in the elementary schools became so interested in learning Spanish that the program had to be expanded to include Spanish language instruction for the children in the elementary schools. The program has been successful both in terms of the children in the elementary school and the students at the high school. The Spanish cadet teachers have worked with the elementary curriculum director in designing, implementing, and revising the special curriculum; they have learned the importance of motivating their students by making the curriculum relevant to their needs. The program has been expanded to include 3rd-, 4th-, and 5th-year Spanish students and has received the wholehearted support of the administration, parents, and students throughout the entire school district.

A relevant program

Another area in which the foreign language profession can offer needed assistance to bilingual programs is in teacher preparation. It is true that bilingual teachers need a variety of competencies that cannot all be provided by foreign language departments (Michel, 78). However, persons planning to teach in a bilingual program must not only be fluent and literate in both languages but must have some knowledge about the nature of language, language learning, bilingualism, and contrastive linguistics. Foreign language departments can impart this knowledge. To teach in a bilingual program the teacher should be able to function in both cultures and in both languages. However, it is not enough to be born into biculturalism (Gaarder et al., 51); teachers need to learn about the history, sociology, folklore, values, aspirations, environment, and the ways in which all these factors interact with the language and culture of the target population. This is an area where foreign language departments could make a great contribution, not only to future bilingual teachers but to regular classroom teachers and to students planning to go into public service fields. Since the linguistic ability of children in bilingual programs is as varied as the number of children within any given program, foreign language education departments should train future teachers to diagnose the individual needs of the child and to adapt the curriculum and teaching

Bilingual teacher preparation

Qualification and skills

119

strategies to meet his needs. Prospective teachers, whether in foreign language or bilingual education, must be given more widely applicable skills "to be utilized more uniquely and consciously in learning situations" (Jarvis, 62, p. 203).

Even in the preparation of teachers of English as a second language, foreign language departments can make a contribution. Alatis (3) states that teachers of English to speakers of another language should have at least some knowledge of the language of their students. In this manner they can not only communicate better during the initial stages of instruction but can anticipate areas in which the child's language may interfere with learning certain structures in English. ESL teachers should also be knowledgeable of the different cultural backgrounds that the student brings to the classroom. Cobb (35) suggests three ways in which the ESL teacher can use the child's culture as a point of departure: initial classroom exposure using visual aids that relate to the child's culture, specific language-learning activities that are relevant to the cultural background, a variety of reading materials that represents the literature from the student's heritage as well as American reading materials. Learning the student's language, Cobb maintains, leads to a greater rapport and sensitivity between the teacher and student which will result in better achievement.

Preparing ESL Teachers

Learning the student's language can also help the foreign language or bilingual teacher gain the confidence of the student by showing him that his language is a viable means of communication. Foreign language departments should prepare teachers to recognize that local dialects spoken in the United States are in every linguistic sense as worthy of study, and in the cultural sense as worthy of use, as any other regional variety throughout the world (Gaarder et al., 51). But mere recognition is not enough. Future teachers and even regular students should have the opportunity to listen to recordings of everyday conversations among Mexican-Americans, Puerto Ricans, Cubans, French-Americans, Italian-Americans, depending on the language they are studying. Perhaps then they will realize that what they passed off as Tex-Mex or Cajun is not any more foreign to Spanish or French than the language of New York cabdrivers, jazz musicians, or computer operators is to American English. As stated in a report commissioned by the Executive Council of the American Association of Teachers of Spanish and Portuguese, we must "close the gap which has so long separated the academic or elitist bilingualism in our schools and colleges from the real world of bilingual people in the nation's streets, shops, and homes" (p. 620).

Local dialect

120

In recognition of the special educational needs of the large numbers of children of limited English-speaking ability in the United States, Congress hereby declares it to be the policy of the United States to provide financial assistance to local educational agencies to develop and carry out new and imaginative elementary and secondary school programs designed to meet the special educational needs (Andersson and Boyer, 8).

1 This Declaration of Policy of the Bilingual Education Act marked the beginning of a new era in American education. It was recognized that the traditional school system was not meeting the needs of children from non-English-speaking homes and that in too many cases schools were causing grave harm to the self-concepts and self-esteem of these children. Bilingual education was a response to this reality.

2 Although during the past five years the number of bilingual education programs that have been implemented in 33 states and United States territories is reaching the 500 mark, this represents only a very small fraction of the need.

3 A parallel movement among ethnic minorities wishing to preserve their linguistic and cultural heritage has begun to exert pressure on American institutions to recognize that the melting-pot philosophy is nothing more than a myth that fosters Anglo ethnocentrism to the detriment of all ethnic minorities. In response to this pressure, state and local agencies are increasingly moving toward the establishment of special bilingual programs on their own. In some states laws have been enacted making bilingual education mandatory; in other states funds for bilingual education have been appropriated; and in a number of states legislation that favors bilingual education is being considered.

4 Public schools are not the only institutions where change is in progress. Colleges and universities are responding with special programs on ethnic studies; public news media have increased the number of features and programs in ethnic languages; social institutions too are recognizing the important role of the ethnic language in reinforcing the sense of identity, of self-esteem, and of self-confidence that all human beings need to function effectively in society (Ely, 45).

5 Bilingual education has a long way to go. Modifying a long-

121

established system presents all sorts of problems; changing long-maintained attitudes is even more difficult. Nevertheless, bilingual programs are making headway. Although it is too soon to predict the long-range impact of bilingual education, preliminary reports indicate that children in bilingual programs achieve at the same rate in English and other subject areas as comparable groups in regular school programs. They have the added advantage of maintaining their native language fluency, learning about their cultural background, and feeling good about themselves (Weffer, 135).

6 By helping meet the educational needs of the different ethnic minorities in the United States, bilingual education will not necessarily bring about the cultural and linguistic assimilation of ethnic minorities (Gaarder, 50), but it will foster greater sensitivity in both the ethnic minority and the Anglo majority, thereby making headway towards cultural pluralism.

References, Bilingual education: the national perspective

1 Abrahams, Roger D., and Rudolph C. Troike,eds. *Language and Cultural Diversity in American Education.* Englewood Cliffs, New Jersey: Prentice Hall, 1972.

2 *Action Goals for the Seventies: An Agenda for Illinois Education.* Springfield, Illinois: Superintendent of Public Instruction, 1972.

3 Alatis, James E. *Guidelines for TESOL Teacher Preparation.* Washington, D.C.: Georgetown University, 1972.

4 Allen, Harold B., and Russell N. Campbell. *Teaching English as a Second Language: A Book of Readings.* New York: McGraw-Hill, 1972.

5 Alvarado, Helen. *Curriculum Materials for Bilingual Programs.* (Spanish-English, Pre-School–Grade 12) Mt. Prospect, Illinois: Bilingual Education Service Center, 1973. [List of commercially available materials.]

6 Andersson, Theodore. "Bilingual Education:The American Experience." *Modern Language Journal* 55(1971):427–40.

7 —— Personal Communication, 1973.

8 —— and Mildred Boyer. *Bilingual Schooling in the United States.* 2 Volumes. Washington, D.C.: United States Government Printing Office, 1970.

9 Angel, Frank. "Social Class or Culture? A Fundamental Issue in the Education of Culturally Different Students," 37–47 in Bernard Spolsky,ed., *The Language Education of Minority Children.* Rowley, Massachusetts: Newbury House, 1972.

10 Aragón, Juan. *Cultural Conflicts in the Traditional Curriculum.* Sacramento, California: State Department of Education, 1973. [Keynote address, International Multilingual-Multicultural Conference, San Diego, California, April, 1973.] [Videotape.]

11 Arciniegas, Tomás. "The Ethnocentric Response of Public Education to the Chicano: Implications for School Administrators," IX 1–69 in Manuel Reyes Mazón,ed., *Adelante: An Emerging Design for Mexican-American Education.* Austin: University of Texas, Center for Communication Research, 1972.

12 Armand, Yvette D. *SCDC Field Guide 1972–73.* Miami Beach: Spanish Curricula Development Center, 1972.

13 Badillo, Hermán. "The Politics and Realities of Bilingual Education." *Foreign Language Annals* 5(1972):297–301.

14 Balasubramonian, K., H. Ned Seelye, and Rafaela Weffer. *Do Bilingual Education Programs Inhibit English Language Achievement?: A Report on an Illinois Experiment.* Mt. Prospect, Illinois: Bilingual Education Service Center, 1973. [Paper presented at the Seventh Annual Convention, Teachers of English to Speakers of Other Languages, San Juan, Puerto Rico, May, 1973.]

15 Ballesteros, David. "Toward an Advantaged Society: Bilingual Education in the 70's." *The National Elementary Principal* 50, ii(1970):25–28.

16 Barrera, María. *Bilingual Education.* Austin, Texas: Region XIII Education Service Center, 1973. [Report presented to the Texas Legislature.]

17 ——— Personal Communication, 1973. [Questionnaire.]

18 Batllé, Ana, Lydia Carcino, Eliezer Rodríguez, and Eleanor Sandstrom. *The Puerto Ricans: A Resource Unit for Teachers.* New York: Anti-Defamation League of B'nai B'rith, 1973.

19 Bauer, Evelyn. "A History of Bilingual Education in BIA Schools," 29–32 in Robert J. Rebert,ed., *Bilingual Education for American Indians.* Curriculum Bulletin Number 3. Washington, D.C.: United States Bureau of Indian Affairs, 1971.

20 *A Bilingual Education Program for Puerto Rico.* [Application for Continuation of a Bilingual Education Program under the Provisions of Title VII ESEA.] Hato Rey, Puerto Rico: Department of Education, 1972.

21 Bowen, J. Donald. "Local Standards and Spanish in the Southwest," 153–63 in Ralph W. Ewton and Jacob Ornstein,eds., *Studies in Language and Linguistics 1972–73.* El Paso, Texas: Texas Western Press, 1972.

22 Bradley, Ruth. Personal Communication, 1973.

23 ——— and Odette Coussan. *Kindergarten Curriculum Guide.* Lafayette, Louisiana: Lafayette Parish Bilingual Program, 1973.

24 ——— *Social Living I.* First Grade Curriculum Guide in Social Studies. Lafayette, Louisiana: Lafayette Parish Bilingual Program, 1973.

25 ———and Alain Marchal. *Education Physique I et II.* Lafayette, Louisiana: Lafayette Bilingual Program, 1973.

26 Brisk, María. *Directory of Bilingual Educational Programs in the United States 1972–73.* Washington, D.C.: Center for Applied Linguistics, in press.

27 Cárdenas, Daniel N. "Compound and Coordinate Bilingualism-Biculturalism in the Southwest," 165–80, in Ralph W. Ewton, Jr. and Jacob Ornstein, eds., *Studies in Language and Linguistics 1972–73.* El Paso, Texas: Texas Western Press, 1972.

28 Cárdenas, José A. "Politics and Education," VII 1–14 in Manuel Reyes Mazón,ed., *Adelante: An Emerging Design for Mexican-American Education.* Austin: University of Texas, Center for Communication Research, 1972.

29 Casso, Henry. *Implications of the California EMR Lawsuit for National Bilingual-Bicultural Education Strategies.* Sacramento, California: State Department of Education, 1973. [Paper presented at the International Multilingual—Multicultural Conference, San Diego, Caifornia, April, 1973.] [Audiotape].

30 Castañeda–Shular, Antonia, Tomás Ybarra-Frausto, and Joseph Sommers. *Literatura Chicana, Texto y Contexto:Chicano Literature, Text and Context.* Englewood Cliffs, New Jersey: Prentice-Hall, 1972.

31 Christian, Chester C.,Jr. "Criteria for Cultural-Linguistic Subdivision in the Southwest," in Paul Turner,ed., *Bilingualism in the Southwest.* Tucson, Arizona: University of Arizona Press, in press.

32 ——— "Language Functions in the Maintenance of Socio-Economic Hierarchies," 181–91 in Ralph W. Ewton, Jr. and Jacob Ornstein,eds., *Studies in Language and Linguistics 1972–73.* El Paso, Texas: Texas Western Press, 1972.

33 ——— and John M. Sharp. "Bilingualism in a Pluralistic Society," 341–75 in Dale L. Lange and Charles J. James,eds., *Foreign Language Education:A Reappraisal.* ACTFL Review of Foreign Language Education, Volume 4. Skokie, Illinois: National Textbook Company, 1972.

34 *The Christian Science Monitor,* [17 February 1973]:13.

35 Cobb, Martha K. "Multi-Ethnic Materials in Secondary Language Program Classrooms." *TESOL Quarterly* 6(1972):339–49.

36 Comeaux, Jane. *La Boucherie: Grade Two.* Breaux Bridge, Louisiana: Title VII Bilingual Education Program 1972. [Interdisciplinary Curriculum Guide.]

37 Coombs, L. Madison. "A Summary of Pertinent Research in Bilingual Education," 9–27 in Robert J. Rebert,ed., *Bilingual Education for American Indians.* Curriculum Bulletin Number 3. Washington, D.C.: United States Bureau of Indian Affairs, 1971.

38 *Culturally Democratic Learning Environments:A Cognitive Styles Approach.* A Manual for Teachers. Riverside, California: Systems and Evaluations in Education, 1972. [Multilingual Assessment Project, Riverside Component.]

39 Davis, A.L.,ed. *Culture, Class and Language Variety.* Urbana, Illinois: National Council of Teachers of English, 1972.

40 De Granda, Germán. *Transculturación e Interferencia Lingüística en el Puerto Rico Contemporáneo (1898/1968).* Río Piedras, Puerto Rico: Editorial Edil, 1972.

41 Delahoussaye, Hazel. *The French Bilingual Program in St. Martin Parish:An Overview*. Breaux Bridge, Louisiana: Title VII Bilingual Program, 1972. [Mimeo.]

42 Del Rosario, Rubén, and Isabel Freire de Matos. *ABC de Puerto Rico*. Sharon, Connecticut: Troutman Press, 1968.

43 Dubé, Norman, and Roger Paradis. *La Forêt*. Elementary Social Studies. St. John Valley, Maine: Project Brave Title VII Bilingual Program, 1971.

44 Dulay, Heidi C., and Marina K. Burt. "Goofing: An Indication of Children's Second Language Learning Strategies." *Language Learning*. 22(1972): 235–50.

45 Ely, Roland T. *Interdisciplinary Criminology:An Inter-American Approach*. ALAS: Bilingual-Bicultural Wings for Spanish-Speaking Prisoners in Illinois. [Paper presented at the Second Inter-American Congress of the Inter-American Association of Criminology and the American Society of Criminology, Caracas, Venezuela, November, 1972.]

46 Estupinián, Rafael. "A Tri-Partite Development for the Cultural Arts in the Education of the Mexican-American," VIII 1–40, in Manuel Reyes Mazón,ed., *Adelante:An Emerging Design for Mexican-American Education*. Austin: The University of Texas, Center for Communication Research, 1972.

47 Figueroa Luciano, Amílcar. "Aguántate Muchacho, Aguántate Hijo Mío. . .," 40–41. in Robert Muckley,ed., *Notes of Neorican Seminar*. San Germán, Puerto Rico: Inter-American University, 1972.

48 *Final Evaluation Report: Fiscal 1972*. ESEA Title VII Bilingual Education. Chicago: Board of Education, 1973.

49 Fishman, Joshua A. *The Sociology of Language:An Interdisciplinary Social Science Approach to Language in Society*. Rowley, Massachusetts: Newbury House, 1972.

50 Gaarder, A. Bruce. *Language Maintenance or Language Shift:The Prospect for Spanish in the United States*. Washington, D.C.: U.S. Office of Education, 1971. [Paper presented at the Conference on Child Language, Chicago, November, 1971.]

51 ——— Donald D. Walsh, et al. "Teaching Spanish in School and College to Native Speakers of Spanish." *Hispania* 55(1972):619–31.

52 Garcelon, Ann. *Process Evaluation of Bilingual Programs in Illinois:A Team Approach*. Chicago: Illinois Office of Public Instruction, 1973.

53 García, Robert, and Carlos Truán. *State Legislation in Bilingual Education*. [Reports presented at the International Multilingual-Multicultural Conference, San Diego, California, April, 1973.] [Audiotape.]

54 García-Passalacqua, Juan M. "Puertorriqueños Todos," 18–24 in Robert L. Muckley,ed., *Notes of Neorican Seminar*. San Germán, Puerto Rico: Inter-American University, 1972.

55 Gardner, R.C., and W.E. Lambert. *Attitudes and Motivation in Second Language Learning*. Rowley, Massachusetts: Newbury House, 1972.

56 Gorena, Minerva,ed. *Information and Materials to Teach the Cultural Heritage of the Mexican-American Child*. Austin, Texas: Dissemination Center for Bilingual-Bicultural Education, 1973.

57 *Guide to Title VII ESEA Bilingual-Bicultural Projects in the United States: 1972–1973*. Austin, Texas: Dissemination Center for Bilingual-Bicultural Education, 1973.

58 Hall, Marian, and Dorothy Sturm. "Spanish Cadet Teaching—Its Own Excuse for Being." *Hispania* 56(1973):110–11.

59 Hernández, Marco, Carlos Pérez, and José Vázquez. *The New York Experience*. Sacramento, California: State Department of Education, 1973. [Report presented at the International Multilingual-Multicultural Conference, San Diego, California, April, 1973.] [Audiotape.]

60 Huntsman, Beverly. "Some Sociological Factors in Bilingual Schooling." *TESOL Quarterly* 6(1972): 255–61.

61 *Inventory of Project Developed Materials for Bilingual Programs*. Austin Texas: Dissemination Center for Bilingual-Bicultural Education, 1973.

62 Jarvis, Gilbert A. "Teacher Education Goals: They're Tearing Up the Street Where I was Born." *Foreign Language Annals* 6(1972):198–205.

63 Jessen, Mariana,ed. *Kindergarten Curriculum Guide for Indian Children*. Curriculum Bulletin Number 5. Washington, D.C.: United States Bureau of Indian Affairs, 1972.

64 Kennedy, Graeme. "The Language of Tests for Young Children," 164–81, in Bernard Spolsky,ed., *The Language Education of Minority Children*. Rowley, Massachusetts: Newbury House, 1972.

65 Kjolseth, Rolf. "Bilingual Education Programs in the United States:For Assimilation or Pluralism?" 94–121, in Bernard Spolsky,ed., *The Language Education of Minority Children*. Rowley, Massachusetts: Newbury House, 1972.

66 Kuenster, John. *The Mexicans in America*. Chicago: Claretina Publications, 1972.

67 Lambert, Wallace E., and G. Richard Tucker. *Bilingual Education of Children:The St. Lambert Experiment*. Rowley, Massachusetts: Newbury House, 1972.

68 "La Vergüenza de Hablar Español." An Editorial. *La Raza*. (17 February, 1973), Chicago.

69 Leal, Luis. "Mexican-American Literature: A Historical Perspective." *Revista Chicano-Riqueña*, 1,i(1973):32–44.

70 Leibowitz, Arnold H. "A History of Language Policy in American Indian Schools," 1–6 in Robert J. Rebert,ed., *Bilingual Education for American Indians*. Curriculum Bulletin Number 3. Washington, D.C.: United States Bureau of Indian Affairs, 1971.

71 Leavitt, Sr. Sharon,ed. *Project Brave Bulletin, Volume III*. St. John Valley, Maine: Title VII Bilingual Education Program, 1973.

72 Mackey, William F. *Bilingual Education in a Binational School*. Rowley, Massachusetts: Newbury House, 1972.

73 Mangers, Dennis H. "Education in the Grapes of Wrath." *The National Elementary Principal* 50,ii (1970):34–40.

74 Martínez, Gilbert T., and Jane Edwards. *The Mexican Americans*. Boston: Houghton-Mifflin, 1972.

75 *Mascenic French Bilingual Educational Program: ESEA Title VII Project*. Greenville, New Hampshire: Mascenic Bilingual Program, 1973. [Brochure.]

76 Mazón, Manuel Reyes,ed. *Adelante:An Emerging Design for Mexican-American Education*. Austin: The The University of Texas, Center for Communication Research, 1972. [Draft manuscript for field review.]

77 Mazzone, Ernest. Personal Communication, 1973.

78 Michel, Joseph. *The Preparation of the Teacher for Bilingual Education*. [Speech presented at Edinboro State College, Edinboro, Pennsylvania, February, 1972.] [EDRS: ED 063 830.]

79 Miller, Wick R. "Obsolescing Language:The Case of the Shoshone," 1–12 in William R. Slager, Betty M. Madsen,eds., *Language in American Indian Education*. Salt Lake City: The University of Utah, Winter, 1972.

80 *The Milwaukee Bilingual Education Program*. [Application for Continuation of the Bilingual Education Program, Title VII and Title I ESEA.] Milwaukee, Wisconsin: Milwaukee Public Schools, 1973.

81 Molina, Hubert. "Evaluation During Development of Spanish Materials on the Kindergarten and First-Grade Level." *Hispania*. 55(1972):899–903.

82 Muckley, Robert L.,ed., *Notes of Neorican Seminar*. San Germán, Puerto Rico: Inter-American University, 1972.

83 Natalicio, Diane S., and Fred Williams. "What Characteristics Can 'Experts' Reliably Evaluate in the Speech of Black and Mexican-American Children?" *TESOL Quarterly* 6(1972):121–27.

84 *The National Elementary Principal* 50,ii(1970). [Entire issue devoted to Education for the Spanish-Speaking.]

85 Nieto, Sonia. *Curso de español para estudiantes hispanoparlantes de primer grado*. New York: Board of Education, Public School 25, 1971.

86 Orta, Awilda. *Multiethnic Cooperation in Bilingual Education*. Sacramento, California: State Department of Education, 1973. [Address at the International Multilingual-Multicultural Conference, San Diego, California, April, 1973.] [Videotape.]

87 Pacheco, Manuel T. "Approaches to Bilingualism: Recognition of a Multilingual Society," 97–124 in Dale L. Lange,ed., *Pluralism in Foreign Language Education*. ACTFL Review of Foreign Language Education. Volume 3. Skokie, Illinois: National Textbook Company, 1973.

88 Palomares, Uvaldo. "The Psychology of the Mexican-American," X 1–30 in Manuel Reyes Mazón,ed., *Adelante: An Emerging Design for Mexican-American Education*. Austin: The University of Texas, Center for Communication Research, 1972.

89 Pasquariello, Anthony M. "The President's Corner: La AATSP Respalda el Movimiento Bilingüe." *Hispania* 55(1972):339.

90 ——— "Una causa en busca de comprensión y dirección: La educación bilingüe y bicultural." *Hispania* 56(1973): 27–34.

91 Peña, Albar. *Federal Legislative Funding for Bilingual Programs*. Sacramento, California: State Department of Education, 1973. [Paper presented at the International Multilingual-Multicultural Conference, San Diego, California, April, 1973.] [Audiotape.]

92 ——— Personal Communication, 1973. [Questionnaire.]

93 Pérez, Carmen. Personal Communication, 1973.

94 Pérez Martínez, Aurelio, and Delia Díaz de Villar. *Conociendo a Borinquen. Estudios Sociales para los Grados 4–8*. Guatemala, C.A.: Cultural Centroamericana, 1971. [Colección Cultural Puertorriqueña.]

95 Picard, Omer. *Les Acadiens*. Curriculum Unit for Elementary Social Studies. St. John Valley, Maine: Project Brave Title VII Bilingual Program, 1971.

96 *Planning Culturally Democractic Learning Environments: The Home Interview. A Manual for Teachers*. Riverside, California: Systems and Evaluations in Education, 1972.

97 *Preliminary Report on the Achievement of Children in Bilingual Programs*. Chicago: Illinois Office of Public Instruction, 1972.

98 *Proceedings, National Conference on Bilingual Education April 14–15, 1972, Austin, Texas*. Austin, Texas: Dissemination Center for Bilingual-Bicultural Education, 1973.

99 *Programs under Bilingual Education Act (Title VII, ESEA): Manual for Project Applicants and Grantees*. Washington, D.C.: Office of Education, 1971.

100 Ramírez, Alfonso. "Bilingual Reading for Speakers of Spanish." *TASCD Journal* 3,i(1972):4–6.

101 Ramírez, Manuel, III "Cultural Democracy:A New Philosophy for Educating the Mexican-American Child." *The National Elementary Principal* 50,ii(1970):45–46.

102 Ramírez, Manuel. "Current Educational Research: The Basis for a New Philosophy for Educating Mexican-Americans," VI 1–46 in Manuel Reyes Mazón,ed., *Adelante:An Emerging Design for Mexican-American Education*. Austin, Texas: The University of Texas, Center for Communication Research, 1972.

103 Rebert, Robert,ed., *Annotated Bibliography of Young*

People's Books on American Indians. Curriculum Bulletin Number 12. Washington, D.C.: United States Bureau of Indian Affairs, 1973.

104 Redbird-Selam, Helen Marie, and Leroy B. Selam. "Cultural Conflict in the Classroom." *Social Education* 36(1973):512–19.

105 *Revista Chicano-Riqueña.* Bloomington, Indiana: Latin American Studies Department, Indiana University, 1973.

106 Robinett, Ralph. "Developing Curriculum for Bilingual Education," 485–500 in Theodore Andersson,ed., *Conference on Child Language.* Quebec, Canada: International Center for Research on Bilingualism and Les Presses de l'Université Laval, 1971. [Conference preprint.]

107 Robinett, Betty Wallace. "The Domains of TESOL." *TESOL Quarterly* 6(1972)163–66.

108 Rodgers, Don, and Diego Rangel. "Learning for Two Worlds." *American Education* 8,viii(1972): 28–32.

109 Roscoe, Carole. "Developing Instructional Material for a Bilingual Program." *TESOL Quarterly* 6(1972): 163–66.

110 *Rough Rock Demonstration School: A Continuation Grant Proposal.* Title VII ESEA. Chinle, Arizona: Rough Rock Demonstration School, 1972.

111 Sancho, Anthony R. "Spanish:A New Approach for Bilingual Program." *TESOL Quarterly* 6(1972): 333–38.

112 Santiago, Jorge, Francisco Torres, Sonia Maldonado, and Minerva Deane. *Estudio Cultural de Puerto Rico.* Resource Manual for Teachers and Secondary Students. Austin, Texas: Dissemination Center for Bilingual-Bicultural Education. [Developed by Project ARRIBA, Philadelphia.]

113 *St. John Valley Bilingual Education Program.* [Continuation Application, Title VII ESEA.] Madawaska, Maine: St. John Valley Bilingual Education Program, 1973.

114 Saville, Muriel, and Rudolph Troike. *A Handbook for Bilingual Education.* Washington, D.C.: Teachers of English to Speakers of Other Languages, 1971. [Revised.]

115 Seelye, H. Ned, and K. Balasubramonian. *Evaluating Cognitive Growth in Illinois Bilingual Programs.* Chicago: Office of Public Instruction, 1973.

116 *Selected Bibliography for Chicano Studies Curriculum.* Riverside, California: Systems and Evaluations in Education, 1972.

117 Silen, Juan Angel. *Hacia una visión positiva del puertorriqueño.* Río Piedras, Puerto Rico: Editorial Edil, 1972.

118 Slager, William R., and Betty Madsen,eds. *Language in American Indian Education.* Salt Lake City: The University of Utah, Spring, 1972.

119 ––––––– *Language in American Indian Education.* Salt Lake City: The University of Utah, Winter, 1972.

120 Spolsky, Bernard. "The Language Education of Minority Children," 1–10 in Bernard Spolsky,ed., *The Language Education of Minority Children: Selected Readings.* Rowley, Massachusetts: Newbury House, 1972.

121 ––––––– "Advances in Navajo Bilingual Education 1969–72," 1–5 in Robert J. Rebert,ed., *Bilingual Education for American Indians, Volume 2.* [Curriculum Bulletin Number 13.] Washington, D.C.: United States Bureau of Indian Affairs, 1973.

122 ––––––– and Wayne Holm. "Literacy in the Vernacular:The Case of the Navajo," 239–51 in Ralph W. Ewton,Jr. and Jacob Ornstein,eds., *Studies in Language and Linguistics 1972–73.* El Paso, Texas: Texas Western Press, 1972.

123 Spolsky, Bernard, Penny Murphy, Wayne Holm, and Allen Ferrel. "Three Functional Tests of Oral Proficiency." *TESOL Quarterly* 6(1972):221–35.

124 *State Guidelines for Bilingual-Bicultural Education Programs.* Chicago: Office of Public Instruction, Bilingual Education Section, 1973. [Revised.]

125 Swanson, María Medina. *Inservice Programs for Bilingual Teachers in Illinois.* Mt. Prospect, Illinois: Bilingual Education Service Center, 1973. [Report presented at the International Multilingual-Multicultural Conference, San Diego, California, April, 1973.]

126 Tennant, Edward. "The Bilingual Education Act and the American Indian," 33–37 in Robert J. Rebert,ed., *Bilingual Education for American Indians.* [Curriculum Bulletin Number 3]. Washington, D.C.: United States Bureau of Indian Affairs, 1971.

127 Teschner, Richard V. "Spanish and Portuguese Cease to be Foreign: The 1972 AATSP Meeting." *Modern Language Journal* 57(1973):125–31.

128 Toronto, Allen. *A Developmental Spanish Language Analysis Procedure for Spanish-Speaking Children.* Evanston, Illinois: Northwestern University, 1972. [Doctoral dissertation.]

129 ––––––– *Standardization of Language Evaluation Procedures in Spanish for Spanish-Speaking Children.* [Preliminary Report.] Mt. Prospect, Illinois: Bilingual Education Service Center, 1973. [Mimeo.]

130 Ulibarrí, Horacio. "Bilingualism," 229–58 in Emma M. Birkmaier,ed., *Foreign Language Education:An Overview.* ACTFL Review of Foreign Language Education, Volume 1. Skokie, National Textbook Company, 1972.

131 Valdez, Luis. *No saco nada de la escuela.* [Play presented by the Teatro de los Barrios of Chicago at the Third Statewide Bilingual Inservice Workshop, Mt. Prospect, Illinois, February, 1973.]

132 Vargas, Herminio. *Curso de español para estudiantes hispano-hablantes del kindergarten.* New York: Board of Education, Public School 25, 1971.

133 Vázquez, Hector I. "Puerto Rican Americans." *The National Elementary Principal* 50,ii(1970):65–71.

134 Ward, James H. "Spanish Teachers and Spanish-Speaking Minorities." *Hispania* 55(1972):893–95.

135 Weffer, Rafaela Elizondo. *Effects of First Language Instruction in Academic and Psychological Development of Bilingual Children.* Chicago: Illinois Institute of Technology, 1972. [Doctoral dissertation.]

136 Zintz, Miles V. "What Classroom Teachers Should Know about Bilingual Education." 39–58 in Robert J. Rebert,ed., *Bilingual Education for American Indians.* [Curriculum Bulletin Number 3.] Washington, D.C.: United States Bureau of Indian Affairs, 1971.

5

Interdisciplinary studies

Introduction

A comprehensive or exhaustive overview of the phenomenon of interdisciplinarity as it relates to the teaching of foreign languages is not within the scope of this chapter. What follows can best be characterized as a selective review of the most recent theoretical pronouncements and practical applications of the interdisciplinary approach which are of significance to foreign language teachers and learners. Much ground has already been covered by Helen Warriner (60) in her chapter on interdisciplinary programs in Volume 3 of the *ACTFL Review of Foreign Language Education*. Consequently, this treatment will be limited primarily to developments in the growth of interdisciplinarity since 1970. The continuing semantic problem of terminology will require attention at the outset, along with some discussion of currently prevalent varying opinions. The central focus of this chapter is, however, on problems and solutions within the two broad areas of institutional structures and curricula. Subsumed under the heading of interdisciplinary curricula will be a brief analysis of innovations in teaching methods and teacher training.

Thomas E. Kelly

Purdue University

Scope of chapter

Terminology

The proliferation of prefixes added to the single word *discipline* makes any attempt at seeking sharp definition of the term *interdisciplinary* a singularly frustrating exercise. A survey of the literature related to

Thomas E. Kelly (Ph.D., University of California, Berkeley) is Associate Professor and Chairman for French in the Department of Modern Languages at Purdue University where he teaches courses in bibliography and literary criticism and medieval Arthurian literature. In 1954–55 he received a Fulbright Travel Grant and taught as an *assistant d'anglais* at the Lycée Malherbe in Caen, France. While teaching French at Dartmouth College (1962–67), he directed the Dartmouth Foreign Study Program in France at the Universities of Montpellier, Dijon, and Caen in 1963 and 1966. He has studied Romanesque art and architecture at the Université de Poitiers—Centre d'Etudes Supérieures de Civilisation Médiévale (1968) and is currently active in the interdisciplinary CARA (Centers and Regional Associations) Committee of the Medieval Academy of America. He has written articles on courtly love in French medieval literature and interdisciplinary approaches to teaching culture through literature and art for *Romanic Review* and *French Review*.

this topic finds the following terms used, with varying degrees of frequency: *multidisciplinary, polydisciplinary, cross-disciplinary, transdisciplinary, pandisciplinary, intradisciplinary, metadisciplinary,* and *unidisciplinary*. Secrest (53) suggested some time ago that "all of this play on words is artificial and smacks somewhat of rhetorical justification for our behavior as Parkinsonian bureaucrats" (p. 1). Nonetheless, he admits to sidestepping the semantic problem by emphasizing his own uncertainty as to what constitutes a basic discipline. He rejects the experimental scientist's approach of an operational definition that identifies disciplines with academic departments currently in vogue. The humanist's resistance to any attempt at fragmenting by definition the totality of man's knowledge is a stance equally unacceptable to Secrest. He ultimately falls back on a paraphrase of Alice's statement, saying that "the word discipline shall mean precisely what I want it to mean, no more and no less" (p. 1).

Proliferation of prefixes

Warriner's solution to the problem was to approach *discipline* as a term limited to curricular references. For the purposes of her study the word meant primarily "an area of study." Within such a broad and nonspecific definition, *interdisciplinary* activities in foreign language programs cannot be easily identified. As Warriner herself acknowledges, "the term *discipline* in its curricular frame of reference is not clearly definable simply because no clear lines separate one discipline from another" (60, p. 128).

Discipline as curricular reference

The basic problem, as Warriner and others have pointed out, is that foreign language teaching and learning are far from being "pure" disciplines. They represent areas of endeavor made up of components from a multiplicity of subjects in the curriculum.

Foreign languages as multicurricular subjects

Yet, obscured as it is in a constantly shifting semantic field, the term *interdisciplinary* continues to generate a considerable amount of intellectual enthusiasm and activity. Rather than trying to formulate *the* definition of the term, it would seem more helpful at this point to sample the variety of descriptions currently being given to it. For, if we accept Dwight Bolinger's (7, p. 218) view of man as a meaning maker, we have perhaps more to learn by juxtaposing subjective opinions than we do from consulting dictionaries.

Were we to plot a definitional graph of the most recent meanings given to the term *interdisciplinary* and *discipline,* the line would cover a wide range from the very loose to the very rigorous. On the lower end of the scale we have statements such as that of Rosenmeyer (49) who asserts that we "need not worry about the precise differences between *interdisciplinary, cross-disciplinary, multidisciplinary,* and the like.

Recent meanings of discipline *and* interdisciplinary

130

What we are interested in is doing things differently from the way they were done, say, ten, or twenty, or fifty years ago" (p. 19). Of more substance is the definition given by Halloran (27) for whom the term *interdisciplinary studies* means "cooperation in courses and programs of study among faculty members from the various disciplines that have become defined in our schools as departments" (p. 33). For language departments this means cooperation across linguistic and national boundaries. But any attempt to define courses and programs would be to imply limits where, in Halloran's view, none exist. The essential point Halloran makes about interdisciplinary programs is that "their worth and vitality depend upon the energy and quality of mind of those who conduct them" (p. 33). From this perspective, the only solid basis for interdisciplinary studies is energetic men and women with ideas, and the perseverance to see their ideas through in cooperation with colleagues and students from other fields as well as their own.

People with ideas

While Halloran stresses the role of the teacher, Nelson (40) focuses on the student, who must be *multi*disciplinary before he can hope to be *inter*disciplinary. It is the students who have to "put it all together" and become *inter*disciplinarians under the direction of *intra*disciplinarian teachers. The faculty member, Nelson suggests, "stays within his nest, but the student is expected to make a veritable bird house out of all the nests he is asked to enter in search of its particular golden egg of knowledge" (p. 211).

Student-based approach

Methodology and spirit are the key components in Brennan's (12) assessment of the interdisciplinary approach. We have created departments as convenient administrative units and have identified these units with segments of knowledge (called disciplines), and finding "that each such discipline has developed into its own methodology, we are now faced with the difficult problem of integrating diverse methodologies" (p. 6). Within this frame of reference, interdisciplinarity is seen as a renewal of the search for comprehensiveness of knowledge, which has been delayed by increasingly separatist methods both in teaching and in scholarly research. But renewal, says Brennan, "does not prescribe new methods so much as a new spirit" (p. 8). The spirit called for is one of seeking to overcome C. P. Snow's notion of the two cultures. We are in need of "one culture in which the humanities and the humanistically oriented social sciences define the context of science" (p. 7).

New spirit for separatist methodologies

Perhaps the most rigorous definitions of *discipline* and *interdisciplinary* in recent pronouncements specifically pertinent to foreign language teaching is that of Roger Shattuck. Speaking before the Association of

131

Departments of Foreign Languages Summer Seminar, Shattuck (54) compared the equally slippery words *discipline* and *culture*. Both terms originally were used in a highly active sense, but we have unfortunately compressed them into predominantly static molds. *Culture* at first meant tillage, the process of individual self-development, rather than a collection of society's observable characteristics. Similarly, *discipline* referred to the *process* of education, as distinct from doctrine. The predominant meaning of *discipline* today, however, has become that of a "branch of instruction." Consequently, when we talk about *interdisciplinary*, we are in fact suggesting two very different things. We mean the relations among separate curriculum subjects or among different areas of knowledge. But the term can refer equally to the relations among quite different processes, methods, or approaches to knowledge. We thus assume, albeit tacitly, that *discipline* in the first sense is congruent with *department* as a word describing where we are and what we teach within the universe of knowledge. *Discipline* in the second sense, is an active process connoting dedication or even punishment; "submission and final mastery, we leave for the most part in outer darkness, unexamined except in a few maverick instances like language teaching. And the emphasis falls entirely on the performance of the teacher, not on the self-discipline of the student" (p. 13).

Discipline and culture

Static and dynamic connotations of interdisciplinary

From all the foregoing definitions it appears that we can synthesize the central ingredients of the phenomenon of interdisciplinarity in its current stage of development. The diversity of the opinions expressed is more apparent than real, although great patience is required at times to overcome the annoyance at having to cut through a rhetorical jungle before reaching clear meanings. The current vogue of the term *interdisciplinary* stems in large measure from the recognition that we have probably gone too far in specialization. With increasing urgency, present cultural needs demand that separate disciplines integrate their concepts and methods as they apply to both teaching and research. The turn to "interdisciplinarity" also derives from the further discovery that solutions to the problems of our cities, environmental pollution, racism, and institutional reform cannot be found uniquely within the narrow frames of reference of traditional disciplines. There is, then, a growing consensus that while existing disciplines need not be abolished, they should be taught in the context of their dynamic interrelationships and societal problems.

Synthesis of opinions on terminology

For teachers and students alike, as well as policy-makers and administrators, the appeal is clearly for solidarity and a growth in conscious awareness of essential unity in the face of apparent institutional, conceptual, and methodological diversity. Interdisciplinarity is, in short, an adaptive response to a widespread malaise within the house of academe. The causes of dissatisfaction are complex, but the responsive forces at work combine to make us reach toward what seems to be a cure-all, or at least a hope for the future: interdisciplinary studies.

Interdisciplinary studies: a panacea?

Interdisciplinarity and institutional structures

A twofold process of change is gathering momentum on the academic scene. Mutations in our educational institutions and new developments in scientific knowledge are occuring with ever-increasing speed. Interdisciplinarity appears to lie at the meeting point of these two currents, and it comes as a direct consequence of them. To meddle with disciplines is to meddle with the social, economic, and power structures of educational institutions, for disciplines form the basis of such organizations and are at the very heart of any structure in which knowledge is discovered, processed, applied, or transmitted. Interdisciplinary studies thus emerge as one key factor in any solutions to the current problems faced by educational institutions at all levels. Significant interdisciplinary changes are taking place at all stages within the organizational patterns of higher, secondary, and elementary education. Since the greatest amount of such activity most immediately pertinent to the foreign language scene is occuring in higher education, it seems appropriate to examine this level first.

Interdisciplinarity as consequence of institutional reforms and knowledge explosion

Beginning with the top of the pyramid we find an important study of the impact of interdisciplinarity on the university in a 1972 report (30) prepared by the Organization for Economic Cooperation and Development in Paris. One major section (pp. 201–16) of this report studies problems and solutions related to institutional structures. The authors preface their analysis with the observation that universities of various ages (old, middle age, and new) are currently facing common challenges with varying degrees of success (p. 185). This categorical division of universities into three "ages" is particularly significant as it draws attention to a major obstacle to the creation of interdisciplinary strategies. However desirous traditional universities may be of changing their approaches in the light of new developments, they are inhibited from doing so by their rigid and frequently anachronistic forms of organization.

Impact in higher education

The fact that it is easier to create new structures than to change old ones is demonstrated in the Paris Report by reference to the University of Sussex (England) founded in 1961 on the principles of interdiscip-

Interdisciplinary university at Sussex

linarity. This new university is designed to operate with an innovative curriculum based on an original form of internal organization. The unit of development is not the single-subject Department but rather a multisubject school headed by a dean, with interdisciplinary courses in each division. The first three schools established were: English and American Studies, European Studies, and Social Sciences. Later additions, which have direct relevance to foreign languages, include: African and Asian Studies and Culture and Community Studies. One detail of particular interest for language teaching is the fact that the School of European Studies requires every student to spend the third year of a four-year degree course studying in Europe, but what is most unique in the Sussex model is not the particular organizational entities that have been created so much as the broad commitment to interdisciplinarity as the basic structuring principle. Although some bold new interdisciplinary departures have appeared on the American scene, few, if any, major structural innovations match this British example in scope.

Multisubject schools

In the most recent literature related to interdisciplinary developments in higher education, the organizational unit most discussed is, however, not the larger structure of the university, or even the collegiate division. The smaller organizational units within the university—departments, research or teaching centers, institutes, and curricular units—elicit the most critical comment as well as the most striking interdisciplinary innovations. To avoid losing track of reality as we survey the present state of such activity, we must examine the concrete situations of the subordinate institutional structures within the diversity of their problems and adaptive responses. Let us look first at the department, which surfaces as the organizational unit currently provoking the greatest dissatisfaction.

Criticism of departmental structures

One prominent cluster of criticism specifically pertinent to foreign languages centers on the apparent confusion of departmental aims and functions, as reflected in the multiplicity of organizational designations. According to the list published by Rütimann (50), who used figures for the year 1968, there were at that time 119 different designations covering 2,382 departments of foreign languages. On the basis of this same list, Brod (14) discusses the implications for the profession of the fact that combined (or multilingual) departments outnumber single-language departments by a considerable margin. The percentages are 62.1 percent for combined and 37.9 percent for monolingual designations. In this brief article Brod does little more than raise questions concerning the relative advantages of one kind of departmental organization over another. Of significance in the present context is the low number (14 percent) of interdisciplinary designations in which foreign languages are administered together with other areas such as Humanities, English, or "Studies" (e.g., Asian, European, Indian, Uralic). In a longer monograph Borenstein (9) reports the results of a separate study of single-language and combined departments at 22 liberal arts colleges. By comparing the relation between departmental structures and a number of objective and subjective criteria (such as interdepartmental or interdisciplinary involvement; enrollment; faculty size, rank, and status), Borenstein attempts to show that, at least in some institutions, divided (or single-language) departments appear to have a distinct advantage over combined deparments— specifically in matters such as total enrollment, budget, rank and tenure of faculty. He also sets forth a number of opinions, mostly negative, concerning the role of the department chairman in a combined unit as a powerful force often inhibiting the development of interdisciplinary projects. The conclusions reached in Borenstein's study tend to interpret the data as demonstrating the distinct advantages of a divided pattern of departmental structure. Paradoxical as it may appear, greater fragmentation is thus proposed as the route not only to increased power and prestige for language departments but more particularly as the best strategy for improving contacts and relations with other disciplines (p. 48).

Combined versus monolingual departments

Whatever the merits of the conclusions reached by Borenstein, his pilot study is significant for its drawing attention to the fact that problems of departmental structure, an area of vital importance to language teachers as they seek to interrelate with other disciplines, have until now been objectively studied by almost no one. Such considerations have been left to informal discussion within the profession, all too frequently in the context of faculty "gripe" sessions.

Departmental organization patterns

A partial exception to the dearth of studies of the basic suborganizational units in foreign languages is the renewal of attention to the concept of *Romania* in Romance Language structures and, in particular, as the topic relates to Spanish. It transcends the notion of national boundaries that compartmentalizes much of our thinking. One common theme in three recent articles is the lament that little conceptual substance exists in the criteria adopted for the academic groupings of languages. Bulatkin (15) finds "little rationale for the clusters beyond that of economic or organizational expedience" (p. 6). Since most groupings arise from convenience, expedience, and economy,

Fragmentation and aimlessness of purpose

Wardropper (59) can see few instances of departments having "an internal reason for being" (p. 10); and the same message is echoed by Murray (37), who explains the trend toward the formation of departments of individual languages in the 1950s and 1960s as happening "more for reasons of administrative ease than through the reasoned application of scholarly principles" (p. 414). Contrary to Borenstein's findings, the phenomenon of "segmentation" (15, p. 6) is blamed for exacerbating further the isolation from other disciplines, which has grown apace with the widespread opposition to language requirements.

This fragmented and aimless state of affairs prompts Rosemary Thomas (56) to call for a new "paneducational" orientation of goals and governance procedures in language departments. She criticizes departments for their attachment to vested interests and narrow loyalty to programs unrelated to larger institutional goals and societal needs. One of the principal causes of such a parochial situation is, according to Crawford (17), the fact that loyalties are engendered and priorities are developed within a budgetary unit: the department. Particularly in matters of support for programs that cross over departmental lines, "the operative adjective for the trouble source is not interdisciplinary (nor poly-, nor trans-, nor multidisciplinary) but rather interdepartmental" (p. 2). Benveniste (5) adds the further thought that single, fashionable pacesetters in academic departments often "tend to monopolize control on funds and have their own, or at most, the objectives of their departments and schools to advance" (p. 11). Departmental budgetary realities clearly pose formidable obstacles to the development of interdisciplinary studies. As Rosenmeyer (49) notes, departments are strong principally because they are already "on the books" (p. 21) and can thereby direct their full energy to teaching and research. Proponents of interdisciplinary programs, however, have to expend considerable time and effort acquiring an account number or the authorization to disburse funds. Getting "on the books" means "to get space, in an environment where space is available only if a rival gets eliminated or at least dislodged" (p. 21).

Narrow loyalties in budgetary environment

In addition to budgetary considerations, analysts of the departmental unit in its relation to interdisciplinarity give considerable attention to a cluster of realities that might best be categorized as "people" problems. The rubric is far from scientific and no statistics are forthcoming. While it is clear that we are dealing here with opinions based ultimately on local situations or personal experiences, it seems useful to examine a small sampling of the thorny issues raised. By so doing we can perhaps identify a few general patterns that have implications for interdisciplinary developments.

Even among established departments, some organizational reshuffling in the form of "splits" or mergers can undoubtedly be traced to conflicts of personality (Brod, 14, p. 37). Such conflicts in the average department of Romance Languages come about, according to Wardropper (59), because the organizational unit lacks both coherence and unity. In consequence, the staff members "feel insecure, aimless, demoralized, fractionalized, and factionized" (p. 10). Department meetings in such an environment furnish continually fresh grounds for animosity and even hostility among colleagues specialized in separate languages and competing with one another for staff and program funds. The temptation is indeed great to relax such tensions "by consigning competitors to the Sheol of a completely separate department" (p. 11). The implication for interdisciplinary organizational realignments seems clear. One must seriously examine the motives behind any structural mutation. Changes should be based on the relative advantages of an interdisciplinary unit within or across departments rather than on the questionable strategy of merely getting around or away from troublesome colleagues.

Departmental splitting caused by personality conflicts

A second set of "people" issues in foreign language units can be detected in an apparent tendency toward dualistic, at times almost Manichean, categorization when describing departmental patterns in terms of the constituent members. A distinct "us and them" semantic operative repeatedly polarizes teachers, researchers, and administrators according to the dominant thrusts of their activities. We have problems of "pure" and "applied" scholars (Crawford, 17, p. 2): the "culture-and-literature" group set up against the proponents of the "daily-life" approach to language curriculum (Borenstein, 9, p. 46), also known as the "Culture-versus-culture" debate (Nelson, 40); the "French" dominance of the "Spaniards" in Romance Language departments (Murray, 37, p. 418); and even the "stars" against the "stewards" (Thomas, 56, p. 40), usually referred to in more banal terms as "research scholars" and "department chairmen." Anyone with an interdisciplinary bent must, therefore, be keenly sensitive to potential opposition from disciplinary-minded colleagues! Also to be kept in mind is the sobering realization that it is far easier to create new structures than to change old ones, and it is even more difficult to reverse a thought process, which we might label "adversary-think," than to modify an organizational unit within an institution. If inter-

The "us and them" semantic

disciplinarity as a new direction needs anything, it certainly requires a departmental environment of cooperation and teamwork.

Faculty recruitment and the rewards system prevalent in the departmental unit form still another problem area with serious implications for the growth of interdisciplinary studies. Administratively speaking, departments frequently seem to encourage "an old boys' mentality in hiring and promoting" (Rosenmeyer, 49, p. 20). Since academic jobs exist in departments and rarely, if ever, in organizational units of interdisciplinary studies, any program that trains graduate students interdisciplinarily has the difficult task of preparing them to find positions within a "traditional" mold (Kuhn, 33, p. 8). The realities of academic "politics" dictate that graduate students trained in an interdisciplinary program are "badly handicapped when they need jobs in a tight market" (Leyerle and Ohlgren, 35, p. 9). For the moment it would thus appear that "straight" language and literature Ph.D.'s have the edge in finding jobs, since by hiring them "the department thinks it gets more for its money." Once in a department, junior faculty may soon acquire habits as fixed as those of their tenured peers and prefer not to risk their careers on what could be a mere adventure or passing fad (interdisciplinary studies), "thereby bolting down the system from one generation to the next" (30, p. 192). *Problem of staff recruitment and rewards system* *Realities of departmental politics*

When viewed only in a negative light, the present general situation of the department within the landscape of higher education appears decidedly bleak. Departments of foreign languages, in particular, reveal the continued existence of bitter ideological differences and internecine feuds, where one would hope to see professional cohesion and cooperation. The Paris Report on Interdisciplinarity sums up the current scene by describing the Department in universities today as having the combined characteristics of: (a) a confusion of aims and functions; (b) an anarchically complex and disorderly structure; along with (c) an anachronistic pattern of subdivision (p. 194). *Summary of current departmental scene: a negative picture*

As might be expected, however, all is not bleak. To counter the confusion and disorder in patterns of organization, a new burst of energy has been directed into structural innovations. Most of this activity falls explicitly under the umbrella term *interdisciplinary* or one of its cognates. A review of the literature on the subject reveals a considerable variety of strategies that are either being revitalized or tried for the first time, both within and across departmental or disciplinary lines. Some additional promising proposals remain for the moment in the theoretical stage. *Revitalization through innovative strategies*

Alpert (3) advises that if universities want to address themselves to today's issues, they must create interdisciplinary centers that are staffed and administered differently from the innumerable inter-departmental institutes and laboratories established on American campuses within the past 25 years. He differentiates three distinct structures: the cross-disciplinary center in which scholars with problems in one discipline seek new methodologies, problems, or solutions from another discipline; the multidisciplinary center wherein individual researchers from several disciplines share common facilities or a common research approach, but each works on problems posed by his own discipline; the interdisciplinary centers where the problem determines the selection of personnel involved in a given project. Most universities have established multidisciplinary centers that essentially serve the separate departments. But the complex problems of today require a much different organizational framework and can best be met, says Alpert, within the interdisciplinary unit. He outlines three critical conditions that must be met in such centers: an environment in which faculty and students may commit themselves to joint inter-disciplinary efforts without making any permanent organizational commitment; a university administrative structure in which the inter-disciplinary center and a group of departments may pursue very different objectives with interim joint appointments but without sub-ordinating one administrative structure to the other; the development of institutional mechanisms for selecting and rewarding a new breed of professional academic staff members, who are not only willing but competent to assume a leadership role for interdisciplinary programs. For the position of director of an interdisciplinary center, Alpert suggests the creation of a new type of position, the "all-university professor" without tenure (p. 8).

On a much less theoretical note, considerable success in meeting the critical conditions for interdisciplinary centers as outlined by Alpert has been accomplished in the field of medieval studies. The creation by the Medieval Academy of America in 1969 of a standing committee on Centers and Regional Associations (CARA) has provided a unique forum for project-oriented, rather than talk-oriented, programs that have direct relevance to the language teaching profession. This committee serves as a clearing-house for information concerning interdisciplinary medieval centers (or institutes) and their organizational and curricular innovations. Documents (e.g., 31, 34, 35) describing existing programs, practical advice for starting programs, and demonstrations of interdisciplinary methodologies and applications are available through the present Chairman of the Committee, Professor Stanley J.

Interdisciplinary centers

Categorization of types

Critical conditions for centers

A new creation: the "all university professor"

Medievalists' contributions to interdisciplinary studies

139

Kahrl at the Center for Medieval and Renaissance Studies of The Ohio State University.

Within the past five years, Brown University (Kuhn, 33) has effected several radical innovations that alter traditional departmental patterns. A first step was the development of the Human Studies Program that allows students to concentrate in areas that transcend the narrow limits of individual disciplines and departments. Since 1967 this program has grown until it now graduates more seniors than many of the formally organized departments. At the graduate level two recent changes have potentially far-reaching implications. The first is the adoption of a new Doctor of Arts degree much different from similar degrees considered or adopted elsewhere. The degree is not a "teaching degree" but rather a noncareer-oriented framework that permits each individual student and each separate department a maximum amount of liberty to devise a program specifically suitable to the student and to the department. A second, more revolutionary departure is the creation of a Special Graduate Studies Program. In this program graduate students enroll in the Graduate School rather than in specific departments, thus allowing them to formulate completely individualized transdepartmental programs of their own creation. The Department of French Studies at Brown was instrumental in the general university reforms, and some of the major transformations in this department preceded those on the university level (pp. 7–8).

Innovations at Brown University

New Doctor of Arts Degree

Special Graduate Studies Program

The move to studies designations is a growing trend in departmental structure. Nelson (38) is one of the principal proponents of a comprehensive Department of French Studies. Acting on his proposal, the French Department at the University of Illinois has recently added majors in "French and History" and "French and Fine Arts" to its two traditional majors: "French and Literature" and "French and Linguistics" (Nelson, 39, p. 31). The movement to a studies structure, at least in French, has grown to the point that at its first international meeting the Association des Universités Partiellement ou Entièrement de Langue Française (4) recommended to the representatives of some 200 university departments and centers from 61 countries the establishment of an international federation of departments and centers of French Studies. A second recommendation called for the creation of separate national information centers (p. 7) on an interuniversity model. In Spanish there seems to be a double movement, either toward the creation of departments of Hispanic studies (Murray, 37) or toward a resurgence of the "ideal" department of Romance Languages (Bulatkin, 15; Wardropper, 59).

Trend toward studies concept

French studies at the University of Illinois

Hispanic studies

A number of other organizational innovations less comprehensive in scope than the various studies structures have also been tried or proposed. Benveniste (5) describes the structural advantages of a metadisciplinary committee unit as developed at the University of California, Berkeley. The meta coalition, which serves as a communication linkage in the overly compartmentalized structure of the university, is intended as a less permanent organizational entity than the department or the specialized research institute. The meta committee has the dual characteristics of "rotation" and "commitment" that counteract many of the human and bureaucratic evils inherent in formal institutional units. An attempt to apply a "resource" philosophy to foreign language department planning is in the initial stage of implementation at Forest Park Community College in Saint Louis. Thomas (56) describes this experimentation in allocating departmental resources to conform to the current priorities of the college and to societal needs. The most extensive of the new projects involved in this approach is a program called "Insights into Language" which seeks to find more effective use of resources available in the departments of foreign languages, English, speech, and reading. The means to this end is a series of language "packages" focusing on specific objectives. One specific example among other "packages" involves cooperation of the library with the departments of history, foreign languages, and industrial engineering to make use of a recently acquired set of plates from the French Encyclopedia. This cooperative venture will produce a historical unit on some aspects of industrial development.

The metadisciplinary *strategy*

A resource approach: Forest Park Community College

"Insights into Language" packages

A much more theoretical minor strategy is that of a "transdepartmental referee" as proposed by Crawford (17) at the University of Minnesota. The role of this new type of administrator would be to control budgetary and position allotments and to iron out disagreements betwen departments and interdepartmental programs. The experience of three German universities (Boning and Rolloffs, 8) in resolving problems involving the obligation or possibility of teachers belonging to two or more constituent units of the university leads to the conclusion that interdisciplinary innovations can be introduced more quickly in the domain of teaching and research. Here they do not affect the distribution of authority within the university. New forms of coordination and cooperation are being proposed in the three universities (p. 167); however, the process is much slower at the organizational level than at the curricular level.

Transdepartmental referee

Innovations in three German Universities

Another professional resource—department chairmen—has through the creation of the Association of Departments of Foreign Languages

(ADFL) also begun to assert its unique leadership opportunities for institutional reform. Through the forum provided in the ADFL *Bulletin,* as well as in the Association's annual summer seminars, chairmen have started to exchange ideas more directly and to share with each other the fruits of their local institutional innovations. The importance of this new flow of ideas for interdisciplinary studies was highlighted in the most recent annual Report of the Executive Secretary of the Modern Language Association (Schaefer, 51, p. 138). There is a growing realization that of all the interdisciplinary strategies that have been tried or proposed in higher education, the agent holding perhaps the greatest potential for change is the department chairman. In his key position as mediator between his department and the institution that supports it, the chairman has the opportunity both to explore and to exploit interdisciplinarity for the common good.

Growth of ADFL

Department chairmen as key institutional mediators

In organizational and institutional developments at secondary and elementary levels, we find that a basic problem to which interdisciplinarity addresses itself appears to be the same in many countries, namely the sharp break between the realities of "school" and "university" (30). A corollary of this problem is the growth of a more generalized trend toward the desirability of "continuing education" (pp. 227–36). This does not mean adult education in the sense of remedial schooling or "catch-up" training. What is meant by *continuing education* is the notion that a person's life is not be be broken into stages —one in which he learns and a second in which he "lives off" acquired knowledge. The process of education continues throughout life. The pattern of spending long periods of time assimilating basic (elementary and secondary) education followed by a shorter but still cloistered life period acquiring more specialized knowledge (university) must give way to a form of activity wide open to the outside or "real" world.

Problem of school and university "break"

New dimension of continuing education

Within the limits of the present chapter, it would be far too ambitious to try to do more than draw attention to a few representative examples of interdisciplinary activity that have come in response to the development of continuing education.

The growth of community or junior colleges in America must be understood, at least in part, as a movement to establish a sense of continuity that might overcome the "break" between school and university described above. Developments in pre-university colleges in a number of countries appear to be prompted by the same problem. In Britain there are the Polytechnics and in Yugoslavia the Visa Skola— two-year post-secondary schools that offer terminal and transfer courses. In Quebec the Collèges d'Enseignement Général et Profes-

Pre-university colleges in other countries

sionnel have direct relationships with universities and provide the first cycle of university studies along with terminal and vocational training. Experiments with interdisciplinary strategies in these foreign systems (30, pp. 201–16), as well as in the United States represent a major direction of organizational change. A national survey of American community college presidents (Tillery, 57) indicates a widespread receptivity to interdisciplinarity as a basic pattern for future growth. Nearly 40 of the presidents in the survey plan to change organizational structures by 1975. These administrative leaders consider interdisciplinary studies an attractive option within a division, a framework which they prefer to departmental organization.

Survey of American community colleges

A preferred organizational unit: the division

An interesting interdisciplinary approach to bridging the school and university "break" is the Twelfth Street School Project reported by Bosco and Robin (10). The project illustrates how the development of a new structure, a Center for Innovations and Research, can bring together university faculty and school system personnel to work jointly and cooperatively. The structural entity created represents the embodiment of several premises: (a) the collaboration of educators and researchers can best occur on the neutral ground of a center; (b) a close relationship between university researchers and school practitioners is necessary; (c) research contacts should be sustained and cohesive; (d) the research findings can contribute to a disciplinary body of knowledge and the solution of real problems of teachers and administrators. Although this project involves only the relation of social scientists and educators (not in foreign language education), it offers an excellent model that might profitably be exploited by interdisciplinary efforts in the humanistic disciplines, where foreign languages ought to play a key role.

Center for Innovation and Research

Current practices and problems of interdisciplinary Arts and Humanities programs in the elementary schools are analyzed in a major study by Purcell (46). The role that higher education plays in innovative interdisciplinary programs is particularly noted in this report. The evidence presented seems to indicate that public school programs frequently take their cues from traditional humanities offerings that sift down from the college level. One particularly useful bit of information contained in this study is a description of the Humanities Center at Baldwin-Wallace College, which functions as a clearinghouse and seems to be one of the most complete sources of up-to-date information regarding interdisciplinary activity at the elementary school level. Purcell includes an extensive bibliography, along with appendixes that analyze more than 140 interdisciplinary programs in elementary

Arts and Humanities programs in elementary schools

Humanities Center: Baldwin-Wallace College

schools across the country. Few of the programs described reflect the input from foreign languages that one might hope to find incorporated into such projects. For administrators and teachers interested in applying the interdisciplinary approach to the organizational planning of middle schools, a recent book by Pumerantz and Galano (45) is an important guide. Structuring and scheduling interdisciplinary programs for grades 6, 7, and 8; teaching strategies; and the design of a new plant or redesign of an old one are all covered by the authors. Useful appendixes including lesson plans, proposals, and source lists conclude the book.

Establishing interdisciplinary programs in the middle school

As we sum up the foregoing institutional applications of a broad variety of interdisciplinary strategies at the different levels of education, it is still much too early to tell just which innovations represent major transplants of suborganizational life. Only time will allow us to sort out the vital grafts from the more ephemeral experiments, or what might be thought of merely as "cosmetic" surgery. While foreign language units have effected increasingly substantial structural changes, the conservation of traditional structures remains the rule and not the exception. The adoption of interdisciplinarity as a primary motivating principle of organizational reform is far more modest in foreign languages than in other disciplines, especially the natural and social sciences. Whatever active role foreign languages play in modifying institutional structures is also more evident at the level of higher education than elsewhere. This is not to say that foreign language units are not involved in considerable interdisciplinary activity at all levels, but such activity seems to be channeled more readily into changing curricular patterns rather than institutional or structural patterns. It is, therefore, to the curricular dimension of interdisciplinary studies that we must now turn our attention.

Summary of structural and organizational innovations

Interdisciplinary studies: programs, courses, and methods

Interdisciplinary courses by their very nature most frequently develop as spontaneous, local experiments. This fact, more than any other, explains why the conclusion reached by Warriner (60) is unfortunately still valid: "More is appearing in the literature to advocate interdisciplinary activities than is available to describe programs that are already functioning" (p. 157). The backlog of material awaiting publication in professional journals with the resultant time lag in sharing results of curricular innovations with colleagues also accounts for the difficulty in obtaining details on specific interdisciplinary develop-

144

ments. There is, moreover, a paucity of evaluative studies on the effectiveness of the interdisciplinary approach, explained in most instances by the trial-and-error newness of methods and materials. On the basis of such incomplete data, what follows is at best only an approximate view of interdisciplinary studies in their curricular context.

Few evaluative studies of interdisciplinary programs

In the absence of any thorough national survey of trends in interdisciplinary experimentation within foreign language units at all levels of education, it is especially hard to situate available information into clear patterns. The most complete nationwide survey is Warriner's (60), but the results of her questionnaire are, for the most part, limited to activity at the secondary level. Given the thoroughness of Warriner's survey of high school programs, this chapter includes a proportionately heavier representation of college and university innovations. Where information permits, some attempt is made to provide brief follow-up commentary on several programs described earlier by Warriner. The primary criterion determining the selection of items for inclusion, however, is the representativeness of a course or program in reflecting as wide a range as possible of individual problems and solutions. But with the diversity of American universities, colleges, and schools of all types in which foreign languages are taught, it is at best doubtful that the interdisciplinary experiences gained in one curricular context can ever be transferred directly to others. With this thought in mind, it is perhaps most useful for us to begin with a sampling of the "do's" and "don'ts" involved in the interdisciplinary approach, as expressed by those who have described the successes and pitfalls of their own experiments.

Warriner's questionnaire

Some "do's" and "don'ts"

A common theme running through a number of reports on interdisciplinary activity is the cautionary note to avoid the mere "flashiness" of interdisciplinary labels that lack substantive content. Shattuck (54) suggests that the flight to interdisciplinary teaching can signify "weakness as much as it does any creative seething of ideas" (p. 16). Rosenmeyer (49) puts one whole category of hybrid or narrow ad hoc constructions, "mix-teach courses" as he disparagingly calls them, "on the lunatic fringe" (p. 24). One example he cites is a course on Thucydides and South East Asia taught by a colleague during the Cambodia crisis several years back. An excellent statement of the obstacles facing any departure into interdisciplinary work is provided by Milburn (36). He advises teachers motivated toward integrating academic disciplines not to be discouraged by (a) the anxiety-provoking nature of this area of endeavor, which causes most people to withdraw to the "safe" problems in their own disciplines; (b) the tendency to regard only

Flashy labels

Lunatic fringe

Obstacles to interdisciplinary work

145

topics in one's own discipline as problematic and outside topics as givens; and (c) the defensiveness and jealousy that can and do exist between disciplines. While it is not obvious how interdisciplinary projects should be organized, one way to overcome the obstacles involved is to benefit from others' mistakes as well as from successful attempts at cooperation between disciplines. Ready access to concrete and descriptive details of such efforts is, therefore, a critical need.

To fill this need for interdisciplinary information, a number of projects are currently under way. Chapman and Kellander (16) have recently published the results of a nationwide survey of educational trends in Romance Language departments. They report that area studies, in particular Latin American studies, are flourishing, and other interdisciplinary programs (comparative literature, medieval studies, French-speaking area studies, and Western European studies) are also receiving increased emphasis (p. 27). References to descriptive details of these programs are, however, not included in the survey. The *Bulletin* of the Association of Departments of Foreign Languages, starting with the May 1973 issue, has begun to include a selection of interdisciplinary course descriptions as a regular feature. This same journal has announced (vol. 4, iii, p. 2) plans to publish the results of a national survey of interdepartmental and interdisciplinary courses and programs involving language faculty. There also appears to be a growing trend among teachers to respond to current needs by undertaking ad hoc independent news gathering projects for more specialized audiences. Giese (24) provides a useful outline of suggested interdisciplinary courses intended to promote greater educational relevance in French studies, and he announces a proposal for a News Sheet on the same topic. In the field of medieval studies, a group of young medievalists has announced a forthcoming *Newspaper of Medieval and Renaissance Studies* (41). The purpose of the newspaper will be primarily to meet the practical needs of teachers of undergraduate courses in medieval and renaissance art, architecture, history, literature, music, and philosophy. It will incorporate the following regular features: course syllabi; available resources (media materials, films, recordings); bibliographies of readily available materials; different ways of teaching a given text; suggestions for relating medieval and renaissance matters to contemporary ones. Such a publication, which fills a need not currently met by any traditional scholarly or professional journals, appears to be a model that might profitably be adapted to a variety of specific solutions involving language teachers.

Filling the need for practical information

Course descriptions in ADFL Bulletin

Ad hoc news gathering trend

Newspaper for medievalists

146

Among specific interdisciplinary projects, Shattuck (54) outlines a useful taxonomy of courses. He distinguishes four types of courses.

Interdisciplinary courses: a taxonomy

University courses. Independently designed outside traditional departmental programs and subjects, generally taught by a distinguished professor with a streak of unorthodoxy. The ratifying authority for such courses is usually a "rubber-stamp" faculty committee.

Extramural courses. Normally part of a loosely defined program of interrelated disciplines (e.g., American Studies, Comparative Literature, Medieval Studies). This category has developed to substantial proportions in many institutions and leads to popular majors, interdepartmental committees, and team teaching.

Intramural courses. Traditional courses within regular departmental programs but given interdisciplinary scope by individual professors. The importance of this type of interdisciplinary study is hard to measure and is apparently widespread but uneven.

Independent study. Usually tutorial courses that carry students across fields of knowledge where the professor may not necessarily have personal expertise (p. 15).

A survey of variations within and among these four categories presents a wide diversity of course and program offerings involving language faculty.

Content Courses—American University. Content courses called "topics" and "colloquia" are taught by qualified members of the Department of Language and Foreign Study, members of other departments, visiting scholars, and experts in the Washington, D.C. area who work for governmental agencies or international organizations. The topics are undergraduate lecture courses with a language prerequisite of two college years or four high school years. Examples of topics from a current course list include: French (Survey of Arts, The Woman); German *Examples of topics* (Customs and Manners, East and West); Hebrew (Israel Today, Life in Kibbutz); Russian (Political System, The Press); Spanish (Regions of Spain, Social Scene in Latin America). The term *colloquia* denotes more demanding courses, open to graduate students and advanced undergraduates, combining lectures and discussions. The language prerequisite is three college years or its equivalent. A sample of colloquia presently offered on countries or regions includes: Germany *Samples of colloquia* (The Nazi Era, Intellectual Life); France (The Common Market, Overseas Commitments); Latin America (Urban Problems, Population Explosion); Soviet Union (Semantics of Communism, Soviet Marxism) (Huberman and Medish, 29).

Modular Interdisciplinary Courses—Colorado College. In the Colorado College Plan begun in 1970, courses are designed in flexible modules labeled "blocks" and offered in units of time ranging from three to ten weeks. Interdisciplinary courses form one of several varieties of sequential courses and involve more than one professor and larger groups of students than other courses. Under this format two or three faculty members from different departments team teach within the available time unit of one or two blocks. One such course is a two-block unit on Greek Philosophy and Literature jointly taught by the Departments of Philosophy and Classics (Wishard, 61).

Interdisciplinary block course

Theme Seminars—Center for Arts and Literature, Prescott College. Course structure in the Center is on two levels. Level I comprises basic courses ("Perspectives"), while Level II stresses theme seminars wherein certain ideas and essences of human existence are explored in depth. "Literature" is defined as encompassing the religious, philosophical, and esthetic expressions of man and includes not only poetry, drama, and fiction but also writing from other fields of human activity. One quarter of all the courses in the program are conceived as seminars or "encounters" (e.g., The Literary Experience, Interlacing Experiences). One half of the entire academic experience is set aside for Directed Studies and Independent Studies (Horwath, 28).

Encounter seminars

Tutorials and General Literary Studies for Spanish—Grinnell College. Recent innovations in the area of literary and interdisciplinary study, involving courses in English and open to all students include: a freshman tutorial, Revolution and Counter-Revolution in Latin America; an interdisciplinary course, The Latin American Mind and Society, which examines the multiple facets of twentieth-century society against the background of historical, political, and social developments in Latin America; a course on the works of several prominent Latin American writers today, offered by a member of the Spanish Department under the General Literary Studies Program, an interdepartmental program of the Humanities Division (Nobel, 42).

Courses in English at Grinnell College

Research Seminar on the Science of Literature—Paris X, Nanterre. This seminar groups approximately 20 senior professors, lecturers, assistants, and advance research workers in several disciplines: French literature, comparative literature, linguistics, psychoanalysis, semiology, and characterology. A first stage in this project, which has been going on for more than six years, was "linear" interdisciplinarity: The sciences of sociology, psychology, esthetics, and structural linguistics were regarded as ancillary to the study of literary texts. In the second stage, the attempt has been made to effect a convergence, in the context of

Linear interdisciplinarity

"structural" interdisciplinarity, of a linguistic and literary approach. *Structural interdisciplinarity*
A primary result of this stage was the definition of a common termin-
ology. The outcome of this experiment is significant for several reasons: *Success of Paris experiment*
Because of its continuity over a period of years, it demonstrates that the
participants reap benefits from it; because of its fruitfulness, interdisciplinary teamwork has proved profitable for current individual
research projects; and because of its effectiveness for teaching itself,
the teacher participants have benefited and have introduced into
their own courses the interdisciplinary spirit and methods worked out
in common (30, p. 233).

*Introductory Courses for Medieval and Renaissance Studies—The Ohio
State University.* The Center for Medieval and Renaissance Studies has
developed a series of five undergraduate interdisciplinary courses in
which faculty from different disciplines participate on an overload
basis. These courses focus on specific topics rather than attempting to *Courses in early European
culture*
survey a broad area. Titles of the courses are: The Court of Charle-
magne, Idealism and Scepticism from the Twelfth to the Fourteenth
Centuries, The City of Florence from 1200–1500, The Impact of
Christianity on Medieval Slavic Civilization, and The Golden Age of
Islamic Civilization: Hârûn Al-Rashîd and His Sons. In each case a
single professor on a "regular" assignment is the course coordinator,
with others participating as guest lecturers. The courses are intended to
introduce beginning students to early European culture while stimulating further interest in the subject studied. They are conceived as
components of a liberal education rather than as requirements in a
program of specialization and have attracted several hundred students
each year (Kahrl, 32).

Seminar on Modern Woman—University of Minnesota at Morris. A research
specialist on the role of women in modern Spanish drama describes a
test-case interdisciplinary seminar, Modern Woman: A Cross-Cultural
View, and offers ten specific recommendations based on the results
of his experience. These suggestions apply to a type of interdisciplinary
course in which experts present the tools and data of their own fields in *Interdisciplinarity applied to
themes*
application to a theme or problem, in this case the role of women in
differing cultures—Spain and the United States. The careful analysis
of student reactions provides excellent hints and helps for others (Turner
58).

*School of Literature—University of Warwick, England; and Center for
Modern Literature—Case Western Reserve University.* The new University
of Warwick has undertaken a boldly innovative course of study, called
a School of Literature, with various "major" tracks following common *The Warwick model*

149

courses for all students. The tracks are broadly conceived in several fields, each with ramifications in a number of other departments. Crocker (18, p. 13) draws attention to this British program while comparing it to innovations at Case Western Reserve University where a new Center for Modern Literature will bring together English, Romance Languages, German, Slavic, and comparative literature departments. An executive committee will design interdepartmental majors (in a subject, genre, or period) and will counsel students wishing to develop an independent major. This committee will also serve to promote interdepartmental cooperation.

Fusion of disciplines through executive committee structure

Two articles less descriptive in nature are worth citing in connection with the foregoing courses and programs. Rose (48) advocates a more general adoption of interdisciplinary studies programs for small liberal arts colleges, and he recommends a redefining of the whole concept of departments and divisions in response to political and ideological exigencies. He cites the example of Alma College in Michigan where restructuring has resulted in six divisions, with individual faculty members being encouraged to associate themselves with as many of these as may meet their particular needs (p. 24). Halloran (27) advances a firm opinion that there cannot be widespread movement toward interdisciplinary studies in foreign language units, especially for undergraduate students, until there is a broader acceptance of the validity of teaching literature in translation. In most of the nation's colleges there are not sufficient numbers of undergraduates "who are competent enough in two languages—even if one is English— to justify the development of multilingual interdisciplinary courses" (p. 33). The experience of comparative literature departments is cited as proof of this contention. Halloran dismisses comparative literature as the appropriate vehicle for interdisciplinary programs both at the graduate and undergraduate levels, since "political forces within the university," primarily the reluctance of foreign language departments to see their enrollments moving over to a "rival" department, tend to work against this solution. One final recommendation is that interdisciplinary programs should all have a "self-destruct component" so that they may be easily phased out when they have lost their viability and attractiveness (p. 34).

New Divisions at Alma College

Literature in translation

Comparative literature and interdisciplinary programs

Need for "self-destruct component"

By way of follow-up on interdisciplinary programs at the high school level reported by Warriner (60), two examples serve to indicate that such endeavors are apparently committed to one of two possible fates: quick demise after initial short-term success or continued prosperity and growth. In the Spring 1973 semester, I had a student participant

Follow-up on earlier reports

from the Gary, Indiana interdisciplinary magnet school program in a French course at Purdue University. The student wrote a term paper about her experience in the Gary program, describing it as one of the most formative experiences in her education; but she also reported that the project was discontinued after only two years, due to the exhaustion of grant funds and lack of support by the school administration. The Foreign Language Innovative Curricular Studies Project (FLICS) developed in Michigan, however, continues to have a significant impact on a national scale (23). Drawing on his experience gained as Director of the Humanities-in-French Program of the FLICS project, Eddington (21) has formulated an extremely practical set of suggestions for those planning to undertake curricular changes involving interdisciplinary instruction, especially at the 11th to 12th grade high school level. The *Teacher's Manual* prepared for the Humanities-in-French Program is a gold mine of practical information on materials, teaching strategies, and course planning.

Short-term duration of Gary magnet program

Continued success of Michigan FLICS project

Along with proportionately more abundant references to interdisciplinary courses and programs, a slow trickle of information specifically related to suitable methods and materials has begun to appear in professional literature. Duffy (20) analyzes some of the findings of linguistics, sociology, and psychology and how they might be integrated into a new foreign language teaching methodology and consequent classroom procedures. She raises the basic problem of transferring theoretical knowledge into practice, but she offers no concrete suggestions or solutions. Of more substance is a series of four papers on interdisciplinary approaches to language, wherein sociolinguists and psycholinguists address themselves to problems of interest to foreign language teaching (Perren, 43). The last paper "Describing the Language Learner's Language" by Corder, for example, defines what constitutes "error" in a learner's use of a second language (pp. 57–64). In an article on measuring proficiency Brière (13) concludes that any real break-through in testing techniques must come from an interdisciplinary team of teachers, testers, psychologists, sociologists, linguists, and others. The sociolinguistic work of Cooper and Fishman at Yeshiva University, along with that of Ferguson at Stanford and Labov at Columbia are, according to Brière, providing data that could lead to such a breakthrough in testing (p. 391).

Interdisciplinary methods and materials

Problem of transferring theory to practice

Interdisciplinary approach needed in testing

Practical advice to writers of textbook dialogues is given in a "how to" report by Stevick (55). Although the techniques of ethnography described here are directly applicable to African languages, they may profitably be consulted by language textbook authors in any spoken

Helps for authors of textbook dialogues

151

language. There are for the moment, however, very few truly interdisciplinary textbooks on the foreign language market. This is not to say that useful materials for teachers with an interdisciplinary bent are not forthcoming. Among others, two recent textbooks by Allen and Valette (2) and Biggs, Chicken, and Leeson (6) are excellent cases in point. Nonetheless, publishing house advertisements and bookjacket blurbs notwithstanding, the mere inclusion in foreign language texts of readings and materials from other disciplines (especially sociology, anthropology, economics, and political science) does not in itself qualify them as "interdisciplinary" constructs.

New textbooks

In the area of teacher training, as in the case of materials development, systematic interdisciplinarity appears to be still at an early stage of evolution. At least in foreign language education, there is little evidence in the professional literature to signal any widespread shift to adopting interdisciplinary training patterns. One notable exception is the Doctor of Arts Program in Modern European Languages at the Claremont Graduate School (19). This program of training, which became operative for French in 1971 and for German and Spanish in 1972, leads to a teaching degree designed to be completed in three years. A year abroad and a full year teaching internship are basic components in an interdisciplinary approach to a broad study of the major language(s). This study takes place in the context of a given cultural-geographic area and one of five related academic fields: Humanities (including history, philosophy, religion, and political science); Creative Arts (art, music, theater); Social Sciences (sociology, psychology, government, history, and economics); Linguistics (theoretical, socio- and psycholinguistics, and philosophy of language); another Modern Language (not necessarily European).

Developments in teacher training

Claremont Graduate School— Doctor of Arts Program

A more modest proposal for adapting the interdisciplinary approach to the training process is that of Akenson (1). He suggests a means of incorporating environmental education in the classroom through the preparation of teachers. The method proposed is one of training teachers to use literature in the humanities as focal points around which environmental issues can be analyzed and discussed by students, but by far the most common pattern of adjusting to the new interdisciplinary dimension in training foreign language teachers appears to be less than programmatic in scope. Concomitantly with the growth of the twin phenomena of "Culture-culture" and "individualized instruction" teacher candidates in recent years have been directed by their mentors, attracted by their own interests, or prodded by societal demands to cross over disciplinary barriers into a wide variety of studies that lend

Teaching ecology through literature in humanities

Most common pattern of interdisciplinary training

152

themselves to exploitation in the language classroom. Subjects such as anthropology, and especially its newer subfields such as "proxemics" developed by Hall (25, 26), have had a major impact in breaking the narrow training molds of language and literature cum "methods" courses. The results of this trend are abundantly manifest in other chapters of this and earlier volumes of the ACTFL *Review*, and they need not be repeated here.

"Proxemics"

One final point in connection with interdisciplinary studies and teacher training which does need to be stressed, however, is a disturbing question raised by an increasing number of critics. The doubt has been expressed that teachers trained in foreign languages and literature are really not competent to teach such things as foreign civilization or interdisciplinary courses—either in the foreign language or in English. Edgerton (22), for example, thinks that "the vast majority of people now teaching foreign languages in this country have no sound linguistic knowledge of the *English* language and at best only a superficial knowledge of the language they teach" (p. 10). Preparation for a teaching career, says Edgerton, should involve course work in basic linguistics, cultural anthropology, and aspects of philosophy, especially epistemology, that are relevant to the needs of language teachers (p. 9).

Disturbing question of amateurism

Foreign language teachers and English

In a similar vein, Remak (47) submits that we are presently "engulfed by a wave of amateurism" in the United States, as evidenced primarily in the teaching of courses and seminars by staff not fully qualified to treat the material under study (p. 21). The plea for a reduction in the amateurishness pervading interdisciplinary effort is very analogous to the negative criticism that more theoretical researchers leveled in the recent past at efforts in "applied" linguistics (e.g., Sebeok, 52, p. 5). In both areas, interdisciplinary studies and applied linguistics, people on the "firing line" of practical endeavors must not forget that their success will depend on the degree to which they gain respectability in the eyes of theory-minded colleagues and the general public. Superficial or indiscriminate application of the term *interdisciplinary* does little to increase respectability. Yet public pronouncements that apply the interdisciplinary label very loosely are continually made by modern language educators. One recent example implies that the study of literature in graduate school prepares a teacher, apparently automatically, as an expert on linguistics, as a connoisseur of the arts, and even as a social scientist: "When we study Molière's problems with the censors, isn't this but one aspect of political science? Castiglione and Machiavelli are clearly political" (Pincus, 44, p. 22)!

Plea for reduction of superficiality

Competence and respectability

Literature teachers as amateur social scientists

From the moment that interdisciplinary courses become too amateur-ish, or, "at their worst, too propagandistic, they threaten our very *raison d'etre* as part of the intellectual enterprise" (Remak, 47, p. 22). If, however, these courses are clearly offered as experiments by one or several teachers, they can be very successful—but only on the double condition that they be presented with proper modesty on the part of the teachers and in a true spirit of learning.

Need for avoiding pretentiousness

Conclusions

1 An initial consideration in drawing conclusions about the current state of interdisciplinary studies is to review the 15 conclusions and implications of Warriner's earlier study (60, pp. 157–159) in the light of new developments and increased interdisciplinary activity since 1970. Two thirds of her conclusions remain completely valid today. For the remaining third, two points call for slight modification, while three others are open to major qualification.

2 With the rapid spread of interdisciplinary experimentation, efforts to integrate the disciplines are no longer at an "embryonic" stage (cf. Warriner, 60, p. 157, no. 5). Dominant patterns still cannot be clearly discerned, but there is at least some evidence of disciplines successfully attaining a stage of "structural" inter-disciplinarity, for example, the convergence of linguistics and literary criticism at the Nanterre seminar on the science of literature (30, p. 233).

3 It cannot now be accurately stated that too few foreign language teachers are engaged in interdisciplinary programs (cf. Warriner, 60, p. 158, no. 11). There are no hard statistics, but the number and variety of course descriptions appearing in professional literature appears to indicate a much higher incidence of inter-disciplinary activity in language units at almost all levels. The one notable exception remains the elementary school language programs.

4 The exponential growth of new courses and programs bearing the label "interdisciplinary" would appear to argue that "content" has at last become a central preoccupation of language teachers, with concern for "methods" fading somewhat into the background (cf. Warriner, 60, p. 158, no. 7).

5 The lack of appropriate instructional materials can no longer be viewed as a temporary but regrettable situation blocking the

154

development of interdisciplinary curricula (cf. Warriner, 60, p. 158, no. 9). In an age of ever-constricting budgets one cannot expect vast sums to be spent on bringing materials together, especially when the "half-life" of a given interdisciplinary course is frequently one semester or less! By the very nature of interdisciplinary endeavor, a given program presents complex variables that require developing materials to fit specific objectives and conditions. Waiting for the ideal materials "package" or "module" to plug into local programs is unrealistic. Time, effort, and resourcefulness are more productive than multimedia spectaculars; and talented, knowledgeable teachers are ultimately more necessary than materials, no matter how excellent they might be.

6 The hope that the interdisciplinary movement will hasten the day of bilingualism needs now to be tempered with the cold fact that, at least on the American scene, the vehicular language of interdisciplinary courses is becoming predominantly English (cf. Warriner, 60, p. 158, no. 13). The rush to "content" courses and literature-in-translation often masks or avoids the difficult problems involved in adapting to new realities without giving up a *raison d'être* of foreign language teachers: proficiency in at least one language other than one's own.

7 While great pains have been taken administratively and curricularly to integrate the disciplines and foster their interrelationships, one very essential factor has been almost totally ignored. The simple realities of architecture—buildings, rooms, and walls —work to maintain a system of discrete isolation for each discipline, and most frequently for subclassifications within fields as well. A French teacher might as profitably benefit from contact with a German teacher as from interdisciplinary interaction with an anthropologist. Yet the patterning of offices and classrooms often makes the first relationship just as difficult to establish as the second.

8 Probably the most serious threat to continued growth of interdisciplinary studies is the mounting cry of amateurism being directed, quite justifiably in some instances, at curricular innovations employing interdisciplinary titles in one form or another. True interdisciplinarity is motivated by curiosity and the desire to explore new questions rather than trying to answer old ones. The exploration must proceed, however, from a base of competence informed by hard knowledge. Students still feel more

155

secure working with interdisciplinary teachers who have had *formal* training in the fields under study in a given course.

9 Of lesser magnitude than the problem of competence, but still a serious question, is that of "what to do next" raised at the termination of an exciting course taught by an enthusiastic interdisciplinary teacher or team of instructors. Another dimension of this problem is the difficulty encountered by interdisciplinarily trained graduate students when they seek positions in traditional language departments. The time has come to give increased attention to the administrative, organizational, and programmatic implications of interdisciplinary activity. Longer range adaptive strategies need to be set up, where basic institutional reform is not feasible, especially in the suborganizational entities of foreign language units. But the lessons already learned by those who have successfully instituted cross-disciplinary structures must not be forgotten. Although it takes some doing, it is still far easier to change an organizational structure than a way of thinking; and a good new idea that does not engender cooperation can sometimes do more harm than an outmoded technique or approach.

10 The time may not be quite ripe for trying to formulate any higher synthesis of interdisciplinary studies with the parallel trends toward Culture-culture and individualized instruction. Still, all three phenomena appear to be the brightest facets sparkling on a single diamond of contemporary reality: the field of foreign language learning and teaching. One might at least reflect on the tentative hypothesis that individualization may be the *rationale*, culture the *content*, and interdisciplinarity the *process* behind a common thrust of activity that at present appears terribly fragmented and uncoordinated. It is indeed possible that a unity of purpose is beginning to coalesce in an age marked by incredible diversity and lack of uniformity.

11 Interdisciplinary studies seem, therefore, to be caught for the moment at the junction of two strong counter currents. Widespread interdisciplinary experimentation in curricula, methodology, and teacher training encounters the powerful forces of conservatism inherent in educational institutions at all levels. To be sure, such conservatism can have a salutary effect. As Brennan (11) points out, institutional conservatism "acts as a shield against untested ideas and as a buffer against the cyclical swings of fashion, preventing the fashionable from converting

stable progress into chaos" (pp. 16–17). There is, nevertheless, growing concern that the conservatism of schools and universities has become a major obstacle to progress at a point in history when the larger society is undergoing fundamental change. The next few years will be crucial in determining whether interdisciplinary studies form part of a fundamental change or represent only a "cyclical swing of fashion."

References, Interdisciplinary studies

1 Akenson, James E. *Environmental Quality and a Humanistic Approach to Teacher Education.* [Paper delivered at the Annual Convention of the National Council for the Social Studies, New York, November 1970.] [EDRS: ED 046 796.]

2 Allen, Edward D., and Rebecca M. Valette. *Modern Language Classroom Techniques: A Handbook.* New York: Harcourt, Brace, Jovanovich, 1972.

3 Alpert, Daniel. *The Role and Structure of Interdisciplinary and Multidisciplinary Research Centers.* [Address to the Ninth Annual Meeting of the Council of Graduate Schools in the United States, Wash-

ington, D.C., December 1969.] [EDRS: ED 035 363.]

4 Association des Universités Partiellement ou Entièrement de Langue Française. *Rapport Général de la Première Rencontre Internationale des Départements d'Etudes Françaises à l'Université Laval.* Montreal: University of Montreal, May 1972.

5 Benveniste, Guy. "The 'Metadisciplinary' Approach to Policy Research in Developing Countries," in *Notes on the Work of the Professional Schools' Committee at Berkeley.* Berkeley: University of California, 1968. [EDRS: ED 030 375.]

6 Biggs, Patricia, Paule Chicken, and Richard Leeson. *La France: aspects sociaux, politiques et économiques.* New York: David McKay, Company, 1971.

7 Bolinger, Dwight. *Aspects of Language.* New York: Harcourt, Brace and World, 1968.

8 Boning, E., and K. Roeloffs. *Three German Universities: Aachen, Bochum, Konstanz.* [Case Study on Innovations in Higher Education.] Paris: Organization for Economic Cooperation and Development, 1970. [EDRS: ED 049 696.]

9 Borenstein, Walter. *The Combined and the Divided Language Department in the Liberal Arts College.* New Paltz: State University of New York at New Paltz, 1969. [EDRS: ED 036 218.]

10 Bosco, James, and Stanley Robin. *Reconstruction in the Relation of Social Science and Education.* [Paper delivered at the American Educational Research Association Meeting, Chicago, April 1972.] [EDRS: ED 065 412.]

11 Brennan, Michael J. *A Cannibalistic View of Graduate Education.* [Address to the Ninth Annual Meeting of the Council of Graduate Schools in the United States, Washington, D.C., December 1969.] [EDRS ED 036 252.]

12 ——— *Research Component: Social Sciences and the Humanities.* [Address to the Tenth Annual Meeting of the Council of Graduate Schools in the United States, Washington, D.C., December 1970.] [EDRS: ED 047 627.]

13 Brière, Eugène J. "Are We Really Measuring Proficiency with Our Foreign Language Tests?" *Foreign Language Annals* 4,iv(1971):385–91.

14 Brod, Richard I. "Single Language and Combined Foreign Language Departments." *Association of Departments of Foreign Languages Bulletin* 1,iv(1970): 37–40.

15 Bulatkin, Eleanor W. "Romance Studies: Integration versus Segmentation, an Administrative View." *Association of Departments of Foreign Languages Bulletin* 2,iv(1971):5–8.

16 Chapman, Hugh H. Jr., and Donald H. Kellander. "Educational Trends in Romance Language Departments: A Report of a Survey." *Association of Departments of Foreign Languages Bulletin* 4,iv(1973): 26–32.

17 Crawford, Bryce. *The Support of Interdisciplinary and Transdisciplinary Programs.* [Address to the Ninth Annual Meeting of the Council of Graduate Schools in the United States, Washington, D.C., December 1969.] [EDRS: ED 035 364.]

18 Crocker, Lester G. "The Future of Foreign Languages and Literatures in a Free Market Curriculum." *Association of Departments of Foreign Languages Bulletin* 2,iii(1971): 11–13.

19 "The Doctor of Arts in Modern European Languages at Claremont Graduate School." *Association of Departments of Foreign Languages Bulletin* 2,iii (1971):43–46.

20 Duffy, Carolyn B. *Foreign Language Teaching: A Brief State of the Art.* Washington, D.C.: Department of Health Education and Welfare, Office of Education, 1970. [EDRS: ED 040 380.]

21 Eddington, George T. "Beyond Skill Building." *Northern California Foreign Language Newsletter* 19 (1971):5–6. [EDRS: ED 051 713.]

22 Edgerton, Mills F. "A Philosophy for the Teacher of Foreign Languages." *Modern Language Journal* 55(1971):5–15.

23 *Foreign Language Innovative Curricula Studies.* Summary Report, USOE 3–7–704431–056. Lansing, Michigan: Ann Arbor Public Schools, 1969. [EDRS: ED 032 538.]

24 Giese, Frank. "How Can We Keep French in the Curriculum—or Should We?" in *Proceedings of the 1971 Pacific Northwest Conference on Foreign Languages.* Portland, Oregon: Pacific Northwest Conference on Foreign Languages, 1972. [EDRS: ED 060 713.]

25 Hall, Edward T. *The Silent Language.* New York: Doubleday, 1959.

26 ——— *The Hidden Dimension.* New York: Doubleday, 1966.

27 Halloran, William F. "To Reverse a Trend: Foreign Literatures and the Humanities." *Association of Departments of Foreign Languages Bulletin* 4,i(1972):28–35.

28 Horwath, Peter. "Innovations in the Curriculum of the Center for Arts and Literature at Prescott College." *Association of Departments of Foreign Languages Bulletin* 4,iii(1973):57–59.

29 Huberman, Gisele, and Vadim Medish. "Content Courses in Foreign Languages." *Association of Departments of Foreign Languages Bulletin* 4,i(1972): 62–64.

30 *Interdisciplinarity: Problems of Teaching and Research in Universities.* Centre for Educational Research and Innovation, Paris. Washington, D.C.: Publications Center of the Organization for Economic Cooperation, 1972. [EDRS: ED 061 895.]

31 Kahrl, Stanley J. *Constructing an Interdisciplinary Major in Medieval and Renaissance Studies.* Columbus, Ohio: The Center for Medieval and Renaissance Studies, Ohio State University, 1971. [Brochure.]

32 ——— *Course Syllabi for Medieval Studies 210, 211, 212, 213, 214.* Columbus, Ohio: The Center for Medieval and Renaissance Studies, Ohio State University, 1973. [Mimeo.]

33 Kuhn, Reinhard. "Graduate Education: the Case for a Revolution." *Association of Departments of Foreign Languages Bulletin* 3,ii(1971):5–9.

34 Leyerle, John, ed. "Marriage in the Middle Ages." *Viator* 4(1973):476 ff.

35 Leyerle, John, and Thomas Ohlgren, eds. *Interdisciplinary Medieval Programs and the Training of Students.* Proceedings of the Medieval Academy's Committee on Centers and Regional Associations

at the Universisy of North Carolina, April 1971. Lafayette, Indiana: Purdue University, 1971.

36 Milburn, Thomas. "Problems of Integrating Academic Disciplines in the Study of War, Violence, and Social Change." in *Diablo Valley Education Project—Berkeley, California*. New York: Center for War and Peace Studies of the New York Friends Group, Inc., 1970. [EDRS: ED 058 106.]

37 Murray, Frederic W. "Trends in Departmental Structure in the field of Hispanic Studies." *Hispania* 55(1972):412–18.

38 Nelson, Robert J. "A Modern Curriculum in French Studies." *Association of Departments of Foreign Languages Bulletin* 2,ii(1970):25–31.

39 ――― "Further Remarks on Interdisciplinary Programs." *Association of Departments of Foreign Languages Bulletin* 3,ii(1971):31–34.

40 ――― "Culture and Culture:An Integrated, Multidisciplinary Approach to Foreign Language Requirements." *Modern Language Journal* 56(1972): 210–17.

41 *Newspaper of Medieval and Renaissance Studies.* [Announcement of publication made by Miriam Dahl Burno (Roosevelt University) et al. at Conference on Medieval Studies of the Medieval Institute, Western Michigan University, April 1973.]

42 Noble, Beth. "After the Storm." *Association of Departments of Foreign Languages Bulletin* 3,i(1971): 25–28.

43 Perren, G.E.,ed. *Interdisciplinary Approaches to Language. CILT Reports and Papers 6*. London: Center for Information on Language Teaching, 1971. [EDRS: ED 054 696.]

44 Pincus, Michael S. "Foreign Languages in the Service of the Liberal Arts:Look, then Leap!" *Association of Departments of Foreign Languages Bulletin* 3,i(1971): 19–23.

45 Pumerantz, Philip, and Ralph W. Galano. *Establishing Interdisciplinary Programs in the Middle School*. West Nyack, New York: Parker, 1972.

46 Purcell, Edna J. *Interdisciplinary Arts and Humanities Programs and Cultural Centers for Elementary Schools*. Title III Final Report. Muncie, Indiana: Ball State University, 1969. [EDRS: ED 033 124.]

47 Remak, Henry H.H. "Foreign Languages and Literatures in the Free Market Curriculum." *Association of Departments of Foreign Languages Bulletin* 2,iii(1971):18–23.

48 Rose, Michael J. "Interdisciplinary Studies:A Program for the Small Liberal Arts College." *Association of Departments of Foreign Languages Bulletin* 4,ii(1972):22–24.

49 Rosenmeyer, Thomas G. "Interdisciplinary Studies: Forms and Limits." *Association of Departments of Foreign Languages Bulletin* 4,i(1972):19–27.

50 Rütimann, Hans. "Departmental and Language Information Available in the MLA List of Chair-

men." *Publications of the Modern Language Association* 84(1969):685–87.

51 Schaefer, William D. "Report of the Executive Secretary." *Publications of the Modern Language Association* 88(1973):536–41.

52 Sebeok, Thomas A. "Linguistics Here and Now." *American Council of Learned Societies Newsletter* 18(1967):1–6. [EDRS: ED 024 921.]

53 Secrest, Leigh. *The Rationale for Polydisciplinary Programs*. [Address to the Ninth Annual Meeting of the Council of Graduate Schools in the United States, Washington, D.C., December 1969.] [EDRS: ED 037 151.]

54 Shattuck, Roger W. "Remarks on Interdisciplinary Programs." *Association of Departments of Foreign Languages Bulletin* 3,i(1971):13–18.

55 Stevick, Earl W. *Interdisciplinary Cooperation in the Making and Use of Field Tapes in African Languages: A Preliminary Statement*. Washington, D.C.: Foreign Service Institute, Department of State, 1966. [EDRS: ED 012 452.]

56 Thomas, Rosemary H. "A Resource Approach to Foreign Language Department Planning." *Association of Departments of Foreign Languages Bulletin* 4,i(1972): 40–43.

57 Tillery, Dale. *Variation and Change in Community College Organization:A Preliminary Report*. Berkeley: University of California, 1970. [EDRS: ED 061 931.]

58 Turner, Thomas C. "A Test Case Interdisciplinary Seminar:Reactions and Recommendations." *Association of Departments of Foreign Languages Bulletin* 4,iv(1973):42–44.

59 Wardropper, Bruce W. "The Resurgence of the Department of Romance Languages." *Association of Departments of Foreign Languages Bulletin* 2,iv(1971): 9–11.

60 Warriner, Helen P. "Foreign Language Interdisciplinary Programs and Activities," 125–61 in Dale L. Lange,ed., *Pluralism in Foreign Language Education*. ACTFL Review of Foreign Language Education, Volume 3. Skokie, Illinois: National Textbook Company, 1973.

61 Wishard, Armin. *The Teaching of a Foreign Language in a Modular System of Instruction*. [Paper delivered at the Annual Meeting of the American Association of Teachers of German, Chicago, November 1971.] [EDRS: ED 056 609.]

6

Career education

Introduction

The critics of education are ever with us. Just as ubiquitous are the educational leaders who crouch, waiting for some new gadget, a new concept, or a promising technique that can be emblazoned in a catchy slogan on a banner (or a bumper sticker). These educators spring forth to rally around the flag and then march out to proselytize the educational establishment.

The cause of career education appears to have gained impetus in January 1971 when Sidney F. Marland, Jr. assumed the office of United States Commissioner of Education, he called the attention of the nation to the failure of our schools to provide youth with the skills and concepts necessary for productive and rewarding lives. He proposed a reformation of schooling so that "educators would be bent on preparing students either to become properly and usefully employed

Kenneth A. Lester
Connecticut State Department of Education

and

Toby Tamarkin
Manchester Community College

USOE and career education

Kenneth A. Lester (Ed.D., Boston University) is Consultant in Foreign Languages, ESOL and Bilingual Education for the Connecticut State Department of Education. He has taught French and English at the secondary school level in Connecticut as well as serving as Director of Audio-Visual Education for a public school district. While employed regularly at the public school and the state level, he has served part time as a lecturer at Central Connecticut State College and has been part of NDEA Summer Language Institute faculty at the same institution. He has had articles published in the *French Review* and the *Modern Spanish Teacher* and has written numerous editorials for the Connecticut newsletter, the *FL News Exchange*, as well as editing several state publications. Dr. Lester's activities in professional associations include positions of leadership in ACTFL, NCSSFL, New England FLA, Connecticut COLT, AATF and Connecticut ASCD. He is also an active member of Phi Delta Kappa, ConnTESOL, AAPBC (Portuguese), the Connecticut Education Association, and the NEA.

Toby Tamarkin (M.A., University of Connecticut) is Chairman of Foreign Languages at Manchester Community College in Connecticut. She is also enrolled in a Ph.D. program at the University of Connecticut. Previous experience includes six years as a secondary teacher of business and language, and three years as teaching consultant for the bilingual elementary school program in Enfield, Connecticut. Her publications have appeared in *Hispania*, *Accent on ACTFL* and the Connecticut *FL News Exchange*. She has served as Vice-President of Connecticut COLT, Secretary of Connecticut AATSP, Board Member of New England FLA, Member of the Connecticut State Advisory Commission, as well as being a member of ACTFL and NECLAS. Other community services include involvement in the Puertorican Businessmen's Association Bi-lingual Business Education Program.

immediately upon graduation from high school or to go on to further formal education" (6, p. 3). A flood of speeches, papers, and pamphlets has subsequently flowed from the U.S. Office of Education on the subject of career education. Support for career education was immediately proffered by certain educators, many of whom were in the field of vocational education, for Marland's words not only described a means of making learning relevant but also promised a curriculum that would "eliminate the artificial separation between things academic and things vocational" (6, p. 3).

The way in which career education was born and fostered may tempt us to reject it as a phase that we will eventually outgrow or as a fad that will pass even more quickly. This would be a grave mistake. The concept of career education has a great deal to offer the foreign language educator, and the foreign language teacher can strengthen career education programs.

Career education K–12

As defined in Washington, D.C., career education is seen as a program with five levels of development: awareness, orientation, exploration, preparation, and specialization. Beginning with career awareness in Grade one, the approach moves toward more specific orientation to the world of work at the upper elementary grades (7). The student explores several "career clusters" at the junior high level in anticipation of in-depth exploration and preparation at the senior high school level. "In senior high school, students pursue their selected occupational area, exercising one of three options: intensive job preparation for entry into the world of work immediately upon leaving high school, preparation for postsecondary occupational education, or preparation for four-year college" (8, p. 2). The student who is preparing for postsecondary education will get practical work experience as well as pursuing academic subject areas related to the professional area for which he is preparing. In this manner, students preparing for specialization will gain the academic skills necessary for further education, and those preparing for postsecondary education will also develop entry-level job skills in an occupation.

Fifteen career clusters have been identified by the U.S. Office of Education (6) which cover the entire field of possible occupations. They are: Agri-business and Natural Resources, Business and Office, Health, Public Service, Environment, Communication and Media, Hospitality and Recreation, Manufacturing, Marketing and Distribution, Marine Science, Personal Services, Construction, Transpor-

Career clusters

162

tation, Consumer and Homemaking Education, and Fine Arts and Humanities. Foreign language teachers who try to use these clusters in defining jobs related to languages will find that this system is different in many respects from traditional classifications. For example, there is no single cluster that includes the field of diplomatic service, a career sometimes suggested to foreign language students. The various jobs available in diplomacy are found under such clusters as personal services, hospitality and recreation, or public service. Language teachers may wish to familiarize themselves with the current career clusters to derive a new orientation that will be more helpful in counseling students interested in exploring employment opportunities according to these 15 basic categories.

New classifications for careers

A booklet has been prepared by the Madison, Wisconsin Public Schools (11) for use in advising students. It lists the areas under each career cluster that can be related to foreign language. For example, under Hospitality and Recreation, one finds Airline Personnel, Bus Personnel, Hotel Personnel, International Clubs, Resort Personnel, Recreation Personnel, Ship Personnel, Tour Guide, Train Personnel and Travel Agent. Related fields are Business, Health, Personal Services, and Transportation (p. 21).

Madison career booklet

The implication for languages is clear. In a career-oriented curriculum many of the students in foreign language classes will be there because they are trying to develop certain language skills that will be of benefit to them in their chosen occupations. The small, hard-core group of students who are taking a language because they like language study will still be with us. Therefore, we must resist an overemphasis on job-oriented motives that would demean the desire to investigate an area simply because the student experiences satisfaction in his study of it, as pointed out by Nash and Agne (30). Up to this point, however, foreign language teachers may have been guilty of gearing language courses too much to the student who is studying language for language's sake. It is timely to give more consideration to language as a practical tool.

Career-oriented student

Emphasis on many motives for study

Career education in foreign language

Technological development, particularly in communication and transportation, and societal changes are making the practical value of language study ever more evident. The "shrinking world" argument has been so often used that it has become trite, and the general public tosses it off without giving due consideration to its full implications. The rise of viable economic systems that are highly competitive with

Competition in world market

that of the United States, such as the Common Market and expanding countries like Japan and Germany, are requiring us to work more diligently at capturing a fair share of the world market. As we are put in the position of selling our products and services abroad rather than finding others coming to us because they need what only we can offer, communication in the language of the prospective buyer becomes more critical.

Imhoff (17) cites a survey of United States firms that do business abroad in which several kinds of experiences were listed as desirable training in addition to language skill. Among them were international business administration, engineering, finance, marketing, statistics and computer science, advertising, area studies, political science, civil engineering, and law. The large majority of companies contacted for the survey recognized the value of language training combined with specialized training in another area such as those mentioned.

Combination of skills with foreign language

A representative list of prospective employers of students who have developed foreign language skill follows: U.S. Information Agency; public school systems; junior colleges; Immigration Service; various colleges and universities; Department of the Army, Navy, and Air Force; international banking, marketing, and import/export; Pan American Airlines; Charles E. Merrill Publishing Company; UNESCO; United Nations; Department of Defense; Peace Corps; Voice of America; U.S. Department of State; National Security Agency; Pan American Union's Division of Education; Agency for International Development; Inter-American School Service (Imhoff, 17, p. 2). Almost half of these employers are directly related to the federal government. International business and the federal government appear to be the two great sources of career opportunities for students of a foreign language.

Prospective employers

The fact must not be overlooked that it is not only change in the international situation that is increasing the practical value of foreign language skill for United States citizens, but also societal change within our own borders. Although one might wonder if there has been a change in attitude towards Americans who speak a language other than English, there is no doubt but what public policy has changed. Bilingual programs, most of them in Spanish-English, in which the child has the opportunity to study the content of his school work in his native language while he is learning English, have spread across the country. Public services such as health, welfare, police, and tax departments have found that there are large groups of the public with whom communication is difficult or impossible unless they have employees

Societal changes

164

who can speak certain languages other than English. There is a growing demand for various public service personnel who have a command of certain foreign languages. Specific programs described later in this chapter will illustrate the extent to which opportunities exist in these fields.

Career education in adult education and higher education

General trends in the direction of career education are not limited to K–12 school curricula. The influence is being felt in adult education and higher education as well, although the former area has been limited in its chances to respond to the pressure. Teachers who have specialized in adult education should be especially qualified to deal with teaching mature adults career development skills and concepts. However, adult *Limitations in adult programs* programs have not been allowed to offer career-oriented courses since they would infringe on the vocational area, a field that receives extensive federal support as does adult education.

Foreign language courses are a regular part of many adult education *Adult education foreign* programs, however, and in addition to adults who take them to gain *language study* skill in a language to use in travel or for other enrichment purposes, it is a fact that certain businessmen, doctors, social workers, and others enroll in adult education courses because they have actually encountered or foresee the necessity to speak a foreign language that is widely used in the community.

Higher education in the United States is becoming more and more *Careers important in higher* an area where career education is of primary importance. There are *education* many areas of our higher educational system that can provide a career education thrust.

First, let us examine the traditional four-year college or university *Four-year college* that is either state supported or privately endowed. Most of these institutions enjoy a selective entrance policy and provide their students with the opportunity to select a combination liberal arts and vocational program. These more sophisticated, potentially rewarding programs range from anthropology to urban sociology and offer the student the skills necessary for employment along with a core of "liberal arts learning." Until recently the foreign language departments considered themselves only as part of that small core of humanities courses avail- *Humanities orientation* able to students for their enlightenment and intellectual growth. Several foreign language departments felt it a duty to offer translation and interpreter courses in the career area. These offerings have become numerous enough to necessitate the formation of an American Trans-

165

lator's Association which recently printed a set of guidelines for use by colleges and universities (37).

A more recent attempt to integrate the foreign language department's existing courses with a career potential is the development of a "double major" program involving the language department and another department. Mary Jackson of Northwest Missouri State University prepared the booklet *What and How for Foreign Language Students* that describes many career opportunities involving foreign language skills and presents interesting combinations of existing language courses with classes in business and economics, office administration, sociology, political science, and history (47). This type of program is a good beginning, but changes must also be effected in the content of the language courses offered. Some innovative programs are beginning to emerge at the four-year colleges; they will be described at the end of this chapter.

Attempts at career emphasis

The community college, that special breed of higher education that follows an open-door policy and tries to fill multiple needs, has begun to move away from a basic liberal-arts transfer policy and toward the development of a two-year terminal career program. These programs allow the student the option of filling an employment slot upon graduation in a special field for which he has been trained or continuing in a four-year institution toward completion of higher levels of achievement. Business departments and the social service areas have been leaders in the preparation of special curricula designed to prepare students for employment and to expand the training of workers already in the field. Preparation programs for many fields—secretarial; hospital assistant and social-service assistant; educational aide; police science; and accounting, sales, and marketing—are innumerable. Recently communications programs have begun emphasizing careers in radio and television as well as journalism, and fine arts departments are even becoming career-oriented.

Community colleges and career programs

Where does foreign language fit into this career picture? Unfortunately, at most community colleges the bulk of the language programs are directed to the four-year, liberal-arts, transfer student. At a time when language departments should be discovering how their talents could improve existing programs within their schools, most are still concerned with maintaining the skills levels and objectives set by their local universities.

Directions of foreign language departments

Some language departments in two-year colleges have recently begun to examine the various career training programs that do exist and are trying to incorporate foreign languages into the total school picture.

166

Special language courses for policemen, hospital workers, social-service personnel, and business employees are beginning to emerge. A few of these innovative courses are presented in detail at the end of this chapter.

Special language courses

Extension courses offered in the higher education institutions are a means of presenting specific classes for credit or noncredit to provide various opportunities to the student body and the community at large. There may be high school equivalency options; in-service training for professional workers or paraprofessional staff; experimental career options such as real estate sales; or fun courses in arts and crafts, music, dance, theatre, and so forth. These courses may be offered at night or on weekends; often they are less expensive than the regular college classes, and they are quite flexible in course content.

Extension courses

In foreign languages these courses are especially useful in providing specialized vocabulary and language practice to community residents who are not full-time college students. William J. Beck (2) at the Virginia Commonwealth University offers specialized courses for adults meeting one evening a week for ten weeks in two-hour sessions. Although the vocabulary emphasizes foreign language in travel, businessmen and secretaries attend classes with couples who are planning vacations. This specialized program is offered in Chinese, French, German, Italian, Russian, and Spanish. The spring 1973 term had more than 110 people registered and enough interest to add a class in Portuguese. Several colleges offer this type of course with great success, particularly when the language is predominant in their communities. Community reaction at Middlesex Community College, for example, has been so favorable that the school offers intermediate and advanced conversation programs in Italian, German, and Spanish.

Language for travel

Technical and junior colleges are becoming increasingly important as centers for preparation in special career skills. At present language learning in the technical colleges is practically nonexistent except for the bilingual training programs that are being implemented for students who are not fluent in English. An interesting example of language learning at a technical university is the University of Missouri, which offers a special course in scientific German and Russian in the second year following two semesters of elementary German or Russian (Law, 23). The course provides the student with a good reading proficiency in the language, a skill that will be helpful even as he does the research necessary to complete his remaining course work.

Technical colleges

Junior colleges differ from the community colleges in that they are usually privately owned and not part of a state school system. Like the

Junior colleges

167

community college, they provide students with a liberal arts transfer option or a technical career program. Language curricula at present are geared toward the more traditional transfer credit goals, and little effort has been made to coordinate existing career programs with language department course offerings.

The need for career-oriented school programs is underlined by the number of private schools that tend to specialize in preparation for jobs. In Connecticut alone there are 59 such schools approved by the State Board of Education (34). They range in specialization from welding to computer programing.

Private vocational schools

Private language schools also seem to be thriving. Since these schools exist for profit and at least two large corporations, American Express and Behavioral Research Laboratories (Marottoli, 29), have recently entered the field, there must be a need for them. Students, who have either avoided foreign language study or have remained impervious to the attempts of their teachers, find themselves coming back to learn a language in a private language school. Some students study for recreation or enrichment, and others are trying to qualify for a career opportunity or studying under a contract their company has made with the language school to train their staff in preparation for a business venture.

Private language schools

Community schools

A concept that is significant in career education is the community school. Flint, Michigan is a leader in this approach to education according to publications of the National Community School Association (9). In this educational model, the whole school system, kindergarten to adult, is integrated. An integrated system under one administration could address itself to community problems, including career education and training, and avoid overlapping of effort and potential squabbling over "territorial rights," particularly at the post-secondary level. The administration could call upon the strengths of various components of the educational establishment according to the particular contribution each might be able to make. A proposed Community School Act is currently pending at the federal level, but its fate is uncertain. The stimulation federal funds could bring might expedite a more rapid development and dissemination of the community school approach to education.

Integrated school system

Community School Act

The most easily attained means of combining foreign language and career education is for the individual teacher to relate the content of his course to students' career goals. This integration can readily be accomplished during the development of language skills by presenting the students with dramatic settings and current vocabulary related to the world of work. The modern emphasis in foreign language education on learning to *speak* the language demands that examples of contemporary oral usage be part of language classes. Some of these examples can be drawn as easily from everyday life in career areas as from academic, family, or other social situations. This means of relating instruction to some students' goals can be an effective way to motivate them and provide needed support for both foreign language learning and career education.

Examples from career areas

The desire to learn a language for use in a job can be defined as instrumental motivation. According to Lambert (Hancock, 14, p. 149–50), instrumental motivation is not so effective as integrative motivation (a deep desire to identify with the people and culture of a language community). However, some students remain resistant to identifying with a language community and may never be reached via integrative motivation, but they may be attracted by the careers that can be opened to them if they have a command of a foreign language. In fact, the student who perseveres in language study for instrumental reasons may eventually embrace the more humanistic aims inherent in the integrative domain. Certainly no potentially effective means of motivation should be ignored by the language teacher. The instrumentally motivated student will undoubtedly be a better target for language study than the unmotivated student.

Instrumental motivation

The school system with a large-scale commitment to career education demands more of foreign language programs than a superficial treatment if they are to be part of the total effort. Through a technique known as "blending," the goals of the career education program are partially accomplished by integrating these goals into disciplines already in the curriculum. In this type of program, career awareness might be part of the FLES program. In addition to listing possible careers that might involve foreign languages, highlighting career-related topics that may appear as a regular part of the FLES materials might be a larger contribution. As an example, the occupation of the father in a Spanish family might be mentioned in a dialogue. The teacher could specifically isolate the word, ask students to do projects

Blending technique

Career awareness and FLES

on that job or related areas, and present a list of vocabulary items relating to that job area. An effective follow-up might be to ask students to play roles in dramatic situations the teacher writes based on the projects the students have done. By doing this with many items throughout the FLES program, students can become aware of and sensitive to different kinds of work as part of life.

At the junior high level, orientation toward choosing a career and exploration of several career clusters might be shared by two or three disciplines including foreign languages. At the exploratory stage the clusters investigated in the foreign language classes are those that have a direct bearing on the use of language skills. The blending of career education and existing disciplines must be well coordinated so that the career awareness, orientation, and exploration are carried out on different fronts. Obviously, programs and students suffer if the same material is repeated in several content areas. An overall guide should be developed, and the portions to be covered in each class should be agreed upon in advance.

Exploration in the junior high school

Avoiding unnecessary repetition

The emphasis at the senior high school should be on preparation for a career or for postsecondary study. The blending of career education and foreign language instruction can be complete for some students during their junior and senior years. A student who starts language study in the FLES section of this hypothetical sequence will have enough skill to undertake a variety of pursuits in language in his last two years. Courses such as French or Spanish typing and stenography, now offered at Franklin K. Lane High School in Brooklyn, New York (31), present an opportunity for skilled students to maintain their ability and to sharpen their language competency for use in a particular manner.

Career preparation in the senior high school

Another category of students is comprised of those who are just beginning language study in the senior high school, because they may have transferred late into the school system, were excluded from language study at earlier levels, or have just discovered that foreign language skill will be helpful in their chosen careers. Such a student poses a particular challenge. If he is highly oriented towards a certain career goal, he may not be receptive to the usual beginning language course content and procedures. He must develop language skills quickly to use them for a practical purpose. Because he does not have four or five years to work at the task he must be presented with reorganized language courses that limit the breadth of his study and permit him to develop in depth the skill he needs in a narrower area. A promising technique for accomplishing this is illustrated by the learning capsules being developed in

Need for reorganized language courses

170

Dade County, Florida (Alonso, 1), which are described in some detail later in this chapter.

The task given to higher education in this career model is further preparation and specialization. Certain areas of specialization such as teaching, translating, or simultaneous interpretation require more training than can be done at the elementary and secondary levels, even in an eight- or nine-year sequence. Such careers demand post-secondary specialization training.

Work experience programs and job placement

The time has come for secondary schools and the various institutions that make up our higher education system to recognize the value of foreign language learning as a special skill that aids in student work experience programs and job placement. The only effective way to insure language skills as a tool is to involve language department members directly with work experience and job placement program directors. Language teachers must assume the responsibility for discussing career opportunities with students to show how foreign language competency can enhance future professional opportunities. They must talk with students who have demonstrated an interest in languages, although another program may be the student's "major." When the student's program includes either work experience or job placement, a language teacher should be an accepted member of the placement team. As a general rule school guidance counselors and business, social service, and medical departments in charge of special work programs do not consider foreign language skills when they place students in jobs. We must teach the students to discuss language skills with all future employers and placement officials, and we must be prepared to serve with the other departments so that language competency as an employment tool is recognized by our institutions.

Language teachers and counseling

Roger Johnson, Jr. of the University of Southern Mississippi feels that good career training is dependent upon two factors: an effective system of student advisement and interdepartmental cooperation in establishing curricula that will provide students with marketable skills (19). Land and water resource managing, nursing, social work, business administration, for example, can be combined with language skills if foreign language advisors can communicate with freshmen to outline the various curricular possibilities before the student has earned many credits.

D. A. Roos of Winston Churchill High School in Potomac, Maryland,

171

has been given released time to develop a career awareness program involving the relationship of foreign languages to possible future professions (41). He has met with each of the school's 50 foreign language classes and has encouraged students to discuss with him their goals and how a language skill might relate to them. Roos plans to begin placing students in internship experiences that involve foreign languages in the Washington, D.C. area.

The above examples reflect what must be done by all language departments if they accept the basic premise that language skill is a tool that provides students with additional employment opportunities.

The reality

Considering the several theoretical bases on which career and foreign language education could cooperate, we conducted a survey to determine the extent to which there was blending of the two in practice. The survey identified actual programs in fewer than ten states. In arriving at this figure, regular career programs that have been in operation for years at the college level—for example, teacher preparation and training for translators—were not counted. Language training at the college level for certain careers has obviously not been totally lacking. What we searched for were *different* programs at the higher education level and the initiation of any foreign language career programs at the elementary and secondary levels. Does a significant level of activity in foreign languages and career education, based on the definition given, exist? The answer must be a firm *no, not yet.*

Survey of new career programs

The basic reason for the lack of development in this area can probably be traced to an attitude growing out of the place foreign language instruction traditionally has held in the curriculum at both secondary and college levels. In medieval Europe, the learned man had to master Latin because it was the common means by which scholars communicated, particularly in writing. With the growth of national languages and the development of writing systems for them, the practical value of Latin was diminished. However, as the practical value waned, the prestige value increased. Latin became the tool of the scholar whose principal concerns were in the realm of philosophy, unsoiled by the practicality of everyday life. Thus, to know Latin was to be identified with that elite group.

Prestige value of foreign language

The addition of modern languages to the curriculum has followed a similar course to that of Latin. It is only within this century that modern languages have lost the taint of practicality in the curricula of the

172

European models on which the schools of the United States were based. Modern languages have only recently been considered worthy of inclusion in the academic or "liberal" course of study in these countries. In the United States these languages were of dubious practical value from the beginning to nearly all but the highly educated. Their symbolic use as emblems of liberal education was accepted early in the development of the curriculum, a distinction that has remained with us. Until fairly recently knowing French or German was the mark of an "educated man." An ironical aspect of this syndrome must be noted here. Knowledge of these languages was a mark of distinction only if they were learned in school. The native speaker of a language other than English merited no special credit in the minds of the educated American public.

Foreign language and the educated man

Rapid changes in the past several years demand a new definition of a liberal education and of the place of foreign languages in the curriculum. Practicality can no longer be used as a major criterion for rejecting certain educational pursuits as part of liberal studies. If a liberal education frees the individual from constraints that prohibit him from becoming the kind of person he wishes to be and permits him to be more self-directed, many of his educational activities may indeed be very practical in nature. However, *immediate* use cannot be the sole measure for the validation of such activities.

New definition of liberal education

Foreign language can serve the ends of both short-term and long-range relevance to the liberation of the American student. Short-term relevance can be attained by joining language skill with the relatively immediate prospect of obtaining a better job. The longer-range goal of positively influencing the student's attitude towards a means of communication that differs from his native language and towards a culture that is different from his own is a goal even the career-oriented foreign language course must retain. If this latter aim were ignored, the foreign language teacher would be guilty of failing to consider one of the most liberating aspects of the study of a second language.

Short-term and long-range relevance

The fact remains that in spite of a new definition of liberal education and in spite of a changing society that gives a new value to the study of a foreign language, the use of a second language as a practical tool rather than as an end in itself is new in the thinking of many foreign language educators. Furthermore, this different concept is probably completely alien to the thinking of much of the general public.

We must begin to understand that just as the typing skill offers personal rewards and serves as an employment tool, competency in a foreign language can also fulfill these dual objectives. The student

Foreign language as an employment tool

173

should be aware that when job applications ask for "additional skills," an ability to communicate in a second language is an important plus factor that may earn him the position over other candidates. If the student's interest lies in the public service, medical, or business areas, he must understand that his ability to secure a good position could depend on his language proficiency. We, as teachers, must apprise our students of this important advantage of a second language, and we must design our courses with this extra dimension in mind.

What is needed?

How do we approach the many career needs and their relationships to our language classes? We must assess the interests of our own students. We must question them: for what do they intend to use this special skill? We must examine very carefully the various programs that our schools now offer and must prepare language classes that will meet student needs and blend with other school programs.

Student career interests

We must realize that students will select certain goals in language study and will reject others. Not all *teacher goals*, even though they have been selected for a specific language course, will be appropriate for all students. The course materials and methodology must be flexible enough to allow each student to progress and fulfill his own ambitions. Attempting to individualize—working sometimes with the entire class and often with the class divided into groups according to their interest choices—will help to keep each student motivated toward his own goals.

Teacher flexibility

Obviously new and different materials are required when we begin to add the career-oriented dimension to our language programs. Commercial materials are not currently widely available, and this requires that we prepare programs on our own. Administrators are very interested in a career approach and will often provide released time, extra money, or other incentives to those teachers who are willing to prepare materials necessary for these classes.

Need for new materials

Representative examples of career-oriented foreign language programs

An exhaustive search for examples of new career-oriented programs that include foreign languages revealed several that represent an excellent combination of student goals and coordination with other existing programs or motivational forces in the school and community.
One of the most thorough and carefully devised programs is the

Model career development program

174

Cobb County Occupational and Career Development Program in Marietta, Georgia (12). Farris Foresman, Career Development Specialist, and Joel Smith, Programs Director, along with teachers, principals, and special curriculum writers and secretaries planned and prepared the project, which grew out of a state grant beginning in September 1969 and a federal fund in 1970. The program is one of orientation and information for students at the elementary level, information and exploration at the middle school level, and exploration and preparation at the secondary level—all built around a career development theme. Included are: (a) the student's evaluation of self-characteristics, (b) exploration of broad occupational areas, (c) introduction to the economic and sociological values of work, (d) introduction to the psychological and sociological meaning of work, (e) explanation of educational career avenues, and (f) development of the student's process of decision making based upon the foregoing items.

Analysis of the above goals led to the development of six elements now incorporated into all units on all grade levels. The elements are: "hands on" activities, role playing, field trips into the community, bringing resource people into the classroom, subject-matter blending, and introduction to occupations in the community that are relevant to each unit. A unit approach was chosen as a structural framework for implementing career development. Career Development Specialists *Career development specialist* work with grade level teachers in selecting activity-centered units, in their planning, in procuring materials and supplies, in arranging field trips, and in bringing resource persons into the classroom. The function of the Career Development Specialist is thus one of *support* to the implementing teacher. The teacher, in turn, incorporates career development activities into the curriculum.

At the 10th grade level, students may choose a class in career exploration and then rotate through the six occupational areas of training offered by the Spayberry High School, an institution selected to experiment with this project. Students who choose occupational goals in the professions are exposed to the unit approach through their language arts, science, mathematics, and social studies classes. As in the middle schools, subject area concepts and skills are presented in such a way that they can be applied to individual career choices.

"French Language Skills in the United States" is the name of one *Example of career development* 10th-grade career-development unit. The behavioral objectives of this *unit* unit are:

1   Upon completion of this unit, the student will be able to spell

175

and define correctly at least 80 percent of the French vocabulary words introduced.

2 The student will be able to demonstrate verbal language techniques by employing proper accent, word formation, and emphasis in oral communication.

3 At the end of the unit, the student will be able to demonstrate oral composition skills by participating in simulated conversation, oral drills, sentence formulation, and question-and-answer sessions.

4 Given a subject topic, the student will demonstrate written composition skills by writing simple sentences and paragraphs. The criteria for evaluation will include proper use of parts of speech, correct arrangement of subject, predicate, and punctuation.

5 Given a list of five clusters that use French as a job skill, the student will select one occupational area and research it to find this information: nature of work; places of employment; training, qualifications, and advancement potentials; employment outlook; earning and working conditions; and sources of additional information.

6 The student will be expected to discuss briefly in written and oral form, occupational information on at least one career area related to French language skills.

7 Given a group of careers within various occupational clusters, the student will be able to distinguish between those careers requiring only a "working knowledge" of French and those requiring "fluency" in this language.

This French unit contains ten parts:

1 Motivational activities
2 Presentation of subject matter
3 Introduction to French language skills as a potential career area
4 Introduction to occupational information related to use of French language skills
5 Research activities on occupational fields within the United States
6 Simulated work activities
7 Analysis of relationships between career choice and individual personality variables
8 Classroom visitations by resource persons
9 Field trips to actual work environments
10 Evaluation activities

Listed in the unit are study activities in the form of a lesson plan that   *Lesson plan*

176

the classroom teacher may follow. The following is an excerpt from that plan, which contains over 40 activities:

A   Initial Activities

1   *Motivation.* Bring French magazines, money, restaurant menus, and airline tickets to class. Allow students to attempt to translate the words and exchange the currency for American dollars.

2   Initiate a discussion on the use of French in the United States. Points to discuss could include ordering food, communicating with French-speaking visitors, exchanging money, trading with foreign countries, reading French literature, listening to French radio stations.

3   Introduce the concept: Many jobs in the United States use French as a job skill.

4   Occupational Correlating Activity. Discuss occupational clusters that provide the services mentioned in Activity 2. These could include: human services such as transportation, traveling accommodations, food services, customs and immigration services; business, clerical, and sales services such as money exchange and foreign trade; general culture careers including writers, broadcasters, and language teachers.

5   Have a planned discussion on levels of language proficiency. Introduce the concept: Communication in French, as in other languages, can be accomplished through mastery of basic vocabulary and knowledge of language structure. Distinguish between a "working knowledge" and language "fluency."

6   Identify basic vocabulary to be covered in this unit. Examples of nouns, pronouns, adjectives, and verbs could be discussed in relation to their use in various occupational areas.

Special activities are also included that are planned around student visits to the school guidance center to teach students to use occupational information related to the exploration of careers involving French skills. Student-teacher planning sessions enable students to develop a research format they may then use in their individual research projects. This 10th-grade career-development unit is being offered to between 150 and 200 students each year.

Community-based career program

"Fasten your seat belts," and "Clear the runway" are dialogue sentences that show up frequently at August Martin High School in

Jamaica, New York, where, according to Foreign Language Department Chairman, Samuel J. Larocca, most courses have an aviation slant (22). In 1971 the school, which is located just one mile from Kennedy International Airport, was converted into a comprehensive high school that offers a full academic curriculum and has courses related to aviation and the air transport industry. Students can elect programs leading to higher education, employment in business and industry, or specialized work in aviation-related fields. Among the school's requirements for all students are one year of typing, one year of practical arts, and two years of foreign language study. In 1974 the school will be filled to its capacity of 2400 students in Grades 9 to 12.

Language courses are offered in French and Spanish, and although standard texts and methods are used, aviation vocabulary is integrated into the regular lessons whenever appropriate. For example, in a unit on food, students might simulate a dialogue between an air hostess and passengers having a meal on board. In a unit on travel, *takeoff* and *landing* would naturally be worked into a dialogue between a tourist and a ticket agent. Career *electives* are being planned in both French and Spanish as more students move into advanced levels of language learning in Grades 11 and 12. Language students visit the Air France and Iberian Airline terminals at Kennedy Airport and a class at a stewardess training center. Throughout the first year, five airline hostesses who speak French and Spanish volunteered to work as teacher aides in the resource center, as their flight schedules permitted. In addition to assistance from a paraprofessional or teacher in the resource center, a student may practice with taped drills in a laboratory that was donated by Pan American Airlines.

Another example of career awareness in foreign language instruction is a program headed by Meshach Browning of the Fort Hill High School in Cumberland, Maryland (5). Browning is a guidance counselor who feels that a career emphasis should be combined with foreign language study as early as the junior high level so that the student becomes aware as early as possible of the need for career exploration.

Guidance counselor's plan for developing career awareness

To integrate career awareness into a foreign language instructional program, according to the Fort Hill High School plan, the following steps should be utilized:

1 Define objectives and/or goals.
2 Review the materials of instruction currently in use to determine present areas of career awareness.
3 Survey the community for sources of possible assistance and added depth.

4 Train the teacher or teachers in career awareness activities via workshop, consultant (guidance counselor or librarian), etc.

5 Develop a set of activities to enhance the current program and implement awareness.

6 Evaluate activities, materials, and goals periodically to see if they are meeting student needs.

7 Redefine objectives or goals yearly to keep current with local student needs and regional career demands.

Sample objectives or goals:

1 To develop an awareness of the world of work by making students more aware that vocabulary being studied in the French language has occupational denotations.

2 To develop an awareness of the world of work by making students more aware that the pictorial presentation of the culture of France being studied has occupational connotations.

3 To develop awareness of the avocational opportunities students may gain by the continued pursuit of a foreign language.

The students participating in the language experiment (language classes including career awareness) felt that learning about jobs at such an early stage was very important to them and made them think about several job possibilities instead of just one career goal.

An individualized career program in German is being taught by Gerald Logan at the Live Oak High School in Morgan Hill, California (25). The school offers career education and German in six general areas: secretarial, stewardess, commercial employment, restaurant and motel work, scientific German, and home economics. These individualized courses consist of extensive collections of materials in each area. When a student expresses interest in doing work in one of these fields, the teachers discuss with him his general goals, show him the materials available, and then write a semester contract with the *Independent study* student including specific detailed objectives. In this program, 80 hours of work constitute a semester course and a semester's credit. Student and teacher come to an agreement as to just what an hour of work will consist of—for example, four pages of reading, a page of composition, an hour by the clock—and then each student may complete the 80 hours at his own rate and convenience. The minimum performance criterion is 90 percent. These are related to the particular student's written objectives—to be able to give English equivalents for 90 percent of the vocabulary presented in the materials, to be able to answer 90 percent of the questions on content presented in the materials, and so on.

179

There is not a large number of students in any one area in these courses. In the last two years three students were in secretarial German, four students in home economics, two students in science, one student in commercial German, and two students in photography. There are also two girls in the "stewardess" course and one student in agriculture.

As an example, in home economics the students enroll in a two-hour block of time, dividing their work between the German learning center and the home economics room. Two of the students worked in foods and two in clothing. The department has 20 books on foods, plus several magazines. One student in the clothing area used the magazines, *Neue Mode, Brigitte,* and *Schöner Wohnen.* She read articles on clothing, selected certain fashions from *Neue Mode* to study in detail, mastered the German directions for making several dresses and blouses, and used the German patterns that were included. In her time in the home economics room she worked with the teacher and sewed the articles. She received one semester of credit in German and one semester of credit in home economics for her 160 hours of work in both departments.

Logan's department has over 1,000 items of materials that could be called career oriented. Students are eligible for this special semester project after having completed at least two years of general German. Some students complete only 40 hours of work and receive one-half credit. One student did 528 hours of work in one year and received 6.6 semester hours of credit.

A unique concept at the secondary level for complete career education is the Skyline Center in Dallas Independent School District (18). This facility houses a $21 million Center for Career Development and is a comprehensive high school for students living within its attendance zone as well as an extensive center for community service. The Career Development Center bases itself on the many career clusters outlined by the United States Office of Education, and if a student is interested in any area of the arts, humanities, science, or technology, he has the opportunity to explore all the careers that are related to his area of interest instead of being channeled into one narrow, specific field. Students from Grades 10 to 12 in the Dallas Independent School District are eligible to attend, but time spent at the center depends on student individual needs. He may spend part of his day in his selected field of interest, the remainder in academic studies—either at the center or back at his home school. Transportation is provided from all schools in the district to the Center on a scheduled shuttle system. In "World Languages," students have the opportunity to study advanced courses in language as well as specialized courses designed to help students who

Career development center

180

are preparing for a profession such as medicine, law, science, foreign service, engineering, or religion.

An innovative Title III grant program is being developed in the Dade County Public Schools under the direction of Elizabeth B. Alonso, Foreign Language Consultant, and Mirta Vega, Program Co-ordinator (1). The materials will embrace five vocational areas when completed: automobile services, barber/beauty work, food services, radio/TV work, and retail sales. The materials are divided into *cursillos*, which provide minimal steps of learning as in true programmed texts and also furnish opportunities for group work and constant teacher contact. The student instructs himself with a package consisting of tapes, visuals, and printed material. Teachers using the materials receive special in-service training. They are selected from both public and private schools, community adult schools, and Miami Dade Junior College. The materials can be used by any age level from Grade five to adult.

A programmed career language course

The *cursillos* are divided into an academic branch (grammatical presentations), a trunk (general vocabulary), and a vocational branch (specific career vocabulary). For example, in the Radio and TV Services Vocational Branch, packages include: *Reemplazando resistencias y bobinas* (Replacing the Resistors and Coils), *Reemplazando tubos y condensadores* (Replacing the Tubes and Condensers), *Ajustando el equipo* (Setting Up the Equipment), *Instalando la antena* (Installing the Antenna), and *Ajustando el vertical* (Adjusting the Vertical). There is a large listing of additional packages to be prepared in this field.

The Dade schools have also developed several short-term courses (quinmesters) entitled Spanish Shorthand Theory, Spanish Shorthand Speedbuilding, Spanish Shorthand-Dictation, Transcribing, Spanish Business Communications, and Spanish Office Procedures.

A successful course in Career Spanish has been prepared by Toby Tamarkin at Manchester Community College in Connecticut (44). Realizing the need for a more practical approach to language learning in the Northeast, especially at the community college level, Tamarkin completed materials for an audiovisual "Career Spanish" course. She wanted to draw from the community at large those workers whose jobs called for an understanding of Spanish as well as those students in the college enrolled in a specific program that would place them in contact with the Spanish-speaking community.

Career Spanish program in the community college

This course has three focal points: medical careers, public service careers, and business careers. There are 24 lessons in all, which consist of the following materials:

181

1 Three- to four-minute television dialogue (often filmed on location for better role simulation)
2 Overhead transparency containing the written dialogue
3 Three-page student lesson

> Page 1 presents new vocabulary.
> Page 2 is a grammatical review.
> Page 3 contains additional questions related to job procedures.

4 Audio cassette

> Part 1 is pronunciation practice with the dialogue and vocabulary list.
> Part 2 includes grammatical exercises using present, preterite, imperfect, and future tenses.
> Part 3 is an oral practice using the additional questions in the student lesson.

5 Mimeographed materials—

> welfare applications, charge account applications, hospital admissions questionnaires, etc.

As an example, the lessons in the medical section include: emergency situation 1 (possible appendicitis), emergency situation 2 (nausea and fainting), hospital admissions (personal and medical history), pregnancy, taking a blood test, taking an X-ray, occupational therapy, dental hygiene, and the visiting nurse.

This program is considered a second-year language course and, after visitation by representatives of other colleges, received full transfer credit in Connecticut. Any student or member of the community with two years of high school Spanish or a year of college Spanish may take the course, which is given in the evening to accommodate everyone. At the end of two semesters, students and workers in this program are actually well able to understand and speak Spanish within their chosen professions. They do not merely utter commands, in an effort to escape involvement, but can actively communicate and handle their entire occupational roles in the second language.

The results are directly related to the materials (which took three years to prepare), which completely immerse the student in the second language. These materials bombard all of his senses—sight, sound, and even his sense of touch as the student handles the different instruments necessary in his future or present occupation—while simulating the job procedure in the classroom.

The student begins with the televised dialogue. He recognizes the type of job and essentially what is happening because it is television. The native speakers do not slow their speech, and all extraneous noises on the job have been retained on the television tape so as to keep the situation as close as possible to what will happen. The teacher reviews the specific vocabulary with the student, acting out and gesturing to show word meaning wherever possible, prior to the initial viewing of the televised dialogue. The students know that only Spanish is spoken unless the teacher is discussing some cultural aspect or a very difficult point in the lesson. After the first viewing of the filmed dialogue, the students see the script on an overhead transparency. The teacher asks simple questions of all the students who use the dialogue as an aid. The teacher points to the answer so that the student is not at a loss for words. The students watch the dialogue on television a second time. This time they understand a great deal more and again use the dialogue transparency, although the teacher now discusses each question or bit of information in a personalized manner. For example, "Did you ever take a blood test?" "Where did you take it?" "Were you comfortable in the office?" "Did you like it?" "Does it hurt?" "Why did you need the test?"

In the next class meeting there is the preparation of a synthesis of the job procedure, which teacher and students write together (on the overhead with everyone contributing). An example follows of a student-prepared synthesis, Taking a Blood Test. This part of the lesson is always done in Spanish.

1 *Identificación: "Buenos días. Yo soy el técnico."*
2 *Explicación de por qué el paciente está aquí.*
3 *Explicación de la prueba de sangre: "No se ponga nervioso."*
4 *"¿Ha comido o bebido desde la medianoche?"*
5 *La prueba: "Suba la manga; la banda apretada, haga un puño; guarde el brazo derecho; pequeño pinchazo; no le dolerá. No se mueva."*

The synthesis is necessary to get the actual sequence of events in that particular job in focus in both the instructor's and the student's minds. The students work in groups of two or three, playing different roles until they have mastered the lesson. When they are ready, they tell the teacher and take an oral exam. Either the classroom teacher, another Spanish-speaking person (friend or colleague of the teacher), or another student in the class will play the opposite role (patient, client, customer), since the burden of getting and giving all pertinent information rests with the students being tested.

The program has been so successful in reaching the stated main goal —the student shall be fluent in his occupational situation—that these materials will be tried experimentally this year for members of the community who have never studied Spanish and will be used for an in-service course at Hartford Hospital.

Using these materials as a first approach to learning Spanish necessitates a much slower pace with each dialogue, and specific lesson arrangement (beginning with the shortest, grammatically easiest lesson and progressing to the more difficult unit). Although the beginning student cannot be expected to be fluent in the language, he should be able to master a great deal of necessary vocabulary, basic verb and pronoun use, and adequate pronunciation in Spanish.

During one semester the teacher allowed students to choose the lessons they wanted to learn. Out of necessity, no more than three different units could be studied at one time in the classroom. This enabled the teacher to work with each of the three groups on the overhead transparency during the class period. The teacher did not allow this freedom of choice until the students had worked together through the first two units and understood the methodology employed and the routine involved in learning each lesson. This technique is especially well suited to a classroom where a teacher aide or student helper is available.

This is an exciting program using all possible attention getters. The teacher is rewarded with appreciative students, happy times with a "fun" method, and real results.

Staten Island Community College has established an extensive internship program in order to provide students with a valid comple- *Internship program* ment to their academic experience, according to Marguerite Bomse (3). Students are working in government agencies, culture groups, research organizations, health organizations, and others, under the supervision of a faculty sponsor. In Spring 1973, four Spanish-speaking students participated in an independent studies program in Modern Spanish Theatre that included an actual internship for each student with the Spanish language theatre group *Nuestro Teatro* in New York City. The program combines literary analysis with actual work experience. Students study selected works by Sastre, Solórzano, and Lorca and participate in productions of Sastre's *Escuadra hacia la muerte* and Lorca's *Don Perlimplín*. Their participation involves observing rehearsals, distributing publicity materials, and working in the off-stage functions during actual performances. Staten Island Community College is also developing and teaching some functional conversation courses for *Conversation courses* hospital personnel, child care and community workers, and airline personnel.

David Pilkenton at Mesa College in Grand Junction, Colorado (33) is teaching an occupational foreign language program that includes Spanish for law enforcement officers, retail sales people, child care workers, hospital personnel, and employers of seasonal Spanish-speaking help (growers of apples, peaches, beets, and wool).

St. Norbert College in De Pere, Wisconsin has begun an International Business and Language Area Studies Program under the co-direction of David Luciano (26). The development came about through cooperation between the departments of business, economics, political science, and foreign languages. The college established an International Business and Faculty Advisory Group, composed of businessmen from local, national, and international companies in the Wisconsin area, as well as St. Norbert College faculty members with foreign backgrounds and experience.

Summary

1 When teachers become involved with the concept of career education in foreign language and begin to make the necessary changes in course offerings and content, materials to be used, and methods to be employed, the student is offered an expanded horizon. There is no longer one single predetermined path of language mastery. The pupil who never before pursued the study of a second language may realize the value of learning another skill that is closely linked to his career interests.

2 The foreign language teacher has a chance to work hand-in-hand with the other disciplines in the school toward the creation of programs that are meaningful and enable the student to expand his views as well as his skills. These "liberalizing" programs will become an integral part of a student's education, whether his career interest is in business, public service, or medicine. The newly defined career education courses, including foreign languages, may liberate the type of student who formerly left school without the firm basis in skills and concepts necessary to lead a full life.

3 The foreign language department must examine the community and assess both the needs and work placement possibilities that exist. As foreign language teachers become involved in the plans and implementation of the career education programs, they will, of necessity, work with students individually in a guidance capacity. They will also help in the placement of students in the

work experience segment of the curriculum, and they may even have some responsibility for posteducational job placement.

4 Career education offers a new dimension to foreign language instructors. Some representative examples of the efforts of a few who have seized the challenge offered have been given in this chapter. If the profession does not recognize this opportunity, build on the work already completed, and strike out in a bold new direction, a chance to make a significant contribution to the education of America's youth will have been lost.

References, Career education

1 Alonso, Elizabeth B.,ed. *Individualized Spanish for English Speakers.* Miami, Florida: Dade County Public Schools, 1972. [Mimeo.]

2 Beck, William J. Personal Communication, 1973.

3 Bomse, Marguerite. Personal Communication, 1973.

4 Brod, Richard I. "Non-Academic Vocational Opportunities in Foreign Languages." *Bulletin of the Association of Departments of Foreign Languages* 3,i(1971):53–54.

5 Browning, Meshach. *Career Awareness in Foreign Language Instruction.* Cumberland, Maryland: Fort Hill High School. [Mimeo.]

6 *Career Education.* Washington, D.C.: United States Office of Education, December 1971.

7 *Career Education:Description and Goals.* [Draft of a paper for discussion purposes only.] Washington, D.C.: Division of Vocational and Technical Education, July 1971. [Mimeo.]

8 *Career Education:A Model for Implementation.* [Revised draft of a paper for discussion purposes only.] Washington, D.C.: Division of Vocational and Technical Education, May, 1971. [Mimeo.]

9 *The Community School and Its Administration* 11,iii (1972).

10 Ford, James F. "A Foreign Language Educator Looks at Career Education." *Arkansas Foreign Language Newsletter* 7,ii(1973):1–8.

11 *Foreign Language:Key to Career Development.* Madison, Wisconsin: Department of Curriculum Development, Madison Public Schools, 1972.

12 Foresman, Farris. Personal Communication, 1973. [Letter and project descriptions.]

13 Froning, Dorothy. "Vocational Opportunities for the Foreign Language Major." *Wichita State University Foreign Language Summary* 6,ii(1971):3–6. [EDRS: ED 066 091.]

14 Hancock, Charles R. "Student Aptitude, Attitude, and Motivation," 127–55 in Dale L. Lange and Charles J. James,eds., *Foreign Language Education:A Reappraisal.* ACTFL Review of Foreign Language Education, Volume 4. Skokie, Illinois: National Textbook Company, 1972.

15 Hardesty, Richard T., compiler *Translating Foreign Language into Careers.* Bloomington: Indiana Language Program, 1964.

16 Holstein, Herbert B., Billy J. Burton, Daryle G. Elkins, and Thomas E. Woodall. "Sample Teaching Unit Level Six," 68–78 in Levene A. Olson,ed., *Awareness Education:Introduction, Instructional Resource Units, and Annotated Bibliography.* Huntington: West Virginia Department of Vocational-Technical Education. [EDRS: ED 060 510.]

17 Imhoff, Paul G. *Major in Foreign Languages and Related Areas,* 1971 [EDRS: ED 054 697.]

18 Johns, H.H.,Jr. "Career Development Becomes FL Objectives." *Accent on ACTFL* 3,i(1972): 16–17, 20.

19 Johnson, Roger,Jr. Personal Communication, 1973.

20 Keesee, Elizabeth. "Vocational Opportunities." *Hispania* 55(1972):632–43.

21 Lafayette, Robert C. "Diversification:The Key to Student-Centered Programs." *Modern Language Journal* 56(1972):349–54.

22 Larocca, Samuel J. *August Martin High School Foreign Language Program.* Jamaica, New York: August Martin High School, 1972. [Mimeo.]

23 Law, David A. Personal Communication, 1973.

24 Lipton, Gladys. "Curricula for New Goals," 187–218 in Dale L. Lange and Charles J. James eds., *Foreign Language Education:A Reappraisal.* ACTFL Review of Foreign Language Education, Volume 4. Skokie, Illinois: National Textbook Company, 1972.

25 Logan, Gerald E. Personal Communication, 1973.

26 Luciano, David. Personal Communication, 1973.

27 Marland, Sidney P.,Jr. *Career Education Now.* [Speech delivered before the convention of the National Association of Secondary School Principals, Houston, Texas, January 1971.] [EDRS: ED 048 480.]

28 ——— *Meeting Our Enemies:Career Education and the Humanities.* [Paper delivered before the Conference on English Education, National Council of Teachers of English, Minneapolis, Minnesota, November 1972.]

29 Marottoli, Vincent. "The Success of Private Language Schools:A Lesson to Be Learned." *Foreign Language Annals* 6(1973):354–58.

30 Nash, Robert J., and Russell M. Agne. "Career Education:Earning a Living or Living a Life?" *Phi Delta Kappan* 54(1973):373–78.

31 Neuhaus, Nicholas. Personal Communication, 1973.

32 Petrello, George J., and Barbara Petrello. "Help Wanted:Vocational Training for the Bilingual Job Market." *Business Education Forum* 27,iv(1973): 7–8.

33 Pilkenton, David. Personal Communication, 1973.

34 *Private Schools for Trade Instruction and Special Occupational Training.* Hartford: Bureau of Compensatory and Community Educational Services, 1973. [Mimeo.]

35 *Proceedings of the Conference on Career Education.* Princeton, New Jersey: Educational Testing Service, 1972.

36 Prol, J. *Occupational Opportunities Through Learning Foreign Languages.* Largo, Maryland: Prince George's Community College, 1973.

37 *Proposed Guidelines for a College-Level Translator Training Program.* Tucson, Arizona: Committee on Translator Training of the American Translator's Association, 1972. [Mimeo.]

38 Reinert, Harry. "Truth in Packaging . . . for Foreign Languages." *Modern Language Journal* 56(1972):205–09.

39 *Revolution in Relevance.* Los Angeles: Parthenon Films, 1972. [16 mm. sound film.]

40 Rivers, Wilga M., Louise H. Allen, Sandra Savignon, and Richard T. Scanlan,eds., *Changing Patterns in Foreign Language Programs: Report of the Illinois Conference on Foreign Languages in Junior and Community Colleges, 1972.* Rowley, Massachusetts: Newbury House, 1972.

41 Roos, D.A. Personal Communication, 1973.

42 "Russian in Your Career," 8–11 in *Why Study Russian. The AATSEEL Answers the Question.* Tucson: University of Arizona, 196. [EDRS: ED 035 344.]

43 Swan, Robert J.,ed., *NVGA Bibliography.* Washington, D.C.: American Personnel and Guidance Association, 1969.

44 Tamarkin, Toby. *Career Spanish.* Manchester, Connecticut: Manchester Community College, 1973. [Mimeo.]

45 Teitelbaum, Sidney L. *The Selling of Foreign Languages.* May 1972. [EDRS: ED 063 846.]

46 Walser, F. LeRoy. *A Preliminary Look At Potential Job Alternatives for Bilingual Students and Students of Foreign Languages:A Career Education Concept.* [Paper presented at the Association of Departments of Foreign Languages Annual Meeting at the Modern Language Association Convention, New York, December 1972.]

47 *What and How for Foreign Language Students.* Maryville Missouri: Northwest Missouri State University, Department of Foreign Languages, 1972.

7
Literary studies in a broader context

Introduction

This chapter is a review of literary works—literary works that have the potential for enriching and expanding the curriculum. This chapter is *not* a review of pedagogical methods and techniques for the teaching of literature. The reader who is interested in teaching methodology is directed to the Literature Section of the 1972 *ACTFL Bibliography on the Teaching of Foreign Languages* (Lange, 23), as well as to earlier editions of the *Bibliography*.

The content of the chapter is a response to a felt need of many of our high school and college students, who do not feel an affinity to the traditional literary content of our courses. It deals with the writing of authors who are not associated with a European "metropolis," although they write in Portuguese, Spanish, French, and English. It is concerned with the writing of authors who often share a geographical proximity to the United States and whose lives even more frequently exemplify a process of acculturation that has genuine relevance and meaning for many of our students. It is concerned with the literature that may have meaning for the emigrant from Europe or Africa who feels no closeness to the traditional content of our curricula.

This chapter deals with literature as literature. The language in which it was originally written or the languages into which it has been subsequently translated matters little. Furthermore, the organizational structure of the university, college, or high school in which it is used is inconsequential. The validity of the literature for a student remains whether he discovers it in a Department of Foreign

O. R. Dathorne
The Ohio State University

Response to a felt need

Nonmetropolis writers

Literature in any language

Irrelevance of institutional structure

O.R. Dathorne (Ph.D., University of Sheffield, England) was born in Georgetown, Guyana. In addition to his B.A., M.A., and Ph.D. degrees in English, he holds two diplomas in Education from the University of London. He has taught in universities in Nigeria and Sierra Leone as well as at Howard University and the University of Wisconsin. Currently he is Professor of Black Studies and English at The Ohio State University. Dr. Dathorne has published two novels, *Dumplings in the Soup* (1963) and *The Scholar Man* (1964). In addition, he has edited anthologies and written widely on Afro-American, Caribbean, and African literature. His new book *The Black Mind*, a study of black literature (in English, French, Portuguese, Latin, and local African languages) will be published in February 1974 by the University of Minnesota Press.

189

Languages or Literatures, a Department of Comparative Literature, or a Department of Black Studies. Indeed, our narrow conceptualizations are often perpetuated by our tendency to compartmentalize and to maintain our compartments through many generations of students.

The literature reviewed here is obviously not limited to 1972. It spans the mid-portion of the century and dates to 1972. Considerable background information and a moderate amount of explication are provided because of the generally limited familiarity of the profession with the content.

Background and explication

The organization of the chapter content is principally according to the language in which the literature was originally written. After the introductory discussion, Portuguese, English, Spanish, and French literatures are each examined.

Even the most cursory examination of the teaching of foreign literatures in the United States reveals that there is an emphasis on associating them with an European "metropolis." This tendency can easily be understood when one is dealing with Polish or German, Hindi or Chinese, or any language that is limited to one country or region. But regarding Portuguese, Spanish, and French in this way is a distortion, for these languages have an immediacy, albeit geographical, with the continental United States. In addition, one must remember that aspects of the new world process of acculturation, which has gone into these languages in this part of the world, give them definite significance for Americans. That even teachers of English Literature refuse to take either the writing of United States Blacks or Caribbean writers into consideration is particularly ludicrous. This makes for a sorry and paradoxical "parochialism."

New world acculturation

Basic skills and the metropolis

A language student first encounters the bias against nonmetropolitan language in his introductory courses. Only occasionally at the level of the acquisition of basic language skills, does one find that use is made of "dialects" other than the metropolitan ones. Thus, for instance, *Portuguêse Contemporâneo* by Maria Isabel Abreu and Cléa Rameh (1) is sometimes being used in the undergraduate curriculum. But there is an almost apologetic note by the authors: "The language used in the lessons is the dialect of Portuguese spoken in Central Brazil. But the exercises may be adapted to the dialect of any major area of Brazil or Portugal" (p. vi).

An example of use of a dialect

One is painfully aware that the statistics of sales do affect the most idealistic endeavors on the part of authors, but the fact also remains that publishers need to be convinced of the viability of the argument that students would respond more easily to what is closest to them—closest from both a geographical and cultural framework. Use of dialects can provide this closeness.

Portuguese in Africa and the curriculum

Portuguese has rather unique status as a language. The assumption is frequently made that Brazil and Portugal are the definable areas for language learning and, *ipso facto*, for literary studies. Areas of Africa are virtually ignored—Cape Verde, Guinea, Angola, Mozambique— not out of some deep-seated prejudice, but because of a lack of information on the part of educators. Likewise, the instructor and the publisher are often unaware that the literature of these latter countries can very often be close to the student's interest and his world. The literature is available, both in Portuguese in an anthology by Mário de Andrade (4) and in translation.

Portuguese-speaking areas

In my own anthology *African Poetry* (15), I made use of four African poets in translation—Aldo da Espirito Santo (São Tomé), Terêncio Casimiro Anahory Silva (Cape Verde), Antonio Jacinto (Angola) and Jorge Barbosa (Cape Verde). I believed that these writers could be utilized at the secondary and university levels (in translation or in Portuguese). The format included a brief explication at the end of the verse (where I hoped to avoid destroying the poem), some brief notes on the poem, and questions about it. The four poems provided below seem to have the potential for enriching and enlarging the curriculum. The background and explication material are intended both for information and as a model of pedagogical strategies (which can be generalized to other works).

Portuguese poetry

There in Agua Grande

A poem of Aldo da Espirito Santo

There in Agua Grande on the way to the farm
young black women use a stone for a scrubbing-board;
they beat and they sing little songs of the region.

They sing and they laugh mockingly
5 about stories that have been told, spread by the wind.

They laugh with a loud sound and the water sings.
They amuse themselves, happily, frolicking in the water . . . .
and watch the little black one in the grass.

191

The plaintive songs of the black women at the river
10 fall silent at the hour of return. . . .
   then they are quiet on their way home from the farm (p. 10).

About the poem

Poets can be moved by the most ordinary experiences: here an African poet who writes in Portuguese describes the songs that women sing at the river as they wash their clothes. The poet shows how their songs share a common oneness with the wind and water round them and how, after their work is finished, they go home quietly from their farms. The tone therefore varies; it is loud, almost boisterous, in the first three stanzas, and plaintive, silent, almost sad in the last one. One feels that the poet idealizes the women as they wash at the river, but his descriptions do not jar.

Notes

Information useful in instruction

1   *Agua Grande:* in São Tomé, an island off the west coast of Africa.
5   *spread by the wind:* the tales have gone from one person to another.
8   *the little black one:* as they wash and talk, they keep an eye on their children.

Sample Questions

1   What does the poet tell us about the hard work of the women?
2   How does she communicate their happiness to us?
3   Why do you feel that they are silent as they return to their farms?
4   An attempt is made at contrast in this poem. What is it? Does it succeed (pp. 76–77)?

About the author

Aldo da Espirito Santo (b. 1926) was born in São Tomé. She was educated locally and is now a schoolteacher. She writes in Portuguese and has published in local and overseas magazines as well as in anthologies.

A poem of Terêncio Casimiro Anahory Silva

Midnight

It is midnight in the *tabanco*
quiet and silence
walk hand in hand in the moonlight
through the badly marked lanes
5 which separate the huts from each other.
the tom-tom put there in the corner
says there is no feast-day today.
the extinguished fireplace
does not invite one to the *djumbaçao.*

10 Méssinho, high on the palisade,

keeps watch over the sleep of the village
and keeps away
bad spirits, dead souls,
wretches and thieves.

15 No stray dog
neither cattle nor human being. . . .
Midnight like many others (pp. 14–15).

Interpretation

Description forms the basis of this poem translated from Portuguese, but underlying the detailed account of midnight in the village is a note of protest. The poet is dissatisfied with the poverty of the life of the villagers; he criticizes the dullness of their lives. Finally he emphasizes the emptiness of their existence by stating that "there is no feast-day today" and that it is "midnight like many others."

Certain local words are used to give a quality of directness and realism to the piece. Also, the poet enters into the beliefs of the people and quite candidly adds that the god watches over them. In many ways the poem is full of movement—quiet and silence are said to work, the tom-tom speaks, and the god is active in his protection. This contrasts strangely with the scene of silence and tranquility midnight has brought about.

Notes

Items requiring specialized information

  1 *tabanca:* village.
  4 *badly marked lanes:* the poet criticizes the way in which the village has been laid out.
6–7 The reference to the tom-tom and the absence of a feast-day signifies the unhappiness of the villages.
  9 *djumbaçao:* palaver-tree, where people would normally meet to talk and sing.
10 *Méssinho:* a god who gives protection.

Sample Questions

  1 What does the poet tell us about midnight in the village?
  2 How does the poet sympathize with the plight of the villagers?
  3 Describe in your own words the function of Méssinho.
  4 Where does the protest in the poem lie?
  5 Which lines describe the silence and desertion of the village at midnight? Why does the poet emphasize these (15, pp. 81–82)?

About the author

Terêncio Casimiro Anahory Silva (b 1934) was born in Cape Verde Islands. He writes in Portuguese and his poetry has appeared in anthologies. He studied in Lisbon and now lives in Guinea.

Monangamba   *A poem of Antonio Jacinto*

On those large plantations there is no rain
It is my sweat that waters all the plants
On those large plantations there is ripe coffee
And its red cherries are drops of my blood turned sap.

5 Afterwards the coffee is toasted
trodden on and tortured
Turns black, black like those damned to forced labour.

Black like the colour of those damned to forced labour.

Ask the birds that sing
10 the rivulets that flow along
the strong winds of the forest:

who wakes up early, who goes the *tonga*
who carries on his long way
the stalks with the heavy load of the oil fruit
15 who tills and receives contempt for his wages?
Rotten flour, rotten fish
and bad cloth, only fifty *angolares*
and the rod of the whip when he is stubborn?
Who?
20 Who makes the corn grow
the orange grove bloom?
Who?
Who gives the master the money to purchase
cars, machines, women
25 and heads of black men for running the machines?
Who helps the white man to acquire this wealth
to get fat bellies, money?
Who?
The birds that sing
30 the meandering rivulets
the forest winds
they answer you
—Monangambéée . . .
Oh! Let me climb on my palm-trees
35 And let me drink palm-wine, palm-wine,
oblivious, disembodied in my drunkenness
—Monangambéée . . . (pp. 34–36).

194

The author of this poem, like the author of "Midnight," lives in a Portuguese-speaking part of Africa. Quite naturally these poets protest about life under a colonial system. However, in *Monangamba* the protest is more on the surface—the poet objects to the life of a slave which the farmers are compelled to lead. His tone varies from loud protest to lyricism and complaint, back to loud protest, and finally to resignation.

Part of the effect of the poem is achieved by the neat balancing of appropriate images; the rain on the plantation is compared with the sweat of the workers, the ripe coffee with drops of blood, and the toasted coffee with the color of laborers. The poet identifies himself with all this, which adds to the vivid realism of the piece. Everything in the poem is channeled toward protest. The birds, the rivers, and the winds, which follow on from the plantation imagery, are other aspects of nature that emphasize the wrong done to the black farm workers. The interrogation of nature is followed up in the last stanza by the answer—the laborers are only slaves. However, the directness of the vicious attack beginning with "who" in the central part of the poem, and concluding with the same monosyllable toward the end spoils the poem. True the word *who* is bitter and explosive, but it makes the poem too personal, too much like a pamphlet. Even though we may share the poet's sentiments, we nevertheless may not approve of his approach. It belongs more to the public platform and is only redeemed by our anticipation of the response of birds, rivers, and winds. After the jeer, the poet seeks solace in palm-wine; it is ironic that the plantation that should have given him real satisfaction in work can only provide him with an illusory despair in pleasure.

Notes

1 *large plantations:* the reference here is to the coffee plantations of Angola.

12 *tonga:* plantation, a working place on the farm.

14 *oil fruit:* probably palm oil.

15 *contempt for his wages:* the worker is despised by his Portuguese employers. The poet has a definite case, for under a decree of 1914, the Portuguese authorities introduced compulsory labor. It was not until as late as 1953 that a law made payment of labor for public purposes compulsory.

17 *angolares:* money.

32 *Monangambéée:* a contemptuous term for a slave.
   Monangamba is the Kimbundu word for the son of a slave.

195

Sample Questions

1 Show examples of comparisons which the poet uses to show us the unhappy plight of the workers.

2 Consider the stanza beginning "Ask the birds that sing . . ." How is the poet's question answered later on in the poem?

3 Is there anything that distinguishes the 6th, 7th and 8th stanzas? Or are they too much like political speeches?

4 Contrast the lot of the peasant and the Portuguese landowners, as expressed in the poem.

5 What solution does the poet advocate for himself and the workers? How serious do you think he is (pp. 112–113)?

Antonio Jacinto was born in Luanda, Angola. He writes in Portuguese and his poems describe exile and longing. They stem from an identification with his land and its people. *About the author*

Poem of the Sea *A poem of Jorge Barbosa*

O drama of the sea!
O unrest of the sea!
Ever
Ever
5 In us.

Oh sea!
That surrounds
Grasps the islands
Washes out the rocks of our islands
10 And leaves the tang of salt on the faces of our fishermen,
Roars on to the sand of the beach
And thunders its voice against our mountains.
It cradles the small ships over to those shores . . .

O sea!
15 It wears prayers on its lips,
It leaves in the eyes of those who have stayed
A futile longing for distant lands
Which come to us in coloured pictures
And in strips of cinema films,
20 In the strange looks of foreign passengers,
When they step ashore to see the poverty of our land.
O sea!
The hoped for letter from a wide distance
Which may never come after all.

25 O sea!

Memories of the sailors, the stories of times past,
Stories of the whale that once overthrew the boat. . .
Of drunkenness—of fights—of women
In foreign harbours. . .

30 O sea!
    In us
    In the song of the Morna
    In the body of brown young girls
    In the hip-swaying of black women
35 In the love of travel which remains a dream for many.

    The demand at every hour
    to go away is brought to us by the sea.
    The despairing hope for the long journey
    and yet to be always forced to stay (15, pp. 47–48).

Interpretation

Cape Verde poets are concerned with longing for release from the arid earth, for the liberating journey over the sea, and with frustration because of the compulsion to stay. This is stated in unequivocal terms at the end of this poem, but the imagery in the poem leads up to this conclusion.

From the first stanza it is apparent that the poet is not so much concerned with describing the sea as in seeing the people of his island in terms of the sea. The sea is linked with their past, he says. Then in the second stanza, the violent images suggest the repressed violence that is in the people themselves. This stanza contrasts with the next, which emphasizes timidity. Lines follow in which the poet simply writes down what the sea evokes in him. Then he returns to the personal element, and the poem concludes on the couplet that clinches what for the poet is the meaning of the sea.

There is a sadness about the whole poem. This is partly achieved by the invocation to the sea and by certain references like the way in which the sea "cradles the small ships over to those shores" and how "it wears prayers on its lips." In addition to the lyricism there is a harshness about some of the lines, especially in the fifth stanza. The harshness is also present in the factual way in which the poet refers to postcards and the cinema. All these elements contribute to the poet's assessment of the personality of the people who form the subject of his poem. They are partly dreamers, but they also have to face up to the harsh realities of life.

On the whole, you will probably agree that this is a successful poem. Not only does it sing, even in translation, but it builds up the agony of life in evocative flashes. We feel part of the poet's world through the use of the sea image, and we can share his nostalgia for the unattainable. The note of protest against Portuguese colonialism is there, but it never obtrudes. One might, however, object to the over-romanticizing of black women in the sixth stanza.

Notes

13 *It cradles . . . those shores:* in spite of the violence of the sea, it still allows the tiny fishing vessels to go to other nearby islands. *Items requiring specialized knowledge*

15 *prayers on its lips:* the sea does not willfully destroy.

16 *those who have stayed:* many people try to leave Cape Verde to find work in the nearby islands. Some even go as far as America.

32 *Morna:* a melancholy folk-song of Cape Verde, usually sung in Portuguese Creolese.

Sample Questions

1 Are we told anything in this poem about life on the island?

2 Describe in your own words the frustrations which the poet mentions.

3 Contrast the notes of violence and lyricism that are present in the poem and account for their use.

4 What two qualities does the sea symbolize for the poet?

5 Explain "drama of the sea" with close reference to the poem.

6 Do you feel that the poet expresses a yearning for travel? How is this done (pp. 131–132)?

Jorge Barbosa was born in Cape Verde Islands. His poetry was published in an anthology of African verse in Portuguese in 1954 as well as in two separate volumes. He writes in Portuguese, and his poetry frequently describes the frustrations of life in Cape Verde. *About the author*

The anthology (15) that includes these four poems was intended for use by African students in former British territories or, in other words, for students whose one European language was English. The poets included could be profitably used in American institutions, because their cultural framework is one with which the American student— black and white—could identify. The writers in Portuguese speak frequently of ghettoism and poverty, or racism and its evils. They, like us, hope for a better society.

American culture and instant solutions

One must ask what can be achieved by the use of these new types of literature? And, more importantly, why include them in the *Why the new types of literature?*

curriculum? To answer these questions one must backtrack a little.

The sour 1960s saw the front doors of the universities blown wide open. There was much idealistic talk of "minority" education and the neglect of Blacks, Chicanos, and Indians in the academic pattern. Hastily—with a great deal of liberal goodwill but with a mere flavor of either good sense or sound planning for future development—programs, divisions, centers, institutes, and in a few cases, departments were set up. They were going to "take care of" what was now seen to be wrong with the American system. A Black Studies Program—varying from a "paper-program" where the only visible sign of "Black Studies" was a tiny office in a run-down building to the "complete works" (a full department with the rights and privileges of any other university department)—was supposed to right the wrongs of a century of miseducation.

Liberal goodwill

This pattern is mentioned in the context of what we are discussing in order to illustrate a salient feature of American life—the fetish of instant solutions to urgent problems. These departments, divisions, centers, were supposed to deal *in toto* with what had come to be called "the black experience." However, the "black experience" is not a U.S. monopoly; problems equally real and significant affect vast areas of the "black world"—the complex mass we dismiss as "Africa," the polka-dot culture that makes up the Caribbean and South America. Obviously no one department can handle all of this; in fact few pretended to. But the nationwide overconcern with academic caveats provided a feeling that anything "black" had to be handled only by an Afro-American Studies Department or an African Studies Department. Hence the neglect. Where does Angolan Portuguese, Haitian or Martinique French, St. Martaen Dutch, or Cuban Spanish fit into such a program? These areas were not included. Their omission was probably also due to our lack of knowledge about them, to our inability to relate the relevance of their experiences to the United States as well as to the political excommunication of some countries. It does not take close reading to see that the experience of Portuguese poetry is relevant for our world and our time because it speaks of some of our social evils. This is the main reason for seeking to make use of new materials. Within literary output in contemporary America complaint (in the manner of black spirituals) and protest (in the manner of latter-day black American poetry) are analogous to the poetry just considered. One could add that both types of black American poetry speak out against oppressive conditions, as does Portuguese verse.

The fetish for instant solutions

Omission of language areas

Relevance through treating social evils of today

The young people who do not feel a part of the mainstream are faced

199

with a dilemma we have bequeathed them. What should the manifestation of American culture be? Should it take the path of retracing the immigrant's journey to Europe or the slave's passage to Africa? Those who have come to these lands are basically a people without a culture and hence without a language or literature. We came here with scant clothing, and the vestments of our culture were discarded in the search for the "American dream." But the gods the land offered were either destroyed or outright rejected; hence the dilemma. There can be no return. We are centuries removed from the ancestry of the cultures of our skins. The journey, even in physical terms, back to Europe or Africa can be painful for the person of American extraction—painful because there are no citadels of home, no families of kin, no true society of likes, into which black or white may confidently enter. The reason? There has been no real initiation into the mores of the parent society. The Swahili or German language drills have become mere mechanical exercises in our doggedness as Americans and are as distinctive as "Afros" and "Bermuda shorts" to those whom we seek to know and identify with but whose way of life we can never wholly share. Only through the study of their literature can we become initiated to the mores of the parent society and thus ultimately know ourselves.

A people without a culture

No familiarity with the parent society

Literature: an answer

The Caribbean and the English language curriculum

This predicament of the cultural marginality of the American in the United States is shared by people of all complexions throughout the Americas. This is perhaps the most important reason we ought to become familiar with the wisdom of other people because they tell us about ourselves—living as we do in a pluralistic society. Therefore, if one is to think in strict geographical terms of the limitations of the present curriculum in literature, the realization comes that even in English (either as a first language or as a second language) we are sorely deficient. With the exception of the program at Boston University, there is little attempt being made to reach out, for example, to the literature of the English-speaking islands of the West Indies. Belatedly, the University of Texas has had two West Indian authors as writers in residence for short periods, but they were not engaged in teaching either the craft of writing or Caribbean literature. They were required to teach standard English courses. Courses on Caribbean Literature in English could admirably fit into Departments of English, Comparative Literature, or Literatures, but again one reflects on the academic phobia for compartmentalizing: "Such studies belong in an

Institute of Caribbean Studies." (Indeed there is one in Puerto Rico!)

The Caribbean recommends itself from a language viewpoint as well as from geographical and cultural affinities. Signs of a beginning are evident, for Derek Walcott's play *Dream on Monkey Mountain* was produced on Broadway in 1973, and *Ti Jean and His Brothers* was aired on the television program "Black Journal" in 1972. Recently Andrew Salkey has brought out his anthology *Breaklight* (41), and George Lamming has published his last two novels in this century—*Natives of My Person* (21) and *Water with Berries* (22). This is only the tip of the iceberg, and even though a case may be made for author Paule Marshall, she is "home grown" like Shirley Chisholm. Several Caribbean novelists who write in English and are mature and worthy of consideration: Jan Carew, Wilson Harris, and Edgar Mittelholzer (Guyana); John Hearne, Roger Mais, Orlando Patterson, V. S. Reid, and Andrew Salkey (Jamaica); Austin Clarke and George Lamming (Barbados); and Michael Anthony, V. S. Naipaul, and Samuel Selvon (Trinidad). Here I discuss only one—the Jamaican Claude McKay. He more than any other seems to have understood the nature of the "New World experience."

Caribbean literature

Novelists a teacher might consider

Claude McKay appears at an interesting stage in the history of the Caribbean novel. He rose from a very lowly position, and though he came to America, he never entirely forgot his humble origin. If America made Marcus Garvey into a nationalist, it made McKay into a man strongly conscious of his racial origins.

An example: novelist Claude McKay

The lives that McKay's heroes live are a protest against the society in which they find themselves; in all of his novels an attempt is made to contrast the life of the black who lives closest to his own instincts and the one who prefers to ape the ways of the Europeans. No doubt McKay had his own ambiguous position in mind when he painted some of these portraits; in his biography *A Long Way from Home* (31), he had referred to himself as "a truant by nature and undomesticated in the blood" (p. 150). His own life had borne testimony to this, and the lives of his chief characters in the novels demonstrated the triumph of the blood over the intellect. His early work was poetry, written in Jamaica, and it lacks this assertiveness.

In his first novel *Home to Harlem* (30), the chief character, Jake, is returning to Harlem after the World War I. The contrast is already there; he has been subjected to many years of a discipline he did not like in pursuit of a goal that had little to do with him. When he returns to Harlem he picks up a "tantalizing brown," but she leaves him during the night and returns the $50 he had given him. The *raison*

Home to Harlem

d'être for the rest of the novel is therefore not at all artificial: Jake sets out to look for her. It gives McKay an opportunity to describe Harlem lowlife, as Jake seeks her from cabaret to gambling den, from the docks to the dining rooms of trains. It gives the author a chance to display something of Jake's animal exuberance and his gluttonous love of life. As McKay put it, "Jake took what he wanted of whatever he fancied" (p. 269). But the girl represents some absolute kind of sensuality to which he aspires.

In *Banjo* (29) Ray, the black idealist, appears with Banjo, a character like Jake. At the end of *Home to Harlem* Ray leaves for Europe, in search of the very civilization he had castigated as decadent. At least Jake's final actions are more in character; he finds his girl Felice, the consummation of his love for life.

Banjo

By the time McKay had written *Banana Bottom* (28) he had perfected his art; he was still constructing a conflict of opposites, but he was going to deal on a smaller canvas, with fewer characters, to make the predicament more pronounced. For this novel, McKay chose a woman as his chief character; at age twelve Bita Plant is seduced by an idiot and is consequently adopted by a missionary couple who bring her up and send her to an English university. She comes back, much to their astonishment, something of a rebel, as she says, "I never wanted to be anything but myself. I take pride in being coloured and different" (p. 169). She is, in a way, the female equivalent of Jake and Banjo, but she is much more subtle and sophisticated; she has known European values and has rejected them for intellectual reasons. The position is now set for her to go in search of the sensual values that McKay equates with the Black race.

Banana Bottom

Banana Bottom contrasts strongly with the screaming overenergetic prose of the previous novels. It was perhaps McKay's most studied and solemn statement and was in many ways a fitting swansong to his novel-writing. McKay fits neatly into the pattern of novelists whose contemporary relevance cannot be disputed.

Claude McKay is only one example of the possibilities for extending our teaching of literature. His books are available, and he should offer exciting and inciteful comparisons with writers of many nationalities and languages. Other Caribbean writers also offer a good opportunity to come to terms with the inquiry and resolution that is a part of a valid American experience. As colonial men they share the ghetto experience and speak and write about a past of servile imitation and the present desire to throw off the shackles of a dead gaoler. The Barbadian poet, L. E. Braithwaite (11), states it well:

The colonial and ghetto experiences

202

       To hell
       with Af-
       rica
       to hell
       with Eu-
       rope too. . . (p. 10).
The beginnings of the sensibility of New World man.

Africa and the English curriculum

African writers in English have fared badly, although their relevance
is very striking when one considers who they are and what they have
said. Chinua Achebe, Cyprian Ekwensi, and Amos Tutuola (Nigeria); *Significant African writers*
Ama Ata Aidoo and Ayi Kwei Armah (Ghana); James Ngugi (Kenya);
Okot p'Bitek (Uganda); and Peter Abrahams and Alex la Guma (South
Africa) are names that are uttered only within the sacred confines of an
African Literature course. For a moment let us consider how some of
these writers establish a relevance that is crucial for the American
reader. Some of them are available through Collier-Macmillan
Publishing Co., others through Humanities Press which distributes for
Heinemann Educational Books.

Even as far back as the eighteenth century, one writer, Ouladah
Equiano, is noteworthy. His book (16) is an adventure story that
relates his capture in West Africa, various incidents on the Middle
Passage, and his brief visits to parts of the New World, including
America.

Closer to our time is Ama Ata Aidoo. Her excellent play *The Dilemma
of a Ghost* (3) makes for good and spirited classroom discussion concerning where the home of the black man is. In her plot, Eulalie, an
Afro-American, marries Ato, a Ghanaian, and returns home with him.
Her first romantic illusions of Africa are soon proven wrong, and in
fact she comes up against the hostility of the village women, for they
dismiss her as someone who needs machines to wash her clothes and
cook her food. They chide her that she cannot have a machine for
making babies. The truth is that the young couple does not want to
have children and is practicing birth control. There are some ugly
scenes when Eulalie is forced to come to terms with the reality of Africa.
In the end she proves to them that she can be accepted, and they prove
to her that they are indeed members of the same family.

Very different in resolution is J. P. Clark's *America, Their America* (13),
different because Clark is writing a first person account of prejudices

and difficulties that a young, sensitive Nigerian encounters when he accepts a fellowship at Princeton. Both *The Dilemma of a Ghost* and *America, Their America* have the advantage of being books that look at the American from outside and attempting to compare, for better or worse, various aspects of the parent culture in Africa and the offspring culture in the United States. *An outside view of the American*

A useful way of introducing African Literature in English at any level is to make use of *An African Treasury* (Hughes, 19). It has the advantage of being inexpensive and available. Langston Hughes, the editor, makes use of material that has parallels in this country. The dominant themes of the prose and poetry selections are the condition of servitude, the search for freedom, and the new renaissance. Although this framework has necessarily imposed a slant upon the literature, many eminent writers from various parts of the continent are represented in this anthology. Ezekiel Mphahlele has become known in this country, for he teaches and writes here.

Wole Soyinka's *The Interpreters* (44) (where the Afro-American Joe Golders appears), and Enriko Seruma's *The Experience* (42) (about an East African's confrontation with racial prejudice in this country), and some of Senghor's poetry about the American scene, all lend themselves to critical examination in classes devoted to literature. These courses can be housed in English, International Studies, Afro-American Studies, Black Studies, Ethnic Studies, or Comparative Studies; if education means extending the concepts of ourselves to take in others and if it is to be relevant, contemporary, and honest, the literature curriculum must include works by black Americans, Caribbeans, and Africans. *Irrelevance of departmental structure*

Spanish and the curriculum

Much of what has already been said about the geographical and cultural relevance of Portuguese applies equally to Spanish, but in the case of Spanish the omissions are even clearer. Apart from Cuba, now often drawn on maps with a bare outline which, therefore, has ceased to exist, the whole of Central and South America remains. Even more important, Puerto Rico is as politically within the United States as the West Coast. To have no Spanish in Nevada, New Mexico, Texas, and Southern California is to be without a *lingua franca*. However, the Spanish literature we do learn is nearly always "peninsular." By this single arbitrary choice, we take sides with the Conquistadores and omit what is more relevant to us—the Zambo and the Mesticho. How many *Prejudice implied in choice of literature*

TABLE 1

College/University	Source	Courses in Spanish Culture and/or Literature of the Americas at Undergraduate Level	Courses in Spanish (Total)
Federal City College	*Guide to Degree Program* (1971)	6	40
Michigan State University	*Catalog* (1970)	8	60
University of Michigan	*Bulletin* (1972–1973)	8	46
University of Nevada, Las Vegas	*Bulletin* (1972–1973)	11	47
University of Wisconsin	*Bulletin* (1970–1972)	4	48

of us know the language of Northern Venezuela? How many textbooks exist that help us acquire the speech of Central Mexico? The infatuation with Europe certainly reflects itself in the teaching of Spanish literature, as indicated in Table 1. The proportion of courses dealing with literature from the Americas is indeed small, although attempts have been made to make the "language" content less biased. This table shows that less than 20 percent of all the courses in Spanish (except at the University of Nevada) deal with the Americas. These are only five institutions, but they were chosen because they are representative of many more significant institutions. In addition, one is predominantly black, and another is situated in a Spanish-oriented area of the United States. Closer scrutiny of the courses that do exist in Spanish-American literature indicates that in many cases they are infrequently taught; they are devised for post-sophomore students, and they are frequently limited to a single academic term. In other words, a student can major in Spanish (or Portuguese or French) without *A biased major* ever learning about the literature of the peoples who are our neighbors.

A great deal of the experience of these writers can be understood easily by our students. On the level of rhythm, these writers, using the so-called Afro-Hispanic theme, bring a new sound into Spanish and even into English translation. Consider, for example, Emilio Ballagas (5), the white poet from Cuba, in "The Masquerade with the Lantern."

> The masquerade with the lantern
> —bamba uenibamba bó—
> is passing with beating of drums
> and the devils in my blood
> awaken in rum and light. . . (p. 8).

Or Marcelino Arozarena's "We Rehearse the Snake Dance" (6).

> Show us the dance of the snake!

205

Sharpen your beak:
"Alaalá-a-lá
alaalá-a-laaa . . ."
Sing without a break (p. 8).

Both poems have a dexterity of movement that is distinctly American, and since these rhythms are very much a part of the musical heritage of our own young people, it is not difficult for us to see excellent ways in which we might "sell" these pieces. As Valdez-Cruz (45) has commented, "The dance-theme is the most characteristic and popular of Black poetry of the Americas [and is] a vital function among the descendants of African races" (p. 41). Even in these few lines one notes how the use of onomatopoeic neologisms helps to bring about this dance effect.

In addition, other extremely pertinent reasons recommend the use of New World Spanish literature in the curriculum. The black in Spanish America (Mexico, Costa Rica, Venezuela, Columbia, Peru, Ecuador, etc.) is not only the creator of the literature, but owing to his presence as myth and reality, there is an exhaustive literature of the black theme in the nineteenth century literature of the Americas. A discovery of ethnic awareness, which parallels that in the United States, began in the 1920s. The Cuban studies of Fernando Oritz revealed the importance of the black contribution. The fashionable European taste for "blackness" helped the writers to be noticed so that they might well have become dilletantes. Several however, took their roles seriously, and some of these are commented on briefly.

Luis Palés Matos was born in the island of Puerto Rico in 1898. As early as 1915 he had published *Azaleas*, but not until 1937 was the theme of third world consciousness—the black man—to become uppermost. The allusions are delicately fused with rare poetic feelings. In "Mulata-antilla" there is the stated reason for our interest: *Luis Palés Matos*

En ti ahora, mulata,
me acojo al tibio mar de las Antillas.
Agua sensual y lenta de melaza. . . (Palés Matos, 34, p. 10):
(In you, mulatta woman, I shelter in the warm
seas of the Antilles. Sensual and languorous
molasses water. . . .)

Luis Palés Matos would argue that the hybrid result of the ethnic melting pot of the neo-Spanish world was significant since it was the microcosmic possibility for the whole world. A teacher does not have to be an ardent advocate of interracial socializing to understand that in the United States alone, cultural cross-breeding is a clear, precise, and indisputable reality. To teach about the snake-dance and the masquerade is to reintroduce American students to their own neglected past.

In the work of Alejo Carpentier and Nicolás Guillén, both available in translation in this country, there is much that is concerned with this reaching back toward a cultural past and questioning of present assumptions. These writers attempt to put up a magnificent defense of a way of life under assault in that they recognize no compromise with a world where real values seemingly matter no longer. In ¡Ecue-yamba-ó! Carpentier (12) used the black man as a starting point for investigating the whole phenomenon of New World beings. If in the Spanish literature of the nineteenth century one finds the use of stereotypes to hide the reality of noble savage, peasant, and worker, certainly with Carpentier and Guillén there is a restoration of historic dignity.

Alejo Carpentier and Nicolás Guillén

A great deal of Guillén's work has been published in a bilingual edition. His poems show a celebration of love for his country and for its lifestyle. Contrasting pieces reflect real-life experiences in various parts of the world. He is concerned with the imposition of segregation and its effects on victim and agent. This part of a long poem speaks to us about a mixed cultural heritage we call "America":

> *Viajé en ferrocarril.*
> [*Vuelvo a hablar de la URSS.*]
> *Y nunca vi*
> Para blancos. Para negros.
> *Ni en el bus.*
> *ni en el café. . .* (18, p. 22).

> (I went by train
> [speaking again of the USSR]
> and never saw
> *White Only. Colored Only.*
> Nor on the bus
> or in a cafe. . .) (Guillén, 18, p. 23).

One identifies with Guillén on the level of his concern with the peasant, the idealization of the black woman, the ironic asides of the middle class, the concern with blackness and the dualism of cultures, as well as his concern with this country and events that occurred here. All of us—black, white, yellow, red—know of the sacrifice, voluntary or not, that we have had to make on the altar of cosmopolitanism. If this is indeed part of the American dream, it cannot be included "*en acquel mundo faubus.*" We have to recognize the duality of the inheritance

Identification with Guillén's work

207

and come to terms with it. "*Balada de los abuelos*" (Ballad of the Two Grandfathers) is a moving poem in this vein:

> *me escoltan mis dos abuelos*
> *Don Federico me grita*
> *y Taita Facundo calla;*
> *los dos en la noche sueñan*
> *y andan, andan.*
> *Yo los junto* (Guillén, 18, p. 68)

> (I'm watched by my two grandfathers.
> Don Federico yells at me
> and Taita Facundo is silent;
> both dreaming in the night
> and walking, walking,
> I bring them together) (Guillén, 18, p. 69).

In this poem too the dance theme is present, and the possibilities of being able to dramatize this for use in the classroom are apparent. It would be worth pointing out to students that the two grandfathers are aspects of contrasting cultures. The New World man is locked in a vice between them, and as he attempts to bring the parts closer to him, to make the dualism one, he brings about self-destruction. This is the nature of the ambiguity to which our experiences here have committed us.

Classroom dramatization

Although work in Spanish by Africans is sparse and difficult to come by, the instructor in Spanish is fortunate in being able to obtain materials that are culturally relevant and geographically near. The instances are numerous. In Puerto Rico, Luis Rachani Agrait has written *Tres piraques para un día de calor* (*Three Ice Balls for a Hot Day*) (2), three different plays with a central theme—the quest for Puerto Rican identity. In Venezuela Rómulo Gallegos uses African songs and dances in his *Pobre negro* (17), and in Ecuador Adalberto Ortiz's novel *Juyungo* (33) has its setting in the river country between Ecuador and Columbia and is about a black man's quest for home. Use of these materials will make the student who comes to Spanish out of curiosity or because he wishes to major in the language, benefit much more. Hopefully, this type of thinking will be able to penetrate to the high schools.

Accessability of literature in Spanish

Available relevant material

French and the curriculum

Focus in this section is on writers in French who are normally excluded from the French syllabus. Again the reasons are more or less the same: the obsession with the metropolis. But it becomes increasingly difficult to understand why the French of Louisiana is virtually unread and definitely untaught, why there is little concern with the experience of writers from the French-speaking Caribbean and from Guyana. Here again one finds that these writers are culturally one with us in that they share our problems and our potentialities for a solution. They expose us to a much wider area—all of French-writing Africa—again virtually ignored except in very special instances. The comments that follow are merely ways of suggesting writers who might be used in extending the boundaries of French. Any such course might include the large amount of writing by Frenchmen relating to the new world and Africa. In particular in this context, Henri Grégoire, Blaise Cendrars and André Gide must be mentioned. But if we seek to focus on the contributions of the Black writers in French, there is a well-deserved place for René Maran, and later when considering the *négritude* writers, for Aimé Césaire, Léon Damas, and Léopold Senghor, as well as the numerous authors who have been recently published.

The French of Louisiana

French-writing Africa

Maran published poetry first in 1909 and 1912. Later he collaborated in founding *Revue du monde noir*, which had six issues, and *Présence Africaine*. During the 1930s he was in Paris and was helpful in bringing about the meetings of blacks from the United States, the Caribbean, and Africa.

René Moran

An *evolué*, Maran was suspect by whites (whose standards he criticized) and by blacks (because of his association with the French Colonial Service). But he did join with the African writers of the *négritude* period, and much of his novel writing reflects his interest in Africa and in the predicament of the "divided" man.

Batouala (24), Maran's first novel, describes the indigenous society. Batouala, the chief, has eight wives and he looks forward to a circumcision ceremony to be held shortly. The ceremony becomes an excess of sex and alcohol, and soon Batouala's own father collapses, a victim of his excesses. Maran suggests that the intrusion of whites had caused the change in the weaning of the rituals of this society.

The novel describes the breakup and abuse of tribal life; Batouala's father and Batouala himself die because they are equally to blame. The novel's importance is not so much in its qualities but in that the preface acted as a catharsis.

Djouma, chien de la brousse (Maran, 25) is a second novel. The harshness of colonialism is the theme, and one incident clearly indicates the provocative nature of the book. Batouala does not turn in enough rubber and is warned by the commandant that unless he does, his wives will be sold and his property taken away. Batouala feels that this is unjust and soon finds himself in prison.

Maran has not yet written his best novel, but he is setting a precedent—the open criticism of the *evolué* of French values, the honest denunciation of French colonial policy. In his subsequent novels one finds more and more that artless criticism is giving way to a utilization of African folklore. Animals and the natural world become more significant.

Le Livre de brousse (Maran, 26) adapts the creatures of African folktale and gives them symbolic importance. *Un Homme pareil aux autres* (Maran, 27) is different and deals with interracial love. The setting is not Africa but Bordeaux. Jean Veneuse, like Maran, has had to live through long periods of loneliness in a boarding-school in France and being black, has taken to conversing with the ancestors (in this case French writers) as any African might do. When he fails in love with Andrée Marielle, a white woman, he cannot accept the consequences of what this means—a complete repudiation of his blackness. His position is made somewhat worse by the fact that he is a colonial administrator. When he does go back to France he is unable to speak to the woman he has loved for months.

The *négritude* movement, to which allusion has been made, is well known and will not be documented here. Two anthologies, easily available, are specially recommended: Marie Collins' *Black Poets in French* (14) and Norman Shapiro's *Négritude: Black Poetry* (43). For the instructor who wishes to go beyond anthologies, the following writers are especially recommended: Seydou Badian, Francis Bebey, Mongo Beti, Olympe Bēhly-Quenum, Nazi Boni, Bernard Dadié, Birago Diop, David Diop, Jean Ikellé-Matiba, Cheikh Hamidou Kane, Camara Laye, Aké Loba, Jean Malonga, Yambo Ouloguem, Sembène Ousmane, Jean-Joseph Rabéarivelo, J. B. Seid, and Félix Tchicaya U'Tamsi. Most of their work is published by Présence Afrìcaine in Paris, although local publishing is increasing in Cameroon and Upper Volta. Some of these writers have been translated into English and are easily available here. Four of them—Beti, Kane, Niane and Rabéarivelo—are examined here.

Négritude movement

Recommended authors

Beti's first prose attempt was "Ville Cruelle," which was published in *Trois ecrivains noirs* (7). It deals with a theme Beti was to explore later on in his work: the crisis of growth. Banda's education was brief; he had spent his time picking potatoes and not being educated. *Le Pauvre Christ de Bomba* (8) is better; purporting to be the journal of Denis, a 15-year-old altar boy, it describes the shortcomings of the missionary en-

Mongo Beti

deavors in Africa. This book makes use of a gentle irony. Because Denis seems to be the complete innocent, all that happens is very funny. Denis, like Banda, matures. A better study of growth is *Mission terminée* (9), centering on Medza, the failed scholar who returns to his village. The fact that at the end he can face up to his father and admit his failure as a scholar and the fact of his marriage are proof that the "village learning" had helped mature him. The book is beautifully written, and in parts the author evokes the lost world of innocence in charming, poetic terms. Comedy and serious purpose blend beautifully to display the viewpoint of the individual who rebels against his society.

Beti's latest novel is *Le Roi miraculé* (10). Again he returned to the missionaries for the theme. Here Father Le Guen tries to bring about the conversion of the Chief of Essazam. The chief resists, but when he falls ill, Yosifa liberally pours water over him, in her effort at baptism. On the whole, Beti's work is most successful. The novels make for enjoyable reading, yet the "punch line" is there—the maturity of the boy, the group, the people; the hypocrisy of colonial administrators and the sorry lot of missionaries who seek to do good. In all the novels Beti suggests that the Africa of the past is the one that survives since its values are more real than those of church and school.

Kane's work *L'Aventure ambiguë* (20) is a novel of ideas and differs in this way from Beti's. The dialogue is artificially structured between the traditionalists—those who advocate that the spiritual oneness in African Islam is the only way of life—and those who opt for the alternative in which the Western world with its emphasis on the superficial (the body and the material) is the only viable alternative. Between these two extremes, Samba Diallo, the chief character, falls victim.

Cheikh Hamidou Kane

Built into the apparent wholeness of Samba Diallo's world, with its sunsets that link him securely to the sky, are evidences of disintegration. Dialogues between Le Chevalier (Samba Diallo's father) and M. Lacroix (a Frenchman), between Samba and his father, between Samba and the young Jean Lacroix expose some of the predicaments. Materialism and spiritualism cannot fuse, and Jean stands amazed as he watches Samba Diallo in prayer.

The plan of this exquisitely contrived novel lies in the debate, which takes place at various points; and this is carried on from Africa (with the stern setting of desert) to Europe. In Europe Lucienne and Adèle complete the dialogue. The result is to make a "marginal man" of Samba Diallo, a man who cannot pray, who cannot accept the faith of his fathers, one who must therefore die. Le Fou (as he is ironically termed) had been exposed to Europe but had returned firm in his convictions. He had hoped that Samba would take the place of Le Maître. Le Fou dresses in clean Moslem clothing topped by dirty Western gear; he is the outer enigma of what Samba Diallo is within. He went mad; Samba Diallo died. Instead, Demba, with whom Samba had fought as a schoolboy, will inherit the master's place and affect the final compromise.

If we sometimes feel that our society lacks heroes, Niane's *Soundjata* (32) is an excellent palliative. With the help of nearby groups Soundjata beats the wicked king Soumaoro Kante of Sosso and begins to establish Islam in the Kingdom of Mali. Soundjata obtains the loyalty of the 12 proud Savannah kings by giving them back some of their power. Through the mouth of a griot the tale of ancient Mali is told: how Soundjata is born, the son of a "buffalo woman" and a king. Soundjata returns in triumph to Niane and begins to establish a reign of peace. The griot tale ends here; it is an affirmation of the presence of legend. The style has made use of praise-phrases, of the apparently fantastic, and of myth-making. (The date is 1230.) Not much is said in this account about what little is known of the "historical" Soundjata and how he transformed the small kingdom of Kangaba into the great Mali Empire and of how after killing Sumanguru he was able to annex the Sosso Empire as well. Niane's purpose is different; it is to construct an elaborate praise-song to Soundjata. In this way it succeeds. *Djibril Tamsir Niane*

In contrast, the work of Rabéarivelo has little that is noble in it. The poet's life was grim; he came from a poor family, was a drug addict, and committed suicide in 1937 by drinking poison. Though only 36 years old, he had published nine volumes of poetry. But this writing is very contemporary and will appeal to students at all levels. *Jean-Joseph Rabéarivelo*

Rabéarivelo's work showed his interest in traditional Malagasy lore. For instance, *Vieilles chansons des pays d'Imerina* (40) are praise-poems in French based on traditional Malagasy love poetry. But his earliest volume, *La Coupe de cendres* (35) is very imitative of French poetry from France. Only with *Presque-songes* (36) and *Traduit de la nuit* (39) he established his claim as an African poet.

The poetry is depersonalized, blending cosmic and terrestrial imagery. The poems are concerned with transitions of being; very often one finds the imaginative unity of sky and earth fused in one poem—the unification of opposites. People are almost totally absent in Rabéarivelo's poetry. Life is suffering and evolves to little purpose; death is omnipresent. When people are mentioned, they seem to represent something elemental: "rude sailor" or "a blind glassmaker."

Rabéarivelo dismantles the world we know and then brings about a cosmic reordering. The cosmos, paradoxically, is then "humanized," the moon, in one image, is a "cake on which a rat knaws;" in another he alludes to a "bird without color and name." Use of seen images helps to sustain the visual quality of the poetry.

Frustration, despair, catastrophe, death are the themes of the poems. The poems are essentially "moods," and the paradoxical imagery conveys the confusion of the moment—"rootless trees," "dumb birds," "fingerless hands," "unknown birds," and so on. Violent images such as "dawn marauding in the orchards of the night" and one in which the "sun capsizes" are used to emphasize, along with repetitive devices, the horrible nature of the mood of despair, hopelessness, and failure.

Often Rabéarivelo can take his art and its inspiration from the natural world. In *Volumes* (38) the poem "Désert" demonstrates this:

> Complete and warming joy of the desert!
> Nowhere is the sky as blue
> than on these hills of sand and fire. . . (p. 41).

This is not merely nature description but again the balance of opposites, not operating through paradoxical imagery this time but culminating in paradox. Only the *empty* desert is *full* of art—the art of poetry.

Presque-songes (36) continues the observation of the natural world but with the type of opposing emphases pointed out before. A poem called "Cactus" is no mere eulogizing verse but one that seeks out the apparent lack of beauty and finds it in "hands without fingers" in "lepers bearing flowers." As a result:

> *le sang de la terre, la sueur de la pierre*
> *et le sperme du vent*
> *qui coulent ensemble dans ces paumes*. . . (p. 12).
> (the blood of the earth, the sweat of stone
> and the sperm of wind
> which flow together in these palms. . . .)

In the original French the *s* sounds convey a feeling of silence. What *Presque-songes* show above everything is that there is little self-centered observation (as in "Désert"). Instead the poet enters into the world he describes and the sexual imagery enhances the point he wishes to make —rebirth.

In *Sylves* (37) the romantic agony is still apparent, the sadness in life, constant references to death; but always associated with the poet. In *Presque-songes* (36) poems such as "Naissance du jour" and "Autre

213

naissance du jour" relate natural phenomena without the use of any intermediary. The private agonies of the poet are subjected to the larger cosmic miracle of dawn. So in one poem he says of dawn:

> The trapped ones one by one escape
> the birds which she caught in her net. . . (p. 12).

In another poem, again of dawn:

> in their coops pierced by the stars
> and the other spears of darkness
> the cockrels crow to each other. . . (p. 17).

And again "lovingly [dawn] cuts the prism [of darkness]" in a third poem. Dawn releases birds and all living things. The new days break violently; "*transpercées par les étoiles*" (pierced by the stars) is a violent and successful image to relate dawn as is: "*taille amoureusement le prisme*" (lovingly she cuts the prism). The poet is left out.

As Rabéarivelo continued to write, he moved away from slavish imitation of French writers. In his first volume he could put down with a straight face such trite expressions as "my tomb is always my tomb" or express the usual romantic love. Even in "Filao," in *Volumes* (38) he can address the "brother of [his] sadness" and as late as 1931 he published "Mourir de ne pas vivre" (certainly "un-African" in its concepts) where he shows his earlier obsession with death. By 1935 when *Traduit de la nuit* (39) was published, the images were more vigorous and the presence of death, more fearful, less "literary," and used to show the inhumanity of mankind. The second poem, for instance, uses symbols of a rat that leaves "the marks of bloody teeth," drunk card players, and a lost coin to state dejection, expressing in a few words the total lack of concern. Man is "shining and silent . . . where dumb birds live." Here in *Traduit* is the country without name, the confused landscape that has been intentionally distorted of "a bird without color and without name," of cockrels who "sing in dreams/and are fed by the stars," of the mythical spider of African lore which weaves a web between heaven and earth. Here Rabéarivelo is in home country, and the backdrop is stark and grim, as in the Malagasy folktales; the telling is everything. This is a place "where all Religions meet/and poems too," and where "*mon frère errant*" is a lime tree. As the poet says "all seasons have been abolished."

The final point of reconciliation is where all life is cancelled out so that only what is truly elemental is important. "Zébu" and "Valiha" from *Presque-songes* had anticipated this. In "Zébu" the bull's life anticipates his death, and in "Valiha" the bamboos, once alive (even though "buried living by moonlight") will become a means toward the achievement of love. In the latter poem as in many others in *Presque-songes* and *Traduit*, the artist-figure is the savior for he will "shatter their god-like youth."

Rabéarivelo comes closest to his own tradition with *Vieilles chansons des pays d'Imerina* (40). Many of the songs can be founded in the traditional *hainteny* or love poetry of Malagasy. The poem is divided into some 30 sections, and the poet speaks from "Imerina," a high mountain in the Republic. His own voice and the responses of the *parente* (lover) give the poetry the form of a duet, with long passages being reserved for soliloquy and self-comment. The poetry is not the love poetry of his first volume; nor does one find the disenchanted world of *Traduit* and *Presque-songes*; this is the true coming together of the living heart and adoring nature ("I am the most beautiful star in the constellation.") Repetition (in the manner of the folklore) serves to increase the effect:

—Can I come in? Can I come in?
—Who is there? Who is there (40, p. 12)?

This type of stylistic device helps each section of these songs to move forward gracefully. Rabéarivelo seems to have not merely translated, but created these songs anew in French. Rabéarivelo's despair, so clear in his poetry, made him deny his own poetry and finally take his own life. He had hinted in *Traduit* (39) and *Presque-songes* (36) of some great cosmic disaster. Eventually it was to engulf the poet himself.

Summary

This article does not claim to be exhaustive. I have merely attempted to show that there is a rich reservoir of literature in Portuguese, English, Spanish, and French that relates very directly to us in the United States and is not being taught for a variety of reasons. Some of the problems that these writers relate parallel the issues that are pertinent in this country at present. The liberties that many of the authors take with the language of expression are not unlike the freedom American authors display. Fortunately they and we are removed from the stultifying environment of the "mother country." Their rhythms appeal to us, for in many instances we have borrowed songs and dance-patterns and incorporated them into our own cultural life in America. Where else in the world does the rhumba, the waltz, the calypso and soul fall so neatly together?

Seemingly then in this country we have vast potentialities for cultural maturity and the manifestation of a world destiny—the meeting point of all men at a common cultural rendezvous. This indicates that once and for all we can banish the narrow parochialism that has been part of the process of learning in other parts of the world. By extending the frontiers of literature, we enlarge imaginative possibilities; we leave our old world forbears alone and in search for a new thread of discovery, discard their static mold and regain a new focus of intensity, a novel turbulency of spirit.

References, Literary studies in a broader context

1 Abreu, Maria Isable, and Cléa Rameh. *Portuguése Contemporâneo.* Washington: Georgetown University Press, 1971.

2 Agrait, Luis Rachani. *Tres piraques para un dia de calor.* Performed at the Festival de Teatro 1971, Institute of Puerto Rican Culture.

3 Aidoo, Christiana Ama Ata. *The Dilemma of a Ghost.* Accra, Ikeja: Longman, 1965.

4 Andrade, Mário de. *Antologia da poesia negra de expressão portuguesa, precedida de Cultura negro-africana e assimilação.* Paris: Pierre-Jean Oswald, 1958.

5 Arozarena, Marcelino. "We Rehearse the Snake Dance," in *Black Orpheus* No. 3. Ibadan, Nigeria, n.d.

6 Ballagas, Emilio. "The Masquerade with the Lantern" in *Black Orpheus,* No. 3. Ibadan, Nigeria, n.d.

7 Beti, Mongo. *Ville cruelle* in *Trois écrivains Noirs* (pseud. Eza Boto). Paris: Éditions Africaines, 1954.

8 —— *Le Pauvre Christ de Bomba.* Paris: Laffont, 1956.

9 —— *Mission terminée.* Paris: Buchet/Chastel, Corrêa, 1957.

10 —— *Le Roi miraculé, Chronique des Essazam.* Paris: Buchet/Chastel, Corrêa, 1958.

11 Braithwaite, L.E. *Rights of Passage.* London: Oxford University Press, 1967.

12 Carpentier, Alejo. *¡Ecue-yamba-ó Historia afro-cubana!* Madrid: Editorial España, 1933.

13 Clark, J.P. *America, Their America.* London: Andre Deutsch, 1964.

14 Collins, Marie,ed. *Black Poets in French.* New York: Charles Scribner, 1972.

15 Dathorne, O.R.,ed. *African Poetry.* London: Macmillan, 1969.

16 Equiano, Olaudah. *The Interesting Narrative of the Life of Olaudah Equiano, or Gustavus Vassa, the African, Written by Himself.* London: Printed for and sold by the author 1789.

17 Gallegos, Rómulo. *Pobre negro.* Buenos Aires: Es pasa-Calpe, 1961. [5th ed.]

18 Guillén, Nicolás. *Man-Making Words: Selected Poems of Nicolás Guillén.* Amherst: University of Massachusetts Press, 1962.

19 Hughes, Langston,ed. *An African Treasury.* New York: Crown Publishers, 1960.

20 Kane, Cheikh Hamidou. *L'Aventure ambiguë.* Paris: Julliard, 1961.

21 Lamming, George. *Natives of My Person.* New York: Holt, Rinehart and Winston, 1972.

22 —— *Water with Berries.* New York: Holt, Rinehart and Winston, 1972.

23 Lange, Dale L.,ed. "1972 ACTFL Annual Bibliography." *Foreign Language Annals* 6 (1973): 537–658.

24 Maran, René. *Batouala:véritable roman nègre.* Paris: A. Michel, 1921.

25 —— *Djouma, chien de brousse.* Paris: A. Michel, 1927.

26 —— *Le Livre de la brousse.* Paris: A. Michel, 1934.

27 —— *Un Homme pareil aux autres.* Paris: Editions Arc-en-Ciel, 1947.

28 McKay, Claude. *Banana Bottom.* New York: Harper, 1933.

29 —— *Banjo:A Story Without a Plot.* New York, London: Harper, 1929.

30 —— *Home to Harlem.* New York, London: Harper, 1928.

31 —— *A Long Way from Home.* New York: Furman, 1937.

32 Niane, Djibril Tamsir. *Soundjata ou Pépopée mandingue.* Paris: Présénce Africaine, 1960.

33 Ortiz, Adalberto. *Juyungo. Historia de un negro, una isla y otros negros.* Buenos Aires: Editorial Americalee, 1943.

34 Palés Matos, Luis. *Poesia 1915–1956.* San Juan: University of Puerto Rico Press, 1968. [3rd ed.]

35 Rabéarivelo, Jean-Joseph. *La Coupe de cendres.* Tananarive: Pitot de la Beaujardière, 1924.

36 ——— *Presque-songes*. Tr. ex. Hove. Tananariva: Henri Vidalie, 1924.

37 ——— *Sylves:Nobles dédains, Fleurs mêlées, Destinée, Dixains, Sonnets et poèmes d'Iarive*. Tananarive: Imprimerie de l'Imerina, 1927.

38 ——— *Volumes:Vers le bonheur, La guirlande à l'amitié, Interlude rythmique, Sept quatrains, Arbes, Au soleil estival, Coeur et ciel d'Iarive*. Tananarive: Imprimerie de l'Imerina, 1928.

39 ——— *Traduit de la nuit*. Tunis: Éditions de Mirages, 1935.

40 ——— *Vieilles chansons des pays d'Imerina*. Tananarive: Imprimerie Officielle, 1937.

41 Salkey, Andrew. *Breaklight*. London: Hamish Hamilton, 1971.

42 Seruma, Enriko. *The Experience*. Nairobi: East Africa Publishing House, 1970.

43 Shapiro, Norman,ed. *Negritude:Black Poetry from Africa and the Caribbean*. New York: October House, 1970.

44 Soyinka, Wole. *The Interpreters*. London: Andre Deutsch, 1965.

45 Valdés-Cruz, Rosa E. "Tres poemas represantivos de la poesia Afro-Antillana." [EJ 033 501].

8

Individualization and personalization

Introduction

The concept of individualization or personalization of instruction is the most frequent response toward meeting the realities of the 1970s. The current literature in foreign language education reflects the growth of this curricular innovation. Individualization subsumes so many other responses that its influence is heightened. Programs in career and urban education as well as interdisciplinary and cultural studies draw upon personalization as their *raison d'être*, and individualization plays a major role in their format.

Reviewed in this chapter, individualization is presented from two vantage points. The historical and theoretical background of individualization provides the rationale for its position in the field at present. A resume of these foundations will guide the interested reader to sources of information but is of necessity limited in detail. The second area of investigation is more comprehensive in scope. Aspects of various extant individualized programs are described so that they may serve as models for adoption or stimuli for adaptation. Concentration is on the literature and programs as developed in the 1971–73 period. The very innovative early programs have functioned long enough to have undergone change. Extensive reviews of those curricula are available in earlier volumes of the *ACTFL Review of Foreign Language Education* Series (86, 87, 88). The reader is directed especially to chapters by Logan (94), Gougher (53), Lipton (92) and Kalivoda and Elkins (80). The current literature, as reviewed here, provides updated descriptions and reveals new perspectives and trends as individualized programs have evolved and matured.

June K. Phillips
Indiana University of Pennsylvania

A look to the past

A view of the present

June Kemmler Phillips (B.A., University of Pittsburgh) is Associate Professor of Romance and Classical Languages at Indiana University of Pennsylvania where she teaches the methodology courses and supervises student teaching. She is currently a candidate for the Ph.D. degree in Foreign Language Education at The Ohio State University. She has taught at the secondary level where she designed and implemented individualized classes in French. Professional affiliations include ACTFL, AATF, NFMLTA and PSMLA.

Definition: What has individualized instruction become?

As a form of instruction, individualization began to grow in practice before it was adequately defined in the literature. Definitions have evolved from the characteristics of programs. Classroom teachers are actively involved in this curricular change; they are not operating under a methodology imposed upon them. The nonprescriptive and flexible nature of individualization makes it amenable to change; indeed, its lack of rigidity in implementation may contribute to a successful and long-term influence that was impossible for the narrowly defined audiolingual method.

Flexibility at the grass-roots level

Logan (96) emphasizes that individualization must be viewed as an instructional approach, not a methodology. It exhibits a variety of forms that tend to be teacher-designed. Hanzeli and Love (58), reporting on the Seattle Symposium on the Training of Foreign Language Teachers, define individualization as an "attitude of teaching students as individual persons" (p. 329). Altman (5) considers it a philosophy of education and cautions against its being interpreted as either a method or a technique. It is many different strategies, operations, and kinds of behavior. Interestingly, these formulations accentuate teacher or curricular aspects of instruction.

An approach, an attitude, a philosophy

Jarvis (72) conceives of a *theoretically ideal* form of individualization as one "implying a unique curriculum for each learner, where objectives, learning activities, and pace all depend upon the *individual*" (p. 375). In practice, however, Altman and Politzer (8) describe individualization as occurring in any of three areas: The goals may be individualized; the means of attaining them may vary among individuals; or the speed at which they are met may be individualized. Mickelson (105) differentiates between personalized and individualized instruction. The latter provides the learner control over the pace at which he works, but the curriculum is imposed upon him. Personalized instruction, however, is a particular approach to individualization where the activities are consistent with the learner's goals and needs. Although this formulation resembles those of Jarvis and Altman and Politzer, it implicitly favors variation of activities and goals over variation in pace.

Personalized instruction

The function of pace in individualized instruction has undergone change since the beginning of the decade. Although Logan (94) cited seven types of individualization, the majority of programs at that time used self-pacing as the *sole* element of individualization. Hanzeli and Love (58) call for individualization to move away from pacing toward independent study and student-oriented content. Their rationale is

More than pacing

220

valid, but their exhortation comes after the fact. Such a move is already well under way. Today, self-pacing is an integral part of most individualized programs; few are designed without it, but few are based solely upon it.

Altman (5) and Gougher (52) have each compiled an itemization of the features of individualized programs. The listings overlap and reinforce one another. A synthesis of their work identifies the following characteristics of individualized instruction:

Definition by characteristics

1 The student is allowed to progress at his optimum rate.

2 Learning for mastery is emphasized; this implies sequential learning, performance objectives, criterion-referenced testing.

3 The learner's interests, abilities, and needs determine the kind of curriculum.
   a Instruction is tailored to the student's readiness.
   b Work may be done independently or in a small group.
   c Provision is made for individual learning styles.
   d If personalization is lacking, the individualization may be insensitive to student needs.

4 Credit is awarded on an individual basis for completed work.

5 Criteria for evaluating the success of the individualized program seek to assess student attitudes toward the learning, the language, and the culture.

6 The student's learning "how" to learn becomes a factor.

Historical background

The concept of individualization of instruction is not a new one to the field of education. Historically, it dates from the late nineteenth century. Mickelson (105) traces its beginnings in the elementary schools to John Dewey's search for a way to break the lock step, age-grade pattern of school organization. In recent times, too, we owe the impetus for development of individualized instruction to the elementary schools. Projects and research money invested in open classroom concepts, individually prescribed instruction, and programmed learning techniques all provided information and possibilities for more specialized fields. The literature in elementary education has been a valuable source for the foreign language teacher, in suggesting designs and models. We needed only to adapt them. The entire open classroom concept with its flexible space, assorted materials, and new teacher role is transferable to the foreign language context.

Insights from elementary education

Forces for individualization

In the late 1960s individualized programs began to appear in scattered parts of the country. Prescribed techniques and strict methodologies had not proven effective in solving the problems faced by foreign language education. Audiolingualism had crested; research studies had failed to support its tenets adequately. The Pennsylvania Project (Smith, 131), both hailed and criticized, did encourage educators to question their practices once again. This swing away from a reliance on methodology for answers was crucial to the growing interest in individualized approaches and the concept of many paths. A cutback in government support and NDEA monies, coupled with high attrition rates, were also factors forcing the profession to look for new responses.

Toward a more eclectic approach

Several trends gaining visibility in the general field of education also supported the concept of individualization in foreign languages. Only a cursory view of these concepts and their relation to the field of foreign languages is introduced here. Guidelines for their implementation follow in the section on existing programs.

Theoretically, individualization has a sound foundation in learning psychology. Educational psychologists have long known that individuals exhibit vast differences as learners. Now educators are acting on that premise. Gagné (50), in his book *The Conditions of Learning*, presents a compelling argument for abandoning the lock step approach to learning. He stresses mastery of subskills as prerequisites for further learning. Each learner approaches a task with a different degree of mastery and needs to be individually guided through a set of procedures. Theoretical grounds for self-pacing and mastery, concepts central to the practice of individualization, are clearly set forth by Gagné. Academic areas, especially mathematics and the sciences, forthwith translated this theory into programmed learning. In the language area, however, little work has been done, although programmed learning is now enjoying a rebirth as part of many individualized programs. Mueller (110) suggests the terms *programmed* and *individualized* are synonymous when describing materials designed for individualization. This justification lies in an abnegation of the narrow Skinnerian definition of programming for one implying optimum sequencing of materials. Instruction and practice in the grammar acquisition phase is especially amenable to programming, for it frees class time for active use of the language.

Mastery and sequence

The arrival on the education scene of performance objectives and criterion-referenced testing was another event that facilitated the implementation of individualized programs. Mager's (100) instructional book has become a classic. The focus shifted from teacher actions to student performance, and this had a tremendous effect on foreign language instruction. Steiner (133) presented a comprehensive case for behavioral objectives in foreign language curricula. Workshops and articles are still advocating their use in classroom planning. This is not to say that behavioral objectives have no detractors. Adams (1) and Grittner (55) reject them as dehumanizing in both concept and practice. They seem, however, to overextend the role these objectives play in the classroom. Performance objectives identify behaviors in the *sequence of instruction* and aid the teacher in making students aware of what they are to do. Applied to measurable skills, the objectives are not meant to describe creative endeavors.

Performance objectives: pro and con

Criterion-referenced testing has been closely tied to the use of performance objectives and new goals for language teaching. Jakobovits (67) calls for an entirely new type of testing. Evaluation should be consistent with the individual's ultimate purpose in studying the language. If the goal is communicative competence, tests must be designed to assess that ability. Jakobovits suggests possible approaches, such as questionnaires and role playing. An investigation of the changing role of testing in individualized programs has been made by Clark (30).

Testing what is taught

The literature of the social sciences has also had an impact on educational practices. The individual and his place in the group context is the theme of numerous studies in group dynamics. Rogers (122) extols the interpersonal relationship in teaching and learning and applies this philosophy to the "facilitation" of learning. The learner, not the teacher, becomes central to the educational process. Foreign language education, however, had adhered for years to the supremacy of "how-to-teach" articles. Jakobovits (69) challenged that traditional thinking by observing: "that people can learn is an undeniable fact of life; that people can teach is an interesting hypothesis, but unsubstantiated" (p. 91). The professional journals of 1972 reflect this sharp change in focus.

Teaching versus learning

As the learner comes to the forefront, concerns for student factors other than achievement take on significance. Interest in motivation, aptitude, and attitude increases, but unfortunately, minimal research is available. Hancock (57), in exploring those areas, underlines the diagnostic role aptitude testing is assuming. Jakobovits' (67) idea of "compensatory" instruction, a theoretically ideal proposition at the

The affective domain

223

moment, is predicated on the teacher's awareness of the learner's motivation, aptitude, and attitude. The subsequent instruction is provided on an individuated basis. It is often the negative manifestation of student attitudes or motivation that compels the individual teacher to search for a new way of organizing his class. Disick (37) offers a variety of procedures aimed at motivating intermediate students. These include small-group work, pass/fail grading, and provision for self-expression. Either in a traditional or individualized class, the procedures are designed to foster positive attitudes among students.

How individualization responds

Given the developments in learning psychology, the educational use of performance objectives, interest in group dynamics and a learner-centered approach, why has Politzer (118) deemed individualization "the best response which foreign language education can make in the present crisis situation" (p. 212)? The answer lies in the unique way in which individualization responds to today's needs.

A strong response

First of all, the nature of learning is given unprecedented prominence in individualized instruction. In his analysis Bockman (15) takes John B. Carroll's 1963 conceptual model of the learning process as a point of departure. He then demonstrates how individualization facilitates that learning process. Carroll's model consists of five elements:

1　The learner's aptitude (function of time)
2　The learner's general intelligence
3　The learner's perseverance (time allowed by learner)
4　The quality of instruction (sequence, order, etc.)
5　The opportunity for learning (time allowed by school)

Except for general intelligence, all the elements are related to the function of time. Bockman suggests a causal connection between *time* and achievement. Freed from the constraint of time, individualization interacts with the learning process in the following manner:

The key to mastery: time

1　Aptitude: Given sufficient time, almost any learner can master a learning task. Individualization provides for variance in the amount of time required.
2　General intelligence: Instruction is modified to meet the needs of the individual's capacity to understand.
3　Perseverance: Time varies with the learner's degree of satisfaction. Individualized instruction consists of those factors identified as

224

contributing to satisfaction—achievement, recognition, learning itself, responsibility, advancement.

4–5 Quality of instruction and opportunity for learning: Mastery is possible when each student receives treatment best suited to his learning needs. Individualization provides for various sequences and circumstances. Its purpose is to enlarge the opportunity for learning.

In summary, Bockman believes that mastery is an imperative and claims that individualization is the key to adjusting time and conditions so that the needs of each learner will be met. Individualized programs designed for mastery and organized on self-pacing, continuous progress, programmed learning, or independent study formats respond to these diverse aptitudes and abilities of students.

Teachers are also looking to individualization for solutions to motivational problems. Since positive student attitudes are closely linked to motivation, ways to strengthen its effect are being investigated. Smith (130) discusses motivation in terms of anxiety levels and anxiety reduction. Three factors are identified as affecting the degree of student motivation: personal interest, attitude, and ability. Individualization accounts for student interest in the selection of mini-courses or special projects. Personalized instruction might alleviate *Fighting negative attitudes* negative student attitudes toward learning, language, or culture. A diversity of course sequences, content, and goals accommodates individual differences. In-depth study of language and literature does not appeal to many students. Lafayette (84) favors terminal courses to attract them. Teachers, by increasing their own sensitivity to student attitudes, can foster positive conditions. Disick (37) encourages attention to teacher behaviors that reflect enthusiasm, concern for students, and sincere praise; these actions promote interest and reduce anxiety.

In recent years, students have been criticizing foreign language classes for not being "relevant" to their needs. Troyanovich (141) advocates relegating the literature and language skills objectives of most programs to a secondary role. Programs developed with goals other than the traditional ones will be inviting to contemporary students. Strongly attracted to the social sciences, these learners desire *New goals in social sciences* a service orientation in their language study. Language teachers are in an advantageous position because of their "linguistic internalization" of a foreign culture. An emphasis on cultural analysis and anthropology as a concomitant to language teaching should appeal to many students. Individualization has made diversity of course offerings feasible. A new

225

role for cultural studies is also a suggestion of Niedzielski (113). He attributes the growing importance of this area to a shift in the goals held by today's students. Their intellectual concerns result from the diversity of their social and educational backgrounds. Niedzielski foresees instructional systems of the future utilizing self-teaching materials and role playing for personalized involvement. Far from being futuristic, behavioral goal characteristics of the type he proposes already serve as the foundation for many individualized programs in operation. These include practical courses for travel or professional purposes, four-skill programs for foreign language majors, reading or writing courses for other specializations, and interdisciplinary studies.

Individualization as a response is strong because its scope encompasses all these factors. It is a structure as well as a tool for facilitating the learning process. As a framework it accommodates students of different abilities, aptitudes, interests, and degrees of motivation. As an instrument of instruction it provides flexibility in managing the teaching-learning process.

Individualization: It's happening in the high schools

For the teacher, department chairperson, or administrator who is investigating the appropriateness of an individualized approach, considerable study of extant programs is a must. Individualization is not tailored merely to the students it serves; ideally it is custom designed for the districts, programs, and teachers involved. Politzer (118) cautions against excluding the particular goals, aptitudes, and abilities of teachers when contemplating individualization. Professionals must evaluate their own objectives, facilities, and philosophies before establishing a program. Copying another program may be inappropriate, but a study of other plans may supply ideas for adaptation. The purpose of this section is to provide a review of the organizational patterns, a description of functioning programs, and insights into some of the techniques that contribute to personalized instruction.

Individualize in terms of students, teachers, schools

The structural framework for individualized programs follows a continuum from total school and curricular involvement to that of a single teacher working within the confines of a classroom. The John Dewey High School in New York City is a completely individualized inner-city school. This plan continues to receive wide coverage in the literature, with Levy (89, 90, 91) an authoritative source. The school adheres to a philosophy of mastery as the criterion for advancement;

Individualization for a whole school

226

therefore, each student works at his own pace and assumes the major responsibility for his learning. Students of all abilities are enrolled. All the administrative accoutrements to support an individualized curriculum are in evidence.

An ungraded school, John Dewey operates on a system of modular scheduling and five seven-week cycles, and extracurricular activities are incorporated into the school day. The departments are organized on a differentiated staffing basis. Individual progress and independent study are components of the student schedules, and individual progress is accomplished within a seven-week cycle. At the end of each period, the student is evaluated and is rated M (Mastery), MC (Mastery with Condition), or R (Retention for Reinforcement). Students with M or MC are promoted, but MC and R students receive teacher-written *Prescriptions for mastery* prescriptions for areas of deficiency. Retention in a course is for the seven-week period. The use of a "Supportive DISK" (Dewey Independent Study Kit) aids the MC student in overcoming his areas of weakness. The Supportive DISK gives an overview of topics and objectives covered during the cycle and lists exercises and tapes with which to work. Time for completion is negotiated with the teacher, and the work is performed in the resource center.

The independent study phase has several levels. Time for it is built into the student's schedule. He may devote this time to "leisure" *Student choices* activities, "homework" or "remediation" in the resource center, or to enrichment or independent study. The latter is available as a DISK in seven languages. Students who successfully complete the kit receive an MI (Mastery in Independent Study) grade.

Differentiated staffing and the plant facilities at John Dewey assist in the individualization process. Teachers are scheduled into the *Differentiated staffing* resource center where they are joined by student teachers, advanced student tutors, and paraprofessionals. The resource center forms a hub with the classrooms built around it. The language laboratory is nearby, and both these "support systems" are accessible for student use during independent study time.

Buildings and program development do not guarantee a humanizing education. The foreign language classes at John Dewey have evolved from basically a variable-pacing for mastery type of program in 1969 *Expanding the concept* to a more personalized kind of instruction today. Learning activities had earlier been characterized by Levy (90) as largely teacher directed. The time arrangement was flexible, but the one-class/one-teacher setup seemed to have prevailed. Recent developments highlighted by Levy (89) indicate that experimentation with team-teaching and open-

227

classroom techniques is now being pursued. The team-teaching format schedules two classes of the same phase and level back-to-back. Teachers then utilize large and small group instructional plans to offer more individual attention. The open classroom was implemented to involve the student more directly in his learning. He may determine the manner in which he learns as well as his pace, has some choice of activities, and may work alone or as part of a group. The school individualizes for the less able language student in two other ways. For students requiring more time, the Level I work is spread over seven cycles rather than five. There is also a conversational course stressing the oral vocabulary and structures presented in the regular Level I course, which serves as a readiness course for the student who wishes to continue. These innovations inside the classrooms at John Dewey seem to assure that the individualized organization is now lending itself to personalized instruction.

The majority of individualized programs are not predicated on a schoolwide basis, and often the impetus is at a departmental level. *Individualization at the departmental level* Teachers must then work within the space and time allocations of an existing system. Successful programs often prove to be strong arguments for change in the superstructure. Ryberg (125) reports on how the Foreign Language Department at Marshall-University High School in Minneapolis tackled its problems with an individualized approach. This inner-city experimental school's student body is highly diverse in terms of socioeconomic levels, educational backgrounds, and career orientations. In a two-year introductory sequence that is now offered *Language for everyone* to every student, the teachers have tried various forms of self-pacing and ability grouping. Although student contact time with the language was less than in a traditional class, Ryberg states that the time was more effectively used. The language laboratory was reorganized as a resource center containing cassettes and carrels for student work. Credits were entered on records four times a year to accommodate the various rates of achievement. Of particular interest is the revitalization of the intermediate and advanced level courses. Discussions with students revealed that use of authentic language and involvement in their learning were of top priority to them (Ryberg and Hallock, 126). The curriculum was then formulated on relevant, student-chosen content with active student participation an essential ingredient. The new mini-courses could be elected by students for full or partial credit. They *Mini-courses* include language studies (e.g., French Skills Workshop, Spanish Test-Taking) and cultural or personal interest areas (e.g., The Soviets and Their Land, German Correspondence: Business and Personal). They

228

are offered on a demand basis, and options are still open for independent study projects that may be done simultaneously with the mini-courses. Interdisciplinary studies are enabling students to receive foreign language credit for courses outside the department. Flexible scheduling, which is on the horizon at Marshall-University High School, should augment the possibilities for the language curriculum. In the interim, the lack of rigidity on the part of the foreign language department has contributed to the relevance of their courses. After three years, Ryberg and Hallock report that 55 percent of the student body is enrolled in a language course.

Individualization at one school

The other end of the organizational continuum is the situation of one teacher individualizing his classes as a response to a felt need. This is the "grass-roots" level at which individualization has to happen if it is eventually to be effective. Personal experiences with individualized instruction are beginning to appear in the journals. Flynn (48) explains her reasons for individualizing her class at Gunston Junior High School (Arlington, Virginia) in a first person narrative. Faced with a second-year French class of students who had received a D or complimentary C in French I, she administered a diagnostic test at the beginning of the year. After identifying student weaknesses in one to ten areas (e.g., poor intonation, lack of reading skills), Flynn charted each student's learning deficiencies on graph paper. Individual conferences resulted in a checklist of activities for each student, and she gathered materials and formed groups so that the various activities might be carried out. She helped students on what she called a "Baskin-Robbins" take-a-number-to-be-served system. After six weeks another diagnostic test was given with results indicating that 80 percent of the deficiencies had been remedied. The original plan for individualization was meant to terminate at that point. When the teacher thought she could begin to "teach" again, student insistence upon continuing with the new program won out. This is one example of a teacher's seeking a solution to the problems of a given situation. It is difficult to assess the number of such teacher-initiated and teacher-designed classes, for these classroom personnel rarely have free time to devote to giving their programs visibility in writing.

Overcoming weaknesses

Individualization: A tool for learning

It should be clear that inaugurating a program requires many local decisions. Using existing programs as models demands prudence. If one were to liken the various aspects of these programs to the patches

229

in a quilt, one's initial reaction might be that it's very nice but beyond one's means. An additional look might reveal, however, that whereas the whole quilt is not a possibility, some of the patches in another arrangement might be very attractive and more serviceable. Thus, the purpose of this review is to highlight the pieces of individualized programs. The interested teacher's task is to assemble them into a model that is functional and appropriate for him and his students. McKim (101) emphasizes that teachers should identify features of individualization that apply to their schools and to take time to "look" before they take the proverbial "leap." Jakobovits (71) asserts that the classroom teacher must assume the responsibility for decision making and abandon dependence on methods and commercial materials.

Building a program

Aldridge (2) is among those who espouse individualization but prefer the lock step approach for beginning students. An increasing number of programs, nevertheless, are denying the premise that it must be reserved for advanced students. Reinert (121) advocates personalized learning in first-level programs to explore the most efficient and effective learning manner for each student. In addition to self-pacing he feels the student should be offered alternate routes toward achievement. The teacher's role in the beginning level is to determine which skills are important and .to establish the proficiency levels required. He does allow that an ideally personalized program would vary the degree of emphasis on various skills for individual students.

For beginning students?

Of the four characteristics of beginning levels of individualized classes listed by Altman (5), two refer to self-pacing: Students are free to proceed at their own pace, and students are tested when they expect to be tested. The rate of learning can be accommodated in several ways. Logan's program at Live Oak High School (Morgan Hill, California) is individualized at all levels of language instruction, though rate is the variable that is manipulated for the first two (Sutton, 137). Braswell (25) provides detailed information on the operation of the Junior High School programs there. A student may choose from one of four courses. There is an introductory course for those having had no previous language experience. Three individualized courses are designed to meet student preferences or abilities: a standard course, a conversational course, and one for those wishing a slower rate. Each course is broken into "daily" assignments with a minimum number to be completed for the required work. Ninety percent proficiency is necessary for satisfactory completion. Due dates and the issuance of credits for two-weeks' work are motivational devices for keeping young adolescents aware of their progress.

A choice of courses

Materials being used in self-pacing programs are often adapted from conventional texts. Classroom teachers hesitant about writing their own materials find that their experience has furnished them with ideas for revision of text materials. Flynn (48), Campbell (27), and Braswell (25) all worked with conventional texts. They provided study guides or assignment sheets to direct students to activities in the text. Clearly stated performance objectives told students what was expected of them. The material was further supplemented with teacher-prepared exercises, directions, etc. At Greenwich Junior High School (Connecticut) the text was divided into units that were then expanded for remedial inserts for the slower students. Sections of drill and exercises could be skipped if mastery could be demonstrated without them (Fitzgibbons, 47). Kentz (82) modified her text for a group of second-level French students who had been designated as low achievers in the French I course at Oak Knoll School (Summit, New Jersey). Daily objectives were stated at the beginning of each class session. They were "reachable" and mastery was expected. Steps for achievement were suggested, but students could work independently or with a group. They could listen to a tape or get help from a friend who had already mastered the objective. Homework was marked "OK" or "Do over." All quizzes were graded Pass/Fail and could be retaken. The unit tests commercially prepared to accompany the text were administered. "How to study" guidelines were furnished. Any section of the test showing 90 percent mastery was accepted. Other portions were retaken in expanded form after a prescription for study activities aimed at the concepts not mastered was completed. Commercial materials play a role in this program without dominating it and gain their validity from the manner in which they are adjusted to student needs.

Working with text materials

Eliminate the unnecessary

The use of a prescription as illustrated above is common to programs where content is adjusted to the student's previous learning. The student at John Dewey (Levy, 89) with an MC (Mastery with Condition) rating received such a prescription, fulfillment of which was the condition for his advancement. Flynn's (48) students worked on the areas in which a diagnostic test had indicated deficiencies. The prescription in these programs is a formalized manifestation of the teacher's role in individualized instruction. In helping individuals or groups as they need it, the teacher also diagnoses the same problems in an informal manner. Jakobovits' (67) idea of compensatory education emphasizes the role of the teacher in breaking down the obstacles to the student's learning. Altman (5) considers assistance when needed a

Remedies when needed

231

characteristic of individualization and charges the teacher with the task of removing obstacles to learning as they are encountered by the students.

Learning packages in various forms have been developed to adapt existing materials and to create new ones. Examples of these are available through the ERIC (Educational Resources Information Center) Clearinghouse. Helpful information can be shared by teachers as the collection of sample materials grows. ACTFL's forthcoming book, *Options and Perspectives: A Sourcebook of Innovative Foreign Language Programs in Action, K–12,* highlights considerations for adapting the programs surveyed and also provides the names of contact persons. Examples of the instructional materials developed in French, German, and Spanish for the West Bend School District (Wisconsin) under the direction of LaLeike (85) are available through the ERIC system. Included are sample objectives, check lists for students, and tests. A sample unit and lesson from the Morgan Hill District is offered by Braswell (25). Closely coordinated with the Level I text, detailed steps inform the student of objectives and instruct him in procedures. There is provision for recording dates of completion and test results. Example: *(Sharing information)*

Step II Get the set of audio cards or the tape labeled Unit I, Text B and then turn to p. 4 (bottom) and p. 5 (top).

Then

a Listen to Text B carefully several times noting the English expressions, pp. 4–5.

b Listen to each sentence several times without referring to any English, p. 2, making sure that you understand what you are hearing.

c Now repeat the German of each sentence after hearing it and do this until you can imitate the model well.

d You do not need to memorize Text B, pp. 120–24.

Note that the amount of detail included permits the student to proceed without teacher help for routine management tasks. Teacher time can be devoted to learning difficulties. Krill (83) made check lists of 15 to 25 objectives for each chapter of her traditional beginning text. Activities directed toward these goals included exercises, tapes, film strips, and quizzes. *(Better use of teacher time)*

Guidelines for the teacher anxious to adapt existing materials are offered by Carroll and McLennan (28). After an inventory of materials, the following steps are in order: *(Adapting materials)*

1 Determine materials necessary for each student per period of time.

2 Prepare behavioral objectives for each unit (what the student is expected to do plus reference to study materials).

3 List learning activities (check list, handbook), balance of skills, practical oral activities.

4 Prepare orientation sheet for students (study techniques, visual aids, etc.).

5 Determine evaluative criteria for each objective and unit; inform students of criteria.

6 Include additional activities with text (games, skits, film strips, etc.) for motivation.

Teacher-made learning packages

Lorenz (98) developed packets for a continuous progress program in Spanish at Charles Town Senior High School (West Virginia). Thirty Progress Packets are designed for a 36-week school year. These packets stress three skills: speaking, listening, and writing. At the rate of one packet per week, a student would have six weeks to research supplementary cultural activities, or study for additional proficiency, or go into Spanish II. Each packet is constructed to provide maximum activity for skill practice and application. A student might need to do all or only half the activities to meet the required proficiency level.

Commercial packages

Commercially available packages requiring little modification can be used in individualized programs. Carroll and McLennan (28) report that BRL (Behavioral Research Laboratories) in Palo Alto have the first two levels of programmed French, Spanish, and German materials. Single concept packages such as UNIPAC, CPP (Continuous Progress Package), and LAP (Learning Activity Package) are designed specifically for individualized programs. A kit entitled *Prep Kit 16* (distributed by the Center for Planning and Evaluation, 1110 North Tenth Street, San Jose, California 95112) contains information about learning packages. UNIPAC is defined as a "self-contained set of teaching-learning materials designed to teach a single concept and structured for individual and independent use in a continuous progress school program." During discussion at the Stanford Conference, Hanzeli warned that a push for commercially individualized materials is antithetical to true individualization, for teacher involvement in matching software to student needs and goals reduces the tedium of "programmed" units of work (Altman and Politzer, 8).

"Do it yourself" guidelines

Copeland and Papalia's (32) guidelines for the writing of a FLAP (Foreign Language Activity Package) were tested in a workshop sponsored by the Williamsville Central Schools (New York). The uniformity and specificity of this format has advantages for the teacher experimenting with this task. In abbreviated form they are:

1 Topic: one idea, concept or skill imaginatively stated
2 Title page: topic, language, level, author
3 Table of contents: 13 components of the FLAP with page numbers
4 Rationale: reasons for learning the package (to motivate students)
5 Behavioral objectives: student-centered behavioral terms including
  a what the student will be given to work with when tested
  b limitations of content or conditions for testing
  c behaviors or actions expected of learner to demonstrate mastery
  d criterion or standard for evaluation
6 Pretest: items correspond to behavioral objectives
7 Pretest key: separate sheet after pretest
8 Activities: multisensory, skills, diversified methodology, media
9 Self-test: items correspond to and test behavioral objectives
10 Self-test key: separate sheet after self-test
11 Mastery test: each item corresponds to behavioral objectives with level of mastery indicated
12 Mastery test key: separate sheet after Mastery test
13 Quest: optional enrichment activities

Note that these guidelines are for the writing of a FLAP. The material given to the student may differ.

Programmed learning of a formalized nature that lends itself to self-instruction or completely independent study is not in widespread use on the high school level. In this context independent study implies minimal teacher contact for practice and performance of activities. Bockman (17, 19) has experimented in Arizona with an independent instructional system for high-ability eighth graders in an introductory language course. A student at John Dewey may take any of the languages (French, Hebrew, Italian, Spanish) offered in formal classes as an independent study if he chooses. A DISK (Dewey Independent Study Kit) is also available for German, Russian, or Latin (Levy, 89, 90, 91). The DISK contains a letter to the student stating the criteria for mastery. Guidelines for study and a plan for reading and grammar lessons are included. A weekly conference with the teacher is held in the resource center. A voluntary independent study program in French, German, Spanish, Russian, Italian, Japanese, and Huasa is offered at the Hyde Park High School in Chicago. Students may enroll

Independent study and student responsibility

or withdraw at will since the course is noncredit. Sutton (137) has described that program as well as one conducted by the University of Colorado for small high schools unable to support a language course. The university offers two levels of Spanish by organizing students' work with texts, workbooks, audio and visual tapes. A weekly tele-lecture (amplified telephone) permits two-way communication between students and the university faculty. Independent study materials allow students to progress at their own rates.

The high cost of CAI (Computer Assisted Instruction) prohibits its utilization in most public schools. Pope (119) emphasizes its potential however, on the basis of a pilot project at Gunn Senior High School (Palo Alto, California). As part of an individualized French course, an attempt was made to program materials to teach students to write the language. A program based upon phonemic/graphemic association was unsuccessful. In searching for a system that would direct the student in how to do the exercises, give immediate correction, and provide remedial content, a decision was made to try CAI. The lessons are used in conjunction with the individualized program for the teaching of spelling in French. By using the CAI program students learn to associate phonemes and graphemes so they can spell unknown words following a regular pattern and spell the most frequently used irregular words. Harrell (59) programmed reading passages for her *Programmed learning revived* individualized classes so that she could work with conversation groups. Programmed learning plays a supporting role in many individualized high school language classes. By programming the portion of a course most amenable to the process (grammar, reading, writing), more time can be devoted to communicative practice with the language. For the teacher interested in writing programmed materials Mueller (110) provides both theoretical background and guidelines for development. However, these recommendations are for the writing of major textual materials, not for supplemental packets. If quality is to result, the former task requires specialists in several areas, putting it beyond the scope of most classroom teachers.

As one moves from beginning or intermediate courses primarily concerned with language skills to advanced ones, individualized programs pay progressively more attention to the student's personal goals and interests. The mini-course most fully involves the student in curricular planning. As reviewed in detail earlier, Ryberg and Hallock *Student interests* (126) surveyed student interests and designed courses to meet these interests. This plan was effectuated to encourage enrollment at the advanced level, for students had been discontented with the long

235

sequence of similar activities imposed by the audiolingual curriculum. For teachers wishing to probe the diversity of interests in their classes and assess what those preferences might be, several instruments are available. Jakobovits' (70) Foreign Language Attitude Questionnaire and the Student Interest Questionnaire developed by Fearing and Arendt (44) would serve this purpose.

Outlines for six mini-courses have been written by Moore (106) for German IV and V. Texts, supplementary materials, and procedures are suggested. Students at Ridgefield High School (Connecticut) select four of the ten-week courses for one credit. All courses are taught in the target language. Titles reveal the spectrum of interests considered: German for Travelers; German-Speaking Lands and America; Introduction to Scientific German; German-Speaking World: History and Culture; Survey of German Literature; and Recent German, Swiss, and Austrian Literature.

The mini-course concept may provide a solution for small high schools unable to offer advanced language classes because of below minimum enrollments. Wainwright (144) proposed an individualized program for Black Hawk High School (South Wayne, Wisconsin). Instead of labeling courses according to level, they were grouped under the heading Advanced French. Sixteen units of study were designed to repeat on a two-year cycle. Thus, students had the opportunity for advanced study, and the combining of levels resulted in sufficient enrollment figures. No single text was used, and scheduling and earning of credits were flexible. The outline for each unit began with some work in basic language skills or a grammar review. Independent study, in which individuals were required to "do something" with the unit, ensued. Areas included were: French Contributions to Humanities, Teen-Agers in France Today, and French Cinema and News Media. At Live Oak High School, Logan (95, 97) has been able to offer more than 45 German courses through a unique scheduling system. All levels are offered during all periods. Each student has a choice of materials and may work independently or join groups with similar interests. A course may be offered for a single individual.

A new type of mini-course is appearing under the name "quinmester." The quinmester is a time division of five nine-week blocks. Systems using the quinmester operate on a twelve-month school year. The "quin" is a self-contained course worth one-quarter credit (Alonso and Vega, 4). In the Rock Hill (South Carolina) district there are even alternate courses for the beginning levels (Jennings, 74) as evidenced by these course descriptions: *Bonjour* (a more academic introductory course

Mini-courses combining classes

A course for each student

What's a "quin"?

236

designed for the student who wishes to continue in the target language), *Hors d'oeuvre* (an introductory and cultural events course with emphasis on speaking and listening, *no* reading and writing), *Bon voyage* (an introductory course with emphasis on the development of listening and speaking skills and emphasis on French travel and customs).

Advanced students are offered quins of a multi-topic nature.

An example in Spanish: *Los de Habla Española* (an in-depth study of the Spanish-speaking people, their attitudes, goals, philosophies, history, culture, systems, thought patterns, institutions).

Interdisciplinary credits are given for study abroad: *Un été en France* (study abroad for six weeks, stay with a French family for two weeks and then tour through France—one credit French, one credit Social Studies).

Materials for Dade County's (Florida) extensive offering of quinmester courses are available through the ERIC system.

When the mini-course is adjusted for the quinmester, it influences beginning as well as advanced studies. It gives some practical viability to Jakobovits' (71) rejection of the sequential hypothesis of language learning, for students are introduced to the functions and varieties of language at an early stage. Language learning would be directed toward specific communicative behaviors rather than the practicing of systematically controlled linguistic patterns. He conjectures a system of independent "tracks," one for conversational interaction, one for reading, and one in using language for instructional purposes. Flexible packages of mini-courses or modules would provide core content. This theory is being put into practice, and future experimentation should focus on results in that area.

Using the language from the start

For the teacher interested in developing mini-courses, the format proposed by Gunderson for Marshall-University High School serves as a guide (Ryberg and Hallock, 126). The components are:

Writing a mini-course

1 Course title
2 Course description (general description, prerequisites, scheduling, credit)
3 Objectives
4 Content
5 Learning strategy (pretest, conditions of learning, learning activities, functions of components)
6 Learning components (commercial materials, teacher-prepared materials, community resources, equipment, realia)
7 Resources (bibliography, films, records, tapes, etc.)

Another break in the tradition of a long sequence of language in-

For the one-year student

237

struction is the inclusion of a terminal course in the language curriculum. To better meet the needs of students often ignored by language programs Antoine (9) set up a one-year conversational course in Spanish at Lincoln High School (Gahanna, Ohio). Speaking skill was emphasized and grammar study was undertaken only as it pertained to oral language; vocabulary expansion and reading as reinforcement were stressed; all testing was oral. At the end of the year several students enrolled for Spanish I.

Career orientation is another personalized goal for individual programs. Chapter 5 in this volume treats the topic in detail; let it suffice here to cite two programs in which it serves individual student needs. Deutch (35) is investigating a work/study program for city students in Washington, D.C. Nonacademic students would learn language relevant for jobs in restaurants, beauty parlors, and garages. The World Language Cluster at the Skyline Center in Dallas offers specialized foreign language courses for career purposes (Johns, 76). Students attend Skyline for a three-hour block of time; the rest of the day is spent at their local high schools. A student may select from among several possible directions as he progresses through a series of 18 terminal objectives. Upon completion of a minimum of 12, he may specialize in career development courses such as bilingual secretarial training and translation or in supplemental studies including "Spanish for Farm and Ranch Workers" or "French for the World of Fashion." *Language for work*

Individual differences occur in many domains. The programs described have tried to cope with basically two areas: aptitude and ability through self-pacing and motivation and interest through multitopic or specific goal courses. Yet one of the most crucial concerns, adapting to the student's individual mode of learning is in an underdeveloped state. In the literature, many programs claim to include this component; however, in-depth investigation reveals that the claim refers merely to a student's option of working independently or in the group context. Other programs cite a student choice of materials or activities as an adjustment for learning style. Psychologically, mode of learning is a more complex and demanding concept. It involves the complicated study of how humans learn language. Research in the interaction of students with instructional procedures is desperately needed. Some investigation of inductive/deductive learning of grammar, aural/visual presentation of material and audiolingual versus cognitive approaches to teaching has been carried out (Politzer, 118). Until data is organized and converted into a form for classroom implementation, the teacher as diagnostician must operate on a hit-or- *Adapting to how one learns*

Research needed; diagnosis not scientific

miss basis. The "eyeball-to-eyeball" contact, as Altman (5, p. 12) terms it, between student and teacher is a major advantage of individualized programs. Teachers practicing individualization spend a good portion of their time in an attempt to accommodate different learning modes. They eventually discover that one student learns via a discovery method that completely frustrates another, but instruments for facilitating this diagnostic process are lacking. Consequently, compensatory instruction aimed at the way an individual learns is currently dependent on the individual teacher's intuition and expertise.

Some programs are striving to include more provision for the individual's mode of learning. Stern and Weinrib (134) find sequential teaching programs inflexible in that they consider only one teaching style, that of the text's author. They are designing modules dealing with one specific aspect of language, for example, a grammar point. Modules treating these topics can be compiled into a group of units. Conceivably, multiple treatments on a topic could be prepared and the one most compatible with a learning style selected. A program at Bates Junior High (Annapolis, Maryland) is a multimedia project with Terminal Objective Blocks (Sutton, 137). Each TO Block specifies entry and criterion behaviors. A student who passes a pretest to demonstrate the criterion behavior may proceed to another TO Block for which he has entry behavior. While the coordination of materials imposes a kind of lock step, the student has a choice of many routes and establishes his own path and pace through them. A flow chart maps out possible strategies. As far as student preference with textbook methodology is concerned, Ryberg (125) discovered that when allowed to explore multiple texts, student choices were distributed evenly among methods.

Modules encourage flexibility

Individualization: Making it work

The previous discussion centered on the types of individualized programs and materials and how they have been designed to respond to the realities of the 1970s. An equally important facet, especially for those contemplating individualization, is the development of techniques and procedures that make the daily operation of a program successful. These techniques differ sharply from the prescriptive ones abundant in the journals of the 1960s. Flexibility is a key word for these processes that are usually derived from informal classroom experimentation.

239

All programs reviewed here are open classrooms in concept. When students are self-paced, given choices in activities, or pursuing personal goals, the classroom has no alternative but to be "open." In addition to its philosophy the open classroom provides an effective model for space utilization. One teacher, with limited physical facilities, has to abandon conventional arrangements if he chooses to individualize. Barrett's (12) analysis provides a check list for the teacher to consider in reviewing the space at his disposition. An environment is needed for

Opening the classroom

1   quiet student activities
2   small-group planning and learning activities
3   teacher-controlled group learning situations
4   resource materials, books, magazines, papers, etc.
5   audiovisual activities for large and small groups and individuals
6   high-level-noise group activities (singing, etc.)
7   teacher-pupil conference
8   teacher-staff preparation
9   storage of materials, programs, student files, etc.

Variations of three basic arrangements seem to serve most purposes for the teacher operating in a self-contained classroom. The first is demonstrated by Fitzgibbons' (47, p. 100) design where wall space is fully utilized, reserving the center of the room for small group activities not requiring hardware (Figure 1).

Utilizing space

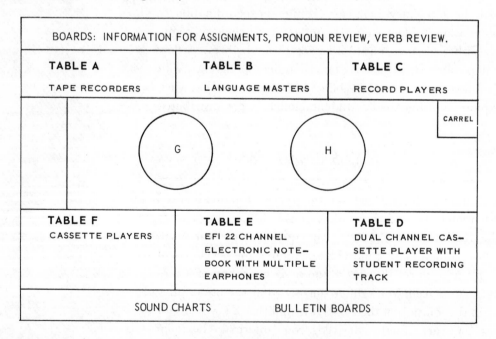

Figure 1. Map of the classroom

Braswell (25, p. 104) moves the space for group work off center. He gains accessibility to the blackboard and can accommodate a larger number of students for teacher explanation (Figure 2).

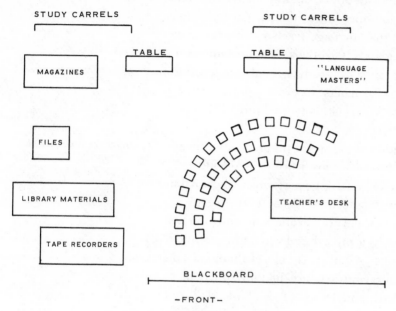

Figure 2. Map of the classroom

De Tullio (34) found another solution by dividing his room into five work areas with five-foot movable partitions. This learning center has areas for

1 Instruction: ten chairs in a semicircle, maps, chalk-board, screen, projectors (overhead, slide, filmstrip, super 8, and television receiver).

2 Conference: teacher's office; partition is bookshelves thus serving as reference area.

3 Work: students prepare materials, accessible to teacher and resources.

4 Audiovisual: students use media individually, porta-screen.

5 Audiolingual: students listen, repeat, record.

Lessons in most individualized programs have been organized in small units prefaced by a behavioral or performance objective. This objective serves a dual purpose. It establishes a goal for the student and informs him of the criteria by which he will be judged. Valette and Disick (143) produced a handbook for the classroom teacher that demonstrates in detail and via case studies how performance objectives and individualization complement one another. Especially informative is a chapter aimed at the teacher under pressure to cover

Using performance objectives

241

a certain amount of material. By using performance objectives in a test/retest approach, students have a chance to achieve mastery within an essentially lock step framework. Rosenthal's (123) listing of performance objectives claims to be adaptable to any materials. This attempt at generality limits the usefulness of the model. For the actual writing of behavioral objectives, the language teacher can experience self-instruction for himself. Mager's (100) book is programmed to provide practice in preparing these objectives, and an exercise specifically for foreign language teachers has been advanced by Hartley and Hartley (60). Disick (38) argues both the "pro" and "con" of the use of performance objectives.

The "contract" has been mentioned in several programs as a means *Contracts for commitment* of securing a student's commitment to his learning. Aldridge (2) defines the contract as a proposal for work to be performed. Included in the formal contract are: expected outcomes (behavioral objectives), alternative means for reaching them or evaluation instruments. Bockman (18) views the contract as a procedure for obtaining student commitment to goals, methods, conditions of evaluation, and acceptance of constraints. Sample contracts are in the Appendix to Bockman's chapter and in Valette and Disick (143). Basic skill and special interest projects can be governed by contracts.

Karrasch (81) drew up contracts listing the requirements for A, B, *Contracting for grades* or C grades in her French classes at Mountain Brook High School (Alabama). Certain activities are scheduled for a daily teacher-led session. The student may attend or work independently toward his contract. There is no penalty for not fulfilling a contract as the student's grade reflects the level he does complete. A similar system was employed by Bornscheuer (22) in an upper division French literature course at the University of Texas. Grades were based on the number of activities for which students contracted. Quality was stressed by the inclusion of a pass/fail clause. Pass was at the B level, but students were permitted to resubmit any work rated unacceptable. Students reacted favorably, and results on the final examination attested to their achievement.

Bockman and Bockman (20) caution against a negative aspect inherent in contracting. Since the formal contract itself is an extrinsic factor, it has the potential to dehumanize the educational process. The instrument aside, the *process* of contracting serves as an intrinsic factor. *Emphasis on the process* The joint effort of teacher-student interaction to set goals and conditions for learning can result in personalized and humanized instruction. The process not the product of contracting has validity.

Hellman (64) uses the contract for motivation. It is short term (for a two-week period), and the fulfilled contract entitles the student to a *certificat de mérite*. Setbacks are compensated for by the possibility of successful goal achievement next time.

When individualized programs are part of the total school organization or the language department, differentiated staffing contributes greatly to an efficient operation. Differentiated staffing plays an important role at John Dewey High School (Levy, 90) and in the West Bend independent study program (LaLeike, 85). Logan's design at Live Oak High School (Morgan Hill, California) owes much of its effectiveness to its differentiated staff concept (Morrey, 107). Two contiguous classrooms provide for both a quiet study or small-group area and a place for work with student assistants. Effective role delineation is needed, for students are scheduled into the facility on a multi-level basis. The staff consists of a senior teacher, a staff teacher, a paraprofessional (native speaker), a secretary, and volunteer student aides. Morrey lists the job descriptions as they relate to the daily program.

Teachers working together

The terms *individual* and *group* are not antonymous as they apply to individualized instruction. In fact, group work is probably the most commonly employed strategy in individualized programs today. Only a few operate under completely independent or programmed techniques. Therefore, knowledge on the part of the teacher in the organization and operation of small groups facilitates the individualized instructional process (Arendt, 11). Horne (65) has defined groups according to their size. He classifies groups of one to four students as individual instruction, five to nine as small group, and ten or more as mass instruction. His research identifies the small group as most effective for teacher-directed intensive language learning. Arendt (10) breaks this latter category into the intermediate group (10 to 35) and the large group (more than 35). He lists activities suitable for large, intermediate, and small groups within the individualized paradigm. The small group is the key mode of instruction, and its activities are subdivided as to levels of sophistication. Arendt emphasizes the importance of close supervision by the teacher or paraprofessional, not as an intruder but as a helper. In the early stages of group work, more teacher involvement or carefully structured activities is essential. As students gain in confidence and in leadership qualities, teacher control can diminish. Disick (36) also identifies supervision and structure as the key ingredients for worthwhile communication practice in small-group situations. Teacher direction should decrease as the group's

The individual and the group

More subtle teacher direction

243

functioning becomes more effective. The teacher's role then shifts from manager to resource person as he circulates among groups.

Groups are formed for various reasons in individualized programs. *Reasons for grouping* One-to-one teacher-student contact is inefficient and necessary only periodically. Students can be grouped because they have similar learning rates; they can be grouped for remedial work (Flynn, 48) and for special interest projects (Ryberg and Hallock, 126). Valette and Disick (143) suggest that real teaching—personal communication—can best take place in the small-group context.

An immediate and negative reaction often expressed toward individualized instruction results from a confusion of the concept with independent study. The question that arises concerns adequacy of *More time to use the oral* communication skills. A closer look reveals that these are not neglected *language* in individualized classes; furthermore, only minimal communication is possible in a class of 20 to 30 students. Harrell (59) shares the opinion of many teachers experienced with individual programs. Programmed reading and grammar practice free her to work with small groups in conversation practice. Teacher-contact time for communication skills is increased in Pope's (119) classes as CAI provides orthographic practice. Various grouping practices coupled with the differentiated staffing system enable the Live Oak High School students to maintain a balance in the four skills (Morrey, 107). A procedure to develop oral fluency begins with a five- to ten-minute whole-class vocabulary drill. Individual practice with Audio-Flashcards aids the student in sentence composition. A brief one-to-one evaluative session with a staff member leads to the conversation group, the key activity for application. This group session is the culmination of the other exercises. A guide-sheet presents a situation (e.g., "You are at an airport . . ."), and students use the vocabulary and structures recently studied in a simulated exchange. The conversation group is here used for recombination activities, not for presentation of new materials. Other levels of conversation are offered as well. Students from 40 courses at Live Oak High School are divided into one of four conversation groups: Basic, beginning, and advanced meet once a week, and an intensive speaking group devotes three sessions to oral practice. They participate in activities such as retelling stories, providing endings for them, describing pictorial events, etc.

Disick (36) advocates small-group instruction for practice in free *Better practice, better attitudes* communication and for drill work. Whether expressing their own ideas or practicing language, students are more comfortable and less inhibited about making errors in the small group. Learning is also more

244

effective, for pupils can't "tune out" or mouth responses. She presents eight techniques in a format giving purpose, procedures, and comments. They encompass all skills and build upon interests and ideas with motivational significance. Heard (63) views the small-group activities from a social-psychological perspective. The helping relationship and interaction inherent in group work contribute toward effective outcomes of language learning. She offers techniques for beginning levels of instruction. Among them are oral composition, remediation and cross-level sharing. An added advantage to both Disick and Heard's ideas are their adaptability to conventional as well as individualized classes. Elkins, Kalivoda, and Morain (61) have devised a scheme for fusing the four skills for communicative exchange. Employed in intermediate classes at the University of Georgia, it involves two groups, subdivided into three more. The process fuses reading, retelling, listening, and writing activities as the groups exchange information. Barrutia (13) identifies 15 examples of natural uses of language in interaction, for example, seeking or giving information, expressing one's reactions, displaying achievements. He then exemplifies how these situations can be simulated by small groups or pairs of students working with procedures to synthesize from drill materials to real language. Niedzielski (112) advocates a recourse to acting methods to inspire the teacher and student to react spontaneously to situations. He would group students with a "teacher-in-the-round" effect. However, the procedure seems teacher-centered while pretending to evoke student participation. Indeed, the class becomes an "ego trip" for the teacher. Thus, group work does not guarantee personalized instruction if the teacher remains center stage!

Reaching the level of synthesis

Some practitioners of individualized instruction advise including some whole-group instruction. Braswell (25) involves the whole class in an initial five- to eight-minute session for announcements and a song. This German "top hit" serves as a warm-up for the individualized work. The entire period on Friday is a culture day with slide lectures, conversation groups, language games, or outside speakers. Braswell feels the junior high student needs both individual and group experiences and that his program seems to provide enough whole-group activities for a feeling of "classness" to develop. Hellman (64) and Krill (83) devote the first ten minutes of the period to total class conversation, changing the topic daily so as to review expressions and structures. Young (145) presents new material to the whole class, which then breaks into small groups for practice and application.

Whole-class activities, too

The transition from conventional to individual instruction can be eased by reducing progressively the amount of full class activity. Since new roles are being assumed by both teacher and student, Valette and Disick (143) suggest that the change occur gradually. Students are not overwhelmed by the responsibility placed upon them, and the teacher can judge the effectiveness of the pieces in his program. In elementary education, Nault (111) attributes failures in open classroom experiences to an all-or-nothing strategy. He advises decentralizing decision-making responsibility first in activities, then in lessons, and finally in the whole subject area. Lourie (99) applies this gradualist approach only to students experiencing difficulty handling freedom.

Gradual changeover

Culture has been touched upon as part of many individualized courses, especially the mini-course. Logan (93) finds that many printed materials for individualized instruction fall short in cultural content. He suggests specific plans and techniques for cultural studies in such classes. A learning center or classroom can be transformed into a "cultural island" with posters, magazines, and realia. Group presentations on given days or at the beginning of class can be devoted to culture (see Braswell, 25). Small conversation groups draw from cultural topics. Native speakers are an excellent "live" source of information. Fiber (45) gives hints at developing the potential of these people.

Including culture

Elkins (39) has designed a procedure to include culture LAPs (Learning Activity Packages) with those for language structure. Employing a system of vertical and horizontal LAPs, the student can study a culture unit commensurate with his language proficiency. The vertical LAPs are required and follow a prescribed sequence. LAPs in various cultural areas (e.g., music, great men, sports) are available at each step on the vertical ladder. At any time the student may branch out horizontally to work on an area of interest to him. For example, a student on Step 5 in the structure sequence might choose a horizontal LAP on sports. This LAP, also at Step 5, would develop sports information using structures comprehensible to him. A student investigating the topic at Step 8 would use a LAP containing different information and more complicated structures. Elkins (40) would also use team teaching to utilize special expertise in these subjects. Savaiano (127) encourages teachers to prepare modular culture units during summer travel. While the suggestion has merit, the danger does exist of the teacher allowing his personal interests and experiences to take precedence over those of the students. John Dewey High School (Levy, 89) devotes the last day of each cycle to a culture activity. All the skills learned are put into practice. Themes have included an international cafe, flight abroad, and a casino. Elkins, Kalivoda, and Morain (42)

Culture packages

Students participation in culture activities

have devised a technique using commands requiring a physical response and props to illustrate a cultural theme. Small- and large-group discussions follow up the experience. Examples of a picnic in four languages demonstrate the procedure.

Evaluation and testing in individualized programs is usually available on a daily basis, although not for every student. There is a need for prompt feedback. A promise of most programs is that the student will be tested when ready, and the test will adhere strictly to the performance criteria established. Clark (29, 30) discusses testing instrumentation and theory and the changes necessary for individualization. Achievement testing of a normative sort is not valid for such programs. The testing structure of individualization contains pretests, self-tests, and mastery tests (Copeland and Papalia, 32). Students' performances are usually judged on a pass/fail basis at a predetermined proficiency level, usually 80 to 85 percent. To carry out this kind of program, most teachers find a need for multiple test forms. Reinert (121) has a solution: One test item is entered on a 3×5 index card. Two or three times the number of items needed for one student are prepared. Cards are shuffled and dealt to each student for tests and retests.

Testing for the known, not the unknown

Grading and awarding of credit are other administrative concerns in individualized classes. Due to the various constraints imposed by districts, teachers have had to develop various means of coping with this situation. Some teachers have individualized within the letter-grade pattern. Lorenz (98) assigns the last grade a student receives as he progresses through units of work. A series of grades such as C, C, C, B, A, A would produce an A for that period. Hellman (64) includes students in their own evaluations; they write a report on their progress and effort. Final exams, rated on a percentage basis, determine the letter grade, but an individual exam for each student covers only material he has studied. Braswell (25) established a base grade of B. Extra-work points could raise it to a higher grade; less than the minimum could lower it. Classes on the contract system have the grade determinant built into the process (Bornscheuer, 22; and Karrasch, 81). Progress reports without letter grades are increasingly acceptable to parents and administrators. In the John Dewey program ratings showing progress toward mastery were used (Levy, 89). Phillips (117) incorporated students' ideas on how to report their work. A system was developed to record the number of units completed with 80 percent oral and 85 percent written mastery, as well as an evaluation of the student's use of time.

Adjusting letter grades

Grading and credit awarding as one operation is perhaps the ideal solution. When a certain level of proficiency is met for X amount of material, credit or partial credit is awarded. In Ithaca (New York) credit is measured in fractions of one-half. Parents are notified when the student completes that amount of work, and totals are printed on the end-of-year report (Teetor, 138). Gilman (51) relates that credit is entered in one-quarter increments at Earl Wooster High School (Reno, Nevada). Campbell's (27) students receive credit when the proficiency requirement of a level is met. Their letter grades indicate the amount of effort put forth as arrived at by teacher/student consensus.

Credit and completed work

Procedures and techniques described here are applicable to secondary- and college-level individualized programs. They have been presented in this section because the motivational and aptitude levels of high school students probably cover a wider range.

Individualization in the college and university

Undergraduate courses are being individualized on campuses for many of the same reasons that secondary classes are. Diminution of the foreign language requirement for graduation is an additional factor. Where it has been abolished, individualization is a means of attracting students to an elective by reducing the chance of failure and appealing to their interests. Where the requirement is still in effect, an effort to increase successful language experiences will assure its existence. Meads (104) reports on an individualized "no-fail" elementary German course at the University of California, Riverside. Four of the lower division courses are merged into a 16-unit series. Students progress as their mastery of material permits. All assignments have been programmed. The self-paced French course at Prince George's Community College (Blanco and Charro, 14) contains a variety of learning techniques. Videotapes and programmed grammar were among the aids receiving high student ratings.

Selling language as an elective

Tracking systems for beginning levels of study offer the student a choice of goal or method from the outset. Each course is not individualized, but the attempt to provide course options for individual learners is a type of individualized instruction. Mueller's (109) program at the University of California, Berkeley, gives the student a choice of four modes of instruction in German. The Basic Course emphasizes the four skills and includes class and laboratory sessions. The Intensive Course covers four quarters of work in two quarters by meeting for ten

Giving the student a choice

hours per week. A Reading course concentrates on translation and discussion in English of language structures. Individualized Instruction is the fourth option. Rate is self-paced, and student-instructor contact time has three forms: class hours for discussion and drill, consultation hours with small groups, and office hours for testing. While students avail themselves of all four courses, figures show that individualization grew from 6 to 28 percent in three quarters, retaining its original students and attracting more from the other courses. French courses at Berkeley provide three options for the first year (Jian, 75). The first is conducted exclusively in French by the direct method; the intensive course resembles the one in German; the third is a reading course requiring passive recognition of structures although the class again is taught in French. A conversation course is to be offered during the second year. After the language requirement was dropped at St. Xavier College (Chicago), Finstein (46) conducted a reading knowledge course. Students were grouped according to their reading skill progress at intervals during the course. Materials and instruction suitable for the level of each group were prepared. By the third semester each student was able to choose readings in his interest area.

Reading courses again

At the intermediate level, Joiner (78) and Zdenek (146) describe the tracking system in Spanish and French at Winthrop College (South Carolina). The three tracks consist of a conversation track (C), a reading track (R), and a multi-skill track (MS). Students may change tracks from one semester to another or enroll in two at once, thereby completing the intermediate level in one term. Grades were improved when students had a choice of courses: B grades increased significantly from 23.1 to 30.9 percent, and F grades decreased from 6.3 to 2.4 percent. Boyse (24) discusses how the University of Wisconsin converted its second-year program into four independent one-semester courses. Designed to be taken in any sequence or concurrently, the courses include written and spoken language combinations. Boyse describes each course and its rationale and reports favorable student reaction to both the courses and the flexibility they provide to the program.

Tracking and options

Individualized instruction was employed at Gustavus Adolphus College (Minnesota) to meet the diverse backgrounds and motivations of intermediate students in French. Everett (43) describes how physical space was utilized in the five-hour-per-week program. Each week began with *un spectacle* at a large-group meeting. Eight rooms were assigned for other class hours, each room provided for instruction in a given skill. There were areas for reading, writing, conversation, listening, music, etc. The student was free to go to the area of his choosing, stay as long as he wished, or move on. The same set of activities/ materials was presented for the week in each area. Students could concentrate on one skill or sample all of them. Testing results show that average students do no better under this system but that the better students had exceptionally high scores.

At the advanced level of language study, individualization is concerned with improving performance for students committed to language study. Kalivoda's (79) model for an intensive oral course in listening and speaking has two phases. Listening comprehension is achieved by a taped program that dictates key words with English equivalents. Monologues, stories, radio plays are followed by questions on the content. The Phase II follow-up provides speaking practice as the student summarizes the listening selection to the teacher or on tape. Students accept responsibility for completion of the lessons and are expected to spend three hours per day (on their own time) with the materials. The radio is the basis for oral work in an advanced class conducted by Savignon (128) at the University of Illinois, Urbana. The broadcasts of *France-Inter*, a French news program, and the materials developed for them increased listening comprehension, contributed toward cultural understanding, and provided topics for small group discussions.

Individualization to increase competencies

Radio for listening comprehension

Brown (26) individualized Spanish literature classes at Ball State University (Muncie, Indiana). Students read at their own rates and participate in discussion groups with other students, progressing at that speed. Student-prepared and teacher-supplemented questions are brought to these sessions. The teacher circulates among groups as a resource person. When the student has reviewed the reading to his satisfaction, he presents himself for an oral exam. Two letter grades of A, B, C, or Repeat are given for content and language usage. Secondary material and reports are included. Student evaluations indicate that 89 percent favor the increased personal aid and instructor contact, and 81 percent react favorably to the self-pacing aspect and testing procedure of the course.

Colleges have more opportunity to benefit from the computer as an aid to individualization. A CAI (Computer Assisted Instruction) program in elementary German has been under development since 1965 at SUNY (State University of New York), Stonybrook (Ruplin, 124). Three hours per week are spent in small sections for recitation, dialogues, word games, and "rapping" in German. This session is the least structured; eclectic methods are used to appeal to individual ways of reasoning. A one-hour plenary session consists of a 20-minute television program (*Guten Tag*) and a half-hour grammar lecture in English. The language laboratory will soon operate on a check-out system allowing students to use materials as needed. The CAI system has a typewriter and TV screen to drill all morphological and syntactic points. Students proceed at their own pace and skip units already mastered. Ruplin claims the machines humanize the course by assuming administrative chores, thereby increasing the affective quality of the teacher-student contact. Statistics from MLA Cooperative tests testify that students are learning more. Dartmouth College (Hanover, New Hampshire) is supplementing its language courses with CAI (Allen, 3). The computer is employed for drilling and practice; it allows for self-pacing, immediate feedback, and avoidance of material sufficiently mastered. The University of Illinois utilizes the PLATO (Programmed Logic for Automated Teaching Operation) system to teach Russian translation to those students who feel they learn most effectively by a decoding process (Curtin et al., 33). The PLATO program individualizes for pace and provides for branching and remedial work. Mastery is an integral concept of the program as the student must respond correctly before proceeding. A group of students using PLATO were compared to those from a conventional classroom on a test provided by the classroom teacher. Although no significant difference in grades was evident, the PLATO students reported their average preparation time per lesson as two hours versus six hours for the non-PLATO group. Boyd-Bowman (23) reports on SUNY-Buffalo's self-instruction course in critical languages. The program is available to requesting institutions.

A humane computer

Individualization and FLES

While the elementary school has been the birthplace of the open classroom, there is a dearth of information on how FLES (Foreign Languages in the Elementary School) is adapting to individualization. Hunter's (66) paper at the Stanford Conference, "Individualizing FLES," dealt with a rationale for individualization, but gave no evidence of any observed programs at that level. Perhaps her argument that the young learner's lack of skills prohibits his involvement in self-instructional situations is an explanation for the lack of literature on individualization in FLES programs. Stewart (135) has written a manual of eight lessons to be used with small heterogeneous groups. Objectives, suggested procedures, and vocabulary cards suitable for 20-

A neglected area

251

minute daily lessons comprise the packet. These less complex packets resemble materials developed for secondary programs.

Personalization for more student involvement

Not everyone is ready to individualize instruction, and unfortunately, not all individualized instruction is personalized. Every teacher can strive to personalize his class, and many of the techniques derived from individualized programs play a role in the traditional classroom. Several recent attempts to personalize the learning situation are worth recounting because their goal is student involvement regardless of the framework. Meade and Morain (103) teach culture through a "culture cluster," several capsule episodes on a central theme. In their example of a French wedding, they present short daily sessions to develop the concept of the civil and religious ceremony. This allows for interaction of language and culture. The climactic activity is a mini-drama that encourages student involvement in a simulated wedding. Tiefenbrun (140) requires her students at SUNY, Brooklyn, to rearrange memorized dialogues so that they better apply to real situations. Groups then dramatize the scenes. Joiner (77) employs a similar technique but provides a prop for students as they work in pairs. The prop serves as a point of departure for their impromptu conversation as well as a control of material.

A feel for culture through simulation

An example of false labeling that personalized instruction must guard against is the implication that procedures are student-centered simply because one wishes them to be. Pfister (116) presents an outline of the structure he deems necessary for an individualized class. He argues for control over classroom activities and suggests that the individualization comes in the form of student response. His evidence for "individualization" is the use of personalized questions, but even that is followed by choral repetition of each response.

Research and experimentation

Data is slowly being evaluated as experimentation with individualized programs advances. Statistical analysis is not limited to achievement scores; attitude, enrollment figures, and student reaction to courses are of primary consideration as well. Valdman (142) cautions against placing greater emphasis on affective outcomes than on cognitive ones. He suggests strategies for evaluating proficiency as it interacts with the various abilities of students. Hartley (61) at the

Achievement as only one factor

Lock step versus self-pacing

252

University of South Carolina compared an experimental self-paced class with a lock step beginning Spanish class. Students in the self-paced program achieved as well or better than traditional students on the MLA Listening and Reading Tests. Hartley also concluded that the combination of the textbook with behavioral objectives was a sufficient tool for study. This research served as the basis for development of an expanded self-paced program at the University of South Carolina (Hartley and Dannerbeck, 62). This elective course has a self-pacing component, as well as small- and large-group activities for speaking practice and culture. "Super-Mastery Units" enable students to concentrate in an area of personal appeal. Fryer and Hartley (49) have evaluated student reactions to the program. Four elements elicited positive response: the self-pacing and testing procedure, prior knowledge of objectives, the self-motivation aspect, and the experience with native informants.

Programming the grammar component

Programmed instruction to teach certain grammar concepts in Spanish was investigated at Southern Illinois University (Prince and Casey, 120). The programmed grammar in conjunction with the normal class activity resulted in significantly higher gain scores on an objective grammar test. Clausing, Mueller, and Voge (31) evaluated the individualized program in German at the University of California, Berkeley, by comparing it with the basic course. Final unit tests for each course were administered to all students; those from the individualized program did as well or better on all measures. An analysis of individualized students' contact time with the instructor revealed that 59.8 percent was of an individual nature and 40.2 percent in groups.

Success of a packaged course

Teichert (139) studied the effectiveness of learning packages with an experimental college German class. Students had to complete one package per week. Two days a week experimental and control groups held similar full-class sessions. The use of the packages had a significant $(p < .01)$ effect on students' midterm and final achievement and on the Listening and Reading portions of the Modern Language Association Cooperative Foreign Language Test (MLA-CFLT). The data imply that information on course objectives, programmed grammar, and deadlines are factors important to successful individualization.

Effect on the social climate of the classroom

Two experiments with individualized instructional techniques were conducted in French classes at Clarence High School (New York) by Papalia and Zampogna (114, 115). The first was to determine achievement and the social climate of an individualized class as compared to a control group. The experimental group of French III students used self-instructional materials and spent most of their time in small-group work. A series of communication games promoted group interaction. Areas of significant difference on The Learning Environment Inventory Scale indicated that the individualized students felt more challenged and satisfied by their work and cared more about one another. The experimental group also scored higher on all four skills of the MLA Cooperative tests (p <.05). The teacher's classroom behavior as related to attrition was chosen for the second study. The teacher of the experimental group received training in interaction analysis and group processes. The experimental treatment included use of learning packets and an integrated model of large-group, small-group, and individual-study activities. Three results were noted: 63 percent of the experimental group enrolled for French IV versus 35 percent of the control; on a Teacher Description Instrument the individualized students gave their teacher significantly higher ratings on categories associated with positive attitudes; and the experimental group achieved significantly (p <.05) higher scores on all four skills as measured by the MLA Cooperative tests.

The teacher and attrition

More experimentation of this sort is needed. While there is justification in measuring outcomes other than achievement, the inclusion of achievement measures guarantees an accountability factor in the program by assuring that cognitive learning is also taking place at a satisfactory level.

Planning for individualization

The teacher or administrator considering individualizing classes needs to evaluate his own unique situation. No two programs encompass identical sets of circumstances. Personal visitations to individualized classes and reading in the professional literature can provide background. Several handbooks can be recommended as an overall yet detailed review. Gougher's (54) *Individualization of Instruction in Foreign Languages: A Practical Guide* and Altman's (6) *Individualizing the Foreign Language Classroom* are informative and realistic. Workshops in Individualization for in-service teachers are increasingly available in all parts of the country. The University of Washington offers one in cooperation with Bellevue Public Schools. West Chester College in Pennsylvania holds two levels of summer workshops. A "Work-In" experience in France, Germany, and Spain is sponsored by the University of Minnesota. Many national and state meetings of

Self-instruction in individualization

Increasing workshops

language teachers include workshops in their conference programs. In these and others, teachers develop materials and examine the new roles and attitudes demanded of them as learning "managers." Altman (7) believes that teachers of individualized classes must be re-educated to the concept of "freedom," to the role of facilitating learning, not interfering with it. Students need to be re-educated to assume responsibility for their own learning. McLennan (102) presents a format and guidelines for planning in-service programs or workshops. On a less formal basis teachers sharing their own experiences with individualization in local in-service programs are untapped resources. Smith (132), a classroom teacher, drew upon her success with supplemental packages aimed at motivating second-year students. She designed a package to teach others the technique. Her colleagues reacted realistically to a self-instructional approach.

A topic for in-service meetings

Thorough and thoughtful preplanning is crucial to a successful individualized endeavor. The innovator must evaluate carefully each constraint and be knowledgeable enough about alternatives so that he can select the best one. Bockman (16) and Bockman and Bockman (21) raise some management considerations and provide a complete check list to identify teacher and student processes as they function in a given district. While Bockman's guidelines consist of a detailed series of questions, Jakobovits' (68) model is an open-ended topical outline. It involves identification of areas for change in curriculum, class activities, etc. Subsequently, these areas are to be ranked for feasibility and concern before action is initiated. A ten-item questionnaire that summarizes planning considerations is offered by Sutton (136). McKim (101) presents case studies in planning and evaluation of school facilities. The use of guidelines is advocated to assure the design of a program compatible to the students, teachers, and school involved.

Designing a program to fit unique needs

Teacher education

A slow but fundamental change is creeping into the undergraduate methods courses. The aim of arming the prospective teacher with techniques for various exercises is undergoing a transformation. Jarvis (73) recommends an approach that would train teachers in flexibility and decision-making behaviors. Ways to develop flexible, humane, sensitive teachers and to equip them with diagnostic, evaluative, and learning expertise are required. Smith (129) integrates individualized techniques into all aspects of the methods course. Students practice grouping, write learning packages, prepare tests. They also participate

The teacher as decision maker

255

in small group activities and work together on unit plans. Students in teams teach Moskowitz's (108) methods course. They research their topics, demonstrate them, and act as informants for follow-up group work. While these future teachers are learning by doing, the instructor's role as a source of information and organizer is crucial. Hancock's (56) concern is sensitizing teachers to individual differences in motivation, attitude, and discipline. Via simulation techniques, they identify and discuss their reactions to realistic classroom situations.

Summary

The phenomenon of individualized instruction is a growing one. It affects students, teachers, and schools, for the changes it implies are not superficial; they will uproot long-held attitudes and convictions. Individualization of language programs has now been in progress for several years, and trends can be identified.

1 Theoretically, the concepts of individualization are well grounded in learning psychology: Students learn at different rates, for different reasons, and in different ways.
2 The number of teachers turning to individualization, as a response to the realities they face, is increasing. The concept is spreading at the classroom level; it is not being imposed "from above."
3 It is becoming difficult to classify programs into neat categories. Programs are gaining in sophistication by incorporating several elements into their design. Self-pacing is a basic component of most courses; seldom is it the sole consideration.
4 Ready-made model programs cannot be effectively packaged and sold. The instructional process and physical facilities are being tailored to the needs of each unique situation.
5 Criterion-referenced testing is replacing normative testing; consequently grading and credit practices are being revised.
6 More research is needed to describe and analyze learning modes, and diagnostic tools must be designed.
7 Experimentation must focus on isolated procedures and techniques as they interact with students.
8 Programs are being evaluated as they affect motivation, attitude, and attrition. This does not mean that achievement should be ignored, only that it assume its proper place.
9 There is a danger in the bandwagon effect. The term can be falsely applied to disguise restrictive and impersonal practices.

10 Planning and evaluation must precede implementation; the boundary between freedom and chaos is easily traversed.

References, Individualization and personalization

1 Adams, Dennis M. "Some Questions Concerning Behavioral Objectives." *Clearing House* 47(1972): 26–27.

2 Aldridge, Hal. "Student Contracts." *Forum* 10 (1971):4–7.

3 Allen, John R. "Individualizing Foreign Language Instruction with Computers at Dartmouth." *Foreign Language Annals* 5(1972):348–49.

4 Alonso, Elizabeth B., and Mirta R. Vega. "Quinmester Courses—What Are They?" *American Foreign Language Teacher* 2,iv(1972):12–13.

5 Altman, Howard B. "Individualized Foreign Language Instruction:Ex Uno Plura," 1–14 in Howard B. Altman,ed., *Individualizing the Foreign Language Classroom:Perspectives for Teachers*. Rowley, Massachusetts: Newbury House, 1972.

6 ———ed. *Individualizing the Foreign Language Classroom:Perspectives for Teachers*. Rowley, Massachusetts: Newbury House, 1972.

7 ——— "The Three R's of Individualization: Reeducation, Responsibility, and Relevance." *Foreign Language Annals* 6(1972):206–13.

8 ——— and Robert L. Politzer,eds., *Individualizing Foreign Language Instruction*. Rowley, Massachusetts: Newbury House, 1971.

9 Antoine, Geraldine. " 'Conversational Spanish': A One Year High School Course." *Hispania* 55(1972):891–93.

10 Arendt, Jermaine D. "The Function and Techniques of Group Work in an Individualized Program," 105–13 in Howard B. Altman and Robert L. Politzer,eds., *Individualizing Foreign Language Instruction*. Rowley, Massachusetts: Newbury House, 1971.

11 ——— "Reports and Recommendations of the Committee on Group Work in an Individualized Foreign Language Program," 114–16 in Howard B. Altman and Robert L. Politzer,eds., *Individualizing Foreign Language Instruction*. Rowley, Massachusetts: Newbury House, 1971.

12 Barrett, Martin. "Space Problems in Individualizing Foreign Language Learning." *Foreign Language Annals* 5(1972):480–81.

13 Barrutia, Richard. "Individualized Procedures and Techniques for Teaching a Second Language." *Individualization of Foreign Language Learning in America* 5(1972):7–11.

14 Blanco, Marjorie B., and Mary E. Charro. "Self-Paced Introductory French at Prince George's Community College." *Foreign Language Annals* 5(1972):350–52.

15 Bockman, John F. "An Analysis of the Learning Process:A Rationale for the Individualization of Foreign Language Instruction," 33–52 in Howard B. Altman,ed., *Individualizing the Foreign Language Classroom:Perspectives for Teachers*. Rowley, Massachusetts: Newbury House, 1972.

16 ——— "A Checklist for Development and Control of Individualized Instruction," 79–85 in Ronald L. Gougher,ed., *Individualization of Instruction in Foreign Languages:A Practical Guide*. Philadelphia: Center for Curriculum Development, 1972.

17 ——— "An Experiment in Independent Foreign Language Study." *Arizona Foreign Language Teachers Forum* 17,ii(1970):8–11. [EDRS: ED 037 135.]

18 ——— "Reports and Recommendations of the Committee on the Process of Contracting in Foreign Language Learning," 122–24 in Howard B. Altman and Robert L. Politzer,eds., *Individualizing Foreign Language Instruction*. Rowley, Massachusetts: Newbury House, 1971.

19 ——— *A Three-Year Research Project on Individualized Foreign Language Learning Based in Programmed Instruction and in Management by Consultation—Summary of Rationale and Principal Findings*. Tucson: Tucson Public Schools, 1971. [EDRS: ED 048 813.]

20 ——— and Valerie M. Bockman. "Contracts versus the Commitment Process." *Foreign Language Annals* 6(1973):359–66.

21 ——— "The Management of Individualized Programs," 51–78 in Ronald L. Gougher,ed., *Individualization of Instruction in Foreign Languages:A Practical Guide*. Philadelphia: Center for Curriculum Development, 1972.

22 Bornscheuer, Joan H. "The Grade Contract and the Language Class." *Foreign Language Annals* 6(1973):367–70.

23 Boyd-Bowman, Peter. "National Self-Instructional Program in Critical Languages." *Modern Language Journal* 56(1972):163–67.

24 Boyse, James A. "D'Ici là:A Second-Year College French Program." *French Review* 45(1972):621–30.

25 Braswell, David M. "Individualizing a Junior High School Foreign Language Program," 103–31 in

Howard B. Altman,ed., *Individualizing the Foreign Language Classroom:Perspectives for Teachers*. Rowley, Massachusetts: Newbury House, 1972.

26 Brown, James W. "Don Quixote Individualized?" *Individualization of Foreign Language Learning in America* 5(1972):4–6.

27 Campbell, Patricia Ann. "Continuous Progress German, Rose Hill Junior High School, Redmond, Washington." *Foreign Language Annals* 5(1972): 477–79.

28 Carroll, Elna R., and Robert McLennan. "Adapting Existing Materials to Individualized Instruction," 177–85 in Howard B. Altman and Robert L. Politzer,eds., *Individualizing Foreign Language Instruction*. Rowley, Massachusetts: Newbury House, 1971.

29 Clark, John L.D. *Foreign Language Testing:Theory and Practice*. Philadelphia: Center for Curriculum Development, 1972.

30 —— "Measurement Implications of Recent Trends in Foreign Language Teaching," 219–57 in Dale L. Lange and Charles J. James,eds., *Foreign Language Education:A Reappraisal*. ACTFL Review of Foreign Language Education, Volume 4. Skokie, Illinois: National Textbook Company, 1972.

31 Clausing, Gerhard, Klaus A. Mueller, and Wilfried M. Voge. "Individualized German Instruction at the College Level—A First Appraisal." *Foreign Language Annals* 6(1972):73–87.

32 Copeland, Josephine E., and Anthony Papalia. "An Integrated Model for the Production of Auto-Tutorial Materials." *Foreign Language Annals* 6(1972): 255–57.

33 Curtin, Constance, Douglas Clayton, Cheryl Finch, David Moor, and Lois Woodruff. "Teaching the Translation of Russian by Computer." *Modern Language Journal* 56(1972):354–60.

34 DeTullio, Thomas. "Chaos and Creativity." *American Foreign Language Teacher* 3,ii(1972):14–15, 32.

35 Deutch, Rachel F. "A Lure for the Reluctant Learner." *French Review* 45(1972):635–41.

36 Disick, Renée S. "Developing Communication Skills Through Small Group Techniques." *American Foreign Language Teacher* 3,ii(1972):3–7.

37 —— "Developing Positive Attitudes in Intermediate Foreign Language Classes." *Modern Language Journal* 56(1972):417–20.

38 —— *Performance Objectives in Foreign Language Teaching. MLA/ERIC Focus Report 25*. New York: MLA/ERIC, 1971. [EDRS: ED 055 522.]

39 Elkins, Robert J. "Horizontal and Vertical LAPs." *Individualization of Foreign Language Learning in America* 4(1972):11–15.

40 —— *Team Teaching and Individualized Instruction*. [Paper presented at Conference of Modern Language, History and Social Studies Teachers,

Wetzlar, Germany, 2 December 1970.] [EDRS: ED 057 644.]

41 —— Theodore B. Kalivoda and Genelle Morain. "Fusion of the Four Skills:A Technique for Facilitating Communicative Exchange." *Modern Language Journal* 56(1972):426–29.

42 —— "Teaching Culture Through the Audio-Motor Unit." *Foreign Language Annals* 6(1972): 61–67.

43 Everett, Aaron B. "Individualized Instruction for Intermediate French." *French Review* 45(1972): 988–98.

44 Fearing, Percy, and Jermaine D. Arendt. *The Extended Foreign Language Sequence:With Emphasis on New Courses for Levels IV and V*. Minnesota State Department of Education, St. Paul Division, 1971. [EDRS: ED 047 586.]

45 Fiber, Louise A. "Using Human Resources Costs Only Time, Energy, Interest." *Accent on ACTFL* 3,iii(1973):14–15.

46 Finstein, Milton W. "French for Reading Knowledge—An Option." *French Review* 45(1972):838–41.

47 Fitzgibbons, Nancyanne. "The Open Classroom: A Case Study," 97–107 in James W. Dodge,ed., *Leadership for Continuing Development*. [Reports of the Working Committees of the Northeast Conference on the Teaching of Foreign Languages.] New York: MLA Materials Center, 1971.

48 Flynn, Mary B. "Individualized Instruction—How I Tried to Resist and Couldn't." *Foreign Language Annals* 6(1972):257–58.

49 Fryer, T. Bruce, and Peggy J. Hartley. *Student. Reaction to Self-paced Spanish at the College Level*. [Unpublished.]

50 Gagné, Robert M. *The Conditions of Learning*. New York: Holt, Rinehart and Winston, 1970.

51 Gilman, Robert A. "Past Results Never Satisfy Nevada Teacher." *Accent on ACTFL* 3,iii(1973): 18–20.

52 Gougher, Ronald L. "Defining Individualized Instruction," 1–5 in Ronald L. Gougher,ed., *Individualization of Instruction in Foreign Languages:A Practical Guide*. Philadelphia: Center for Curriculum Development, 1972.

53 —— "Individualization of Foreign Language Learning:What is Being Done," 221–45 in Dale L. Lange,ed., *Pluralism in Foreign Language Education*. ACTFL Review of Foreign Language Education, Volume 3. Skokie, Illinois: National Textbook Company, 1973.

54 ——ed. *Individualization of Instruction in Foreign Languages:A Practical Guide*. Philadelphia: Center for Curriculum Development, 1972.

55 Grittner, Frank M. "Behavioral Objectives, Skinnerian Rats and Trojan Horses." *Foreign Language Annals* 6(1972):52–60.

56 Hancock, Charles R. "Guiding Teachers to Respond to Individual Differences in the Affective

Domain." *Foreign Language Annals* 6(1972):225–31.

57 —— "Student Aptitude, Attitude and Motivation," 127–55 in Dale L. Lange and Charles J. James,eds., *Foreign Language Education:A Reappraisal.* ACTFL Review of Foreign Language Education, Volume 4, Skokie, Illinois: National Textbook Company, 1972.

58 Hanzeli, Victor E., and F. William D. Love. "From Individualized Instruction to Individualized Learning." *Foreign Language Annals* 5(1972):321–30.

59 Harrell, Marcia. "The Open Classroom in French." *American Foreign Language Teacher* 2,ii(1971):21.

60 Hartley, Ernest B., and Peggy J. Hartley. "Teach Yourself to Write Behavioral Objectives:—An Exercise for Foreign Language Teachers." *American Foreign Language Teacher* 3,ii(1972):16–18,23–25.

61 Hartley, Peggy Johnson. *A Comparison between Achievement in an Individualized Self-Paced Program and a Conventional Lockstep Program in Basic College Spanish.* Unpublished Ph.D. dissertation: University of South Carolina, 1972.

62 —— and Francis J. Dannerbeck. *An Experiment in Self-Pacing and Subsequent Implementation in Basic College Spanish.* [Unpublished.]

63 Heard, Lorraine E. "Foreign Language and the Group Context:Expanding Student Roles." *Foreign Language Annals* 5(1972):313–20.

64 Hellman, Sharon. "You CAN Individualize the Teaching of Foreign Languages!" *French Review* 45(1972):1152–60.

65 Horne, Kibbey M. "Optimum Class Size for Intensive Language Instruction." *Modern Language Journal* 54(1970):189–95.

66 Hunter, Madeline. "Individualizing FLES," 59–63 in Howard B. Altman and Robert L. Politzer,eds., *Individualizing Foreign Language Instruction.* Rowley, Massachusetts: Newbury House, 1971.

67 Jakobovits, Leon A. *Foreign Language Learning:A Psycholinguistic Analysis of the Issues.* Rowley, Massachusetts: Newbury House, 1970.

68 —— "Procedural Steps in Individualizing FL Instruction." *Foreign Language Annals* 5(1971):96–98.

69 —— "Psychological Perspectives on Individualizing Foreign Language Instruction," 88–102 in Howard B. Altman and Robert L. Politzer,eds., *Individualizing Foreign Language Instruction.* Rowley, Massachusetts: Newbury House, 1971.

70 —— "A Relevant Curriculum:An Instrument for Polling Student Opinion," in Joseph A. Tursi, ed., *Foreign Languages and the New Student.* Reports of the Working Committees of the Northeast Conference on the Teaching of Foreign Languages. New York: MLA Materials Center, 1970.

71 —— *A Typology of FL Education with Particular Emphasis on Compensatory and Individualized Instruction.* [Paper presented at the Kentucky Foreign Language Conference, Lexington, April 1971.] [EDRS: ED 062 884.]

72 Jarvis, Gilbert A. "Individualized Learning—Where Can We Risk Compromise?" *Modern Language Journal* 55(1971):375–78.

73 —— "Teacher Education Goals:They're Tearing Up the Street Where I Was Born." *Foreign Language Annals* 6(1972):198–205.

74 Jennings, Margaret. *Why Study Foreign Languages?* Rock Hill, South Carolina School District. [Mimeo.]

75 Jian, Gerard. "Le Programme de première année à Berkeley." *French Review* 45(1972):846–49.

76 Johns, H.H. "Career Development Becomes FL Objective." *Accent on ACTFL* 3,i(1972):16–17,20.

77 Joiner, Elizabeth. *The Self-Directed Dialogue:A Technique for Conversational Practice.* [Unpublished.]

78 —— *Tracking System, Winthrop College.* Rock Hill, South Carolina. [Mimeo.]

79 Kalivoda, Theodore B. "An Individual Study Course for Facilitating Advanced Oral Skills." *Modern Language Journal* 56(1972):492–95.

80 —— and Robert J. Elkins. "Teaching as Facilitation and Management of Learning," 61–96 in Dale L. Lange and Charles J. James,eds., *Foreign Language Education:A Reappraisal.* ACTFL Review of Foreign Language Education, Volume 4. Skokie, Illinois: National Textbook Company, 1972.

81 Karrasch, Ada. "Contracts Cure." *Accent on ACTFL* 3,iii(1973):11.

82 Kentz, Rita O. "The Kids Are More Important than the System:An Experience with Personalized Instruction." *American Foreign Language Teacher* 3,i(1972):35–37.

83 Krill, Carole L. "A Confession:We Need to Individualize." *Accent on ACTFL,* 2,iv(1972):6–8.

84 Lafayette, Robert C. "Diversification:The Key to Student-Centered Programs." *Modern Language Journal* 56(1972):349–54.

85 LaLeike, Fred. *Individualized Foreign Language Program.* West Bend, Wisconsin: Joint School District No. 1, 1970. [EDRS: ED 047 574.]

86 Lange, Dale L.,ed., *Individualization of Instruction.* ACTFL Review of Foreign Language Education, Volume 2. Skokie, Illinois: National Textbook Company, 1972.

87 ——ed. *Pluralism in Foreign Language Education.* ACTFL Review of Foreign Language Education, Volume 3. Skokie, Illinois: National Textbook Company, 1973.

88 —— and Charles J. James,eds. *Foreign Language Education:A Reappraisal.* ACTFL Review of Foreign Language Education, Volume 4. Skokie, Illinois: National Textbook Company, 1972.

89 Levy, Stephen L. "Foreign Languages in John Dewey High School, New York City:An Individualized Approach," 130–48 in Ronald L. Gougher, ed., *Individualization of Instruction in Foreign Languages:A Practical Guide.* Philadelphia: Center for Curriculum Development, 1972.

90 —— "John Dewey High School:Individualiza-

tion in an Inner-City School." *Foreign Language Annals* 5(1972):346–48.

91 ——— et al. *Dewey Independent Study Kit and Course of Study:French, Levels I, II, III, IV; Hebrew, Level IV; Italian, Levels I, II, III, IV; Spanish, Levels I, II, IV.* Brooklyn: John Dewey High School, 1971. [EDRS: ED 054 700.]

92 Lipton, Gladys. "Curricula for New Goals," 187–218 in Dale L. Lange and Charles J, James. eds., *Foreign Language Education:A Reappraisal.* ACTFL Review of Foreign Language Education, Volume 4. Skokie, Illinois: National Textbook Company, 1972.

93 Logan, Gerald E. "A Comment on Including Culture in an Individualized Program." *Foreign Language Annals* 5(1971):99–101.

94 ——— "Curricula for Individualized Instruction," 133–55 in Dale L. Lange,ed., *Individualization of Instruction.* ACTFL Review of Foreign Language Education, Volume 2. Skokie, Illinois: National Textbook Company, 1972.

95 ——— *German Curriculum.* Morgan Hill, California: Morgan Hill Unified School District, 1969.

96 ——— "Individualized FL Instruction:Is It Just Another Fad?" *Accent on ACTFL* 3,iii(1973):6–8.

97 ——— "A Totally Individualized High School Program." *Individualization of Foreign Language Learning in America* 1(1970):8–9.

98 Lorenz, Jean Marie. "Course Description for the Continuous Progress Program in Spanish." *Foreign Language Annals* 5(1972):352–53.

99 Lourie, Elizabeth S. "A Comprehensive Approach to Individualization in a French Class." *French Review* 46(1972):371–74.

100 Mager, Robert F. *Preparing Instructional Objectives.* Belmont, California: Fearon Publishers, 1962.

101 McKim, Lester W. "Planning for Individualization:A Necessary Look before Leaping," 67–87 in Howard B. Altman,ed., *Individualizing the Foreign Language Classroom:Perspectives for Teachers.* Rowley, Massachusetts: Newbury House, 1972.

102 McLennan, Robert L. "A Guide to In-Service Training of Teachers for Individualized Instruction in Foreign Languages." *Foreign Language Annals* 5(1971):241–43.

103 Meade, Betsy, and Genelle Morain. "The Culture Cluster." *Foreign Language Annals* 6(1973):331–38.

104 Meads, William. " 'No-Fail' German:Individualized Program at the University of California." *Foreign Language Annals* 5(1972):481–83.

105 Mickelson, John M. "Personalized Instruction: How New Is It?" *The Education Digest* 38,iii(1972): 38–40.

106 Moore, Merriam M. *"Mini-Course" Curriculum for German IV and German V.* Ridgefield, Connecticut: Ridgefield High School, 1972. [EDRS: ED 050 633.]

107 Morrey, Robert A. "Individualization of Foreign Language Instruction Through Differentiated Staf-

fing." *Modern Language Journal* 56(1972):483–88.

108 Moskowitz, Gertrude. "For Methods Instructors: A Less Visible, Less Verbal Approach." *Foreign Language Annals* 6(1972):232–36.

109 Mueller, Klaus A. *The Student Has A Choice: Four Instructional Modes for College Students of German.* [Paper presented at the Conference of the American Association of Teachers of German, Chicago, 1971.] [EDRS: ED 056 599.]

110 Mueller, Theodore H. "The Development of Curriculum Materials for Individualized Instruction," 148–54 in Howard B. Altman and Robert L. Politzer,eds., *Individualizing Foreign Language Instruction.* Rowley, Massachusetts: Newbury House, 1971.

111 Nault, Richard. "Open Education—A Gradualist Approach." *The Elementary School Journal* 73(1972): 107–111.

112 Niedzielski, Henri. "From Rehearsed Monologue to Spontaneous Acting." *American Foreign Language Teacher* 3,i(1972):16–18.

113 ——— *New Objectives in Foreign Language Teaching.* [Paper presented at the First Annual HALT-HAVA Conference, Honolulu, 1969.] [EDRS: ED 048 787.]

114 Papalia, Anthony, and Joseph Zampogna. "An Experiment in Individualized Instruction through Small Group Interaction." *Foreign Language Annals* 5(1972):302–06.

115 ——— "An Experimental Study on Teachers' Classroom Behaviors and Their Effect on FL Attrition." *Modern Language Journal* 56(1972): 421–24.

116 Pfister, Guenter G. "Individualized Instruction and Control—Are They Compatible Terms?" *American Foreign Language Teacher* 3,i(1972): 29–30.

117 Phillips, June K. "Students Create Report Cards." *Accent on ACTFL* 3,ii(1972):34–35.

118 Politzer, Robert L. "Toward Individualization in Foreign Language Teaching." *Modern Language Journal* 55(1971):207–12.

119 Pope, Ernest. "Modified Individualized Foreign Language Learning." *Accent on ACTFL* 2,iv(1972): 9–11.

120 Prince, Marilyn M., and John P. Casey. "Programmed Instruction Helps Teach Spanish Grammar." *Modern Language Journal* 56(1972):491–92.

121 Reinert, Harry. "Beginners Are Individuals, Too!" 89–101 in Howard B. Altman,ed., *Individualizing the Foreign Language Classroom:Perspectives for Teachers.* Rowley, Massachusetts: Newbury House, 1972.

122 Rogers, Carl R. *Freedom to Learn.* Columbus, Ohio: Charles E. Merrill, 1969.

123 Rosenthal, Bianca. "Individualized Foreign Language Instruction:Performance Objectives." *Foreign Language Annals* 6(1972):253–55.

124 Ruplin, Ferdinand A. *Consistency, the Hobgoblin of the Petty Mind or in Support of Eclecticism.* [Paper presented to the Conference of the American Asso-

ciation of Teachers of German, Chicago, 1971.] [EDRS: ED 057 671.]

125 Ryberg, Donald C. "Student Involvement, Flexibility and Individualization." *Washington Foreign Language Program Newsletter* (February 1971):1–8. [EDRS: ED 048 785.]

126 ——— and Marcia Hallock. "Development of Mini-Courses at Marshall-University High School: Individualization and Interest," 119–29 in Ronald L. Gougher,ed., *Individualization of Instruction in Foreign Languages:A Practical Guide*. Philadelphia: Center for Curriculum Development, 1972.

127 Savaiano, Geraldine. *Individualized Modular Culture Units—A New Dimension for Summer Travel*. [Paper presented at the Conference of the American Association of Teachers of Spanish and Portuguese, Chicago, 1971.] [EDRS: ED 057 673.]

128 Savignon, Sandra J. "A L'Écoute de France-Inter: The Use of Radio in a Student-Centered Oral French Class." *French Review* 46(1972):342–49.

129 Smith, Alfred N. "How to Train Prospective Foreign Language Teachers in the Use of Individualized Instruction." *Foreign Language Annals* 6(1972):220–24.

130 ——— *Motivation*. [Paper presented at the Conference of Washington Foreign Language Teachers Association, Ellensburg, 1971.] [EDRS: ED 050 639.]

131 Smith, Philip D. *A Comparison of the Cognitive and Audio-Lingual Approaches to Foreign Language Instruction: The Pennsylvania Foreign Language Project*. Philadelphia: Center for Curriculum Development, 1970.

132 Smith, Vicki. "A Package on Packaging for Teachers." Pittsburgh: Churchill Area School District, 1972. [Mimeo.]

133 Steiner, Florence. "Behavioral Objectives and Evaluation," 35–78 in Dale L. Lange,ed., *Individualization of Instruction*. ACTFL Review of Foreign Language Education. Volume 2, Skokie, Illinois: National Textbook Company, 1972.

134 Stern, H.H., and Alice Weinrib. *French-Language Teaching Modules:A New Approach to Language-Teaching Materials* Toronto: Ontario Institute for Studies in Education, 1971. [EDRS: ED 047 578.]

135 Stewart, Adela Artola. *Mini-clases de espanol:A Small Group Process To Beginning Spanish Instruction in the Elementary School*. Phoenix: Wilson Elementary School District, 1972. [EDRS: ED 058 801.]

136 Sutton, Donna E. "Preplanning—An Essential Ingredient for Successful Individualized FL Programs." *Foreign Language Annals* 5 (1971): 243–44.

137 ——— "Problems of Individualized Instruction—How Some Successful Programs Deal with Them," 86–114 in Ronald L. Gougher,ed., *Individualization of Instruction in Foreign Languages:A Practical Guide*. Philadelphia: Center for Curriculum Development, 1972.

138 Teetor, Will Robert. "Grading and Awarding Credit on a 'Humane' and Sensible Basis: The Ithaca Experience," 149–65 in Ronald L. Gougher, ed., *Individualization of Instruction in Foreign Languages: A Practical Guide*. Philadelphia: Center for Curriculum Development, 1972.

139 Teichert, Herman U. "An Experimental Study Using Learning Packages in Beginning College German." *Modern Language Journal* 56(1972): 488–90.

140 Tiefenbrun, Susan W. "The Use of Planned Dramatic Scenes with the Audio-Lingual Method." *French Review* 45(1972):855–59.

141 Troyanovich, John M. "Foreign Languages and the Dodo Bird:A Lesson from Darwin." *Foreign Language Annals* 5(1972):341–44.

142 Valdman, Albert. "Criteria for Measurement of Success in an Individualized Program," 66–80 in Howard B. Altman and Robert L. Politzer,eds., *Individualizing Foreign Language Instruction*. Rowley, Massachusetts: Newbury House, 1971.

143 Valette, Rebecca M., and Renée S. Disick. *Modern Language Performance Objectives and Individualization:A Handbook*. New York: Harcourt, Brace, Jovanovich, 1972.

144 Wainwright, Judith. *Individualized Learning in the Foreign Language Program:A Proposal for an Advanced French Curriculum*. Whitewater: Wisconsin Association of Foreign Language Teachers, 1971. [EDRS: ED 055 504.]

145 Young, Robert B. "Individualized Learning of English—The Mexico City Experiment." *Foreign Language Annals* 6(1972):108–12.

146 Zdenek, Joseph W. "Try Tracking." *Modern Language Journal* 57(1973):133-34.

9

Empathy for a second culture: motivations and techniques

Introduction

American language teachers have been attracted to workshops on "the culture" because for them and their students this facet of the discipline has "turned on" a fresh interest in language learning. Will the interest last? Does it warrant the long-range effort, that would be necessary to develop the knowledge of a culture and society the workshops make us realize we need?

We have been so subject to fads that the burden of proof rests on a positive claim: This time, we have something more solid than a fad on which to build. This assertion seems plausible, for reasons we shall look at immediately. The end of this chapter suggests how it may be feasible and, indeed, fun to develop the needed knowledge, whose precise nature will meanwhile become more definable as we explore the need for it.

Among the reasons for expecting a sustained interest is a desire of many Americans for the personal capacity to communicate more successfully with persons of some other culture, particularly for purposes of travel or negotiation. The need for such communication will certainly increase with international contact; and the hazards of cross-cultural misunderstanding, according to the research, require consider-

Howard L. Nostrand
University of Washington

Fad or durable reality?

The need of individuals to communicate

Howard L. Nostrand (Docteur de l'Université de Paris) is Professor of Romance Languages and Literature at the University of Washington. His B.A. is from Amherst, his M.A. from Harvard. His thesis dealt with Greek, Latin, and French literature. He has also taught Italian and Spanish. He has been U.S. Cultural Attaché in Peru, a member of the funding committee for NDEA media research, chairman of the NEA National Commission on Teacher Education and Professional Standards, and a member of the humanities committee for *World Book*. He has been a member of the MLA Foreign Language Program Steering Committee and MLA/ERIC Advisory Board, president of the AATF, Romance editor of the *Modern Language Quarterly*, and Director of an NDEA Institute. He has had a Guggenheim Fellowship and directed seven research projects for the U.S. Office of Education. He has published 95 articles and written or edited 11 books, among them *Le théâtre antique, Ortega y Gasset's Mission of the University, The Cultural Attaché, Dos problemas de educación cultural, Viewer's Guide to College French, Research on Language Teaching: An Annotated International Bibliography, The University and Human Understanding, Film Recital of French Poems: Cultural Commentary,* and *Background Data for the Teaching of French*. He is a member of the ACTFL bibliography committee.

able knowledge of culture patterns, social customs, and institutions, as well as language skills.

The second reason for expecting sustained interest is further from the surface of public consciousness. It is the changed posture of the United States from one of dominating to one of competing, in which successful negotiation will have to involve the ability to persuade, hence the need to see clearly the other person's attitude. Government and industry have been searching for means of developing this communicative capacity in their representatives. We have tried with tragic results the egocentric assumption that Russians, Chinese, Vietnamese, Latin Americans, and the European peoples all react just about as we do—or when they prove uncooperative, that they are the reversed "mirror" image of our virtues. Overcoming our ethnocentrism involves a deep change in public outlook and education. Enlightened policy makers will need the support of a public that is sensitive to the differences in peoples' values, assumptions, and modes of thought and feeling.

The national need to persuade

Fortunately, we are growing conscious of a need for the same sort of sensitivity at home. In our own country, tensions among subcultures have produced a widespread curiosity to know about different lifestyles, and this is a third, independent reason to expect a lasting interest in cultural differences. Both minority peoples and the majority live with conflicts of values, conflicts between ethnic value systems and between the old and the new. The majority person's psychological and material security, is tied to community-wide norms, including a collective work ethnic—the American way of the melting pot. Yet the prejudices and material discrimination inherent in that basis for security are now perceived to conflict with the professed values of liberty and justice for all. The authority that enforced the old norms had a mystique of acceptance that clothed its naked force, but in its clashes with protest and alienation during the 1960s it broke out of that mystique. The psychological effect has been a gradual reexamination of the values in conflict, some anxiety over the proposed alternative of cultural pluralism, and curiosity about reconciliations of old and new attempted by other peoples; for their lifestyles, like ours, are evolving from the industrial ethnic to a post-industrial society—a society perhaps foreshadowed by the young generation's counterculture.

Curiosity about lifestyles

Although our students have further personal motivations for their interest in cultures, these three forces seem to assure a continuing public concern. The culture workshops are decidedly to the point, and the gains made in them are worth sharing. They will not be hard to

264

consolidate. But beyond the gains, participants have been taking home four big questions and have been searching for satisfying answers:

The morning after the workshop

1 How do I select what is worth teaching, for the purposes I want to serve?
2 What are the techniques, viewed critically with an eye to the purposes?
3 How can I get the materials I need?
4 How can I acquire the knowledge I lack?

These questions are also the main concerns of methods-course students, as they prepare to realize the hopes of a fresh generation. If we face each of the four in turn, we should be able to work out solutions we can use.

Selecting what is worth teaching

The first question, basic to those that follow, holds a high potential for improving our ability to generate and sustain student interest. We must be both drastic and critical in our selection of what to teach. External details, presented as though intrinsically important—shapes of doorknobs, lamp posts, once-a-year bonnets—still pass for "teaching the culture." Will Seelye (179) has shocked us at last into a more critical selection by propounding his Great Bellybutton Question—whether a given population's navels predominantly point in or out? A factual, researchable, quantifiable question—but what does it matter? Seelye shows how the asking of significant questions can transform the trivial into the worthwhile.

The surest way to select the significant is to use two approaches in conjunction with each other: *the student's interest* and *the nature of the phenomenon to be grasped.*

Two criteria for selecting essentials

Since Hancock's (75) excellent review chapter of 1972 on student attitudes and motivation, Rivers (167) has brought from psychology an insight into student motivation that can improve our teaching. The fact that the human being is a motivated organism results in two educational resources: the pleasure-pain motive and ego-involvement. Both can be exploited, but to use the immediate-pleasure, pain-avoiding motive alone tends to produce an authoritarian classroom. Even a democracy-loving teacher dominates the scene as he or she intervenes to reinforce the approved behavior. The learner, subordinated and inhibited, adopts contrary strategems to protect his self-image. The remedy lies in the motivating force described by those psychologists who view the individual as "continually seeking that which enhances

The approach from the learner's interest

Pleasure vs. ego involvement

his self as he perceives it. . . . The student is, then, motivated at first in a general, nonspecific way. . . . This initial motivation energizes and directs the student's behavior, causing him to focus on what is new in his environment" (p. 63). If the teacher catches and maintains the student's attention, "a cognitive drive which is self-sustaining then develops. . . . [It is] the best assurance that the student will continue to learn. . . . In this latter view, a student's reaction to a stimulus is not predictable from the external conditions as the teacher sees them, but is determined by the student's individual perception of reality" (p. 64). This conceptualization provides the bridge to connect the concern for alternative lifestyles with the potential curiosity to understand a foreign culture, to manipulate its language, and to explore its literature. The practical consequence of this theoretical synthesis, and of common sense, is that *we must begin where each individual student is*, whatever behavioral changes we may have in mind for him to adopt.

One way to discover the felt needs and aspirations of individuals is simply to talk with them. A teacher can spend part of a first-class hour asking each participant what he or she wants from the course and exploring how to accommodate the different emphases. Then each member of the group can personify a particular area of interest for the rest of the course. Becoming acquainted with a student through visits outside the class often permits involving the student's ego by showing the relation of the course to his or her unique life. It also shows the student that the instructor's intellectual curiosity and sensitivities reach out to meet his own. The more two people learn about each other's lives, the better the chance of discovering a common interest in some exciting frontier of knowledge—in the sciences, philosophy, the arts, or the realization of human values in a post-industrial society.

The first class meeting

The uniqueness of each person lies partially in his particular combination of interests, most of which are shared with other persons, but in different combinations. In a time of change, it is therefore useful to make a systematic survey in the school and the community to see what common interests would support new initiative. A model for this kind of survey is the work of Reinert (164). In 1968 language students of the Edmonds School District near Seattle rated learning about the foreign culture as the most important substantive value of foreign language study; in the case of German it even topped the external incentive of college requirements. A second survey in 1971 (165) showed that efforts in the interim had succeeded in attracting and holding students on the basis of the intrinsic value, though without isolating the factor of interest in the culture. This survey brought to

The survey of local interests

light, incidentally, a close conformity between the attitudes of students and those of parents in a given neighborhood. A 1972 survey (166) revealed that among the students not then taking a language, 49 percent had started one but had dropped it, usually because of the way it was taught. In 1973 Rivers surveyed attitudes of University of Illinois students not majoring in a language and found their interests were generally being satisfied. Such inquiries have at least suggestive value for any age level and any region.

Student interests come out also in language students' essays of the type "What Latin means to me," such as those elicited by the statewide essay contest of the Foreign Language Association of Missouri (110). Of course some students have difficulty in probing their private thoughts when they have one eye on the expectations of adults: They speak one dialect to an interviewer and another among themselves. When the purpose is for them to formulate their own views, perhaps discussions could be led by a student. *Student-initiated ideas*

No other general surveys of attitudes involving the foreign culture seem to have been conducted since Morain (131) summarized the evidence. A few studies specific to certain teaching materials have informally corroborated her conclusion about the high potential of culture for arousing interest; these will be noted in connection with the materials evaluated. Whatever means are used to ascertain the potential motivation, we are likely to find that one of the most attractive items is the foreign culture.

The concern over lifestyles—a causative force underlying the rapid change in the cultures of today—is particularly acute everywhere among young people. Christian and Sharp (26) have pointed out how the much-studied youth protest is related to the subject (pp. 345–46). Besides that direct concern, several widespread motives for studying a language can be shown to involve its sociocultural matrix. *Interest in lifestyles*

How important this matrix is for the common aspiration to communicate with bearers of another culture has been underlined by several recent studies, which will be reviewed in the discussion of the second means of identifying what is important to teach: the approach from the nature of the phenomenon to be grasped. Two aspects of cross-cultural communication should be noted here, however. They are the need to be prepared for culture shock and the need to know about one's own culture. *Culture-related motives: communication*

The symptoms of culture shock, Seelye once remarked, are as scary as those of the common cold *would be* if one were not forewarned. In a strange land, after a "honeymoon phase" of enjoying the novelty, we *Readiness for culture shock* need the ability to take in stride the more or less bitter disappointment that ensues as one feels the frustration of missing the familiar signals and as one finds one's own signals perversely misunderstood. This ability has a further value at home, for if we could all take a clinical view of our behavior toward other peoples, we could then attack with our intelligence the real remaining problems of discrimination.

Recent contributions that will help meet this educational need are Brein and David's (17) description of culture shock as a cycle that follows a W-shaped curve; Katcher's (98) analysis of shock in the acculturation of a minority; Wight's Peace Corps guidelines (Wight and Hammons, 218; Wight et al., 219); and Stewart's *American Cultural Patterns* (189).

Readiness for outsiders' questions

It is not hard to convince a person who wants to communicate with a host of people that he will be asked questions about his country and will win respect or scorn depending on his knowledge and lucidity. Eighteen years of direct experience, or even a venerable 50 more, are of no use here unless they are converted into an *examined experience* of one's home culture. Here again, the need of the sojourner abroad is paralleled by the need arising from our ethnic relations at home.

Books about American culture

Various types of books about Americans will appeal to different curiosities. Many students will enjoy making their way into the subject through science fiction such as Heinlein's (81) story of an earthling returning from Mars, or through the eyes of a real visitor like the Eskimo woman that Washburne (216) tells about, or Wedge's wealth of anecdotes in *Foreign Visitors* (217), or perhaps by seeing the blunders Americans make in Houston's land of *The White Dawn* (83). One can learn a great deal about Americans from Edward C. Stewart's (189) succinct account and from the Peace Corps materials by Wight and his colleagues (Wight and Hammons, 218; Wight et al., 219). Finally, a thorough exposition of our values, assumptions, and social institutions is Robin M. Williams' (220) humane "*Sociological Interpretation*," updated in a third edition of 1970.

Peer-group vs. target-group identification

Lambert (106, 108) and associates corroborate a further involvement of the cultural context, which directly affects language learning. In research summarized by Nostrand and associates (147, pp. 128–29), Lambert had already drawn the distinction between the limited motivation to learn a language as a tool and the ego-involved motive of identifying with the speakers of the target language. Indeed, Brooks had noted still earlier that "schoolgirl French," of the type *Je vais ay-too-di-ay*, is the natural product of peer-group identification overpowering any desire to sound authentically French. The new

Lambert study (Lambert et al., 108), made in the bilingual St. John Valley of Maine, shows a high correlation between language proficiency as a whole and self-identification with the linguistic community concerned. The researchers connect this finding with those of William Labov in New York City and those emerging from a McGill dissertation by B. Brown, to the effect that persons motivated by the aspiration of upward mobility tend to imitate the language of the target group (p. 7). So we are fortunate that most of our students already are spontaneously curious about the foreign people's lifestyles! We clearly should make the most of the attraction. The alternative strategy—to try to diminish our students' solidarity with their peers— would be quixotic, while the tactic of exploiting that solidarity, by extending the self-identification first of all to the learner's age group in the foreign population, has been used with increasing success.

The success is due partly to student interest and partly to the increasing flexibility of teachers who make room for youth-centered materials, but partly also to the improvement in the materials themselves. To select the best materials available for each language, one must consult the critical reviews, which appear chiefly in the respective AAT journals. Here we shall mention only a few teaching materials to illustrate various features. *Toute la bande* (203), for example, lends itself to the possibility of local supplementation. Slagle (184) has provided some lesson plans and exercises. This collaboration between producer and consumer raises the question of how to create a national clearing house that can reduce the duplication of such labor. Bourque's *The French Teen-Ager* (15) reflects not only her perceptive and experienced observation of young Americans and their hosts, but also the exacting evaluation that has distinguished the ACTFL Study-Abroad Program at Arcachon since its first summer, 1970, when it was audited from inside and outside by Bourque (14) and by Bendon (7). Pindur's parallel booklet *The German Teen-Ager in Profile* (159) is based on an extension of her earlier research, brought up to date under the sponsorship of the Advancement Press. Ortali's *Entre nous* (153) is based on taped conversations of teen-agers.

For Spanish, Christian was administering in 1973 some 2,900 questionnaires to 14- and 17-year-old Guatemalans and Colombians, on which it will be possible to base teaching materials that will accurately represent these young people's conceptions of their environments. This research may be the first to provide junior high students with extensive information on age-mates abroad. For a still lower age level, Mauricio Charpenel, of the Institute of Latin American

The peer group in the target area

269

Studies in the University of Texas at Austin, was offering a new course on children's literature: *Escritores, libros y niños de México*. At some age, perhaps younger than we have supposed, children will find it exciting to be told the surprising history of childhood and the family. These are modern concepts that hardly existed in Western Civilization before the eighteenth century, despite the contrary impression given by political oratory. Ariès (4) continues to revise the accepted historical notions of the family, the child, and the adolescent (a concept whose origin is still more recent).

Often a student can be interested in an aspect of a lifestyle that *Individual hobbies* touches a personal hobby or preoccupation—sports, family relations, love, friendship, religion. (Conversion to the Bahai faith proves to be one reason some have chosen Persian.) Sometimes a preoccupying *Individual anxieties* anxiety, such as a family problem, so absorbs a student that he has trouble concentrating on anything else. Without the prompting of a resourceful teacher, it is not likely to occur to him that he could respond to some available discussion of the evolving family in the foreign society, or perhaps a work of literature, because of his need for understanding himself. His foreign language can become much more for him than an academic subject.

Interest in a career creates a potential curiosity about the role of the *Careers* contemplated occupation in the foreign culture—whether the occupation involves cross-cultural communication or not. The increasing needs for language skills in business, industry, and social organizations were surveyed anew by the Modern Language Association (57) in 1972 for a booklet *Foreign Languages in Careers*. Community colleges, which can teach together both full-time students and persons from the community, lead the development of "alternative programs" aiming toward international jobs.

Curiosity about lifestyles can carry students beyond topics of direct *Interests beyond direct* self-identification. Adolescent and adult students, men as well as *involvement* women, are interested in the change in the status of women, a basic change whose repercussions reverberate through the social and cultural structure. Mildred Boyer has planned a new course, Women Writers in Hispanic Literature, at the University of Texas at Austin. The course will explore what the authors observe and also what may be feminine in their way of observing.

The motivation of the minority person to learn about his ethnic heri- *Culture-related interest of the* tage is treated in Chapter 4 of this volume, and the social relations of *minority student* bilingualism have been well explored in the preceding volume of ACTFL *Reviews* by Christian and Sharp (26).

The bearer of a minority culture depends partly on that culture to satisfy his basic human need for a self-concept. The extent of that dependence is determined partly by inner conditioning, and partly by the satisfactoriness of his second identification—with the surrounding culture. Many minority Americans, it is evident, are largely dependent on the ethnic source, which education must consequently respect if it means to respect basic human needs. At the 1972 ACTFL Meeting Lambert (105) expressed the belief that French Canadians and Hispanic Americans adjust better if their heritage is kept alive. He cited his own research and that of Padilla and Long (154), and he proposed employing teachers' aides who know the folk language and wisdom of the ethnic tradition as well as educating teachers to the behavioral aspects of the minority person's feeling of strangeness. Jones and Dean (95), in one of the later volumes of their *Intercultural Education Series*, treat the subject of *The Americas and Self-Identification* from the practical standpoint of classroom teaching. The American educational establishment is making progress in this provision for cultural differences, compared with the recent past when just to soften the first impact of the curriculum on the minority child was felt to be sufficient.

The bicultural child's problem of adjustment to two cultures continues through life. Sophistication is not a panacea for it. Edmund Glenn notes that sophistication can actually decrease a person's cultural stability. The wearing of symbols of mourning, for example, once served to arouse social support for the bereaved person; when these come to be perceived as "mere symbols" which it would be hypocritical to wear, bereavement becomes a major problem for psychiatry and medicine. The contrary solution, of withdrawing into an intense ethnic solidarity, harms society—both the surrounding structure and the minority. It can be used to isolate the group, generate hostility, and degrade individuals, as Boris Erassov (45) warns, apropos of the Third World.

Sophistication

The surrounding sociocultural matrix needs some degree of cohesion to make possible the shared pursuit of civilization. There is no need for agreement on ultimate beliefs, but rather for agreement on working principles and modes of action. The ideal of pluralism is not an absolute, but a mean between extremes. It is whatever combination of diversity and commonality that will best serve the interdependent ideals of individual self-fulfillment and social justice.

Pluralism as a mean

Discrimination and oppression, obviously, have no place among our professed values. The minority person must be enabled to participate fully in the institutions under which he or she lives, or alienation is both inevitable and warranted. But recent literature is pessimistic about the prospect of overcoming discriminatory behavior. This is manifest in the bibliography of Storr's *Human Destructiveness* (190). The grim prospects are, however, no justification for a half-way effort, but for quite the contrary.

Discrimination

Our present practice incurs a basic criticism that follows from this chapter's point of departure. All our enlightened theory leads toward cultural pluralism, in the sense of accepting all the diversity of language and customs, as well as of religion and skin color, that does not harm the essential commonality of national life. Yet our practice consists in modifying the behavior of the minority job-seeker, for example, so that he will not arouse the prejudice of the hiring officer through some discrepancy of dialect. Our practice is to accept prejudice as one of the facts of life. We cannot hope to solve this problem of human relations by moving half the way, from only one side of it. Adult education programs should involve both the minority and the majority participants in the relationship. The hiring officer and the fellow workers need to learn to take pride in their "decoding imagination," as Gerhard Nickel calls it—the skill a host population needs to understand nonstandard speakers of its language, a phenomenon that is inevitable in a world of increasing mobility.

One-sidedness of present policy

Language teachers, who represent awareness of the plurality of cultures in the world, have a responsibility to catalyze thought on the subject through the majority's educational institutions, church groups, service clubs, and the like. In pre-adult schooling, too, the social science teachers who combat ethnocentrism should have effective help from us, the language teachers, who enjoy the unique resource of being able to show, through the *experience* of another culture, that it can make sense in its own terms.

A new role for language teachers

Until recently, cultural relativism has been an unthinkable concept for most of the American majority because of two nineteenth-century realities: the isolation from other continents and the intensive immigration, which led to the fear of cultural disintegration and to the extreme policy of the melting pot. Now for the first time, those realities are overbalanced by realities of the twentieth century. Isolation is yielding to travel, trade, and the public awareness of international negotiation. The fading melting-pot complex is overwhelmed by two forces: the demand for respect on the part of the ethnic groups and a widespread dissatisfaction with the materialism of an over-achieving society, which had been extolled as the only 100 percent American lifestyle.

Favorable forces

The North American WASP is mutating to fit a new cognitive

The new role: intellectual leadership

272

climate in which languages are no longer only a tool subject entrusted to drill masters. Now language teachers have the opportunity to assume a role of intellectual leadership, inducing the public media to look into the everyday life of other peoples—to see the world from *their* windows— multiplying such programs as "World Press" of San Francisco Station KQED and the documentary programs on social and cultural developments abroad that have been pioneered by European television networks. An event like the 1976 Bicentennial gives the opportunity to take stock of the ethnic contributions within the American living space. At the University of Missouri, Schroeder (176) is planning a course on the German contribution, using cultural data collected from local families. Similar initiative in the media, as well as in schools, can provide a cultural climate favorable to multicultural education.

Intellectual leadership means not only consolidating gains, but looking ahead. The West has come some distance from the Crusade mentality that saw the in group as the faithful and out-groups as infidels. But what of the future of cultural pluralism? Its evolution is not likely to stop here. A 1949 book *Ursprung und Gegenwart* came into our English language discussions of pluralism in 1972 (not an unusual lag). In it Gebser (61) impressively documented a thesis that the "age of perspective," which began in the Renaissance, is evolving through and beyond the *multiple* perspective expressed in Picasso's double faces and in polytonal music, toward an age of *non*perspective. This is a concept barely thinkable at present. It has one evident implication: It would deemphasize the perception of cultures as hard-edged, separate things. *Main Currents in Modern Thought*, the magazine that has introduced Gebser's writing, is rich in explorations of ideas that will concern language teachers as the interpreters of an expanding, cross-cultural horizon.

Pluralism's unknown future

All the motives for language study that we have reviewed reach their fulfillment only with understanding of a culture, either as an explicit goal or as a means to successful communication—hence the second, concomitant approach to the problem of selecting what is most important to teach: Precisely what needs to be understood?

The approach to essentials from the nature of a culture

A sociocultural system, and any of its variant lifestyles, is a whole whose parts color one another. This is why a value, a custom, or a word has no one-to-one counterpart in another culture. It is why the cross-cultural contrasting of discrete elements leaves the student with his private belief that only *his* view really makes sense—*unless* he learns to feel the "fittingness" of the detail as perceived by the bearer of the other culture.

The overemphasis on mini-contrasts has led some, like Runte (171), to say that teaching about cultural differences has gone out of date. Her objection against arousing the expectation that every social custom and every culture pattern abroad will be different is well taken. To swing to the other extreme would of course result in an equally misleading expectation. The fault has been to stress the easy "We do this; they do that" at the expense of any feeling for the lifestyle as a coherent response to the human condition. The way to this educational objective takes us into the relatively modest activity of ethnography: the describing of one culture. The easy mini-contrasts have led teachers into the ambitious comparative and contrastive generalizations of ethnology before we have created the prerequisite descriptive knowledge and before our students have accomplished the basic step of feeling at home in their second culture.

Overemphasis on contrast

Ethnography before ethnology

The developmental task of the language learner is to internalize a semantic system independent of his home culture: to develop a "co-ordinate system," rather than a "compound system" in which only the native language is a coherent whole and the foreign one appears as contrastive extrusions atomizing in all directions from the single center. The most effective way for a student to come to feel at home in the new semantic system is to internalize it both experientially and cognitively. Furthermore, it is precisely by bringing together *experience of* and *knowledge about* a phenomenon that we come to "understand" it and to make it count toward the examined life essential to full human development. Without experience of the thing, the knowledge is mere verbalization; without reflective, organizing thought, the experience is only the forgotten past of a programmed organism. Hence the focus on "The Language Learner: Reaching his Heart and Mind" (109), selected by the Toronto-New York Conference of 1971.

"Understanding": experience of and knowledge about

The efficient use of the student's cognitive capacity, and, indeed, of our own, requires the organization of what we know about the socio-cultural whole into some structure. As we unfold the parts of it that progressively come within the learner's capacity we should approximate, bit by bit, either the most understandable model of the whole or the model that most truly represents the reality of its interacting parts—or, ideally, a model both readily understandable and true to fact.

The need to structure descriptive knowledge

Such a structure is unlikely to occur to a student through his own trial and error, even if he had years for the purpose. The efficient approach here is not student centered, and it will strike opposition in any narrowly trained administrator. But actually, even John Dewey,

Reconciliation with Dewey's concept of culture as process

274

far broader than he has sometimes been represented, was not opposed to all integration of knowledge outside the head of the learner. Between 1902 and 1931 he evolved, as has been summarized in *The University and Human Understanding* (Nostrand, 145, pp. 182, 186–88, 429–31), to a position involving the utilization by the learner of prior organizations of knowledge. That study reconciled two types of definition of culture— one as a process and the other as content. The culture of a person, as well as the culture of an historic period, is really an interplay between the process (activity and sensitivity) and a cognitive content, so that the quality of the interplay depends on the quality of both factors.

There is only an apparent conflict between the content-centered synthesis of ethnographic knowledge from which we must teach, in order to use the learner's time efficiently, and the progressive principle with its emphasis on the learner's activity. The real conflict, however, is over the scope of the context in which he lives. Kohlberg and Mayer (103), recapitulating in 1972 the progressive philosophy, conclude with a concept of moral education. Its aim, they propose, is "justice, the reciprocity between the individual and others in his social environment" (p. 455). The implication is that his social environment is limited to persons in direct interaction, and today that environment— even without invoking the learner's imaginative power—clearly reaches beyond his culture area. At a university in middle America, 60 percent of Wilga Rivers' respondents in 1973 reported that they had a friend who spoke a foreign language. There is a further conflict; it is between cultural relativism and the implied assumption that the proper "reciprocity" between persons is everywhere a relationship of democratic equality. We Americans assume we live in a horizontal social structure; others assume it to be vertical. So long as we impute our culture-bound assumption to them, and they do likewise, our reciprocal relation will be one of misunderstanding, latent friction, and outbursts of culture shock. The Latin American, the European, the Asian, feels that the informal American is humiliating him by treating him as an inferior on a vertical scale; the American, unaware of the vertical structure in the other person's subconscious, perceives only an irritating, time-consuming formalism.

If we must employ a culture-centered approach to back up our student-centered teaching, is there a model of a socio-cultural system that is both true to the reality and easy to grasp? Several United States Office of Education grants during the 1960's gave me the chance to examine, with excellent consultants from the social sciences, all the recommended structures: humanistic aperçus, inventories, structural-

Criteria for a satisfactory structure

275

functional and dynamic models, and theme configurations. All of these have merit, and the contributions of some of them have been reflected in selective inventories such as Brooks' (19) 50 highlights and the Seward list of 13 common civilities noted by Morain (131, p. 73). Some appear in methods textbooks such as Brooks' *Language and Language Learning* (18), Jenks' *Planning to Teach Culture* (91), Pillet's culture chapter in *Foreign Language Study* (158), Brooks' projected new "primer" (19), and Valdés' synthesis of current theory applied to Mexico (208).

The structure that best interrelates all these contributions for describing a sociocultural system is a structured inventory, designed with a "handle"—the main themes of the culture studied. If the inventory is structured to represent the actual interplay of forces, it will become a working model of the system, as we learn more about the actual exchanges of energy within it. Such an "emergent model," developed by Howard Nostrand, is described by Seelye (177) in the first ACTFL *Review*. (An improved form, published by Clapper [27, pp. 24–30], is available from H. L. Nostrand, University of Washington Department of Romance Languages, GN-60, Seattle 98195.)

An emergent model

The interacting forces group themselves and divide the model into several subsystems that we may adapt from the sociologist Talcott Parsons. The *cultural* subsystem is made up of the culture's dominant values, habits of thought, and assumptions—the "semantic matrix" or "ground of meaning" of the culture—plus its empirical knowledge, art forms, language, paralanguage, and kinesics. A *social* subsystem comprises interpersonal and group relations, shaped by institutions whose component roles are governed by norms (situation-specific directives that apply one or more of the culture's values). An *ecological* subsystem describes the population's relationships with its subhuman environment. And the last, for our purposes, an *individual* subsystem, describes what a given person does with the shared patterns—conforming, rebelling, exploiting, or innovating. The four subsystems require a total of 30 main headings.

Sociology's contribution to the model

Our focus should be the shared patterns. We would mislead our students if we seemed to promise a recipe for predicting individual behavior. What we *can* validly offer our students is some understanding of the influences the culture exerts on the behavior of its carriers. We thus concentrate on one level of generalization—the regularities of one culture—while keeping in the picture as background both the lower level, generalization about a single individual, and the higher level of abstraction where one generalizes about universal human needs and aspirations.

The many shared patterns can be gathered into a summary of its main forces (in the form of the culture's main themes) which make a manageable "handle." They are never more than a dozen or so, doubtless because value conflicts are painful and a people keeps countering the tendency of the value system to proliferate. A "theme" for this purpose has to be defined carefully as the anthropologist Morris Opler has proposed (Echols, 43; Opler, 151, 152). It does not mean just any "topic," nor even a "value" in the usual restricted sense. It means an emotionally charged concern, which motivates or strongly influences the culture bearer's conduct in a wide variety of situations. If we define a value (or a disvalue) in this broad way, it is convenient to say that a cultural theme has a value at its core. But the theme is more than this core. To comprehend the culture bearer's concern empathically, as he perceives it, one must see it in the light of the accompanying habits of thought and the underlying assumptions concerning the nature of man and the world. A "theme," then, is an expanded definition of one of the pervading concerns that make up a culture's value system. And taken together, the main themes of a culture are coextensive with the first three headings of the emergent model. They are simply a particularly understandable, yet true-to-fact description of the culture's ground of meaning.

Anthropology's contribution to the model

In 1967 a group of students and colleagues helped apply the "emergent model" to a highly complex contemporary culture in *Background Data for the Teaching of French* (Nostrand, 140). The chapters that resulted proved to meet squarely the individual interests of students, and a fruitful college course took shape as students explored their interests while the time spent together was devoted to exploring the meaning of the main themes.

Validation of the model

During 1970–71 the Nostrands' year of research in France showed that the same scheme serves to organize the heterogeneous data of a field study on social and cultural change: The structured inventory accepts findings on any and all aspects of a lifestyle and groups them so that they lead to significant conclusions.

The emergent model, then, helps one to orient oneself and to feel at home in a culture, and it helps us to revise our description of it, including its diachronic dimension. It lends itself, finally, to contrastive research: Gerhard Nickel of the University of Stuttgart was using it in 1973 as the framework of a comparative study for the Council of Europe.

Recent research and experience confirm the importance of the main themes—ground of meaning—of a culture both for descriptive and

Confirmed importance of main themes

contrastive studies and for teaching. Stewart, in Part I of *American Culture Patterns* (189), presents "patterns of thinking, assumptions, and values" as concepts basic for dealing with the differences and conflicts between cultures. Gorden (64), a sociologist whose work is especially helpful to language teachers, has traced to unwitting assumptions the breakdowns of communication between Americans and Colombians. Mueller (133) found that while control groups of students had missed the culture-related humor in a play of Jules Romains, those who had assimilated the main themes of French culture, even the imperfect account of them presented in the *Background Data* (Nostrand, 140, Part A, pp. 77–101), laughed spontaneously at those same points that amuse a French audience.

Lambert, d'Anglejan, and Tucker (107) report that even professional translators fall short of mutual understanding with monolingual persons in one of their languages, unless they share with them, in addition to the surface code, "a common frame of reference." It is not surprising, therefore, that persons from a culturally inbred milieu particularly, as they come to take part in international contact, need to acquire that common ground of meaning. This was demonstrated by a class of boys and girls 15 to 17 years old from rural Devon, as reported by the BBC in the fall of 1972. On an excursion to a German provincial town they encountered difficulties of adjustment and communication quite beyond the anticipation of either their teachers or their hosts. The work of Lee Taylor and others (195) suggests that in this sort of case, rural sociology may provide a bridge of common interests; but the culture gap will remain a hazard. Using such research and experience as a point of departure, Jakobovits and Gordon (88) propose a "transactional engineering" approach to language teaching in which the differences between the semantic backgrounds become the explicit subject of discussion.

Ebling (42) urges the desirability of focusing on a culture's ground of meaning. After admiring the presentation of American culture he observed in France, he concluded that teachers of French in America should utilize the proposed themes of French culture (Nostrand, 140) summarized by Ladu (104).

Of the three sectors that make up a culture's ground of meaning the most elusive, the most out-of-awareness for the culture bearers, is the habits of thought—"the forms of reasoning and problem solving preferred" in the culture, as Edmund Glenn calls them (63, p. 53). This article illucidates how the intercultural differences in cognitive

Defining cognitive styles

style can generate friction. Glenn draws upon his own and others' research in cross-cultural semantics; on his experiences as chief interpreter in the Department of State; and on his familiarity with linguistic, sociological, and psychological theory, including that of the transactional school represented as early as 1952 by his associate Kilpatrick (100). Applying an idea developed by Glenn that cultures differ along certain parameters, one of which is a continuum, stretching from particularism through a preoccupation with relationships, to a predilection for global conceptualizations, my article on "French Culture's Concern for Relationships" (141) shows that the thought processes typical of a culture *can* be illuminated and can help us understand other sectors of an evolving sociocultural whole.

Contribution of linguistics to the consensus

Linguists are now also concerned with describing a culture's ground of meaning. From the death of Edward Sapir in 1939 through the structuralist and transformational-generative periods, the linguistic and cultural components of language learning led in different directions; now they converge. Semantics and pragmatics—the term revived by Oller (149) to designate the relation between an utterance and its situational context—have become essential to linguistic theory. Politzer (162) expresses the judgment that Noam Chomsky's most important influence has been to shake the positivistic faith in the self-dependence of the surface facts. Hymes (86) predicted as early as 1964 that linguistics had to expand into the province of meanings; Bolinger (10) reached the same conclusion about the same time in *Aspects of Language*. Hymes (86) wrote in 1972: "There really is no way that linguistic theory can become a theory of language without encompassing social meaning. . . . There is no way to analyze speech acts adequately without ethnography" (p. 17). Selinker, Trimble, and Vroman (181) are among a growing number of younger linguists who, accordingly, are researching "the notion of presupposition and its effect upon surface syntax," including interference in second-language learning.

The converging advances in anthropology and sociology, in communications and linguistics, mean for the language teacher that a consensus is emerging to support a more purposeful and concerted "teaching of the culture." The working theory that emerges is that we are trying to *understand* a phenomenon, which turns out to be a *system of action and of cognition*. Central to the system and to our problem of comprehending it, is the culture's ground of meaning, whose process and content require a two-pronged approach—experiential and cognitive. The learner can begin from the experience of any surface manifestations

Individualized experience: common concepts

279

that motivate him, but to understand what they illustrate he must sooner or later relate what he experiences to the central features illustrated.

We are also approaching a consensus on another divisive problem of ethnography: to decide on the proper scope of the culture area to be studied. The best solution for our purpose of education is to equate culture area with language area, but to select one sociopolitical subarea (such as one country within the Hispanic area) and one socioeconomic class, where the learner can begin to feel at home. The initial focus should be even narrower for some sociocultural patterns—a single city for observing municipal government, a single age group for leisure activities. The motivation of some students will be strongest if they begin not from the metropolitan subarea, such as Paris, but from one like Senegal or Quebec. A bilingual area adds the problem of being at least sensitive to the presence of a coexisting culture—a complication that can be turned to advantage. Whatever geographical point of entry is selected, many of our students will pick as their target subculture the middle class, with which they are most likely to have contact. But the range of sympathies and comprehension should be broadened from the point of entry to other countries or regions; other social classes; other age, ethnic, and religious groups, just as one does in growing to know one's home country.

Scope of a culture area

The complexity we encounter need not deter us from describing a people's everyday culture, any more than we are deterred from describing its historical achievements in science and invention, in social structure, and in the arts. Indeed, French *popular* taste in the arts is in a real sense less complex, by being more indigenously French, than a movement in painting that was carried on at Paris by artists from many nations or a style of furniture that was designed for the tastes of an international aristocracy by artisans refined in an Italian tradition.

Complexity of elite and folk culture

We may define a culture area, then, on the same principle that serves for selecting what is important to teach of a culture: Start from the student's objectives and place what he wants to know in the context of relationships that will make its true nature understandable.

The techniques, with a critical view to the purposes

If our aim is indeed understanding, directly or because it is necessary for successful communication, it is useful to list separately the devices for achieving the two components of understanding: experience of the reality and knowledge about it. We can thus gain the advantage of assuring that both needs are fulfilled, while recognizing that some procedures provide for both. Taylor (194) has combined devices of both sorts in a useful, selective inventory.

In listing the devices, let us assume that the student-teacher contact time is substantially in the target language from the start (which does not preclude homework at the start in English) and that to make the student at home in the language, the teacher will steadily increase the proportion of time used for real communication, diminishing the proportion devoted to grammar practice and to the intermediate process of pseudo-communication. The progress toward real communication has two hazards in its way: the old tendency to receive messages only superficially in the new language, instead of assimilating them deeply into one's life experience and also a newer tendency to develop "short memory" at the expense of long-term learning. To overcome these hazards, activities in which the student feels emotionally involved—in which he feels impelled to exchange meaningful utterances—are better than those that engage only the intellect; and longer-range, real-life objectives of competence and performance are more effective than an emphasis on the parts separately.

Contact time in the target language

Learning to think in the language

The repertory of techniques for working toward understanding of a culture can usefully be organized into 20 types of devices, 11 conducive chiefly to experience of the culture and nine for the knowledge of its patterns.

Experiential techniques
1 Nonverbal bridges to the new culture
2 Semi-verbal bridges
3 Situational dialogue and representative monologue
4 Literature, the cinema, and the theatre
5 Audio self-instruction, broadcasts, and telecasts
6 The mini-drama and the culture assimilator
7 Native informants and language camps
8 Pen pals, tape pals, and "twinned" classes
9 Role playing
10 The experience-based project
11 Testing affective results

Cognitive techniques
1 Observation and inference, with Socratic prompting
2 The incidental comment
3 Systematic exposition of a topic, including individualized self-information
4 Participatory exposition

5 The writing of simulations
6 Analytical techniques
7 Bibliography
8 Techniques for synthesis
9 Testing cognitive results

The two sets of devices, "experiential" and "cognitive," are arranged here in sequence from those usable early in language instruction to those requiring more language skill.

Experiential 1: Nonverbal bridges to the new culture

Primus (163) interests children in African cultures through a dance presentation, with a musical and architectural background. Knowledge about the values represented can be given in programmed homework or can be postponed if misinterpretations are intercepted. Often this can be accomplished indirectly by the teacher's attitude, as the students watch or act out the dance, trying to catch its spirit. Pindur (160) recommends German and Austrian *Volkstänze* that have enabled the high school students who danced them to outgrow the reaction of laughing at an unfamiliar culture's art form. *The dance*

A bullfight *could* be presented nonverbally, with such materials as Hatton and Jackson's (77) film script, but here the danger of misinterpretation is formidable. This culture-related art form is better utilized after students have reached a point where they can learn in the culture's own terms how the spectator identifies with the courageous battler against the forces of animality. *The bullfight*

While students are beginning a language, they can also be learning visually some of the gestures and other kinesic signals and symbols. But this is advisable only to the extent that it can be done in a spirit of accepting and not of prejudging. Some kinesic features are among the hardest for the ethnocentric mind to accept—the French ceremonial accolade between men, for example, or the Asian men's pattern of holding hands or putting an arm around each other's waist. For students who just cannot overcome their repugnance for a pattern of this sort, there is presumptive evidence that a clinical psychologist could apply the same "systematic desensitization" that is coming to be used against the fear of tests, of speaking in a group, or of attending a class that poses an excessive challenge. *Kinesics*

Experiential 2: Semi-verbal bridges—songs, games, motor and visual aids

Students need not know all the words of a song to feel the thrill of joining in with an ¡Olé! just like a Spanish café audience. In the *Songs*

282

Tacoma (Washington) Public Schools, Carl Dellaccio has had as resident resource persons a real *mariache*, a talented Cuban couple who play and sing their way from school to school. Later can come the realization that all Hispanic culture has this pattern of audience participation in common with the Moorish invaders and with Black Africa. Insight into a people's culture can start from folk songs, as used by Juaire (96). In time, songs of social protest and commentary will give a feeling for the attitudes of present and past countercultures. The music is no mere sugar coating. A troubadour poem is transformed by its musical setting from a technical *tour de force* to a vivid expression of joy or languor.

Games are a semi-verbal bridge whose potential as experience of a culture has still to be exploited. Even at college age, the simple game of "guess who I am" is fun, when played in small groups with the teacher circulating as a resource person. The questions required can be in elementary language, and the activity can internalize basic historical information. If a character is acted out, players gain some feelings for the significance of a culture hero or heroine. At the junior high level Patricia Campbell, of the Lake Washington School District near Seattle, has been experimenting with ten German picture-word games, instead of a textbook, as the core of a first-year course. The vocabulary learned serves well for reading, and the attrition was zero. The sociocultural outcome of such an experiment will not be hard to test—nor deliberately to maximize. *Games*

A kind of semi-verbal game of solitaire is Seelye's device of teaching the connotative meaning of a concept, such as *una mujer*, by having a student collect about 30 pictures of women from magazines and arrange them by apparent social class. This is a beginner's form of the experience-based project (Experiential 10). DuFort (40) describes several games usable in any language.

Games are not the only way of linking language learning to kinetic behavior and memory. Another is the audio-motor unit of instruction, as adapted by Elkins and his colleagues (44). The teacher acts out directions heard on tape for setting up an event like a picnic, and the students learn by imitation, entirely free of English words. In subsequent discussion, they learn what the French, German, or Spanish words actually mean in the situational context of the respective assumptions about what a picnic is. DuVerlie (41) reports an enthusiastic response of college students to a winter intersession of French-related activities in the Baltimore-Washington area, with a one-semester prerequisite in the language. *The audio-motor unit*

Plays and museums

283

Visual aids have long been better exploited than kinetic adjuncts. *Films*
The last few years have produced few innovations that affect the cultural component. Already noted is the improved use of film to immerse students in the atmosphere of their age mates. The Centre de Recherche et d'Etude pour la Diffusion de Français (CREDIF), at the Ecole Normale Supérieure de Saint Cloud, plans to release in 1974 a set of units that exemplify a new standard for combining an enjoyable immersion with high selectivity of significant data. The set of 18 units is designed to occupy about 300 class hours, following a first 300 to 400 class hours that might include the film-strip course *Voix et images de France*. (The new set is separate from the richly documented lessons, of which samples are printed in *Le français dans le monde*.) These audiovisual units, consisting of language-teaching tapes, still pictures, and documentation for reference, go far beyond the usual, diffuse sort of informative conversation, to organize a substantial sociocultural topic as seen from within the culture. An engaging human situation leads to a well-motivated exposé of the social security system, or the pattern of attitudes toward women job-holders. An apartment elevator, for example, which is stalled on Sunday morning with a load of passengers on their way down to freedom, generates an animated conversation that leads to a view of the society's chief leisure activities. Or a visit to the office of the internal revenue inspector motivates an emotionally charged probe of a family budget, as the inspector so legitimately questions the items claimed: How much can a family of these means *normally* be expected to spend on a weekend cottage or a pleasure boat? Such units efficiently join vivid experience with accurate and useful knowledge about a culture.

Despite the vividness of film, still pictures have one advantage. *Still pictures*
Robert Politzer once remarked that when he was learning English, he had wished that *something* in the situation would hold still for a moment.

Comic strips also provide nonverbal cues to the meaning of utterances *Comics*
and so confer the virtue of the semi-verbal devices upon the dialogues in Experiential 3. Hall and Lafourcade (73) have edited comics for beginning and intermediate classes and have discussed the problems and possibilities of their use in teaching. Gerald Fleming of the University of Surrey has begun work on the audiovisual presentation of a more ambitious story: a half-hour animated version of *Max und Moritz*, the classic by Wilhelm Busch.

Fleming has pioneered in several ways. He used culture-specific *Wall pictures*
gestures first in wall pictures (56) and then in a *Grammaire visuelle de*

français (52) whose slides, he explains in a letter, are aimed to present "the gestural components which are the spontaneous extensions of the verbal, arising out of an organized moment in time." These visuals and his audio cassettes with accompanying texts (49) anticpiated the linguists' new interest in pragmatics (the situational determinant of an utterance's meaning). Fleming has also deepened our insight into the culture of the Renaissance by identifying the "gesture significances" (50) in the hand studies of Dürer and in the iconography of Cranach the Elder (53, 54).

Gestures in a culture's past

Experiential 3: Situational dialogue and representative monologue

Culturally authentic dialogues, beginning with elementary terms of address, may illustrate perfectly the central values, thought patterns, and assumptions of a culture. The proportion of culturally significant dialogues can be deliberately increased, as has been done in the second edition of the Encyclopaedia Britannica film course, *Je parle français* (170). The new Level I and Level II each have ten films whose beauty is matched by their careful integration of culturally significant content into the progression. For a textbook where several successive dialogues yield little of cultural significance, a unit on some interest of the age group can be inserted—the adolescent in the family, in school, in leisure activities or the change-generating evolution in the status of women.

If one samples students' ideas about what patterns they imagine are illustrated in a dialogue, one will be convinced that accurate knowledge should be provided on main points as soon as possible. But that belongs to the cognitive ingredient of the instruction.

Danger of misinterpretation

At the intermediate level, students can begin learning from authentic monologues or dialogues typical of a specific subculture's language, thought, and attitudes. Teaching materials are appearing that alert students to differences in social classes, regions, and age groups by immersing them in the language of a milieu. Santoni's (cf. Santoni and Rey, 174) forthcoming French conversation course uses the representative monologue with particular care to assure empathic understanding. He moves in six steps from an exercise ensuring comprehension of the language used to an exercise in describing the subculture the speaker has exemplified. Haac and Bieler (71) have based a language text on interviews taped in France. Film courses have the multisensory advantage over tape, as have the supplementary films obtainable from sources listed in the Illinois Conference proceedings (Rivers et al., 168, pp. 89–91).

The representative monologue

Experiential 4: Literature, the cinema, and the theatre

The best dialogues have the advantage of being works of literature, in the sense of "a verbal composition which elicits contemplation" (Nostrand, 144). If a dialogue is at the same time an authentic manifestation of a culture, its form and content both give subtle experience of patterns that have only to be pointed out in due time.

It is in fact a narrow view that opposes "teaching the culture" to asking the significance of any of a people's historic achievements, and it is particularly myopic to crowd out literature. All the art forms of a culture stand high among the manifestations of its main themes, and literature, the art that most explicitly evokes thoughts and feelings, is quite rightly called the autobiography of a people. A language course that arouses the expectation of enjoying the people's literature will have achieved a crucial objective on the way to understanding, and on the way toward becoming a welcome person in the cultural community.

False conflict of literature and culture

From the earliest lessons, carefully selected poems can give intriguing tastes of a people's imaginativeness, whimsy, or humor; at the same time they can teach phonemic oppositions much more interestingly than can drills of minimal pairs. This Jeanne Varney Pleasants demonstrated at the Columbia University Language Laboratory; and the periodical she founded, *Teaching Language through Literature* (197), continues to help teachers find works of artistic merit that meet the requisite pedagogical criteria.

Poems for teaching pronunciation

Audiovisual recitations of poems and monologues, authentic as to paralanguage and kinesics, can vastly improve a beginner's learning of a piece and also serve at later stages to deepen the reflective experience. Perhaps the profession and publishers are now ready for more teaching materials such as the filmed recital of Pierre Viala and his associates (146), with its accompanying booklet of *Cultural Commentary* to help a teacher formulate the French characteristics exemplified by the selections and by the actor.

The audiovisual recital

Proverbs can be learned early and, as J. Dale Miller (129) suggests, are one way into a folk culture. They are highly significant in certain African cultures where they are used as a way of gently admonishing a child without embarrassing him. They also come in handy for persuading a person of literal mentality. But their sociocultural value is limited because their wisdom is rarely peculiar to the culture, and they often occur in pairs that give opposite directives, the real intent being a presupposed mean between extremes. The experience given by

Proverbs and their limitations

proverbs is thus often misleading unless responsible descriptive knowledge is put with them.

Brief narratives that involve the learner effectively in a significant situation are a welcome change after a few dialogues. Folk tales, particularly, induce a childlike involvement at any age, as Otto Bond appreciated a generation ago when he prepared his simplified readers. In a history of cross-cultural migration, one is likely to find some characteristics of the culture that shaped it in any version studied.

Stories that engross the listener

Literature, including the cinema, can illustrate unforgettably any regularity of a culture, once the regularity has been carefully derived from the widest possible range of sociocultural manifestations. Even the anthology of short selections, usually frustrating for students, can become engaging reading if vivid moments are organized around fundamental life issues, as the Capelles and their coauthors (23) have done in *La France en direct*.

Literature as illustration not as a self-sufficient source

Students at all levels of learning can enjoy a deepening experience of the cultural and social import they find in works of literature, films, and plays. Through this insight they can better comprehend almost every work of art without in the least neglecting that other, equally important context of every literary composition, world literature envisaged as a distinct and universally human form of creative imagination.

Literature's two contexts

The *humanizing* effect of literature depends more, however, on exploring its connection with life than on placing it in the litterateur's structure. Indeed the humanizing effect may be unrelated to the most sophisticated analyses.

Educational value of the sociocultural context

One must also acknowledge that it is the greatest authors who best put proprieties and conformism in their place, because they stand above conformity to their milieu; but for that same reason, they are less illustrative of the culture. A Molière neither needs nor develops in the student the sensitivity to culture-specific humor that Mueller (133) found important for reading Jules Romains.

Value of the greatest and of other good authors

Marquardt (118) cites W. F. Mackey's exhaustive analysis of the language features that make a text harder or easier for a foreign reader and reports that certain types of story induce the most active involvement in the learner of English: "texts portraying Americans interacting with aspects of the learner's culture. . . texts portraying non-Americans interacting with Americans in an American setting. . ." and "texts by Americans attempting to interpret some unique individual, work of art, art form, institution, or feature in the learner's culture to the English-speaking world" (p. 1022–23). Mead (124) has

Topics with affective appeal

used this principle in a course on the United States as seen by Spanish-American authors, including Puerto Ricans, Cubans, and Chicanos. Mueller has used the principle in the third semester of a French course in which the teaching assistants are briefed on the main themes of French culture (Nostrand, 140, Part A, pp. 77–101).

Steiner (188) reminds us, in an excellent list of cultural activities, *Plays* that students enjoy going to a play. Indeed even a play in English that relates to the foreign culture can be an engaging experience. A foreign troupe brought to town provides the opportunity for students to meet the actors. The event motivates the study of the play beforehand. Students who present a play themselves gain immensely in motivation and in cultural experience. The play need not be so long as to damage the rest of a semester's studies.

The teaching possibilities of film, already demonstrated by pioneers *Ways of using films* like George Borglum, Elton Hocking, and Robert Hammond, have been codified by Maynard (121).

Experiential 5: Audio self-instruction, broadcasts, and telecasts

Rand Morton's early vision of the language lab booth as an *The language lab* acculturation chamber, surrounding the learner with a multi-sensory simulation of the foreign environment, is still refreshing and still largely unfulfilled. The *ACTFL Annual Bibliography* continually adds items on the cultural possibilities of the lab, such as E. W. Hawkins' (79) expansion of the list of culturally significant types of lab exercise for Levels I, II, and III that was made for the 1969 meeting of the NALLD (Nostrand, 142). Among experiments to be published as soon as they are evaluated, Hernandez has been modifying participation tapes at the Language Laboratory of the University of Maine, Portland Campus to elicit and record a rejoinder filled in by the student on his second hearing of a master tape. This tape could be further modified to give a useful foretaste of a social situation, by surrounding the learner with a conversation among several persons, with blank spaces in which the newcomer is to try to fill in a rejoinder or an answer to a question. Another of the newer types of exercise that can use the lab well is the culture assimilator (Experiential 6).

After practice by means of audio self-instruction, the student can *Radio and television* enjoy shortwave broadcasts from the culture area and, where they can be received, telecasts. Articles on these resources have become numerous: for radio, those of Wood (222), Savignon (175), Therrien (199), and Garfinkel (60), who is also co-editor of an *LBRIG Newsletter* on the subject (111); for television, the articles by Polcyn (161), Thompson (200), Tidhar (201), and Howlett (84).

Experiential 6: The mini-drama and the culture assimilator

These useful techniques are basically the same two-part device: the experience of an incident, broken off at a climax and followed by an exercise of inferring what caused the climax. The incident may consist of a social error made by an outsider to the culture or a problem of human relations within the society that reveals some significant feature. The mini-drama, or mini-skit, presents the incident in dramatized form; the students observe or play the roles themselves. The assimilator uses the narrative form for its exposition. The inferential exercise can take the form either of a discussion or of multiple-choice explanation. The latter form, usual in the assimilator, is adaptable to less advanced students and to self-instruction. The programmed assimilator exercise often refers one to a different page for each answer, and at each wrong answer agrees that the answer was plausible but explains what is wrong about it. This is one effective way to induce a student to question a cherished stereotype in the privacy of self-instruction. There is of course no magic in following what one is "supposed" to do. All the experiential devices can be used for the expository segment, and all the cognitive devices, for the inferential part.

Overcoming hearsay opinions

Behmer (5) has produced mini-skits for French, German, and Spanish and has reported enthusiastic student response (6). Jenks (93) has discussed both these and Gorden's (65) well-researched Spanish mini-dramas, among them one that explains the unwitting rudeness and the exasperation of Americans in their encounter with the banking system of Colombia. Clapper has printed a workshop's harvest of mini-dramas in French, German, and Spanish (27, pp. 3–22). Bourque exemplifies both the mini-drama and the assimilator in *The French Teen-Ager* (15).

Fiedler and coauthors (47) have described how to develop an assimilator and have given results of validation under laboratory and field conditions. O'Brien (148) has reported an experiment to measure the effect of prior training with an assimilator on community-development personnel in Spanish America. Jane Wright is writing a dissertation on this kind of self-instruction, in The Ohio State University College of Education; and at the University of Illinois, Harry C. Triandis was developing new assimilators to prepare defense personnel for Honduras and Thailand.

Experiential 7: Native informants and language camps

When live representatives of a culture talk with a class, the experience they give of their lifestyle need not be completely exploited at the time. Their presence becomes more purposeful, however, when the students are seeking to understand patterns or institutions they know something about. This is particularly true if the visitor, while authentic, has little background for defining the patterns he represents. One can use whatever the informant does know: If he can tell about a sport, for example, the students will gain some preparation for the further experience of listening to a radio or television sportscast—a difficult kind of authentic monologue, and one that many would like to be able to understand. International exchanges occasionally make possible a visit by a sports figure of another country (87). In the absence of informants, one can use as an alternative introduction to sportscasts the reports of athletic events that are included in general newscasts, such as are available in German through the nearest West German consul.

Newsreels as substitute informants

All the purposes of live visits, except the interaction with a native person, can be accomplished with films or video-tapes, including some available commercials on film (48). In the case of the classical languages, an engaging experience of the culture can be mediated by documentary films and simulated situations from the cinema, as used by Muegge (132). Self-identification can come, too, from putting on a play such as Plautus' *Menaechmi*, even in translation, or from reading an intimate account of everyday life such as Gaston Boissier's classic *Cicéron et ses amis.*

Informants in books

A book has the advantage over the live informant in that it permits a commentator to explain, without embarrassing the informant, where the sample individual does and does not exemplify the shared patterns. A model of such commentary is *Apache Odyssey*, an experiment by Morris Opler in which the anthropologist has narrated a fascinating Apache biography and has inserted, in a contrasting type face, his well-informed observations on the relation of the biographee to the regularities of Apache culture (150).

One lone visitor in a strange classroom can hardly interact as he would at home. The spontaneous language and gestures that are missed can be watched in films. For some purposes, an interview with a group is best. One class gained a vivid feeling for a group attitude and its individual variations from a group of Quebec militants.

If a visitor can stay for weeks or months, students develop a deeper sense of his lifestyle. Two organizations that screen and recommend

Sources of resident informants

290

resident visitors are Amity Institute, Box 118, Del Mar, California 92014, and The Experiment in International Living, Putney, Vermont 05346, whose Teacher and Foreign-Language Assistant Program brings only teachers and prospective teachers to this sort of position.

A language camp can mediate informal contact with diverse *Language camps* representatives of a culture area. Patrick Henry High School in San Diego County has had as many as 200 students at a two-day camp. Alvino Fantini (46) has reported on a camp for college students.

Experiential 8: Pen pals, tape pals, and "twinned" classes

Correspondence with an age-mate in the foreign area has been one of the experiences most productive of a feeling of self-identification. Children too young for this meeting of minds experience some degree of closeness by exchanging handiwork with a "twin" class, as Sister Ruth Jonas (94) has shown. Sellman (182) has described a high school *jumelage* in which some students had already been pen pals before they made exchange visits. Under a program called "Partners States," 5th- to 8th-grade students in 41 states are "twinning" their state with a Latin-American country or province. Teachers prepare social studies materials, inserting bits of the language. An example is Kirk's (102) booklet on Brazil. She made a trip to Rio Grande do Norte for its preparation.

To obtain names of prospective pen pals, the first place to look is *Sources of correspondents* among the services of the respective AAT (American Association of Teachers of . . .). Among the world-scale organizations of tape respondents, one of long standing is World Tapes for Education, Box 15703, Dallas, Texas 75215. Less expensive is Voicespondence Club, Box 207, Shillington, Pennsylvania 19607, which lists its correspondents with their ages and hobbies and gives special help to blind and handicapped members.

Experiential 9: Role playing—actual and simulated

To act out a social situation is such a powerful means of immersion— of overcoming our besetting hazard of skin-deep learning—that we should use it to the fullest. In fact, the explorations beyond the pseudo- communication of linguistic dialogues, mini-dramas, and assimilators have led to other valuable forms of role playing.

Pseudo-communication can very early evolve into a meaningful exchange of utterances, in a simulated situation such as buying and selling. In an imaginative unpublished FLES text, Matkovick, Ybarra, *Activities for beginners* and O'Keefe (120) have a tourist forget to bargain with a handicraft vendor, and the class chimes in with quite real concern, "¡*Hay que regatear!*" Jenks (93) proposes using real money of the country and putting up a backdrop, projecting a street scene through a bed sheet. Seelye has elicited involvement by choosing crisis situations: "What do you say in this culture to a person who has just lost a relative?" This motivation can be appealed to in some types of language laboratory exercises usable as early as Level II: the sleuth type and the "What would you do?" type (Nostrand, 142). The "critical incident" thus has possibilities as a teaching device as well as an attitudinal measuring instrument.

Gestures are an important part of language teaching—the point has been made well by Fleming (51, 55)—and they need to be explicitly taught in exercises of simulation. In real life, they may make the difference between successful and ineffectual communication. Dialogues can be "seeded" with appropriate gestures, and the gestures of the people can be observed on film. They tend to look forced in films where they are consciously modeled but are spontaneous in authentic movies. Readily usable descriptive knowledge of gestures is largely lacking except for the work of Green (66) in Spanish. The best digest for French appears still to be the *Background Data* (Nostrand, 140, pp. 251–65). The French inventory by Tsoutsos (207) is a help, but the gestures are not the most practical selection, nor are they culture-wide. They are adapted from Barult (16), who remarked that none of them "are in general use among the Canadians" (p. 382). For German and Italian, Green's (67) 1971 report, reprinted in 1973, states that nothing exists. A partial response to the need in German is provided by Fleming's historical studies (50, pp. 57–58), which draw upon his seminar at the University of Surrey on German Humor and Satire from 1848 to the Present.

Kinesics

More advanced students enjoy studying to impersonate a culture bearer of a specified social class, age group, geographical region, and political persuasion and to be able to react as such a person might. Santoni (173, 174) has used this device, and Corbin (31) has had each of her students personify a social type, such as a Norman farmer, throughout a semester course. Response has been enthusiastic. Marquardt has employed a similar but more concentrated and intensive experience, with a cognitive emphasis which places his device in type Cognitive 5.

Simulation of specific types

At about Level IV students can improvise a political situation such as a coup d'état (Parker, 156) and can profit by either an interview with an expert who plays the role of a "contrast-American," deliber-

Enacting an episode

292

ately misconstruing every slip the American makes, or a real-life interview with a person of a contrasting culture, followed by a discussion of "do's" and "don't's." When an Edward Stewart or an Edmund Glenn plays the innocent "contrast-American" who engages one member of a class in an interview, inquires into his motives for being in the contrast-country, and ends up aghast, the whole class feels involved as their fellow student finds himself tied in knots of self-explanation.

Intercultural simulation training has benefited from research and development because of industrial and government interest. The Defense Language Institute and Foreign Service Institute, particularly, have seen this device as a main means of improving international contact and negotiation. The research up to 1969 has been well synthesized by DeCrow (36). Evaluation has also been carried on, notably by National Training Laboratories for the Peace Corps (76). Decaroli (35) reports that simulation games in the classroom increase interest—provided the learners are prepared in the subject matter—and that they improve attitudes toward an out-group; but he cautions that the retention of information may fall below that achieved with traditional methods.

Research and validation

Experiential 10: The experience-based project

The Peace Corps articulates "experience-based training" into six steps, explained by DeCrow (36, p. 43), with a focus on some service to the host community. The same term seems appropriate, however, to any project of intercultural education in which the learner plans an inquiry into a lifestyle, inductively formulates some descriptive knowledge, and evaluates his own learning.

In this simplified sense, such a project can be carried out away from the area studied. *The Study of a Culture at a Distance*, by Mead and Metraux (122), makes clear how it was possible during World War II for a few good anthropologists to find out more about predicting Japanese reactions than our government could learn from businessmen who had lived in Japan for 30 years.

Vicarious experience

An elementary form of the experience-based project, if self-evaluation were added, is the collecting of pictures to define the connotative meaning of a word (Experiential 2). Seelye (179, p. 80) has also used a more complex inquiry: Students read the movie announcements in a newspaper, asking not only what is advertised in them, but what time are the shows? Is there evidence of censorship? If so, for what age levels? What are the apparent attitudes, then,

Exercises for beginners

293

toward children and adolescents? Loew (116) gets students to ask equally telling questions about an issue of a magazine. Wylie (223) demonstrated in an article of lasting value that even the *Annuaire statistique de la France* is a potential treasure of ideas. When the student is ready, a comparison with the *U.S. Statistical Abstract* reveals fascinating differences in methods of approach and objects of concern.

It is important to study the culture, and particularly its language, beforehand to avoid producing those hasty inventions—"I get along, all right!"—that impress their inventor more than they do the natives. For those forced to begin from too little preparation, Zinn (97), working with Kaplan and Aqua, on basic adult education for incomers to the United States, has devised some highly practical early exercises: a morning's study of the map of a city and its bus lines followed by an afternoon using the buses, and later, a similar sequence of half-days devoted to the gas company, whose employees were only too glad to be better understood by their new customers. Even for such beginners, study abroad is the most effective when it includes a plan, an inquiry, and an evaluation.

For beginners living in the foreign area

Raymond Gorden's *Initial Immersion in the Foreign Culture* (65) quickly gets newcomers beyond a tourist's acquaintance by a sophisticated approach based on his *Contrastive Analysis of Cultural Differences which Inhibit Communication* (64). The wide variety of field studies open to more seasoned observers, working more on their own, is illustrated by the team reports produced by the teachers in the NDEA Institutes at Rennes organized by the College of Saint Catherine (204).

Purposeful summer visits to Europe by groups of high school students have been organized successfully by school systems across the United States, from Columbia, South Carolina, to Santa Clara County, California, where junior high students have proved to be not at all too young. Criteria for evaluating high school foreign-study programs have been drawn up, notably by Haukebo (78), Leamon (112), and the National Council of State Supervisors of Foreign Languages (70). Numerous evaluations have been conducted and some published, for example, by ACTFL (Bendon, 7; Bourque, 14) and by the San Leandro District (187).

Study abroad: High-school age

For the college level, there is a published description of the California State Colleges' Program, designed by Thomas Lantos and admirably integrated into the curricula (22). Michielli (127) has described an independent-study type of program. And the invention of programs continues. Marquardt was planning for the summer of 1973 a "literary

Study abroad: College age

study tour" by bicycle in Japan and mainland China, for which the students, including a writer and professor of psychology, were preparing themselves by digesting a list of readings in translation. Criteria for foreign study at the college level have been published by the Council on International Educational Exchange (69). Helpful sidelights have also appeared here and there, such as the comment by Royal Tinsley (202) of the University of Arizona. Evaluations of programs abroad have been conducted by the sponsoring colleges, and the experiences of foreign students in the United States have been evaluated by the Institute of International Education and cooperating organizations. One interesting long-range evaluation, by Dow (39), is a study of Chinese students after their return from the United States to their own institutions. They were able to modify only some of the institutions to correspond to American models.

The results of efforts to evaluate training specifically for cross-cultural interaction skills were summarized, up to 1969, by DeCrow (36). One form of training that appeared effective was the self-structuring T group ("T" for training), a sensitivity-training group made up of local nationals and outsiders. A general criticism, made by National Training Laboratories, was that training programs aimed at a too academic, cognitive "understanding" to the neglect of affective commitment and the courage to take risks for an objective (Harrison and Hopkins, 76). Since 1969, Althen (2) has found that intercultural workshops accomplish more than sensitivity training for the adjustment of foreign students.

Evaluation of cross-cultural skills

Experiential 11: Testing affective results

Seelye's 1968 "Measuring cultural achievement" (177) remains the broadest vision of this subject.

Civilized attitudes are the main contribution, surely, that experience of a foreign culture can make to human growth and development. The main justification for giving that experience, therefore, depends on aiming at enlightened attitudes. The measurement of attitudes and attitude change is, however, a branch of psychology and not of ethnography. The encouraging progress made in that field during the past decade is reflected in the psychology and testing sections of the *ACTFL Annual Bibliography;* it falls outside this chapter, except for the implication that it is now possible to test our achievement of the affective aims—acceptance of cultural differences, ego-involvement, commitment—but only as of the moment of testing before or after an experience. Prediction of what the subject *would* do under conditions

Measurement of attitudes

he has not experienced introduces variables that reduce the probability of prediction.

Testing understanding of a culture is subject to a second limitation. *Limits of "objective" testing* "Objective" questions cannot measure the ability to *put together* one's experience and knowledge *unless* the knowledge concerned is an unexceptionable truth—while most cultural generalizations are only useful probability statements—and a truth that the examinees, collectively, can be expected to know, up to an agreed level of proficiency. Such truths are scarce in this field, on two counts: because judgment is involved in one's answers and because we ourselves have still to reach a consensus as to what knowledge is important to teach. Ground of meaning, lengths of rivers, shapes of doorknobs are still competing. No substantial national standard is yet practicable. The Committee on the Advanced French test of the Graduate Record Examination has resolved the first problem—agreement on some items that require the use of significant facts—but only to find that few of these items survive the pretest: They tend to come out with both a high level of difficulty and a low coefficient of the power to discriminate between good and bad performances.

Within those limitations, it is possible to test a person's understanding of a culture pattern—his ability to use his skill and knowledge—in real or simulated situations. *Understanding* here has some nine alternative meanings, all of which call for testing with a cognitive emphasis except for parts of two among them, the first and the sixth listed in Cognitive 9: the ability to act in accord with a conventionalized pattern and the *Measurable skills* ability to react affectively to a problem situation in a way acceptable to the host community. Thus when one reads Clark's *Foreign Language Testing* (28) one should apply in this connection the chapter on proficiency testing, although he treats "culture testing" only under "knowledge testing." Each of the simulation devices that have been reviewed in the present list can in fact provide testing situations. In turn, testing situations can be used for teaching. Jennifer Rogers (169) cannot but induce some self-questioning in her foreign readers when, after quizzing them on their ability to sort out fact from fiction about Britain, she suggests that anyone with a score of 55 believes only what he wants to believe.

Proficiency testing can be made more fun and more motivating if *Festive testing situations* enjoyable occasions are devised for students to demonstrate their skills. An annual declamation contest, for example, at Kent State University has been giving incentive to high school students for nearly three decades, and an annual language fair in which high school students have a part is a tradition at the University of Missouri's Rolla campus. The Mid-Missouri Association of Colleges planned to combine these types of event into a Foreign Language Participation Day at that University's Columbia campus. Lipton (115, p. 207) has reported similar activities, with some reservations.

In sum, the attitude test, proficiency test, contest of wit or skill, and language festival *can* all serve to dramatize goals and motivate students to internalize, analyze, and retain a fleeting experience.

Cognitive 1: Observation and inference, with Socratic prompting

The Socratic technique has two great advantages over any other: that the learner values his hard-won knowledge and that meanwhile he gains experience in the skills of observation, creative imagination, and inferential reasoning. Seelye's writings are particularly helpful for applying this technique, as one sees in the examples already cited, in his "Performance Objectives" paper (178), and in his teaching text based on the mass-media, written with Day (180). He distills three guiding *Three guiding assumptions* principles to make one's interrogating significant (179, pp. 76–78):

1 To approach the particular culture from the concept of universal human needs. One must heed here, however, the observation of the anthropologist Dorothy Day, that this analytical concept is itself culture bound and can obscure how the culture bearer sees his world.

2 To notice that in a given culture, it takes not one pattern but a structure of interacting patterns to satisfy a basic human need.

3 Never to lose sight of the individual—a principle urged by Brooks and well exemplified by Opler in *Apache Odyssey* (150).

These principles can suffuse with significance even the earliest language lessons. Programmed homework exercises, of the sort William *Programmed homework* Bull used for the linguistic component of elementary Spanish, can be worked out in English as soon as students have a first dialogue in mind. A sample, applied to the first dialogue in the Holt, Rinehart and Winston *Ecouter et parler* (Nostrand, 142, p. 35; Clapper, 27, p. 44) leads the student to notice whether terms of address are used in greeting and leave taking and whether *Monsieur* is followed by the person's last name; confirms the regularity observed; and suggests a possible feudal origin, clearly labeling the explanation as a conjecture, in contrast with the verifiable description of the present-day pattern. An equally simple *Inferring change* guide to inferential reasoning, apropos of the documentary film *Four Families* (58), asks the student to observe how the parents in the French family treat the one year old and the older siblings and then to infer

297

from the synchronic data how the child and the parents probably perceive the radical, diachronic change from coddling to the demanding of adult-like responsibility (Clapper, 27, p. 43).

As soon as students can carry on a discussion in simple language, *Comparing impressions* they can compare their impressions of a significant visual cue. Cooke shows a class the pictures of human types in a book such as *The Family of Man*; some students see the diversity; others, the unifying humanity; and a comparison of the two observations leads to the recognition of both (Cooke, 29, pp. 120–21). At this stage it becomes feasible to use "discussion stimulators," as devised at the University of Georgia (for *Discussion stimulators* the audio-motor unit) (Elkins et al., 44, pp. 65–66). This device consists of a general topic put in question form, a checklist of points to be discussed, and some cues designed to spark discussion of the points.

When students are sufficiently advanced to be somewhat at home *Inferring a dénouement* in a culture's ground of meaning, they can see a movie about two thirds of the way through and then discuss what outcome to expect. Margaret Mead used this procedure when she, as well as Martha Wolfenstein and Nathan Leites (221), were analyzing films as manifestations of a culture. The same film can serve for a wealth of material for inductive generalization about kinetics, role relations, age and sex status, artistic concerns, conflict patterns, attitudes toward material things, and quite unpredictable discoveries of data and interrelations.

Finally, when students are ready to talk with persons from the *Culture-free questioning* culture, they can overcome the distorting effect of culture-bound questions by using UNESCO's ingenious device of asking, "What question should I put to you, so that you can tell me about your living style as you see it?" The Peace Corps has also formulated valuable guidelines for "learning how to learn" in the field. The fullest source is the volume of *Specific Methods and Techniques* by Wight and Hammons (218).

Cognitive 2: The incidental comment

Thinking back over one's own teachers' digressions, one will likely find reams of self-narration that proved quite worthless, even for the subconscious purpose of arousing admiration. A few telling observations probably generated repercussions of thought. If one reduces the quantity to these few and uses them to unfold the elements of an adult synthesis that meet with learner readiness, incidental comments become a powerful and compact instrument. The brief moments they take are repaid, even if judged wholly by their contribution to the meaningfulness of the language or literature lesson. It is surprising how soon a class that uses only the foreign language can grasp a linguistically simple remark, provided it bears directly on the material in mind at the moment.

Cognitive 3: Systematic exposition of a topic, including individualized self-information

A teacher can immediately utilize expository material, even while developing the background of knowledge required for the best use of the Socratic inquiry and the incidental comment (which takes knowledge both for the planning and for answering spin-off questions). Students themselves can fill in useful information from expository sources in the form of outside reading, lectures, or interviews, either live or on film. The expounding may be accompanied by factual questions to assure comprehension. The factual questions can be used in multiple ways, as Smithson (186) has spelled out.

A superior instance of the expository genre is Lewald's *Latino-América* (113), which defines values and social conditions, recognizes the complexity of a three-culture area, and yet speaks simply to intermediate students.

In French, Bouraoui (12) has sustained a lively sociocultural and historical exposition, with question and marginal explanations, through the two volumes of *Créaculture*. He has adapted the expository material in an audiolingual course (13) and reports that at York University, where the French enrollment had dropped from 850 to 100 with the abandonment of a language requirement, these two books helped raise the figure in five years to 600. The Valettes have embodied careful sociocultural expositions in a review grammar (210) and are doing the same in a high school program for Levels I and II (211), where they have added ideas for individual and group projects.

German culture is surveyed well in a reader by vonHofe (213), and Troyanovich (206) has pinpointed some key German-American contrasts.

The neglected classical perspective

Classical studies have a long tradition of broad-gauge synthesis—witness the discussions of the Amphictyonic League in the great debate that shaped the American Constitution. Teachers of a modern language as well as the classicists ought to be utilizing this tradition for the long perspective in which it puts the contemporary world. Lieberman (114) has distilled from classical scholarship an eminently accessible introduction to the Greek and Roman cultures.

Individualized expository materials

Besides the survey of essentials, students want opportunities to explore in directions that appeal to them personally. Here is where teachers of all the age levels need many more packages of lively, self-instructional materials to meet individual interests and capacities. We shall return to the problem of international provision for sifting out and sharing the best of the materials that are already being created.

Expositions of facts cannot be counted on to enlighten attitudes. *Exposition and attitude change* Vassiliou (212) found that Americans living in Greece who read an essay on Greek culture came out with changed perceptions but no change in attitudes. To the extent that attitude change is desirable, the expository devices must apparently be used in conjunction with other types.

Cognitive 4: Participatory exposition—culture capsules and clusters

There is a useful way of presenting information that goes beyond straight exposition and factual questions yet not so far as to engage students in the time-consuming process of inductive generalization. In this strategy, students participate in briefer events, calculated to minimize by active involvement the hazards of skin-deep assimilation and short-term learning. The activities emphasize cognitive learning but add an experiential accompaniment.

The culture capsule is a device that a teacher can use before he has *The culture capsule* acquired sufficient background for the other cognitive devices.

The French capsules written by J. Dale Miller and his students (128) present on a single page, in English, a terse description of a pattern, social type, institution, product, or monumental work of art; a picture; the objective of the unit; a contrast between the United States and France; a paragraph of background facts; and suggestions for presenting the unit with realia and activities. These specific suggestions are amplified by a repertory of alternative procedures that use all the media and a wide range of techniques (pp. 103–17). A capsule can be taught in as little as five to 15 minutes.

However, a trap to avoid in using this convenient device is that its *A by-effect to avoid* atomistic approach reflects and abets the American tendency to seek satisfaction in "knowing" isolated particulars, to the neglect of the interrelations that give them their true meaning. Neither the "subjective culture," as seen by the insiders, nor the objective "social reality"—to borrow Triandis' (205) terms—can be rightly seen without attending to the interrelatedness of its patterns. The easy, contrastive view of each pattern impedes further the discovering of the ground of meaning, the fabric that confers meaning on the individual stitch. The student needs more help than this if he is to outgrow his original private conviction that *his* fabric makes sense and the foreign stitches are

300

merely odd additions. He is less likely to feel at home in the new world of meaning if he continually reenters it from reference points such as "Though the French are famous for their 'romantic' tendencies. . ." (Miller, 128, p. 1), and "The French have the reputation of being the world's greatest lovers. . . however . . ." (p. 6). Nevertheless, the teacher wary of these intrusions of middle-America can use to good purpose the valuable material in these and other culture capsules. Examples are given by Bourque (15, pp. 75–78), Clapper (27), Hage (72), and Cudecki (34, pp. 14–17). Meade (125) emphasizes student activity in using the device. She and Morain (126) effectively use clusters of capsules.

The "culture cluster"
The "learning package"

A kind of culture capsule, essentially, is the "learning package." This device is created by first formulating the behavioral objectives for a unit supplemental to a textbook, then identifying component objectives, assembling teaching materials aimed at the component objectives, and finally writing a pretest and posttest. Teichert (198) found that the device significantly improved achievement ($p < .01$) and reduced the number of dropouts.

In a Brigham Young University M.A. thesis, Jameson (89) claims that the capsules "seemed to modify" false ideas, that the contrastive feature "greatly facilitated" the learning of the material, and that the 70 subjects studied became more objective in their assessment of French people and their culture. The Language Research Center of Brigham Young has planned an "Intercultural Data Bank," whose project proposal raises again the question of how far to indulge American particularism and its lack of a felt need for organizing concepts. To the extent that a culture is an organic whole, an enumeration of its organs fails to lead toward an understanding of its nature.

A "data bank"

The recipe of the capsule is only one form of participatory exposition. The type also includes the basic "lecture-discussion" method, and it merits new experimentation where we have unsolved problems. Where cultures in contact generate prejudice and violent conflict, for example, Marquardt (119) proposes that the presenting and discussing of a certain rather rare type of oral or written literature can engage a troubled student in thought, discovery, and attitude change.

The "lecture-discussion" method

The "transcendent message"

How do we impart cross-culture communication skills to ethnic populations living side by side and in increasing confrontation with one another? How do we change a Puerto Rican kid who responds to "Hey you dirty . . .!"—the greeting from the gang down the street his family has just moved into—by swinging and getting bloodied, as described by Piri Thomas in his autobiographical *Down*

These Main Streets? How do we get him and his friends to regard this kind of greeting as a challenge to enter a new world, to see things in a new way, to learn new uses of language, and to help his tormentors to grow, too? . . . The best hope is through the type of literature I call the transcendent message. The TM is a message created by a member of one of the cultures in contact, embodying a vision of how members of his culture might come to understand members of the other through self-understanding and through developing a feeling of openness with all types of human beings." (p. 1).

The devices of participatory exposition also include one contrastive approach that carries out two recommendations made by Margaret Mead: to avoid the "We do this; they do that," and to introduce a third culture for perspective. Lewald has devised a course at the University of Tennessee in which he compares the French and Hispanic cultures, through a series of lectures in English, and the students make a further study of the one or the other through reading and separate discussion sessions. *Third culture*

Cognitive 5: The writing of simulations

One of Francis Bacon's maxims puts a triple challenge to language teaching: "Conversation maketh a ready man, reading a broad man, and writing an exact man."

Jenks (92) finds it useful to write a dialogue based on Mexican current events as reported in an American newspaper. By the third level, students can help write dialogues and imaginary interviews, using sources from the culture area. Writing gives time to "seed" the script with appropriate gestures, as suggested in Experiential 9. Marquardt had his students of ESOL in Africa draft a brief, designed to persuade a specific type of American to accept some contention or to buy a product. *Writing a dialogue*

Writing a brief

Advanced students can sharpen their understanding of the foreign cognitive style by the "stylistics" exercise of carefully translating into the target language a paragraph so conceived to encounter the "refusals" of the target culture's ground of meaning. An English novel of the Romantic period, for example, encounters the refusal of the French language to make vagueness impressive. Eighteenth-century Latinists had a method of consulting a native: They would translate a passage of Cicero into their own language, then set their handiwork aside long enough to forget the original, and later retranslate the passage to test their Latinity against the original. *Studies of literary style*

Cognitive 6: Analytical techniques

The activities grouped in Cognitive 1 began with rudimentary observation and inference, then moved in the direction of field performance. The more advanced activities required much language skill and substantive knowledge but did not involve any increasing sophistication of analytic or synthesizing method. The inferences involved were hypotheses, not conclusions.

If I am right in proposing Cognitive 6 and 8 as separate types, it is because these two groups of devices do something different for the learner. They acquaint him with a method—an explicit theory and rigorous application. This is the all-important element of the humanities and the sciences that distinguishes them from dilettantism. Analytical methods of all the social sciences and humane disciplines can be applied to some sector of a sociocultural system. Language teachers, with a few exceptions, can best concentrate their investigations of primary data within the problems and methods relating to language, literature, and teaching.

Pragmatics

One current problem, at the growing edge of ethnography, linguistics, and language-teaching method, is the question of precisely how language relates to situational context—the rediscovered field of pragmatics. This problem can be investigated by methods of all these fields and also by those of literary analysis, including an analytical commentary called *lecture expliquée*.

The running commentary

A passage from a literary or documentary work can be analyzed from any of various points of view, in fact, by the long-matured procedure, dear to the medieval universities, *lecture expliquée*: a running commentary that not only elucidates the language of the passage, usually in a context of prior history, but relates the sample to the form and content of the work as a whole. The commentary can be concentrated on the cultural or societal regularities exemplified.

Whole works and groups of works can be analyzed for the data they contain on a limited question. Ruple (172) wrote a paper of permanent value on the themes of Hispanic culture that emerged from several Spanish plays of the 1960s.

Sociolinguistic research

Advanced students can benefit educationally, from doing manageable parts of a sociolinguistic project, such as the research of Blanc (9) and others on the tape corpus for the city of Orléans, sorting out the evidences of social structure and culture patterns.

Usually analysis is embodied in an effort aiming directly at synthesis. This subordinate role of analysis will be included in Cognitive 8.

Cognitive 7: Bibliography

At an elementary level the collecting of different observations and opinions on a single point can be an eye-opening experience—the beginning of critical, independent thought. Bibliographical training, guided by an informed teacher or librarian, is at once a discipline and a liberation.

A student still at a stage of rehearsal for creative scholarship, if he is near a library, can assemble a thorough bibliography on a small topic and write a bibliographical essay on it.

With supervision, college and even high school students can go beyond the rehearsal stage and establish parts of the bibliography preparatory to the types of research described in Cognitive 8 as "secondary analysis" and "working synthesis."

The sources for bibliographizing will be discussed following this list of teaching devices.

Cognitive 8: Techniques for synthesis

As in the case of the analytical methods, most language teachers are concerned directly with the deriving of generalizations from primary data only in the fields of language and literature. The *explication de texte* belongs to this set of devices because, unlike the *lecture expliquée* in Cognitive 6, the *explication* is a composition whose structure is generated by the points it makes and the relationships among them. It frees itself from following the form of the work of art studied—the better to observe the work's form—as well as its materials and its presuppositions. Yet, in common with the *lecture expliquée*, this method gains the advantage of approaching the whole work through an intensive examination of a part, and thus it manages to combine breadth and thoroughness. While this is a method of exposition only, not of discovery, it makes manageable the demonstration of a work's social and cultural relations. Its ingenious principle of showing the macrocosm reflected in the microcosm can be exploited without incurring the stultifying effect of following academic recipe books. Manuals and examples that avoid that effect are discussed by Frances Nostrand (138), and further examples continue to appear in *Teaching Language through Literature* (197).

Explication de texte

In a methodology for theme hunting, literary researchers (Nostrand, 144), have explained how one can build inductively from theme expressions to the main themes that are the central import of a literary work, precisely as one can synthesize the data of social behavior.

The main themes of a work of art

304

When we possess such studies on both the arts and the society of a period, we will have a surer basis than at present for saying just where the arts reflect the society, or innovate in the culture, or serve as instruments of social control.

Content analysis

While *explication de texte* and theme study aim to synthesize the import of the work of art itself, content analysis treats the work as document, extracting generalizations that may be irrelevant to its import. Three basic kinds of content analysis, defined by Costner (32), have been used to reveal attitudes and attitude changes, notably in journalism and in government reports. One type weighs, in either qualitative or quantitative terms, the amount of attention given to selected topics. Analyzed in this way, the Russian press revealed the rise and decline of government concerns during the cold war. A second type of analysis inventories the "word companions" of the selected units of communication so as to discover the associative relations of those units in the minds of the writers. This type can be applied to spoken language: Szalay (192) has made sophisticated studies of the connotative meanings of *education* and *educación*, *government* and *gobierno*, by questioning foreign students instead of by analyzing documents. A third kind examines the writers' evaluative assertions on selected topics and records on a scale the degree to which a document evidences certain attitudes, such as satisfaction or frustration, that are of interest to the researcher.

Comparative semantics

Further types of content analysis arise from what we want to know about cultures or their relations. Lambert has adapted from Pareto a type fruitful for research on intercultural attitudes (Dill, 37). Glenn (62) studied cultural differences through the minutes of the United Nations Security Council, in their English, French, and Russian versions. He extracted the discrepancies of language from these very careful translations and drew fascinating conclusions concerning the respective assumptions and cognitive styles. Using this model, less-than-advanced students can play at least a part in valuable team research: One girl with a passion for teddy bears studied a translation of *Winnie the Pooh* and produced conclusions well worth publishing concerning the transformations of Pooh and Christopher Robin.

Secondary analysis

The kind of study called "secondary analysis" is actually a form of synthesis. One begins by assembling all the quantitative research, such as opinion polls, that has been done on approximately the same social group over a period of years. One then traces the changes the group has undergone, as well as the stable characteristics over the time period. Secondary analysis has been defined by Boudon (11) and Padioleau (155), and exemplified by Mimiague and his associates (130) in a study of French teen-agers.

Teachers who devote their lifetimes to understanding a people can contribute a kind of study that refines one of the culture-wide generalizations such as have been common since the eighteenth century and particularly in the books of the 1930s on "national character" by such thinkers as Salvador de Madariaga, Ernst Curtius, André Siegfried, and Count Keyserling. An attempt at the more modest generalization befitting the 1970s is the paper on French "relationism" (Nostrand, 141).

The grain of truth in clichés

Even this last kind of study *can* be used as a teaching technique. Students can collect the evidence to substantiate manageable parts of it. But here we cross the threshold between the *unfolding* of what is known as it comes within the learner's capacity to grasp it, and the building of the adult synthesis in the mind of the teacher.

The weakness in our descriptive knowledge of the complex cultures now takes on a precise and constructive meaning: It lies in the gap between the small empirical findings that "don't get off the ground" and the old clichés that overgeneralize. Both have much good in them. The task of ethnography for the decade ahead is to close that gap, from below with secondary analyses and from above with substantiated refinements of the stereotype descriptions.. The objective is to create a working knowledge empirically based as far as possible. If an anthropologist had spent his lifetime describing a single culture, we could turn to him for this knowledge. Since anthropologists do not, however, typically focus on a single culture, we have no one but ourselves to look to for the work of completing the pieces and putting them together.

A sharpened view of the task ahead

The chief instrument of progress in this task is a sort of organizing study that we may call a working synthesis. It is an essay that aims to describe one of the major articulating parts of a sociocultural system. *Background Data for the Teaching of French* (Nostrand, 140) attempts a set of such essays for France as of 1967; some of the more successful are the chapters on the value system, cognitive style, and assumptions of fact; gastronomy as an art form; the language, para-language, and kinesics; education from the student's point of view; leisure patterns; and attitudes toward minorities.

The implementation

Cognitive 9: Testing cognitive results

Descriptive knowledge is after all only a means—toward generous attitudes, wise judgments, and critical thinking throughout the learner's life. The testing of these educational outcomes belongs to the field of testing and measurement.

To the field of ethnography belongs the testing of the various kind of "understanding of a culture" referred to in Experiential 11. The nine kinds suggested by the Nostrands (139) and taken up by Seelye (179) and Morain (131) comprise the following abilities, whose cognitive component can be tested in behavior: the ability

1 to appeal to a value of the culture
2 to describe a pattern or to ascribe it to a subculture of which it is typical
3 to recognize a pattern in an instance of behavior
4 to "explain" a pattern, either in terms of its functional relation to other patterns or in casual terms
5 to predict a probable reaction to a given situation
6 to select an approved attitude
7 to evaluate the basis given for a descriptive generalization
8 to describe or demonstrate a method of analysis or of synthesis
9 to select descriptive knowledge significant for a common human purpose

To the extent that these are mutually exclusive meanings of "understanding," they require separate performance objectives and separate testing, for which our essay suggests some usable procedures (Nostrand and Nostrand, 139).

It would be useful to have definitions of proficiency levels for evaluating the capability to succeed in cross-cultural communication. Hutchinson (85) has drafted standards parallel to the five levels of language proficiency used by the Defense Language Institute.

The 20 types of technique reviewed above are too numerous to use in any short period of time. But by choosing the most effective technique for an immediate purpose, with a long-range end in view, we can enable a student to use his time and energy with much more effect and satisfaction.

Materials: Sources and resources

The sociocultural component of language teaching poses the problem of where to find several distinct kinds of information and assistance.

The question that logically comes first, for workshop participants and methods-course students alike, is how to consolidate the disparate theoretical contributions into a basis for the practical decision one

The theoretical foundation

307

faces if one wants to introduce "the culture": What should it mean—in view of what educational purposes? The first section in the development of this chapter brought together the recent theorizing and research one may wish to refer to for this question and then endeavored to consolidate a working basis for the decision. That endeavor should help the reader to form his own opinion—if only by virtue of Bacon's principle that "Truth springs more readily from error than from confusion."

The question we strike next is where to find good materials. Part of the answer will arise from the section just completed. Reading the critique of devices with the resources for one language in mind will help a teacher to list some suggestive mentions of materials, which the references at the end of the chapter amplify with addresses and periodicals. Most of these sources will continue producing in their respective lines of development. *Existing materials*

Where the materials are not forthcoming, the 20 types of technique help one to visualize what one may want to create, alone or by team work. There are already numerous sources of films one can incorporate into one's own instruction. A list of these sources, for all languages, was compiled for the Illinois Conference, jointly sponsored by a university and a junior college (Rivers, 168, pp. 89–91). *The need for a clearinghouse*

To create one's own materials, based on the best previous research and development, involves one in the problem of bibliographizing, and here real progress has been made during the 1960s. One can now bring up to date a great deal of the international documentation on a subject in the field of language teaching, by using only a few sources. For many of a teacher's purposes, the first two or three of the following will suffice. *Sources for a bibliography*

1 ERIC (Educational Resources Information Center) stores for retrieval the bibliographical data on all books and unpublished papers listed in *RIE (Research in Education)* and all the articles in the many journals covered by *CIJE (Current Index to Journals in Education)*. A printout, which includes abstracts for the unpublished materials, can be obtained through cooperating libraries at a reasonable cost. Whole texts can be obtained from EDRS (ERIC Document Reproduction Service) inexpensively on microfiches or, if needed, on photocopied pages. The ERIC system is described fully and clearly by Svobodny (191).

2 *FLA (Foreign Language Annals)* publishes in each May issue the *ACTFL Bibliography* for the preceding year, listing by topics and subtopics a wider range of articles and books than the ERIC

308

system. It includes American and foreign textbooks and audio-visual materials, and devotes a separate item to each chapter in the multiple-author "Festschrift" volumes of the year. A cumulative edition is projected. This bibliography can serve as a good point of departure for research and development in the field of applied ethnography, but its coverage has not presumed bibliographic control of all information about the various cultures. Needed is a series of publications for each culture, organized according to a structured inventory, with the documentation subsumed under the concepts worth teaching. This would immensely help the teacher in his continuing development.

3　*PMLA (Publications of the Modern Language Association of America).* The annual bibliography lists topically the preceding year's studies on literary works and movements. (The *FLA* and *PMLA* bibliographical searches are coordinated, and the items of interest to both are listed in both bibliographies.)

4　*MLJ (The Modern Language Journal)* and the AAT (American Association of Teachers of . . .) journals—magazines such as *The French Review, The German Quarterly, Hispania, Italica*—publish many book reviews, of which there is no consolidated list. *AFLT (American Foreign Language Teacher)* adds to these much practical information, as the references of this chapter show. These journals are not covered by the *Bibliographie der Rezensionen,* which constitutes *Abteilung C* of the following series.

5　*Internationale Bibliographie der Zeitschriftenliteratur aus allen Gebieten des Wissens.* Any articles that may have been missed by the ACTFL bibliographical teams may be found, under German topical headings, in this compendium, which is *Abteilung B* of the set, or for German periodicals, in the corresponding *Abteilung A.*

In addition to these convenient sources, a thorough search takes one into the annual record of books published in the language area concerned; the scholarly and scientific journals, which include book reviews in their fields; and the card-file bibliographies of the area's research centers, usually unpublished but accessible to a qualified observer.

As for current research, the "work in progress" bibliographies have been discontinued as being unsuccessful—incomplete and repetitious from year to year. The unpublished items in ERIC replace them except for the most recent information, which one can obtain only by corresponding with the researchers or by hearing them read papers in the meetings of professional associations.

The resources available shape the future of the language sequence, offering a certain opportunity but requiring some steering by the language-teaching profession. Both the opportunity and the danger prominently involve the cultural dimension, for in that dimension lies the relevance of language courses to students' interests, outside activities, and learning in other disciplines. The great drawback is that all this "horizontal" coordination, left to itself, enfeebles the "vertical" progress of the learner toward mastery of a language and empathic understanding of a culture.

The future of the language sequence

Language skills need a sustained sequence of challenges, each step just high enough. Otherwise, the familiar results: short memory ("I *had* x years of it but . . ."), skin-deep impact of reading and spoken ideas, and a reading "knowledge" unreliable wherever the learner would have to outgrow the monolingual person's limits of syntax and cognitive style. Here language merges into culture patterns. These, too, are acquired only by sustained and sequenced learning of an inter-connected whole: the culture's "grammar" of method, world picture, and values.

The "vertical" progression

The one reality that favors the vertical advance is the variously motivated curiosity about lifestyles—persistent, but subtle and fragile. Against this force, the unfavorable realities make a formidable coalition.

Forces favoring "horizontal" expansion

Students want short cycles of satisfying achievement, and the "success" of the teacher and the school, for which they are accountable to society, consists in mediating the student's pursuit of that satisfaction, even where it amounts only to an institutionalized whim. Genuine motivation does result, which after all is better than the old docility, but efficient continuity suffers.

Student satisfaction

Pulling in the same direction as the student's interest is the fact that the liveliest centers of action in the humanities are those that reflect a similar interest in human problems of our time. The University of Birmingham Centre for Contemporary Cultural Studies (183) has task forces investigating both artistic and social manifestations of British, American, and French culture, drawing upon kindred centers, in anthropology—Claude Levy-Strauss' Laboratoire d'Anthropologie Sociale—and in sociology—Pierre Bourdieu's Centre de Sociologie Européenne. The University of Wisconsin-Milwaukee Center for Twentieth Century Studies (Galbreath, 59) decided in 1972 to focus its activities for

Thrust within the humanities

310

several years upon cultural pluralism, conceived to embrace eight interests including "World views and self images," "Synthesis," "Tradition and modernity in contemporary culture." In contrast with this ferment, the most glamorous of the 20 techniques for expertise in cross-cultural communication appear to many of our colleagues only as technical curiosities.

The most imaginative applied forms of the humanities, likewise *Trend in the applied humanities* addressed to the urgent social concerns of our time, attack problems of intercultural relations using interdisciplinary approaches: the Peace Corps, Vista, and within the teaching establishment, certain fresh initiatives from Education and the Social Studies that promise a new official climate for language teachers. In 1966 the American Association of Colleges for Teacher Education began a study of the education of American teachers with respect to world affairs. One result was Taylor's *The World and the American Teacher* (193). In 1972 that Association (136) adopted a strong statement formulated by its Commission on Multicultural Education. At least one Education course of an emerging type, called Multicultural Education, is offered by Richard Cummings at the University of Wisconsin-Milwaukee. The Association for Supervision and Curriculum Development began planning early in 1968 for a Conference on World Cooperation in Education held at Asilomar in 1970 and, in that connection, published four background papers, one of them by Kenworthy (99). The ASCD created a World Council for Curriculum and Instruction (135), which publishes a *Newsletter*. The National Council for the Social Studies has produced an anthropological issue of *Social Education* (196), with a 53-page article on "Teaching about American Indians." The American Anthropological Association's Anthropology Curriculum Study Project directed by Ms. Malcolm Collier, wisely avoiding any proposal to make that discipline one more school subject, has created exciting and worthwhile educational materials.

Government forces converge with the private powers of the *Political concerns and subsidies* establishment. The United States Office of Education has encouraged world-minded education financially as well as through statements like that of King (101) for the elementary school and Caldwell (21) for the university. UNESCO has advanced intercultural awareness by calling attention to "how nations see each other," by publishing its Geography Series, by conducting its "Associated Schools Project in Education for International Co-operation and Peace," with that project's semiannual bulletin, *International Understanding at School*, and not least, by attracting

American educators into international activities involving anthropology and linguistics, of which the latest in 1973 was the UNESCO (3) "Anthropology and Language Science in Educational Development" program.

Alternative language courses

All these influences, and more, are conducive to interdisciplinary developments that are badly needed. American life is richer for the alternative courses that sacrifice something of language learning to more burning interests. Molly Melching, a Teaching Assistant at the University of Illinois, makes a fourth-semester variant course on French culture so interesting that students bring their friends. The courses in translation are also a gain and are worth the time of teachers who can read in the original: It was a significant remark by a classicist, reviewing a monolingual philosopher's book on Plato, that "this was exactly the sort of book Jowett's translation deserved to have written about it." Yet the pull of these developments draws energy away from the vertical sequence essential to mastery of a language and immersion in a culture.

Funds for innovation

The diversion of energy has a powerful economic undertow. The research and development funds that may be expected, at least throughout the 1970s, will be largely for interdisciplinary instruction in which the languages are incidental. Language teachers will have to take the lead in persuading the nation that the exhortations to world-mindedness cannot be fulfilled unless many citizens of the countries in contact benefit by a long sequence such as the St. Lambert bilingual program evaluated by Lambert (e.g., Dil, 37, pp. 111–59), which succeeds demonstrably in enlightening attitudes.

The case for the long sequence

Our case is strengthened by Lambert's careful research in the course of that long sequence, compared to Vassiliou's (212) results with Americans living in Greece. We are helped, too, by the increasing international contact, the career motivation, the opportunity to study abroad, and the opportunity to visit local ethnic groups. The opportunity was always there but could not be used so long as it was fashionable to scorn all but the cosmopolitan versions of foreign cultures. At Harvard, where ethnic studies began with the introduction of Armenian in 1955, Francis Rogers' students of Portuguese study not only Brazil and Portugal but the local Boricua area, whose culture has been analyzed by Adler (1). At the University of Wisconsin-Green Bay, a curriculum in Liberal Education requires a cross-cultural experience, after a semester's preparation for it; Wallach (215) reports that the experience strongly motivates language study. For Grades K to 12, new approaches to the foreign culture are being collected into a book by Love (117) and others, and in the public elementary schools of

312

Washington, D.C. and Philadelphia, Love reports that Latin is being taught with a cultural emphasis that relates Roman culture and society to inner-city students.

The case for the vertical sequence is strengthened, finally, by the progress language teachers have made in defining performance objectives, both for the language skills and for the cultural component. The advances in this latter sector are embodied chiefly in contributions made by Seelye (178), Valette and Disick (209), Steiner (188), Cooney (30), and DuFort (40) who has elaborated the objectives at Level I for French and Spanish.

Should we aim toward a core of performance objectives defining a progression of challenges from level to level? Absolute freedom from any such obligation is most attractive and has been claimed in the cause of local or individual autonomy. The claim is cogent at the FLES stage, on the ground that FLES should be just a "booster" experience. But we destroy our own case for a long stretch of the student's time if we do not use it efficiently; and he cannot actualize much of his potential to learn without a manageable progression of challenges— in the four skills, language analysis, the cultural context, and at least the expectation of enjoying the people's literature. Only teamwork on our part can provide him with such a learning situation. Students now experience discouragement, sometimes to the point of dropping out, as they move from one institution to another—at a time when the mobility of the population is increasing. As for the cultural component, the frustration is less—but only for lack of any substantial expectation! A common core would save even the nomadic students from the exasperation of tasks beyond their preparation and would save the teacher from the extreme discrepancies in student preparation that make it so hard for a class to function as a group. Satisfaction would be more widespread at the end of the year, and the next year would have a fresh plateau on which to build. Individualized instruction adds a further reason for a common core. Individual approaches and short modules can result in just a repetition of beginnings, except in those programs where the modules add up to something—preferably something central rather than peripheral to the phenomenon that is being approached.

The case for considering voluntary adoption of a nationwide, basic core of performance objectives for each level is strong enough to warrant scrutinizing. This is true for both the commonly taught languages and the neglected ones. Jazayery (90) finds reason to urge "a minimum of generally agreed-upon objectives for Persian language instruction"

A core of objectives for each level

313

(p. 20). Objectives by levels have been worked out for the language skills by a conference of Illinois teachers and edited by Castle and associates (24). For the cultural part, Steiner (188) has gone beyond DuFort (40) to Level IV in French (but with a result suggestive for all languages). A proposed progression deliberately limited to a core, and neutral as to the language, was drafted by a committee of the Pacific Northwest Conference, improved in North Carolina, and published by the Illinois State Superintendent (Nostrand, 143), as well as by the Washington Association of Foreign Language Teachers.

The clearinghouse function

Assuming nationally defensible objectives for the language sequence, let us turn to the problem of completing one's collection of needed materials. To overcome the waste of producing the same materials in many schools and colleges, the state foreign language bulletins have been mediating some exchanges of information. At least two state "FL editors" have created an additional serial: *The Gadfly*, which supplements the Arizona *AFLT Forum; Recipes for Teaching Foreign Languages in Oklahoma* (Hammond and Garfinkel, 74); and in Washington, Crosbie's *Project FLITE* (33). Excellent cultural materials produced by school systems are nonetheless still unknown to many who could use them. A case in point is the high-quality production of the Minneapolis Public Schools, such as the lively little chapters for high school German by Waitschies and Mayrs' (214).

National scale

Logically, the exchange should be expanded to a national scale. A small part of the need is filled by ERIC and the national journals. ACTFL has begun to supplement these through *Accent on ACTFL*, through the display of materials kits at its national meetings, and—since March 1973—through the mention in *Foreign Language Annals* of teacher-prepared materials that become available through EDRS.

In addition to these arrangements among language teachers themselves, a few broader frameworks may help. The possibility is illustrated by the Union for Experimenting Colleges and Universities, whose 21 members in 1973 spread from Hofstra University on Long Island to the University of the Pacific, with its president at Antioch College.

International scale

The national coordinating effort of language teachers should aim from the start to become a part of an international clearinghouse structure, which is still more logical. Teachers in all the English-speaking countries, for example, struggle with the same linguistic and cultural interferences. The lack of coordination thus far, even in this one language community, is evidenced by the scant overlap between British and American bibliographies on language teaching. Of 712 books listed in the *CILT Language-Teaching Bibliography* of 1968, Frances

314

Nostrand (137) found only a combined total of 125 listed either in our *Research on Language Teaching* of 1965 (147), the Birkmaier and Lange *Selective Bibliography* of 1968 (8), or Grittner's *Teaching Foreign Languages* published in 1969 (68).

The pedagogical clearinghouse function must include research on the interests and attitudes of students, potential students, and ex-students of languages. Publishers have an interest in this research and might eventually gain by taking part in a clearinghouse despite the loss of what competitive advantage there is in secrecy.

Information on the tastes of learners

When teachers have such aid at their disposal we can have more and better students, a better time with them, and more time for other things than preparing materials. But even so, we can present only what understanding we have—which brings us to the last of the four problems we take home from the workshops on "the culture."

Acquiring knowledge: The future of the teacher's development

Each section of this chapter has sketched some features of a new social role for the language teacher—a new meaning of what it is to *be* a language teacher. The adjustment of American society to cultural pluralism calls for participation in intellectual leadership beyond the classroom. The need for cross-cultural understanding entails an extension of our competence to include a mature form of that understanding. And the evolution of the curriculum—outward at the expense of vertical progression—demands initiative in the making of educational policy.

The language teacher's emerging status

Basic to all three of these spheres of influence is a certain descriptive knowledge of a culture and of cultural differences, knowledge so alien to our majority culture that many insist it is nonsense. The individual teacher must decide for himself whether, or where, the majority is right—not only to argue his way to the influence enjoyed by a convincing idea and not only to avoid teaching trivia that give him a weak case, but above all because the synthesis he personally has arrived at determines what he really means to society. Our indirect, implicit teaching, as Taylor (194, p. 44) observes, is as important as all we can accomplish through explicit techniques.

Consequent importance of ethnographic knowledge

If our descriptive knowledge has this underlying effect, the preservice education of language teachers demands attention and is inseparable from the culminating problem of our self-development after that stage. Both stages raise the question of feasibility in time; both depend on a more ingenious team approach to the syntheses of descriptive knowledge

Implication for preservice education

315

that none of us, and no single college of teacher education, can create alone.

The sociocultural part of preservice education remains weak, even at the graduate level which presumably should complete the rudiments of an understanding worth imparting to students. Hayes (80) and Opler (151), working with specialists in several disciplines, staked out a reasonable standard in a conference of 1962, and the Northeast Conference Report of 1972 (Dodge, 38) reflects essentially the same state of beginning.

In a discussion among representatives of foreign language education centers, held at Atlanta in November 1972, no one claimed to be satisfied with the cultural element in his program. Some were allowing for elective courses in anthropology, history, sociology, social psychology, economics, political science, social and economic geography. But the elective time available, even in a doctoral program, cannot capture the relevant value of more than two or three of those seven disciplines, which are no more interchangeable than seven languages would be. Suppose the student had time and were prepared for enough advanced courses in most of those departments to collect their contributions toward a knowledge of one culture whose language we teach. The candidate would still be left with a collection of jagged pieces that the specialists themselves cannot put together.

Recommendations seem unanimous. In two conferences of 1972, a knowledge of the foreign culture was recommended as indispensable for the Ph.D. in a language. The first conference, devoted to Spanish, was to be reported on in the October 1973 issue of *Hispania*. The other, jointly sponsored by the MLA, ADFL, and ADE (Association of Departments of English), has been summarized by Mead (123).

The time available for imparting what we know is scarcest at the stage of the M.A. and the teaching certificate—the point where the next generation's profession-wide level of competence is determined. Middlebury College in 1972 revised both its Doctorate of Modern Languages and its M.A., adding to both degrees a required component in a foreign culture. The University of Washington adopted in 1972 a new M.A. program in French that makes room for the cultural component by offering it as one of six modules, from which the candidate chooses four. The other modules are three segments of literary history, language and applied linguistics, and teaching methods. A syllabus for the culture module assigns passages from diverse books and articles but still lacks the documented generalizations, nuanced yet organized, that one would like to offer.

The M.A. and certification

316

The NDEA institutes gave impetus to making the culture a part of in-service training—particularly those abroad with field study, as in the College of Saint Catherine institute at Rennes (204). The process of appraising the NDEA institutes, moreover, stimulated advances in evaluative techniques, most recently in the follow-up by Bruck and others (20), studying the effect of the 1968 institute in the Philippines upon the cross-cultural attitudes of the participants. The culture workshops that have carried on from the NDEA have gone on refining the practical training for imparting what we know. But there we come down to the question of how to advance *beyond* what we know.

Evaluation of pre-service preparation

A small part of the answer is that the individual teacher can make a project of reading about one topic at a time—and this enjoyable approach is not to be belittled. But in a larger view, our collective knowledge is not satisfactory. Moreover, it becomes obsolete and inaccurate very rapidly.

The personal project of reading

There is perhaps one strategy that would work, because it would pit economy of energy against the size of the task. It would be to form survey teams, on the model of the ACTFL bibliographical teams, to carry out continuing "working syntheses" of the type mentioned in Cognitive 8. Each team would be responsible for a manageable sector of a given sociocultural system, and each culture area would need some coordinating center like those provided by the MLA and ACTFL for their bibliographies.

Synthesis through teamwork

The coordinating agency for the study of a culture would have one advantage over the bibliographical endeavors, in that ethnography offers more preexisting activity to coordinate—not only the research of individuals but of centers both within their respective culture areas and in other countries. At present one finds centers of this sort in which the same culture is being studied, yet they lack contact with one another. On inquiry one learns that the isolation is not intentional but is usually due to a certain culture barrier, and a proposal to pool efforts in some degree would be welcome as a means to achieve more of the result that is the *raison d'être* of the center.

If some of the working syntheses produced should turn out to be weak at times, the whole would be less harmed than in the case of the bibliographies. Even if some parts should be missing, we would still be ahead. But is it realistic to attempt a continuing synthesis? The past says "No." Why should the future be different?

A funny thing has happened on the way to the twenty-first century. Ever since the Middle Ages, individual meditation, writing, and teaching have been the mode of advance both for the individual and for

The future of the humanities

317

Western civilization. That mode of advance has generated our academic structure. In the present century, however, the realities we seek to understand have escaped the capacity of the best-rounded Renaissance man, necessitating the expansion of that phenomenon to a circle of specialists pooling their different competencies. The necessity became evident first in the sciences, then in the leading centers of the humanities.

The need for more ingenious teamwork is creating a new structure to facilitate it. The French universities, where tradition and innovation both stand their ground, dramatically demonstrate the new structure: New Centers for Teaching and Research, called UER (Unités d'Enseignement et de Recherche) have sprung up to supplant the graduate-*department* structure with research *teams* studying interdisciplinary topics.

It no longer takes much imagination to see team activities in the future of the humanities; it is precisely by seizing on that principle that we may hope to harness the pull of the emerging interdisciplinary interest so that it will strengthen, instead of weakening as at present, the long sequence in a language and culture.

"Working synthesis" teams afford their members the most exciting intellectual companionship if they are international in composition. And this indeed they have to be—for two reasons: first, to balance together the views from different cultures, and second, to relate the outsiders' perspective to the view from inside. The first need is evident. We Westerners are far from overcoming our "Eurocentric" bias, as Chandra (25) reminds us. Every team needs non-Western representation as well as varied representation from the West. The second reconciliation to be made is harder to see because of a jealous feeling that the insider's view is self-sufficient.

Cross-cultural teams

Useful here is the distinction drawn by Edward Sapir and Kenneth Pike, adopted by Smith (185, pp. 154–55) and Marquardt (118, p. 1020), between what they call "the -*etic* and the -*emic* standpoints," on the analogy of *phonetic* and *phonemic*. Phonetically, [e] and [E], [u] and [y] are separate sounds; but in the phonemic structure of Spanish, the [e/E] distinction may only indicate whether a Peruvian comes from the mountains or the coast; an American, who hears in the French [y] nothing more than an Irish or a Swedish accent, is completely baffled by *Monsieur EEss*, equivalent for the French announcer to *Monsieur Heath*. The -*emic* and the -*etic* perceptions *are* different! Triandis (205) reconciles the two in his conception that both the "subjective culture" and the "social reality" are important to a full understanding

Insiders' and outsiders' contributions

318

of the phenomenon. The present chapter adds the caveat that the outsider's view, as well as the insider's, must have both a developed experiential element and a developed cognitive element.

No financial assistance is being offered either to teams or to individual researchers for developing the descriptive knowledge fundamental to our teaching. This is not the "point of application research" preferred by government grantors, responsible to the public for a direct outcome. Nor does it compete well as pure research, for it aims at a working knowledge, and in point of method it falls between the grant classifications of social science and humanities. Yet it is also true that in the long run, imagination attracts funds when it addresses itself to a significant task. Responsible conclusions, wanted by a live branch of the teaching profession to meet a practical, public need for knowledge about cultural differences, will attract the means of development and publication. The desirable series on each culture mentioned above in the critique of the *ACTFL Annual Bibliography* is not at all beyond the reach of a serious collective effort.

By taking part in such an effort—contributing as a specialist on some favorite topic and receiving in return the context that gives the topic its meaning—the individual teacher can keep up with the swiftly changing culture he wants to understand.

A learning situation for ourselves

The fact that no verbal formulation can capture all of the experienced reality it alludes to will always remain. Our implicit teaching must convey the informed distrust of generalizations, which is so different from the misplaced caution of the timid. Perhaps the best way to be a wary consumer of ideas is to take what part one can in their production.

A feeling for the limits of verbal truth

Summary

Concern for cross-cultural understanding is growing in society in general, in the educational establishment, and within the foreign language education profession. Interest in superficial details is being replaced by a greater sensitivity to differences in peoples' values, assumptions, and modes of thought and feeling.

If foreign language education is to capitalize on these concerns, the teacher must be able to respond to four questions:
1   How do I select what is worth teaching for the purposes I want to serve? A rationale has been developed for using two approaches in conjunction with each other: (a) selection on the basis of

319

student interest, and (b) selection on the basis of the nature of the phenomenon to be grasped.

2 What are the techniques for achieving the purposes? Twenty types of devices have been described and have been organized into two groups: those most useful for giving experience of a culture and those most valuable for developing knowledge about it.

3 How can I get the materials I need? Sources that are useful to the teacher have been described and evaluated.

4 How can I acquire the knowledge I lack? The implications of the new social role for the foreign language teacher have been discussed, particularly as they bear upon preservice and in-service education. A proposal is made for teacher participation in a collaborative effort to consolidate the knowledge needed in our pursuit of cross-cultural understanding—an understanding that could become the most significant response of the profession to the realities of the 1970s.

References, Empathy for a second culture: motivations and techniques

1 Adler, James P. *Ethnic Minorities in Cambridge, Volume I (Summary):The Portuguese.* Cambridge, Massachusetts: City Department of Planning and Development, 1972.

2 Althen, Gary L. *Human Relations Training and Foreign Students.* Washington, D.C.: National Association for Foreign Student Affairs, 1970. [EDRS: ED 048 084.]

3 *Anthropology and Language Science in Educational Development.* Paris: UNESCO, 1973.

4 Ariès, Philippe. *L'Enfant et la vie familiale sous l'Ancien Régime.* Paris: Plon, 1960. [Translated as *Centuries of Childhood.* New York: Knopf, 1962. Updated in "Les Ages de la vie," *Contrepoint* 1(1970):23–30, and in his chapter in *Encyclopédie de la Pléiade. La France et les Français.* Paris: Gallimard, 1971.]

5 Behmer, Daniel E. "Cultural Mini-Skits Evaluated." *American Foreign Language Teacher* 2,iii(1972):37, 43,48.

6 ——"Teaching with Wayne State Cultural Mini-Skits." *American Foreign Language Teacher* 3,i(1972):3,38–39. [For description and prices of the *Mini-Skits,* available from Advancement Press, 15 E. Kirby St, Detroit, Michigan 48202, see *American Foreign Language Teacher* 3,iii(1973):26.]

7 Bendon, Benita. "ACTFL in Arcachon:A Program Description Revisited." *Foreign Language Annals* 4(1970):183–86.

8 Birkmaier, Emma, and Dale L. Lange. "Selective Bibliography on the Teaching of Foreign Languages, 1920–1966." *Foreign Language Annals* 1(1968):318–53.

9 Blanc, Michel. *Socio-Linguistic Study of Orleans. Socio-Linguistic Problems: An Exploratory Essay.* London: Birkbeck College, University of London, 1969. [Mimeo.]

10 Bolinger, Dwight. *Aspects of Language,* New York: Harcourt, Brace and World, 1968.

11 Boudon, Raymond. "Analyse secondaire et sondages sociologiques." *Cahiers internationaux de sociologie* 47(1969):5–34. [Translated as "Secondary Analysis and Survey Research . . ." *Information sur les sciences sociales* 8,vi(1969):7–32.]

12 Bouraoui, Hédi A. *Créaculture I. Créaculture II.* Philadelphia: Center for Curriculum Development, 1971.

13 —— *Parole et action.* Philadelphia: Center for Curriculum Development, 1971.

14 Bourque, Jane. "ACTFL in Arcachon:Fifty-five Teenagers Launch a Program." *Foreign Language Annals* 4(1970):179–82.

15 —— *The French Teen-Ager*. Detroit, Michigan: Advancement Press of America, 1973.

16 Brault, Gerard. "Kinesics and the Classroom: Some Typical French Gestures." *French Review* 36(1963):374–82.

17 Brein, Michael, and K.H. David. "Intercultural Communication and the Adjustment of the Sojourner." *Psychological Bulletin* 76(1971):215–30.

18 Brooks, Nelson D. *Language and Language Learning: Theory and Practice*. New York: Harcourt, Brace and World, 1964.

19 —— *Parameters of Culture*. Hartford: Connecticut State Department of Education. [*FL News Exchange 19*, Special Supplement, February 1973.]

20 Bruck, Margaret, et al. *The 1968 NDEA Institute Follow-Up Evaluation*. [Montreal: McGill University, Department of Psychology, 1973. [Mimeo.]

21 Caldwell, Oliver J. "The Need for Intercultural Education in Our Universities." *Phi Delta Kappan* 52(1971)544–45.

22 *The California State International Programs: The Official Study Abroad Program . . . :France, Germany, Italy, Japan, Spain, Sweden, Taiwan*. San Francisco: California State Colleges, Office of International Programs, 1968. [EDRS: ED 026 925.]

23 Capelle, Janine and Guy, Gilbert Quénelle, and Francis Grand-Clément. *La France en direct, 3*. Paris: Hachette, 1971. *La France en direct, 4*. Paris: Hachette, and Lexington, Massachusetts: Ginn and Company, 1972.

24 Castle, Pat, et al. "An Explanation of Three 'Levels' of Competence for Spanish Classes," 150–60 in H. Ned Seelye,ed., *Perspectives for Teachers of Latin American Culture*. Springfield, Illinois: State Superintendent of Public Instruction, 1970.

25 Chandra, Satish. "A Note on the Decentring of History and Apprehension by All People(s) of their History." *Diogenes* 77(1972):92–109.

26 Christian, Chester C.,Jr., and John M. Sharp. "Bilingualism in a Pluralistic Society," pp. 341–75 in Dale L. Lange and Charles J. James,eds., *Foreign Language Education:A Reappraisal*. ACTFL Review of Foreign Language Education, Volume 4. Skokie, Illinois: National Textbook Company, 1972.

27 Clapper, William O.,ed. *ACTFL-FLAM* [Foreign Language Association of Missouri] *Workshop on Teaching Culture*. Jefferson City, Missouri: Missouri Department of Education, 1972.

28 Clark, John L.D. *Foreign Language Testing:Theory and Practice*. Philadelphia: Center for Curriculum Development, 1972.

29 Cooke, Madeline A. "Suggestions for Developing More Positive Attitudes toward Native Speakers of Spanish," 118–39 in H. Ned Seelye,ed., *Perspectives for Teachers of Latin American Culture*. Springfield, Illinois: State Superintendent of Public Instruction, 1970.

30 Cooney, D. *German Culture through Performance Objectives*. Detroit, Michigan: Advancement Press of America, 1973.

31 Corbin, Diane. Unpublished description of French course, with test questions. Cheney, Washington: Eastern Washington State College, 1973.

32 Costner, Herbert L. *Varieties of Content Analysis*, 1964. [Mimeo. Available from H.L. Nostrand, Department of Romance Languages and Literature, University of Washington, Seattle.]

33 Crosbie, Keith, comp. *Project FLITE:Foreign Language Idea and Technique Exchange*. Olympia, Washington: State Superintendent of Public Instruction, 1972.

34 Cudecki, Edwin, et al. "Teaching of French Culture in the Classroom," 11–20 in Charles Jay and Pat Castle,eds., *French Language Education:The Teaching of Culture in the Classroom*. Springfield, Illinois: Superintendent of Public Instruction, 1971.

35 Decaroli, Joseph. "What Research Says to the Classroom Teacher:Simulation Games." *Social Education* 36(1972):541–43.

36 DeCrow, Roger. *Cross Cultural Interaction Skills:A Digest of Recent Training Literature*. Syracuse, New York: ERIC Clearinghouse on Adult Education, 1969.

37 Dil, Anwar S.,ed. *Language, Psychology, and Culture. Essays by Wallace E. Lambert*. Stanford, California: Stanford University Press, 1972.

38 Dodge, James W.,ed. *Other Words, Other Worlds: Language-in-Culture. Reports of the Working Committees, Northeast Conference on the Teaching of Foreign Languages* New York: MLA Materials Center, 1969.

39 Dow, Tsung I. *The Impact of Chinese Students Returned from America, with Emphasis on the Chinese Revolution, 1911–1949*. 1971. [EDRS: ED 062 228.]

40 DuFort, Mary. *Cultural Understanding:French, Level I*. Hayward, California: Alameda County Schools, 1971. [Also . . . *Spanish, Level I*.]

41 DuVerlie, Claude. "The Disappearance of the Academic Foreign Language Program." *American Foreign Language Teacher* 3,iii(1973):16–18.

42 Ebling, Benjamin. "Toward the Teaching of Authentic French Culture at the Secondary Level." *French Review* 46(1973):927–30.

43 Echols, John M. "A Bibliography of Morris Edward Opler," 383–402 in Mario D. Zamora et al.,eds., *Themes in Culture:Essays in Honor of Morris E. Opler*. Quezon City, Philipines: Kayumanggi, 1971.

44 Elkins, Robert J., Theodore B. Kalidova, and Genelle Morain. "Teaching Culture through the Audio-Motor Unit." *Foreign Language Annals* 6(1972):61–72.

45 Erassov, Boris S. "Concepts of 'Culture and Personality' in the Ideologies of the Third World." *Diogenes* 78(1972):123–40.

46 Fantini, Alvino E. "Formula for Success: Camp, plus Young Americans, plus New Language." *International Educational and Cultural Exchange* 8:ii(1972):62–69.

47 Fiedler, Fred E., Terence Mitchell, and Harry C. Triandis. "The Culture Assimilator:An Approach to Cross-Cultural Training." *Journal of Applied Psychology* 55(1971):95–102. [EDRS: ED 042 343.]

48 "FL Commercials Readied for Schools." *Accent on ACTFL* 3,i(1972):10,24.

49 Fleming, Gerald. *Les Aventures des carré.* London: Macmillan, and Basingstoke, 1965. [Swedish translation, 1969.] [With 8-mm film.]

50 —— "Gesture Significances Then and Now: In Honor of Albrecht Dürer's 500th Anniversary." *Lebendiges Wort.* Grillparzerinstitut, Vienna, Heft 2,iii(1971):26–30.

51 —— "Gestures and Body Movement as Mediators of Meaning in our New Language Teaching Systems." *Contact* 16(1971):15–22.

52 —— *Grammaire visuelle de français.* London: Macmillan, 1970.

53 —— "On the Origin of the 'Passional Christi und Antichristi' and Lucas Cranach the Elder's Contribution to Reformation Polemics in the Iconography of the Passional." To be published in *Gutenberg-Jahrbuch*, 1973. [Analyzes 26 woodcuts.]

54 —— "Der reitende Pabst in der Bildpolemik der Reformation" in *Cranach-Festschrift.* Berlin: Humboldt Universität. [In press.]

55 —— "The Role of Gesture in Language Teaching." *Pensiero e linguaggio* 2,v(1971):31–43. [Milan.]

56 —— and Fougasse [pseud. C. K. Bird]. *A Book of Wall Pictures for Guided Composition.* London: University of London Press, 1957.

57 *Foreign Languages in Careers.* New York: Modern Language Association. [In press.]

58 *Four Families* [of France, India, Japan, and English-speaking Canada]. [Documentary film with comments by Margaret Mead.] Montreal: Canadian Film Board, P.O. Box 6100.

59 Galbreath, Robert. *Cultural Pluralism Project. Report Number 1 to the Director.* Milwaukee, Wisconsin: University of Wisconsin-Milwaukee, 1972.

60 Garfinkel, Alan. "Teaching Languages via Radio: A Review of Resources." *Modern Language Journal* 56(1972):158–62.

61 Gebser, Jean. *Ursprung und Gegenwart.* Stuttgart: Deutsche Verlagsansalt, 1949. [See also "The Foundations of the Aperspective World." *Main Currents in Modern Thought* 29,ii(1972):80–88.]

62 Glenn, Edmund S. "Meaning and Behavior: Communication and Culture." *Journal of Communication* 16(1966):248–72.

63 —— "Toward a Theory of Intercultural Communication." *Kultura* 17(1972):55–69 [Belgrade, Jugoslavia]; English ed., 51–66.

64 Gorden, Raymond L. *Contrastive Analysis of Cultural Differences which Inhibit Communication between Americans and Colombians.* 1968. [EDRS: ED 023 337.]

65 —— *Initial Immersion in the Foreign Culture.* Yellow Springs, Ohio: Antioch College, 1968. [EDRS: ED 023 339, 1968.] [Mini-dramas may be purchased from author, Department of Sociology, Antioch College, Yellow Springs, Ohio 45387.]

66 Green, Jerald R. *A Gesture Inventory for the Teaching of Spanish.* Philadelphia: Chilton, 1968.

67 —— "Kinesics in the Foreign-Language Classroom." *Foreign Language Annals* 5(1971):62–68. [Reprinted in Jerald R. Green,ed., *Foreign-Language Education Research: A Book of Readings.* Chicago: Rand McNally, 1973.]

68 Grittner, Frank M. *Teaching Foreign Languages.* New York: Harper & Row, 1969.

69 *Guidelines on Developing Campus Services for Students Going Abroad.* New York: Council on International Educational Exchange, Student Advisory Committee, 1972.

70 "Guidelines for Evaluating Foreign Language Programs Abroad for High School Students: A Reappraisal." *Foreign Language Annals* 6(1973):453–56. [Also in Connecticut *FL News Exchange* 18,v (June 1972):2–5.] [By National Council of State Supervisors of Foreign Language.]

71 Haac, Oscar, and Arthur Bieler. *Actualité et avenir.* Englewood Cliffs, New Jersey: Prentice-Hall. [In press.]

72 Hage, Madeline Cottenet. *The Relationships and Rules of Social Life in France.* Madison: Wisconsin Department of Public Instruction, 1972. [Mimeo.]

73 Hall, Wendell, and Enrique Lafourcade. "Teaching Aspects of the Foreign Culture through Comic Strips," pp. 51–61 in H. Ned Seelye,ed., *Perspectives for Teachers of Latin-American Culture.* Springfield, Illinois: State Superintendent of Public Instruction, 1970.

74 Hammond, Patricia, and Alan Garfinkel,eds. *Recipes for Teaching Foreign Languages in Oklahoma.* Oklahoma City: State Department of Education, 1972.

75 Hancock, Charles R. "Student Aptitude, Attitude, and Motivation," 127–55 in Dale L. Lange and Charles J. James,eds., *Foreign Language Education: A Reappraisal.* ACTFL Review of Foreign Language Education, Volume 4. Skokie, Illinois: National Textbook Company, 1972.

76 Harrison, Roger, and Richard L. Hopkins. *The Design of Cross-Cultural Training, with Examples from the Peace Corps.* 1966. [EDRS: ED 011 103.]

77 Hatton, Robert W., and Gordon L. Jackson. "Fiesta Brava Wins the Ears." *Accent on ACTFL* 3,iv(1973):14–15.

78 Haukebo, Gerhard K. *Summer Foreign Language Programs for School Students.* MLA/ERIC Focus

Report on the Teaching of Foreign Languages, Number 10. New York: MLA/ERIC, 1969.

79 Hawkins, E. W. " 'Language Lab' Should Be the Foreign Environment." *Dialogue* 9(1971):8–9.

80 Hayes, Alfred S. "An Inter-disciplinary Ph.D. in Language and Language Learning," 141–48 in *Seminar in Language and Language Learning:Final Report*. Seattle, Washington: University of Washington Department of Romance Languages and Literature, 1962.

81 Heinlein, Robert A. *Stranger in a Strange Land*. New York: Putnam, 1961.

82 Henderson, George,ed. *Education for Peace: Focus on Mankind*. Washington, D.C.: ASCD, 1973.

83 Houston, James A. *The White Dawn: An Eskimo Saga*. New York: Harcourt, Brace, Jovanovich, 1971.

84 Howlett, Frederick G. "Le Rôle de la télévision dans l'enseignement des langues modernes." *Canadian Modern Language Review* 28,ii(1972):47–49.

85 Hutchinson, Joseph. *Draft Standard for Five Levels of Proficiency in Cross-cultural Communication*. Bethesda, Maryland: Defense Language Institute. [Unpublished.]

86 Hymes, Dell. "The Scope of Sociolinguistics." Social Science Research Council *Items* 26(1972): 14–18. [Condensed from chapter in Roger W. Shuy,ed., *Sociolinguistics: Current Trends and Prospects*. Washington, D.C.: Georgetown University Press, 1972.]

87 *International Exchange—1968*. Washington, D.C.: Bureau of Educational and Cultural Affairs, 1969. [EDRS: ED 036 211.]

88 Jakobovits, Leon A., and Barbara I. Gordon. *The Transactional Model of Talk*. [May be obtained from Transactional Engineering Corp., 48 Palm Island, Miami Beach, Florida 33139.] [Mimeo.]

89 Jameson, Brent L. *Student Attitudes in Culture Capsule Usage*. Provo, Utah: Brigham Young University, 1972. [M.A. thesis.]

90 Jazayery, M.A. "Persian Language Instruction." *Middle East Studies Association Bulletin* 6,i(1972): 9–29.

91 Jenks, Frederick L. *Planning to Teach Culture:An Instructional Manual*. Detroit, Michigan: Advancement Press of America, 1972. [Revised ed., 1973.]

92 ———— "Teaching Culture through the Use of American Newspapers." *American Foreign Language Teacher* 2,iv(1972):28–29,40.

93 ———— "Toward the Creative Teaching of Culture." *American Foreign Language Teacher* 2,iii(1972): 12–14,42.

94 Jonas, Sister Ruth. *African Studies in French for the Elementary Grades:Phase II of a Twinned Classroom Approach to the Teaching of French . . . 1972*. [EDRS: ED 066 994.]

95 Jones, Earl, and Frances Dean,eds. *Intercultural

Education Series. The Americas and Self-Identification*. 1970. [EDRS: ED 052 100.]

96 Juaire, Dennis,O.F.M. "The Use of Folksongs to Develop Insight into Latin American Culture," p. 62–69 in H. Ned Seelye,ed. *Perspectives for Teachers of Latin American Culture*. Springfield, Illinois: State Superintendent of Public Instruction, 1970.

97 Kaplan, Fran, Lorraine Zinn, and Helene Aqua. *Community Orientation:Survival in the City*. Milwaukee: United Migrant Opportunity Services Adult Basic Education, United States Office of Economic Opportunity, 1970. [Mimeo.]

98 Katcher, Roberta. *Culture Shock:What Problems in Acculturation Can Occur in a New Society?* 1971.[EDRS: ED 066 987.]

99 Kenworthy, Leonard S. *The International Dimension of Education. Background Paper II*. Washington, D.C.: Association for Supervision and Curriculum Development, 1970. [EDRS: ED 039 202.]

100 Kilpatrick, Franklin P.,ed. *Human Behavior from the Transactional Point of View*. Hanover, New Hampshire: Institute for Associated Research, 1952. [Revised as *Explorations in Transactional Psychology*. New York: New York University Press, 1961.]

101 King, Edith W. *Worldmindedness:The World Context for Teaching in the Elementary School*. Dubuque, Iowa: William C. Brown, 1971. [EDRS: ED 052 094.]

102 Kirk, Geneva. *Partners States*. Lewiston, Maine Public Schools, 1973. [On Rio Grande do Norte, Brazil.]

103 Kohlberg, Lawrence, and Rochelle Mayer. "Development as the Aim of Education." *Harvard Educational Review* 42(1972):449–56.

104 Ladu, Tora Tuve. *Teaching for Cross-Cultural Understanding*. Raleigh, North Carolina: State Department of Public Instruction, 1968.

105 Lambert, Wallace E. [Address at ACTFL Annual Meeting, Atlanta, 24 November, 1972.]

106 ———— "Motivational Variables in Second-Language Acquisition." *Canadian Journal of Psychology* 13(1969):266–72. [EDRS: ED 031 968.]

107———— Alison d'Anglejan, and G. Richard Tucker. "Communicating across Cultures:An Empirical Investigation." Montreal: McGill University, 1972. [Mimeo.]

108 ———— Howard Giles, and Omer Picard (Project Director, St. John Valley [Maine] Bilingual Education Program). "Language Attitudes in a French-American Community." Montreal: McGill University, 1973. [Mimeo.]

109 *The Language Learner:Reaching His Heart and Mind*. [Proceedings of the Second International Conference.] Toronto: Ontario Modern Language Teachers Association, 1971. [EDRS: ED 055 500.]

110 *Language:Missouri Youth Speak Out*. Jefferson City: Foreign Language Association of Missouri, 1973. [Mimeo.]

111 *LBRIG Newsletter* (Language-By-Radio Interest

Group), Alan Garfinkel, Robert J. Nelson, Sandra Savignon, and Philip D. Smith,Jr.,eds. West Lafayette, Indiana: Department of Modern Languages, Purdue University.

112 Leamon, M. Phillip. *Foreign Study for High School Students*. MLA/ERIC Focus Report on the Teaching of Foreign Languages, Number 5. New York: MLA/ERIC, 1969.

113 Lewald, H. Ernest. *Latino-America:Sus culturas y sociedades*. New York: McGraw-Hill, 1973.

114 Lieberman, Samuel. "Ancient Greek and Roman Culture," 31–40 in James W. Dodge,ed., *Other Words, Other Worlds:Language-in-Culture*. [Reports of the Working Committees, Northeast Conference on the Teaching of Foreign Languages.] New York: MLA Materials Center, 1969.

115 Lipton, Gladys. "Curricula for New Goals," 187–218 in Dale L. Lange and Charles J. James, eds., *Foreign Language Education:A Reappraisal*. ACTFL Review of Foreign Language Education, Volume 4. Skokie, Illinois: National Textbook Company, 1972.

116 Loew, Helene. "FL Magazines Plus Planning Equal Up-to-Date Culture Units." *Accent on ACTFL* 3,iv(1973):6–8.

117 Love, William, et al. *Options and Perspectives: A Sourcebook of Innovative Foreign Language Programs in Action, K–12*. New York: MLA Publications Center. [In press.]

118 Marquardt, William F. "Criteria for Selecting Literary Texts in Teaching Cross-Culture Communication, Especially in English as a Second Language." 4:1019–27 in *Actes du Xᵉ congrès international des linguistes, 1967*. Bucarest: Editions de l'Académie de la République Socialiste de Roumani, 1970.

119 ——— *Sociolinguistic Model for Selecting Literary Texts for Teaching Cross-Culture Communication*. Hays, Kansas: Fort Hays Kansas State College, 1973. [Mimeo.]

120 Matkovick, Edward, Tomás Ybarra Frausto, and Josefina Vargas de O'Keefe. *Elementary-School Course in Beginning Spanish*. Bellevue [Washington] Community College and University of Washington. [Unpublished textbook.]

121 Maynard, Richard A. *The Celluloid Curriculum:How to Use Movies in the Classroom*. New York: Hayden, 1971.

122 Mead, Margaret, and Rhoda Metraux. *The Study of Culture at a Distance*. Chicago: University of Chicago Press, 1959.

123 Mead, Robert G.,Jr. "Reassessing the Ph.D. in Foreign Languages." *Bulletin of the Association of Departments of Foreign Languages* 4,iii(1973):26–29.

124 ——— *The United States Image in Latin America:A Select Bibliography*. Storrs, Connecticut: University of Connecticut, 1972. [Mimeo.]

125 Meade, Betsy. "Let Students Live It Out." *Accent on ACTFL* 3,i(1972):11.

126 ——— and Genelle Morain. "The Culture Cluster." *Foreign Language Annals* 6(1973):331–38.

127 Michielli, James A. "Students Abroad Studying Their Own Thing." *Improving College and University Teaching* 20:3(1972):160–01.

128 Miller, J. Dale *One Hundred French Culture Capsules*. Provo, Utah: Brigham Young University, College of Education, 1972.

129 ——— "Proverbs Supply Gems of Culture." *Accent on ACTFL* 3,iv(1973):9.

130 Mimiague, Michel, et al. *Indicateurs de changements d'opinions et d'attitudes dans les jeunes générations, 1957–1970*. Paris: C.N.R.S. Groupe d'Etude des Méthodes de l'Analyse Sociologique, Maison des Sciences de l'Homme, 1972. [Mimeo.]

131 Morain, Genelle G. "Cultural Pluralism," 59–95 in Dale L. Lange,ed., *Pluralism in Foreign Language Education*. ACTFL Review of Foreign Language Education, Volume 3. Skokie, Illinois: National Textbook Company, 1973.

132 Muegge, Richard L. "The Teaching of *Prometheus Bound*." *American Foreign Language Teacher* 2,iv(1972): 31–33,37,40.

133 Mueller, Theodore H. *Impression d'Amérique:Cultural Commentary*. Lexington, Kentucky: University of Kentucky, 1972. [Mimeo.]

134 ——— *Cultural Notes on Jules Romains'* Donagoo. Lexington: University of Kentucky, Department of French, 1968. [Mimeo.]

135 "New Prospects for Language Teaching . . . Bilingual Schools." *Newsletter* 2,i(1971):1–2. [World Council for Curriculum and Instruction, 2202 Fairmount Court, Bloomington, Indiana 47401.]

136 *No One Model American:A Statement on Multicultural Education*. Washington, D.C.: American Association of Colleges for Teacher Education, 1972. [Reprinted from *AACTE Bulletin* 25,ix(1972):2–6.]

137 Nostrand, Frances. "Review of *A Language-Teaching Bibliography*." *Modern Language Journal* 54(1970):39.

138 ——— *The Teaching of Foreign Literature*. [Monograph commissioned by Modern Language Association of America.][In press.]

139 ——— and Howard L. "Testing Understanding of the Foreign Culture," 161–70 in H. Ned Seelye, ed., *Perspectives for Teachers of Latin American Culture*. Springfield, Illinois: Superintendent of Public Instruction, 1970.

140 Nostrand, Howard Lee,ed., *Background Data for the Teaching of French*. Seattle: University of Washington, 1967. [Part A, *La Culture et la société française au XXᵉ siècle*; Part B, *Exemples littéraires*; Part C, *Contemporary Culture and Society in the United States*.] [EDRS: ED 031 964, ED 031 989, and ED 031 990.]

141 ——— "French Culture's Concern for Relation-

ships: Relationism." *Foreign Language Annals* 6(1973) 469–80.

142 ——— "The Language Laboratory and the Sociological [read: Sociocultural] Context." *NALLD Journal* 4,iii(1970):23–38.

143 ——— "Levels of Sociocultural Understanding for Language Classes," 19–24 in H. Ned Seelye,ed., *A Handbook on Latin America for Teachers.* Springfield, Illinois: Superintendent of Public Instruction, 1968.

144 ———"Theme Analysis in the Study of Literature," 182–97 in Joseph Strelka,ed., *Problems of Literary Evaluation: Yearbook of Comparative Criticism.* University Park and London: Pennsylvania State University Press, 1969.

145 ——— *The University and Human Understanding.* Seattle: University of Washington, Department of Romance Languages and Literature, 1963.

146 ——— et al. *Film Recital of French Poems: Cultural Commentary.* Seattle: University of Washington Press, 1964. [EDRS: ED 044 955.]

147 ——— et al. *Research on Language Teaching: An Annotated International Bibliography, 1945–61.* Seattle: University of Washington Press, 1962.

148 O'Brien, Gordon E., et al. *The Effects of Programmed Culture Training upon the Performance of Volunteer Medical Teams in Central America.* 1969. [EDRS: ED 039 807.]

149 Oller, John W.,Jr. "Transformational Theory and Pragmatics." *Modern Language Journal* 54(1970): 504–07.

150 Opler, Morris E. *Apache Odyssey: A Journey Between Two Worlds.* New York: Holt, Rinehart and Winston, 1969.

151 ——— "Cultural Anthropology and the Training of Teachers of Foreign Languages," 90–96 in *Seminar in Language and Language Learning: Final Report.* Seattle: University of Washington Department of Romance Languages and Literature, 1962.

152 ——— "Themes of Culture," in Wilhelm Bernsdorf and Friedrich Bülow,eds., *Wörterbuch der Soziologie.* Stuttgart: Ferdinand Enke, 1969.

153 Ortali, Raymond J. *Entre nous.* New York: Macmillan, 1972.

154 Padilla, Amado M., and K. Kilby Long. *Evidence for Bilingual Antecedents of Academic Success in a Group of Spanish-American College Students.* Bellingham, Washington: Western Washington State College, 1970. [Mimeo.]

155 Padioleau, J. *Introduction à l'analyse diachronique des enquêtes par sondages.* Paris: University of Paris, 1972. [Unpublished thesis.]

156 Parker, John R., et al. "Political Simulation: An Introduction," 25–28 in H. Ned Seelye,ed., *A Handbook on Latin America for Teachers.* Springfield, Illinois: State Superintendent of Public Instruction, 1968.

157 " 'Partner' Areas Abroad." *Christian Science Monitor,* Western ed., (5 June, 1973):8.

158 Pillet, Roger. *Foreign Language Study: Perspective and Prospect.* Chicago: University of Chicago Press. [In press.]

159 Pindur, Nancy. *The German Teen-Ager in Profile.* Detroit, Michigan: Advancement Press of America, 1973.

160 ——— "They Dance Their Way through German." *American Foreign Language Teacher* 2,iii(1972):34–35.

161 Polcyn, Kenneth A. "The Joint United States-India Educational Broadcast Satellite Experiment." *Educational Technology* 12,vi(1972):14–17, 20–25.

162 Politzer, Robert L. *Post-Chomskian Applied Linguistics.* [Lecture at the University of Washington, October 1972.]

163 Primus, Pearl E. *A Pilot Study Integrating Visual Form and Anthropological Content for Teaching Children Ages 6 to 10 About Cultures . . . A Danced Presentation with Lecture Interpreting Some of the Cultural Values in West and Central African Communities,* 1968. [EDRS: ED 027 095.]

164 Reinert, Harry. "Student Attitudes Toward Foreign Language—No Sale!" *Modern Language Journal* 54(1970):107–12.

165 ——— *Foreign Language Student Opinion Survey.* Lynnwood, Washington: Edmonds School District, 1971. [Mimeo.]

166 ——— *Summary of Foreign Language Nonparticipant Survey.* Lynnwood, Washington: Edmonds School District, 1973. [Mimeo.]

167 Rivers, Wilga M. *Speaking in Many Tongues: Essays in Foreign-Language Teaching.* Rowley, Massachusetts: Newbury House, 1972.

168 ——— et al.,eds. *Changing Patterns in Foreign Language Programs: Report of the Illinois Conference on Foreign Languages in Junior and Community Colleges.* Rowley, Massachusetts: Newbury House, 1972.

169 Rogers, Jennifer. *Foreign Places, Foreign Faces.* Harmondsworth: Connexions, Penguin Education Series, 1968.

170 Rosselot, LaVelle, et al. *Je parle français. Nouvelle édition.* Chicago: Encyclopaedia Britannica Educational Corporation. *Premier degré,* 1973. *Deuxième degré,* 1971.

171 Runte, Roseann. "A Cultural Mini Alphabet." *American Foreign Language Teacher* 3,iii(1973):24–25.

172 Ruple, Joelyn. "Teaching Cultural Themes Using the Spanish Theatre." *Hispania* 48(1965):511–16.

173 Santoni, Georges V. "Un cours de civilisation française au niveau universitaire." *Le français dans le monde* 84(1971):27–33.

174 ——— and Jean Noël Rey. "Langue et civilisation: Ouvriers et étudiants: Préparation à une simulation." *Le français dans le monde* 88(1972):26–34.

175 Savignon, Sandra J. "A l'écoute de France-Inter: The Use of Radio in a Student-Centered Oral French Class." *French Review* 46(1972):342–49.

176 Schroeder, Adolf E. [Personal communication.]

177 Seelye, H. Ned. "Analysis and Teaching of the Cross-Cultural Context," 37–81 in Emma M. Birkmaier,ed., *Foreign Language Education: An Overview.* ACTFL Review of Foreign Language Education, Volume 1. Skokie, Illinois: National Textbook Company, 1972.

178 ———— "Performance Objectives for Teaching Cultural Concepts." *Foreign Language Annals* 3(1970) 566–78.

179 ———— "Teaching the Foreign Culture:A Context for Research," 74–89 in Jerald R. Green,ed., *Foreign-Language Education Research:A Book of Readings.* Chicago: Rand McNally, 1973.

180 ———— and J. Laurence Day.*The Newspaper, Spanish Mini–Culture Units.* Skokie, Illinois: National Textbook Company, 1973.

181 Selinker, Larry, Louis Trimble, and Robert Vroman. *Working Papers in English for Science and Technology.* Seattle: University of Washington Office of Engineering Research, 1972. [Mimeo.]

182 Sellman, Ethel L. "Aberdeen-L'Union Jumelage." Aberdeen, Maryland: Aberdeen Senior High School. [Mimeo.]

183 *Sixth Report, 1969–71* [of the University of Birmingham, Centre for Contemporary Cultural Studies]. Edgbaston, Birmingham: University of Birmingham, 1971.

184 Slagle, Joyce. *Lesson Plans and Exercises for* Toute la bande. Tulsa, Oklahoma: Nathan Hale High School. [Mimeo.]

185 Smith, Alfred G.,ed. *Communication and Culture, Readings in the Codes of Human Interaction.* New York: Holt, Rinehart and Winston, 1966.

186 Smithson, Rulon N. "French Culture and Civilization for American High School Students," 80–87 in Charles Jay and Pat Castle,eds. *French Language Education:The Teaching of Culture in the Classroom.* Springfield, Illinois: Superintendent of Public Instruction, 1971.

187 *Spanish Institute for High School Students:Final Report.* San Leandro, California: San Leandro Unified School District, 1968. [EDRS: ED 027 787.]

188 Steiner, Florence. "Culture: A Motivating Factor in the French Classroom," 28–35 in Charles Jay and Pat Castle,eds., *French Language Education:The Teaching of Culture in the Classroom.* Springfield, Illinois: State Superintendent of Public Instruction, 1971.

189 Stewart, Edward C. *American Cultural Patterns:A Cross-Cultural Perspective.* Pittsburgh: University of Pittsburgh Regional Council for International Education, 1971.

190 Storr, Anthony. *Human Destructiveness.* New York: Basic Books, 1972. [Translation: *L'Instinct de destruction.* Paris: Calmann Lévy, 1973.]

191 Svobodny, Dolly D. "Information Sources for the Foreign-Language Teacher-Researcher," 37–50 in Jerald R. Green,ed., *Foreign-Language Education Research:A Book of Readings.* Chicago: Rand McNally, 1973.

192 Szalay, Lorand B. Psychological studies of associative meanings in English and Spanish. American Institutes for Research, 10605 Concord Street, Kensington, Maryland 20795.

193 Taylor, Harold. *The World and the American Teacher: The Preparation of Teachers in the Field of World Affairs.* Washington, D.C.: American Association of Colleges for Teacher Education, 1968.

194 Taylor, James S. "Direct Classroom Teaching of Cultural Concepts," 42–50 in H. Ned Seelye,ed., *Perspectives for Teachers of Latin American Culture.* Springfield, Illinois: State Superintendent of Public Instruction, 1970.

195 Taylor, Lee, et al. *Internationalizing Rural Sociology: Training-Practice-Recruitment.* Ithaca, New York: State University of New York College of Agriculture, 1970. [EDRS: ED 053 838.]

196 "Teaching about American Indians," 481–534 in Hazel Hertzberg,guest ed., *Social Education: Official Journal of the National Council for the Social Studies* 36,v(1972).

197 *Teaching Language through Literature.* Maxine G. Cutler,ed., Purchase, New York: New York State College.

198 Teichert, Herman U. "An Experimental Study Using Learning Packages in Beginning College German." *Modern Language Journal* 56(1972): 488–90.

199 Therrien, Melvin G. "Learning French via Short Wave Radio and Popular Periodicals." *French Review* 46(1973):1178–83.

200 Thompson, Marion E. "A Study of International Television Programming within the Structure of Global Communications." *Dissertation Abstracts International* 32(1971):3469A(University of Wisconsin).

201 Tidhar, Hava. *Using Television for Teaching a Second Language through Dramatized Everyday Situations.* [EDRS: ED 053 578.]

202 Tinsley, Royal L.,Jr. "Study Abroad." *Arizona Foreign Language Teachers' Forum* 18,iii(1971):2–3.

203 *Toute la bande:Film Program for Beginning and Intermediate French.* Englewood Cliffs, New Jersey: Scholastic Magazines, 1970.

204 *Travaux pratiques de civilisation, Rennes.* Saint Paul, Minnesota: College of Saint Catherine, 1963–68. [Annually.]

205 Triandis, Harry C.,comp. *The Analysis of Subjective Culture.* New York: Wiley-Interscience, 1972.

206 Troyanovich, John. "American Meets German: Culture Shock in the Classroom." *Unterrichtspraxis* 5,ii(1972):67–79.

207 Tsoutsos, Theodora M. *A Tentative Gesture Inventory for the Teaching of French.* Brooklyn, New York: Queens College, 1970. [Unpublished M.S. Thesis.]

208 Valdés, María Elena. *Communication and Understanding: Teaching Language in Context.* 1973. [Mimeo.]

209 Valette, Rebecca M., and Renée S. Disick. *Modern Language Performance Objectives and Individualization. A Handbook.* New York: Harcourt, Brace, Jovanovich, 1972.

210 —— and Jean-Paul. *France: A Cultural Review Grammar.* New York: Harcourt, Brace, Jovanovich, 1973.

211 —— and Jean-Paul. *French for Mastering, Level I and Level II.* Lexington, Massachusetts: D. C. Heath. [In press.]

212 Vassiliou, Vasso. *Attitudes after Reading an Ethnographic Essay: An Exploratory Study.* Springfield, Virginia: Clearinghouse for Federal Scientific and Technical Information, 1968. [EDRS: ED 031 119.]

213 vonHofe, Harold. *Kultur und Alltag.* New York: Charles Scribners Sons, 1973.

214 Waitschies, Heidi, and Eduard Mayr. *So macht man's in Deutschland.* Minneapolis: Minneapolis Public Schools, 1971. [Mimeo.]

215 Wallach, Martha Kaarsberg. "Cross-Cultural Education and Motivational Aspects of Foreign Language Study." *Foreign Language Annals* 6(1973): 465–68.

216 Washburne, Heluiz C. *Land of the Good Shadows.* New York: John Day, 1940.

217 Wedge, Bryant. *Visitors to the United States and How They See Us.* Princeton, New Jersey: Van Nostrand, 1965.

218 Wight, Albert R., and Mary Anne Hammons. *Guidelines for Peace Corps Cross-Cultural Training, Part II. Specific Methods and Techniques.* Washington, D.C.: Peace Corps, Department of State, 1970. [EDRS: ED 059 938.]

219 —— et al. *Guidelines for Peace Corps Cross-Cultural Training, Part III. Supplementary Readings.* Washington, D.C.: Peace Corps, Department of State, 1970. [EDRS: ED 059 939.]

220 Williams, Robin M. *American Culture: A Sociological Interpretation.* New York: Knopf, 1951. [Third ed., revised, 1970.]

221 Wolfenstein, Martha, and Nathan Leites. *Movies, A Psychological Study.* Glencoe, Illinois: Free Press, 1950.

222 Wood, Richard E. "Shortwave Radio as a Teaching Aid for German." *Unterrichtspraxis* 5,i(1972)36–40.

223 Wylie, Lawrence. "A Treasury of Facts about France." *French Review* 33(1960):281–85.

327

Theoretical foundations in linguistics and related fields

Introduction

Terence J. Quinn
Monash University

If one were to try to characterize the postwar period in language teaching—from the early 1940s to the late 1960s—one would be tempted to speak of it as the "era of linguistics in language teaching." During these years it seemed obvious that the science of linguistics had a key role to play in language teaching, that this discipline was indeed the basis of a sound theoretical foundation for foreign language education. In 1973 this era is viewed as coming to an end. The reality is that linguists seldom have much to say about language teaching these days, and language teachers turn to other fields for the stimulus of new ideas. Significantly, Volume 4 in the *ACTFL Review* Series had no chapter on linguistics, and an important recent survey of the field of linguistic science (Dingwall, 20) has no section devoted to language pedagogy. It is therefore appropriate to reconsider the role of linguistics as the principal theoretical foundation of language teaching activities.

Recent evaluations of linguistic influence on language teaching

Even to catalogue the vast literature of "applied linguistics" that accumulated during the 1960s would be a daunting task. The simple *quantity* of enthusiastic work purporting to spell out the implications of this or that linguistic theory made it easy for one to assume that the flourishing science of linguistics should provide the essential theoretical input to language teaching endeavors. Recently, however, the appearance of several major restatements points to a growing gulf between linguistics and language teaching and to a cautious evaluation of the desirable relationship between the two fields. Ronald Wardhaugh's

A mood of caution

Terence Quinn (Ph.D., The Ohio State University) is Senior Lecturer in the Department of French at Monash University (Australia), where he coordinates language courses and teaches French language and linguistics. He has previously taught at the secondary and tertiary levels in Australia and in the United States. He has studied in France and Italy. His publications have appeared widely in Australian pedagogical journals. He is also co-editor (with Paul Pimsleur) of a collection of papers entitled *The Psychology of Second Language Learning*.

(79) important address to the 1972 TESOL Convention analyzes the contribution of various academic disciplines to TESOL and, not unexpectedly, considers linguistics first. His assessment, however, is sobering. He finds little evidence of even basic linguistic sophistication in the attitudes of language teachers and admits that the current preoccupations of theoretical linguists have little if any relevance to language teaching.

Wardhaugh on TESOL

Another paper presented at the same convention by Dwight Bolinger, President of the Linguistic Society of America (5), approaches the subject from an historical point of view. He sees the "organized intervention of linguistics" in language teaching as a relatively recent phenomenon. Bolinger finds good and bad but is largely—and regretfully—negative in his evaluation of the impact of what he calls "post-structural linguistics." Current linguistic theory, he fears, may finally succeed in turning language teachers away from linguistics as a source discipline.

Historical approach of Bolinger

Selinker (70), in an important "state of the art" paper, seems to be somewhat less pessimistic than Bolinger, although he is quite firm in his enunciation of some basic home truths. The idea that linguistics should be the sole basis of a theory of language teaching, he claims, is a discredited hypothesis because many of the problems central to the language teaching situation are of no relevance to current theoretical preoccupations in linguistics. Linguistics itself, furthermore, is in a somewhat uncertain stage of development, marked by doubt, dispute, and promising hypotheses, which are nevertheless constantly under challenge.

Linguistics and a theory of language teaching

Politzer's (62) recent study of applied linguistics represents a somewhat ambivalent position. He exhibits an extensive array of pedagogical assumptions supposedly derived from linguistic theories and yet concludes on a note of doubt, suggesting that linguistics ultimately may not be crucial to effective language teaching.

Finally, in this somewhat gloomy litany of reconsiderations of linguistics in language teaching, one can point to a strong statement by William Bull (9), whose work in applying linguistics to the teaching of Spanish has had considerable influence both in the United States and in Europe. While conceding that linguists have had a very large impact on language teaching, Bull sees this impact as almost completely negative; the audiolingual method, he claims, was a creation of linguists, and it has been hardly less than disastrous in its effects.

The impact of linguistics

330

Given such sobering statements at the end of a long period of enthusiastic "applications" of linguistics, it is illuminating to reconsider the rationale for such applied work. From the vantage point of 1973, the basic lack of validity is easy to spot in much of what passes for applied linguistics. A perusal of journals such as *Language Learning* and *IRAL* over the past decade will reveal a recurring assumption underlying a great deal of work that purports to apply linguistic principles to language teaching methodology. The assumption—which might well be dubbed the principle of transfer of validity—can be quite simply stated: *What is valid in linguistic theory must also be valid in language teaching*. Once the principle is so stated, the inherent fallacy or unjustified logical leap is manifest. Yet a great deal of otherwise careful and sensitive work has been marred by the tacit acceptance of such a view. A striking example is found in the very interesting recent work of T. Grant Brown (7, 8). Arguing from a position in linguistic theory close to that of Charles Fillmore, Brown draws quite specific conclusions about language teaching practice, with no argumentation to justify the logical leap. The terminology and pattern of thought are those of the linguist, while the conclusions supposedly derived from these are clearly intended to be pedagogical. Thus, for instance, the presentation of certain tenses in French is postponed on the grounds that "the other tenses [those being postponed] require the existence of embedded structures [in the deep structure] before they are properly used" (8, p. 275n), a statement that exemplifies the unjustified leap from hypothetical language structure to practical language pedagogy. Such a reliance on extrapolation is not confined to the appliers of linguistic theory. Once the validity of this approach is allowed to pass unquestioned, one is in the realm of what might be termed "pedagogical ecumenism." *Any* discipline can be made to seem relevant to foreign language teaching. Positions that are theoretically valid for *any* field of inquiry can be extrapolated as insights for language pedagogy. With some ingenuity, one can find "applications" and "implications" in many different fields (cognitive psychology, speech perception, anthropology, sociology) for foreign language teaching.

These remarks are not intended to denigrate such work, much of which is very thoughtful and indeed ingenious. Yet, while one admires the ingenuity, one must also question the validity and stress that proposals for a practical field cannot be justified solely by reference to the validity of related positions in a theoretical field. The jump from

A false principle

Attempts to apply case grammar

Linguistic argumentation to justify pedagogical practice

Danger of pedagogical ecumenism

Ingenious applications that lack validity

From principle to application

theory to practice, from principle to application, is no easy one. An oversimplified interpretation of theory and a facile expectation that theoretical constructs must find basically similar counterparts in an applied field represent an abdication of responsible independence. Wilkins' (82) recent book on linguistics in language teaching stresses the importance of such independence and adopts a cautiously sceptical point of view similar to the one expressed here.

A cautious recent survey

The continuing popularity of the principle of transfer of validity is somewhat surprising since its inherent weakness was pointed out very clearly by Chomsky (16) as far back as 1966. His remarks to the Northeast Conference in that year have been widely quoted: Both linguistics and psychology are in a state of very great change, and one should view suggestions about "applications" with caution and scepticism. Language teachers should retain their independence of judgment and expect that the validity of proposals purporting to come from linguistics (or any other discipline) will be clearly demonstrated and not merely assumed. Crystal (18) in his remarks on linguistics as a *science*, and Obrecht (58) in an analysis of pure and applied science, make a similar point: Uncritical reliance on a theory is particularly dangerous at a time when the theory is relatively new and in the process of changing rapidly and making spectacular progress. (One might remark, parenthetically, that it is this very spectacular progress that has made "application" look so attractive. It is tempting for practitioners to seek intellectual legitimacy and prestige by claiming descent from the dazzlingly brilliant world of linguistics.)

Chomsky

Rapidly changing theory

The intellectual prestige of theory

Jakobovits (38) has recently discussed this same phenomenon of submission to what he calls "the tyranny of irrelevant expertise." In his view, foreign language teachers have largely—and unfortunately—given up the sort of independence of judgment Chomsky would have them retain. "Experts" from outside the classroom and from other disciplines "have been elevated to totally unrealistic levels of respect and adoration" (p. 4). Furthermore, says Jakobovits, to expect research in or insights from linguistics and other scientific disciplines to solve our problems represents a dangerous form of *reductionism*—the view that the problems of an applied field can be reduced to those of a theoretical field. The reductionist assumption is that the parameters of a problem in an applied field are isomorphic with those of problems in the theoretical field. A recent important study of semantic theory in linguistics (Katz, 40) considers the reductionist temptation equally dangerous for pure linguistics. Katz sees years of neglect of semantics being caused by a form of reductionism. Progress in the subject was so

Tyranny of expertise

Unjustified reliance on research

Danger of reductionism

slow that it became tempting to work exclusively on less central but more manageable subjects and eventually to define the intransigent problems out of existence. A great many applied linguists have worked on a reductionist principle: When you are not making progress with problems in a particular field, restate them in the terms of a related field where progress apparently *is* being made.

Rejection of just such thinking is what marks the approach of Chomsky, Wardhaugh, Selinker, and Bolinger. Given such an attitude on the part of linguists, one need not be distressed at their withdrawal from language teaching. If such a withdrawal also entails a reemphasis of the independence of the language teaching enterprise, one can happily speak of a "decolonization" of language teaching. We are certainly at the end of the era of what Bolinger (5) has called "the organized intervention of linguistics" (p. 107).

No grounds for pessimism

Decolonization of language teaching

What linguistics has not achieved

Decolonized people seldom say much about the positive contributions (if any) of the departing colonial power and are usually more than ready to stress what the former masters did *not* achieve. Such a point of view is often a necessary prerequisite to true independence and to a solution of pressing problems. In this spirit, we mention the thinking of writers who have recently stressed what the organized intervention of linguistics in language teaching did *not* achieve. Significant failure is evident in two areas: content of pedagogical grammars and attitudes of teachers.

Perhaps the most startling deficiency is seen in the state of pedagogical grammars, the *content* of the language textbooks, the descriptions of the grammatical acts underlying the program of presentation and practice. These seem to have changed remarkably little in the past decade. As early as 1966 Saporta (68) pointed out the curious contradiction in the situation where linguists had much to say about pedagogy and little if anything to say about what should have been their special field of competence—the grammatical facts. The situation does not seem to have changed much since then. Bull and Lamadrid (10) have analyzed the many basic distortions of grammatical fact that still find their way into Spanish textbooks, and Quinn (63) documents the same situation for second-generation audiolingual French textbooks. When one can find statements as gross as the claim that "these two past tenses [French *imparfait* and *passé composé*] sometimes cause some confusion in English" (Langellier et al., 50, p. 278), it is clear that no

The state of pedagogical grammars

strong tradition of accurate grammatical description has found its way into language textbooks. A recent statement on the matter by Freeman Twaddell (76) would suggest—perhaps more accurately— that only the confused remnants of a grammatical tradition can be found in pedagogical statements. Twaddell (75) had earlier pointed to a specific area of deficiency in pedagogical grammars, that of the functions of the past tenses in the Romance languages.

Grammatically impoverished language textbooks

The treatment of this subject has changed little over the years. Linguistic analyses have not been able to provide any illuminating breakthroughs on this matter. An adequate account of the subtle notion of *aspect* (the characterization of an action as completed or in progress, as permanent or impermanent, as instantaneous or enduring, as performed once only or repeatedly, etc.), for instance, is essential to a proper understanding and presentation of the semantics of past tenses in the Romance languages. Yet this is precisely the sort of topic that has not been adequately treated in transformational analyses. In their transformational account of French syntax (generally derived from Chomsky's 1965 *Aspects of the Theory of Syntax*) Dubois and Dubois (22) dismiss aspect in a few unilluminating lines (pp. 93–94). In his very full treatment of the notion of aspect in English grammar, Macaulay (52) indicates the great difficulty one has in fitting the relevant facts into a standard transformational model. Yet these are precisely the facts that need to be incorporated into an adequate pedagogical grammar. The failure of linguistic analyses to respond to these realities and hence to provide a sound descriptive basis for textbook material, may be due to the character of early transformational grammars. Chomsky's earlier version of a grammatical model was not meaning-based: the base component of the grammar dealt with meaningless strings of categorial symbols to which meaning was later attached. Although it was probably not intended, such an approach tended to minimize the importance of meaning in grammatical analysis; hence the lack of any profound new insights into the problems of meaning which have long marred pedagogical grammars. Bolinger (5) is hopeful that this deficiency can still be remedied by current work in linguistics. It is of course true that many of the new generations of transformational linguists reject Chomsky's approach to semantics and are working with several new approaches that restore the primacy of meaning. These new moves, globally referred to as the generative semantics movement, might be seen as a promising trend from the point of view of language teaching.

Aspect: a neglected semantic category

Early transformational grammar

Moves to reassert the primacy of semantics

If the "organized intervention of linguistics" did not radically alter the content of language teaching, did it successfully modify the attitudes of the teachers? Part of the motivation for a linguistics component in so many NDEA Institutes for foreign language teachers was an attempt to *sensitize* teachers to the nature of language phenomena, to help them see beyond the details of jargon, rules, and symbols to a linguistic way of thinking about language. Wilkins (82) still claims that such a feeling for the basic character of the human language phenomenon is the major contribution of linguistics to language teaching: "Anyone who has studied linguistics is sensitized to language and thereby to the complexity of language learning" (p. 299). Yet other recent commentators do not share such optimism. Wardhaugh's negative opinion on this matter has already been cited, and Bolinger (5) finds it unfortunate that the impact of linguistics has chiefly been through its externals, through a tendency to stress the mere apparatus of formalism rather than its purpose. It is a formidable task for specialists in any area to condense the essential principles of their field and to present them to nonspecialists in a comprehensible and undistorted form. One should therefore not be too critical of linguists if they have not succeeded in imparting basic insights to language teachers. "Popularization" is always hazardous. The popularization of linguistics often seems to have emphasized the ritual aspects of the subject, the unmotivated manipulation of arcane algebraic formalism. Gradman (33), writing specifically about contrastive linguistics, warns of the danger of this sort of approach to the training of foreign language educators and highlights the difficulty of ensuring that exposure to linguistics will provide a basic sensitivity to the phenomenon of language. Contrastive linguistics should perhaps *assume*, rather than set out to provide such an attitude: "One might well argue. . .that a better course would be in the sensitizing of students toward language rather than in activities dependent upon that sensitivity" (p. 32).

Attitudes of teachers toward linguistics

Unfortunate stress on formalism

Current emphases in linguistic research

The transformational revolution is far from over, and far-reaching controversies within the movement are still the order of the day.

The generative-semantics controversy might be of interest for those who seek a sounder linguistic base for language teaching. It is necessary to consider the parameters of this controversy since this is the dominant issue underlying a great deal of discussion in contemporary linguistic theory. Compiling a condensed version of complex theoretical issues is a hazardous enterprise, and what follows should be read with

Generative-semantics controversy

Danger of distortion

335

some caution in the knowledge that simplification often brings distortion in its train. However, despite the risk of oversimplification, it is important to try to see the general principles emerging in the discussion, since it is these general principles—not the details of any current specific analysis—that might hold some promise for language teaching.

In the "standard theory," as expounded by Chomsky (15) in 1965, syntax and semantics are sharply separated and a concept of deep structure is central. The base of the grammatical model is syntactic and consists of phrase structure rules (e.g., that a noun phrase can consist of a determiner plus a noun) which generate a string of abstract categorial symbols. A process of *lexicalization* introduces lexical items ("words") into this previously semantically empty string. Lexical items are thus the basic semantic elements. The skeleton string of categorial symbols, now fleshed out by lexical items, constitutes deep structure. This deep structure serves as input both to a set of transformation rules and to a set of semantic interpretation rules. The transformation rules effect such operations as changing the order of elements, deleting certain identical elements, etc.; and the outcome of these operations is a surface structure. This surface structure will be a string of elements or morphemes, and a set of phonological rules will indicate how these elements are to be realized in sound. Meanwhile (this *meanwhile* of course being understood in a metaphorical sense) the semantic interpretation rules will have spelled out the meaning of the input provided by the deep structure. The syntax (the base categorial rules) is thus generative and the semantics, simply interpretive. Furthermore, the semantic rules operate on lexical items—"chunks" of meaning corresponding to the normal vocabulary of the language. There is, moreover, a separate level of deep structure, which is not, however, very much more abstract than surface structure. It consists of a string of lexical items.

Chomsky's standard theory

Deep structure

The standard theory is thus an elegant and coherent account of how a model of language production might operate. It proved to be very fruitful and productive in that it stimulated a great deal of illuminating research into the transformational structure of English and other languages, into the sort of rules that must be presumed to operate to derive the final form of a sentence from "earlier" underlying forms of the same sentence. However, it soon became clear that certain facts of language could not be made to fit into the model. The standard theory assumes a quite close correspondence between the lexical items of

Productivity of the standard theory

Strain on the theory

surface structure and the elements of deep structure. Thus, a verb in the surface form of a sentence will have corresponding to it a single verbal element in deep structure. Some linguists, however, came to realize that one cannot capture the full truth about certain semantically complex lexical items—for example, verbs such as *persuade*, which McCawley (53) has used to illustrate his position—if this assumption is to be made. To do justice to the facts about such verbs, it seems more adequate to posit a *semantic representation* as the base component of a grammatical model. It is then possible to follow the derivational path by which units of meaning or content are *encoded*—combined by a transformational process into the lexical items of surface form. The sharp distinction between syntactic structure and semantic representation thus disappears. The derivational path is from abstract underlying semantic structure to surface phonetic form, and there is no longer any point in a separate level of deep structure distinct from semantic representation. The autonomous syntax of the earlier standard theory is thus rejected in favor of a model that has semantic content as the starting point and surface form as the outcome.

An alternative model

No need for deep structure

Is there anything in all of this for the foreign language educator? Before even a partial, preliminary answer to that question is attempted, the warning given earlier needs to be restated: The generative semantics versus interpretive semantics controversy is still in full swing, and the grounds of argument change constantly. In such circumstances, any attempt to rush for easy "applications" and "implications" would be foolhardy indeed. With this reservation in mind, however, one can see very hopeful signs that the controversy may ultimately be productive from the point of view of those who seek to apply the results of scholarly research in linguistics. The generative semantics position can certainly be said to represent a restatement of the primacy of meaning, an attempt to restore the conceptual structure underlying linguistic utterances to the forefront of linguistic inquiry. Such a trend can only be welcomed by language teachers, since it may well provide new insights into the patterns of semantic structure of the languages we teach. McCawley (52) sees as fundamental the question of "what kind of rules are needed to specify how the content of sentences is related to their surface form" (p. 19). Adequate answers to this sort of question will of course imply close and detailed investigation of semantic representation, and some of the studies already produced under the influence of generative semantics (cf. Karttunen, 39, for example) have revealed aspects of meaning relationships that had not hitherto

Generative semantics vs. interpretive semantics

Generative semantics

been obvious. By virtue of its long-range effects, then, the generative semantics movement may well be of great interest to language teachers.

We must go beyond this broad prediction, however, and try to see in the current controversies an indication of the present preoccupation of linguistics. A perusal of much of the current syntactic literature makes it very clear that linguistics is principally preoccupied with *theory* *Linguistics as theory-building* *building,* with the solution of very basic questions of a high level of generality, such as the nature and legitimacy of evidence and argument in the field. Most professional linguists are aware of the fact that they are taking part in a scientific revolution, as is indicated by the fre- *A scientific revolution* quency with which they refer to the work of Kuhn (42) on this subject. At such a moment of development it is natural for the pendulum of professional preoccupation to swing away from empirical observation to abstract theorizing, from data gathering to concept definition, from close observation of facts to arguments about theoretical constructs at the highest level of generality. In the context of the history and *Observation of data* philosophy of science, as it is set forth by Kuhn, for example, such broad trends are familiar. Yet it must be stressed that the high-level abstractions of theory builders are necessarily remote from the pre-occupations of "appliers." For the mutual benefit of each, the two domains must at times be kept strictly separate and remain quite in-dependent of each other.

High-level, abstract argumentation dominates a good deal of *Examples of abstract theorizing* linguistic discussion these days. Emmon Bach (4) in a 1971 paper set out to survey developments in syntax since Chomsky's 1965 *Aspects.* The argument is largely on the level of abstract conceptualizations: the definition of "theory," the validation/refutation of hypotheses, the mathematical properties of models, the notions of excessive or insufficient theoretical "power," and of "strength" and "weakness" in a theory. Such issues also dominate much of the discussion in a work as important as Katz's (40) recent major study of semantic theory. An attempt to come to grips with these issues also seems to have dominated the discussions at a wide-ranging "survey" conference at the University of Maryland in 1971 (Dingwall, 20). Dingwall reports "a surprising degree of unanimity among the participants" in agreeing that *Power of Chomskyan theory* Chomskyan theory exceeds the generative capacity needed to describe natural language; that many current attempts to revise the theory serve only to expand rather than limit its power; and that, in a theory with rules as powerful as transformations, there is no way to decide among alternative hypotheses (p. 12). Preoccupation with highly abstract theoretical issues is thus characteristic of contemporary linguistic inquiry.

Of course such discussion is thoroughly sound and legitimate scientific argumentation. But it also entails estrangement from a field like language teaching that must necessarily stay close to the observable facts. High-level speculation does not throw light on practical procedures, and the justification for the procedures must be firmly rooted in a data base. In the elaboration of theory, however, close observation of facts and solid grounding in a data base are much less important than considerations such as logically sound argumentation from principles, internal coherence, economy, simplicity, and elegance. To the extent that observable facts (such as data on first- and second-language acquisition) are dealt with at all, they must be regarded as material to be reconciled with the theory.

Different attitudes to data

A very clear example of this divergence can be seen in the frequently quoted Chomskyan notion of language acquisition as hypothesis testing on the part of the learner. This nativist position on language acquisition is frequently referred to in Chomsky's writings; it is set out in detail by McNeill (54) and subjected to critical discussion by Braine (6). The theory emphasizes the active contribution of the learner and proceeds from the assumption that "every normal child constructs for himself the grammar of his native language" (Slobin, 72, p. 299). This emphasis on the *active* role of the learner stems from an awareness of the vast complexity of the language-learning task. The acquisition of a language is so vast and complex an achievement and one carried out with such relative speed and effectiveness, that one must postulate a large contribution by innate factors—what the child possesses "built-in." The nativists claim that knowledge of the universal properties of human language must be innate so that the child "knows" from the start that the language around him must conform to these universal properties or, in other words, must be a possible human language. This limits his learning task, which now becomes one of choosing within a limited range of possibilities. Such a process can be appropriately construed as one of theory construction and hypothesis testing. It is a matter of deducing the structure of the particular language in question, of selecting a grammar that conforms both to the innately known universals and to the speech data of the surrounding environment. The child is assumed to proceed like the speculating scientist: He formulates hypotheses about the grammatical rules of the language he hears; and, on the basis of these hypotheses, he makes predictions about the sentences he will hear; he

Language acquisition as hypothesis testing

The nativist theory

The learner as a constructor of theories

then tests these predictions against his actual linguistic experience. This verification process enables the child to refine his hypotheses about the language in question until he arrives at a virtually complete grammar of the particular language. The language-learning process is thus essentially one of generating hypothetical grammars and testing them against the input data.

Such is language learning as perceived by someone interested in speculative theory construction. Now it should be quite evident that the constructs of such a theory do not correspond in any but the most remote and figurative sense to the observable reality of the nursery or the classroom. Nor should they be expected to correspond, because the theory is not arrived at by simple generalizations from observation of facts like those of developmental history. The conceptual model of the language learner as hypothesis tester proceeds, not from the observation of phenomena, but from general principles of theory to postulated structures and processes that might explain the phenomena. The process is one of logical inference rather than empirical generalization. The account of language acquisition sets out what must be assumed to be the case in the light of certain fundamental principles: If human language is as the theory assumes it to be, the process of language acquisition must be assumed to be like this.

Unfortunately, it is very easy to forget this distinction and to slip from manner of speaking to assumed psychological reality. Linguists giving a nativist account of language acquisition are usually careful to point out that a theoretical model is indeed a "manner of speaking" and cannot be readily assumed to be in any sense psychologically real. Slobin (71) makes the point quite specifically about the "rules" postulated to explain a speaker's behavior. Such an account, he says, does not imply "that the particular rules devised by the scientist are actual entities existing inside the individual in a definite psychological or physiological sense" (p. 55). It is unfortunate that many of the terms used in the construction of speculative theory suggest psychological reality. Terms like "knowledge of the grammar," "rule-governed behavior," "the predictions made by the child," "the child's selection of a grammar" can be readily misinterpreted. These terms are not being used in their familiar sense of conscious psychological operations.

Current linguistics is preoccupied with theory building, and the concepts being elaborated are not likely to be of immediate relevance to language teaching. Thus, for instance, Katz (40), in a footnote to part of his elaboration of a theory of semantic representation, addresses himself to second-language acquisition. He has claimed that semantic

Theory and observable reality

Logical justification for nativist theory

Theoretical model

Potentially misleading terminology

Second-language learning as seen by a theorist

340

projection rules are universal and, on this basis, goes on to assert that the learner of a second language learns phonological and transformational rules, plus a dictionary "in which readings, most of which are already in the dictionary for his native language, are correlated with morphemes in the foreign tongue" (p. 116). The learner, having mastered the second-language phonology and transformations, and being able to "obtain the underlying phrase marker for a sentence," can go on to "use the dictionary he has learned to obtain the meaning of the sentence because he already knows the right projection rules to apply." This, according to Katz, is "a very realistic picture of what happens in second-language learning." One suspects that few foreign language teachers would agree. Of course, from the point of view of a theory builder, such statements *are* realistic in terms of the kind of assumptions analyzed above, and such a comment serves to highlight the point being made here: The key preoccupations of linguistics and language teaching are so far apart at the moment that communication between the two fields is likely to be much more difficult than it has been assumed to be in the past.

Competence and performance

A striking example of divergence between the preoccupations of theoretical linguistics and language pedagogy is to be found in the development of the competence-performance distinction. Chomsky in *Aspects* (15) stated axiomatically that a grammar is an account of a speaker's competence, his presumed knowledge about his language. His competence must be sharply distinguished from his performance, his concrete execution of acts of speech. What the speaker is capable of doing must be considered apart from what he actually does. The investigation of performance was to be excluded from linguistic theory, at least at that stage. Since then, the distinction has been spelled out time and time again, in many varied contexts, by large numbers of writers attempting to set up a linguistic background to many different problems. The competence-performance distinction has served linguistics well. It proved to be extremely productive for theorists because it effectively blocked the inhibiting and irrelevant objection that normal speech is massively irregular. Released from this restraint, the linguist was free to concentrate his attention on underlying regularities and thus infer postulated organizing principles. Such a situation is perfectly adequate for a theory-oriented discipline (or for a discipline at a theory-building stage of development). It is somewhat less than adequate for a

Chomsky's first use of competence-performance distinction

Usefulness of the distinction

341

discipline that needs data. Indeed, insistence on the competence-performance dichotomy may inhibit perception of the data because "data-gathering" comes to look second-rate and unimportant, part of what some would call "mere" performance. Labov (45) points out that the distinction has served to *insulate* generative grammar from "the unreflecting language used by ordinary people in everyday life" (p. 451). Wardhaugh (78) sees it as "more of a slogan than a well-defined concept" (p. 3), a slogan used to justify the relegation of "performance" differences to the status of peripheral issues. A facile acceptance of a competence-performance dichotomy makes it easy to think of natural speech as essentially "degenerate" and hardly worthy of study. This kind of thinking can readily become an attempt to define real but troublesome problems out of existence, a danger that has been pointed out by Halliday (35), writing in the British linguistic tradition. Thus, a basic distinction that has proved fruitful for theoretical linguistics may have an unfortunate effect on a discipline such as language pedagogy which needs a solid data base.

Data observation

Defining a problem out of existence

In view of this danger and under the strain of working within the confines of an unsatisfactory distinction, many writers are seeking to redefine the distinction and to extend the notion of competence to include communicative competence, which might be roughly defined as the ability to use sentences appropriately in a suitable context or situation. One finds in recent literature a renewed emphasis on the act of communication. Savignon (69), for example, found it necessary to use a notion of communicative competence to design a meaningful experiment dealing with the day-to-day realities of the foreign language classroom. Campbell and Wales (13) similarly see the need for a drastic revision of the methodological distinction between competence and performance if answers to basic questions about language acquisition and language use are to become possible. Cazden (14), working in the same area of language acquisition, also emphasizes the need to study language at work in the context of the larger communicative function. Oller (59), uses the philosophical term *pragmatics* to focus attention on "the relation between word sequences and extra-linguistic contexts" (p. 98). Wilkins (83, 84) is currently investigating the possibility of basing language teaching programs not on a linguistically based grammatical sequence, but on *situational* features and *notional* or conceptual categories. The emphasis in this work is on the definition of categories of communicative function and on the communicative needs of the learner. Finally, a lengthy study by Robin Lakoff (47) shows that what is normally attempted in standard transformational grammar—

Communicative competence

Acquisition research and communication

Grammatical rules and social context

342

the definition of the conditions on the applicability of grammatical rules by reference to the superficial syntactic environment only—cannot be achieved. By reference to examples in several languages, she successfully demonstrates that "one must be able to refer to assumptions about the social context of an utterance" (p. 907).

This revived emphasis on the act of communication, on language in use, on language function, is not without its critics. Dillard (19), in his review of a collection of studies on the theme of language and poverty, is quite caustic about those who want to discuss language function as separate from language structure. In his view, such a distinction is a specious one, and talk about it is merely a fad.

Criticism of structure-function dichotomy

New fields of linguistic inquiry

Several attempts are being made to restate the field of legitimate linguistic inquiry, to go beyond the classic competence-performance distinction, in a way that might ultimately be relevant to foreign language pedagogy. Indeed, whole branches of linguistics are developing within the transformational paradigm, but with significantly different approaches that might make these fields promising from the point of view of language teaching. It is appropriate to point to trends in *developmental psycholinguistics, neurolinguistics,* and *sociolinguistics.*

New developments within the generative paradigm

The recent survey of psycholinguistics by Slobin (71) has already been cited. This is probably the most accessible to language teachers, but other valuable surveys can be found in the 1971 *Annual Review of Psychology* (Fillenbaum, 24), in Gough's chapter in the Dingwall collection (31), and in Braine (6), McNeill (54), and Menyuk (55). It is interesting to note suggestions that some of the early work in experimental psycholinguistics was vitiated by an oversimplified reliance on the competence-performance distinction and on the attractive assumption that a performance model would closely resemble the competence model. This point emerges quite clearly from Gough's interpretation of such work. Recently, however, workers in the field of developmental psycholinguistics have been emphasizing the need to work out methods of data gathering that enable them to answer the sorts of questions being asked. Campbell and Wales (13) believe that much greater attention must be paid to the communicative environment of the developing child because they regard as crucial answers to questions about whether parents simplify their speech for children; how parents react to failures in communication; how parents correct, expand, and elaborate children's speech; and so on. Cazden (14) poses

Developmental psycholinguistics

Methods of data gathering

343

similar questions about adult-child interaction. Experimental work in developmental psycholinguistics is a flourishing field, and insights gained from this work will be relevant to the study of foreign language learning. The learning strategies of second-language learners may of course be quite different from those of the native-language learner, but even if this is so, one must assume that in both cases the learner is a richly active contributor. The most important thing we can learn from current work in developmental psycholinguistics may well be a set of observational techniques for measuring the contribution of the learning subject.

The communicative environment

Observational techniques

While neurolinguistics is an equally flourishing example of empirically grounded linguistic inquiry, its relevance to language pedagogy is not so obvious. The basic preoccupation of workers in this field is the attempt to discover physiological evidence to support postulated linguistic constructs. Much of the research is centered on the abundant data from *aphasia*, which Whitaker (80) defines as "abnormal language behavior produced by neurological deficits in adults" (p. 138). In addition to Whitaker's review, an accessible and brief survey of some related questions are found in a recent paper by Lenneberg (51). There are grounds for believing that neurological evidence will play an increasingly more important role in constraining the power of linguistic theory, as is suggested by Patel (61). It is interesting that Whitaker, on the basis of his neurolinguistic investigations, felt constrained first to radically redefine competence and performance and eventually to abandon the distinction altogether (80).

Neurolinguistics

Aphasia

A great deal of flourishing research into sociolinguistic questions is associated with the name of William Labov. His lengthy study, published in 1970 (44), states the case for a social emphasis in linguistic inquiry, for a move away from what he elsewhere calls "the extreme asocial position in theoretical work" (43, p. 43). Labov, too, sees the need to enlarge the notion of competence to include skill in the use of language, the "communicative competence" mentioned above. Language teachers who have been discomforted by the seemingly excessive theorizing of many linguists will probably echo with a hearty cheer Labov's plea for "the removal of the barrier between the linguist and the human being" (p. 43). In Labov's own view, his work raises issues about the very basis of linguistic inquiry, the nature of evidence, and the validity of linguistic argumentation. Such an approach is a healthy antidote to the excessive preoccupation with speculative theory that was discussed above.

Sociolinguistics and Labov

The social dimension

There are, of course, many other approaches to sociolinguistics.

Indeed, the field is expanding so rapidly that it is difficult to summarize even major directions. An earlier collection of readings edited by Fishman (25) is still of considerable interest. He has now made available a two-volume collection (26) intended to update the earlier work. The new collection provides several major statements of basic theoretical positions (Volume 1) as well as papers describing the application of sociolinguistic principles to the description of speech behavior and to practical problems such as language planning (Volume 2). Fishman has also published a basic textbook (27) that is described in its subtitle as "an interdisciplinary social science approach to language in society." An extremely valuable anthology edited by Gumperz and Hymes (34) provides the reader with an indication of the sorts of issues currently being handled in a sociolinguistic framework, and the Dell Hymes lengthy editorial introduction to the new sociolinguistics journal *Language in Society* (36) addresses itself to basic questions of method and definition. The current picture is one of a field seeking to define its lines of inquiry and methodology.

Other approaches

The burgeoning field of sociolinguistics holds much promise for language pedagogy. The phenomenon of bilingualism, for instance, is usually studied within the context of sociolinguistics and has been adequately surveyed in this volume as well as in earlier volumes of the *ACTFL Review*. In addition to directly applicable insights from such research, however, the *methodology* of sociolinguistic inquiry will clearly prove to be fruitful in stimulating and facilitating research in school language learning. If foreign language educators can acquire from sociolinguists a set of effective data-gathering techniques, the way may well be open for much meaningful research in foreign language learning. Fortunately, one can afford to be optimistic about such a prospect, since much of the work inspired by Labov's approach is carried out in school contexts and is thus likely to be suggestive of observational techniques applicable to the foreign language learning situation. Sociolinguistic work may well lead to a deepening awareness of the wider social basis of educational problems such as inadequate foreign language learning programs in schools.

Bilingualism

Importance of methodology

The prospect of progress: From contrastive linguistics to error analysis

Much of what has been said above has suggested the need to expand the data base of research into language learning. Happily one can point to a very fruitful application of linguistic research that promises

Need to expand data base

to achieve that very goal: the study of error analysis, which might profitably be thought of as the successor of the now somewhat outdated contrastive analysis.

The contrastive analysis movement in foreign language education has had a chequered history. The basic principles of the theory, as enunciated by Lado (46), seemed to hold out a great deal of promise as a soundly scientific linguistic basis for language teaching methods and materials. Yet the movement did not live up to such expectations. The several volumes in the "Contrastive Analysis Series" of the University of Chicago Press (Agard and Di Pietro, 1, 2; Kufner, 41; Moulton, 56; Stockwell and Bowen, 73; Stockwell, Bowen, and Martin, 74) vary greatly in quality, and the project was partially abandoned before completion—the French volumes are published only in the ERIC system (Lampach, 48; Lampach and Martinet, 49). The volumes that did appear do not seem to have had any revolutionary effect on language teaching materials and procedures. By the time a Georgetown Round Table (Alatis, 3) was devoted to contrastive analysis, a great deal of fundamental rethinking about earlier assumptions was evident, and a substantial attack on the contrastive analysis hypothesis was launched by Wardhaugh (77), who argued that, in the light of the new insights provided by the Chomskyan revolution, earlier views on contrastive analysis were no longer tenable.

Early promise of contrastive analysis

Subsequent failure

From the point of view of contemporary linguistic thinking, two fundamental reservations about contrastive analysis appear. First, excessive predictive power was expected of contrastive analysis. A comparison of structural descriptions of the phonology and grammar of source and target languages were assumed to highlight the conflict areas and thus successfully predict what errors the learner would make. The key factor of "native language interference" was assumed to be the source of error. However, things do not work out quite so simply: Learners make errors that cannot be explained by native-language interference, and they do not make some of the errors a contrastive analysis would predict. Whitman and Jackson (81) have recently reported an empirical study of "the unpredictability of contrastive analysis." They conclude that not only is contrastive analysis an inadequate predictor of interference problems but also that interference plays a very small role in language learning.

Unwarranted expectation of prediction

The second fundamental objection to contrastive analysis is more theoretical. Contrastive analysis has largely been based on what would now be called surface structure phenomena, which is inadequate. In grammar as well as in phonology, a speaker's linguistic behavior cannot

Limitations of surface structure contrasts

be understood and explained unless it is viewed as rule-governed, that is, the output of an underlying productive system. Attention is now focused on the highly regular and systematic processes that engender surface forms, and the mere cataloguing of the surface phenomena throws little light on the matter. Lists of surface-structure contrasts are not likely to tell us anything about the real sources of whatever conflict exists between the two systems. Labov (43) gives an illuminating example (from the English speech of Puerto Ricans) of the complexities involved in comparing, not the surface outcome of two linguistic systems but the operations of the productive mechanisms underlying each set of forms. He clearly demonstrates that contrastive studies need to go much deeper than the ones we are familiar with: "Whatever the actual mechanism is . . . contrastive analysis must dig deeply into perceptual and productive processes to account for and predict interference" (p. 59).

Need to study underlying productive system

Despite these quite serious reservations, contrastive studies continue to thrive. They seem to correspond to a basic intuitive conviction of language teachers that some student errors, at least, find their explanation in the students' mother tongue. The English-speaking learner of French who says incorrectly "*Le garçon aime son mère*" seems quite clearly to be transferring a feature of his native language system to the foreign language. To go beyond this seemingly simple statement, however, and build it into a coherent account of the nature and limits of interference is a complex task, and one that still attracts the attention of many workers. A major conference on "Contrastive Linguistics and Language Universals" was held at the University of Hawaii in 1971. The full proceedings are available (Jackson and Whitman, 37), and a recent article by Oller (59) reports on trends evident at the conference and their relevance to language teaching. At the Second International Conference of Applied Linguistics, held at Cambridge University in 1969, a section was devoted to contrastive studies and a selection of these papers has now been published (Nickel, 57). A book-length study of contrastive analysis was published by Di Pietro in 1971 (21) and has been reviewed in somewhat ambivalent terms. Gradman (33), whose doctoral dissertation also dealt with the contrastive analysis hypothesis (32), sees Di Pietro's analysis as "a semi-theoretical evasion of what would most help the language teacher," while Rusiecki (67), reviewing the same book in the *TESOL Quarterly*, expresses similar reservations in claiming that both the theoretical assumptions and the procedural recommendations put forward by the author are open to serious criticism" (p. 272). The theoretical status and practical value of

Contrastive analysis

Defining interference

Conferences on contrastive problems

contrastive analysis thus appear to be still a matter of considerable doubt.

Language teaching needs a sound foundation in empirical data. The resurgence of interest in error analysis seems to be effecting a felicitous union between close observation of data (student performance) and insights from theoretical and descriptive work in linguistics. S. Pit Corder (17) seems to have been the first to suggest that, in the light of basic insights from generative-transformational grammar, the study of learners' errors might be very important for research in language learning. Bruce Fraser (29) concluded his study of the relevance of linguistics for teachers of English as a foreign language with the specific suggestion that a book be prepared (with the engaging title of *The Gooficon*!) devoted to the study of errors; it was to draw up a *hierarchy* of errors, not derived from contrast-based predictions, but based on comprehensibility; classes of errors should be established, and in-depth analysis of the points of English grammar relating to them should be provided. Such a book, by Burt and Kiparsky, has been published by Newbury House (12), and a section of the book is also available as an ERIC document (11). This will clearly be a very important work for teachers, an example of "applied linguistics" at its best. The authors demonstrate that from the point of view of teaching strategy not all errors can be corrected, and since the communication of meaning is what matters, a hierarchy of errors ("goof types") must be based on comprehensibility. They illustrate this with specific examples. They then go on to introduce a further criterion for grading errors and selecting corrective teaching material: the *pervasiveness* of parts of the language system—those aspects of the system that apply most widely throughout the whole system. The authors illustrate this principle by reference to the complement system of English and show how the results of recent research in this area of English syntax can be applied to the correction of various kinds of learners' errors.

Dulay and Burt (23) have published an important study based on the same principles. This analysis of "goofing" evaluates the evidence relevant to the contrastive analysis hypothesis, as well as evidence for the claim that children learning a second language use the same acquisition strategies as children learning their first language. The authors effectively demonstrate that neither hypothesis accounts for all of the data available and go on to suggest an alternative account of second-language learning strategies that will explain the data. This is a richly suggestive study.

A somewhat similar approach is found in Selinker's (70) recent

Ambivalent status of contrastive studies

New interest in error analysis

Suggestions for research

The Gooficon

Hierarchy of errors

Major aspects of the language system

Evidence for theories interpreting acquisition data

Importance of studying learning strategies

"state of the art" paper, which is highly recommended, not merely for its perceptive and sensitive insights on various aspects of linguistics and language teaching, but also for its very valuable detailed and classified bibliography. Selinker is realistic about the relevance of linguistics to language teachers, but he produces some very interesting concrete examples of how insights from recent work in linguistics can help teachers to deal effectively with student questions and errors. He also mentions briefly his concept of "interlanguage" and relates his work on this subject to the analysis of learning strategies.

Selinker's review of the state of the art

"Interlanguage"

The study of errors as evidence for strategies is the basis of some very interesting work by Richards (64, 65, 66). This work, too, is solidly data-based and emphasizes the importance of errors as evidence for postulating the existence of certain kinds of learner strategies.

Errors as evidence of learning strategies

In a recent important book-length study, H. V. George (30), uses a simple "input-output" model to analyze learning strategies and claims that the data of input and output are an adequate observational basis for the study of second-language learning. The promising resurgence of research in error analysis is pithily summed up by one of George's remarks: ". . . at the beginning of the sixties the word *error* was associated with correction, at the end with *learning*" (p. 189).

Conclusion

Where then does this survey of linguistics and language teaching leave us?

1 Much of what has been written above is negative, and uniformly gloomy: The major trends in current linguistic research are far removed from the preoccupations of language teachers. It is far better to accept this fact realistically than to proceed with the ill-founded optimism of the postwar period. Given the present state of ferment in linguistics, it would be foolhardy to look for "applications." It is better to be realistic and agree with Selinker that "it is impossible to base teaching materials or a teaching methodology upon linguistics" (70, p. 8). As Barbara Hall Partee (60) points out, the absence of a working paradigm in linguistics is aggravating and distressing, but it is a fact that must be accepted. At the same time, there are signs in the "newer" branches of linguistics that work relevant to language teaching may be forthcoming.

Applicability

Linguistics as theoretical foundation for language teaching

2 The failure of linguistics to provide a sound theoretical foundation for language teaching is not a situation that should be greeted

349

with gloomy pessimism. If it throws the language-teaching profession back on to the resources of its own conventional wisdom, this is surely a good thing. Language teaching is an autonomous art, and it has accumulated over long periods a large body of traditional wisdom and an attitude of healthy eclecticism vis-à-vis other fields. Eclecticism is not an intellectually respectable posture, but it is essential for workers engaged in a practical field. As Wardhaugh succinctly puts it: "We must take what works wherever we find it" (79, p. 302). We must realistically accept what one reviewer (Foster, 28) calls "the sort of non-provable, non-scientific assumptions upon which, when the dust settles FL teaching still appears to be solidly based" (p. 43).

Importance of traditional wisdom

Inevitable eclecticism

3   At the same time, and to end on a note of uncertainty, one must point out that it would be a pity if some sort of training in or at least exposure to linguistics were not a part of the education of language teachers. The Burt-Kiparsky *Gooficon* is probably the most exciting work reported in this chapter. It has a great deal to offer the language teacher, and specifically the teacher of English as a foreign language. Yet it is a fact that adequate use of this work is based on the assumption of the existence of a basic linguistic sophistication, an ability to handle linguistic concepts and follow linguistic argumentation. The same can be said of the valuable linguistic material presented in Selinker's paper. The record of linguists in communicating a linguistic way of thinking to nonspecialist outsiders such as language teachers has not been good, and one hopes that this situation might improve. There is at least one hopeful sign in the fact that a first-rate linguist is willing to address himself to such a task. By the time this chapter appears, Charles Fillmore will have addressed the 1973 TESOL Convention on "things language teachers ought to know from linguistic theory." One hopes that the views of such a distinguished linguist on this subject will receive wide attention within our profession, and will become a part of our response to the realities we face.

Language teachers and linguistic training

References, Theoretical foundations in linguistics and related fields

1 Agard, Frederick B., and Robert J. Di Pietro. *The Grammatical Structures of English and Italian.* Chicago: University of Chicago Press, 1965.

2 ——— *The Sounds of English and Italian.* Chicago: University of Chicago Press, 1965.

3 Alatis, James E.,ed. *Report of the Nineteenth Annual Round Table Meeting on Linguistics and Language Studies.* Washington, D.C.: Georgetown University Press, 1968.

4 Bach, Emmon W. "Syntax since Aspects," 1–17 in Richard J. O'Brien,ed., *Report of the Twenty-Second Annual Round Table Meeting on Linguistics and Language Studies.* Washington, D.C.: Georgetown University Press, 1971.

5 Bolinger, Dwight. "The Influence of Linguistics: Plus and Minus." *TESOL Quarterly* 6(1972): 107–20.

6 Braine, M.D.S. "The Acquisition of Language in Infant and Child," 7–95 in Carroll E. Reed,ed., *The Learning of Language.* New York: Appleton-Century-Crofts, 1971.

7 Brown, T. Grant. "Pedagogical Implications of a Case Grammar of French." *IRAL* 9(1971):229–44.

8 ——— "On Emphasizing Syntax." *Modern Language Journal* 55(1971):271–76.

9 Bull, William. *The Role of Applied Linguistics in Foreign Language Teaching.* [Paper read at the 1971 Annual Meeting of the Washington Association of Foreign Language Teachers, May 1971.] [EDRS: ED 052 645.]

10 ——— and Enrique E. Lamadrid. "Our Grammar Rules Are Hurting Us." *Modern Language Journal* 55(1971):449–54.

11 Burt, Marina K. *Goof Analysis in English as a Second Language.* [Paper presented at Harvard University, October 1971.] [EDRS: ED 061 838.]

12 ——— and C. Kiparsky. *The Gooficon: Errors in Spoken English.* Rowley, Massachusetts: Newbury House, 1972.

13 Campbell, Robin, and Roger Wales. "The Study of Language Acquisition," 242–60 in John Lyons, ed., *New Horizons in Linguistics.* Baltimore: Penguin Books, 1970.

14 Cazden, Courtney B. *Two Paradoxes in the Acquisition of Language Structure and Functions.* [Paper presented at a Conference on the Development of Competence in Early Childhood sponsored by the Developmental Sciences Trust, CIBA Foundation, London, England, January 1972.] [EDRS: ED 063 831.]

15 Chomsky, Noam. *Aspects of the Theory of Syntax.* Cambridge, Massachusetts: MIT Press, 1965.

16 ——— "Linguistic Theory," 43–49 in Robert G. Mead,Jr.,ed., *Language Teaching—Broader Contexts* [Reports of the Working Committees of the Northeast Conference on the Teaching of Foreign Languages.] New York: Modern Language Association Materials Center, 1966.

17 Corder, S. Pit. "The Significance of Learners' Errors." *IRAL* 5(1967):161–69.

18 Crystal, David. *Linguistics.* Baltimore: Penguin Books, 1971.

19 Dillard, J.L. "Review of Frederick Williams,ed., *Language and Poverty.*" *Language* 48(1972):479–87.

20 Dingwall, William O.,ed. *A Survey of Linguistic Science.* College Park, Maryland: Linguistics Program, Universtiy of Maryland, 1971.

21 Di Pietro, Robert J. *Language Structures in Contrast.* Rowley, Massachusetts: Newbury House, 1971.

22 Dubois, Jean, and Françoise Dubois-Charlier. *Eléments de linguistique française: syntaxe.* [Langue et langage.] Paris: Larousse, 1970.

23 Dulay, Heidi C., and Marina K. Burt. "Goofing: An Indicator of Children's Second Language Learning Strategies." *Language Learning* 22(1972): 235–52.

24 Fillenbaum, Samuel. "Psycholinguistics," 251–308 in Paul H. Mussen and Mark R. Rosenzweig,eds., *Annual Review of Psychology Volume 22.* Palo Alto: Annual Reviews Inc., 1971.

25 Fishman, Joshua A.,ed. *Readings in the Sociology of Language.* The Hague: Mouton, 1968.

26 ———*Advances in the Sociology of Language.* The Hague:Mouton, Volume 1, 1971, Volume 2, 1972.

27 ———*The Sociology of Language.* Rowley, Massachusetts: Newbury House, 1972.

28 Foster, David W. "Review of Karl Conrad Diller, *Generative Grammar, Structural Linguistics, and Language Teaching.*" *Modern Language Journal* 57(1973): 43.

29 Fraser, Bruce. "Linguistics and the EFL Teacher." 1–27 in Robert C. Lugton,ed., *Preparing the EFL Teacher:A Projection for the '70s.* Philadelphia: Center for Curriculum Development, 1970.

30 George, H.V. *Common Errors in Language Learning. Insights from English. A Basic Guide to the Causes and Prevention of Students' Errors in Foreign Language Learning.* Rowley, Massachusetts: Newbury House, 1972.

31 Gough, Philip B. "Experimental Psycholinguistics," 252–96 in William O. Dingwall,ed., *A Survey of Linguistic Science.* College Park, Maryland: Linguistics Program, University of Maryland, 1971.

32 Gradman, Harry L. "The Contrastive Analysis Hypothesis:What It Is, and What It Isn't." *Dissertation Abstracts International* 31(1971):6579A–80A (Indiana).

33 ———"Review of Robert J. Di Pietro, *Language Structures in Contrast.*" *Language Sciences* 22(1972): 32–33.

34 Gumperz, John J., and Dell Hymes,eds. *Directions*

in Sociolinguistics:The Ethnography of Communication. New York: Holt, Rinehart and Winston, 1972.

35 Halliday, M.A.K. "Language Structure and Language Function," 140–65 in John Lyons,ed., *New Horizons in Linguistics.* Baltimore: Penguin Books, 1970.

36 Hymes, Dell. "Editorial Introduction to *Language in Society.*" *Language in Society* 1(1972):1–14.

37 Jackson, Kenneth, and Randal Whitman,eds. *The PCCLLU Papers.* [Pacific Conference on Contrastive Linguistics and Language Universals. Working Papers in Linguistics.] Honolulu: University of Hawaii, 1971.

38 Jakobovits, Leon A. *On Becoming a Language Teacher.* [Paper presented at the Sixth Annual TESOL Convention, Washington, D.C., February 1972.] [EDRS: ED 061 830.]

39 Karttunen, Lauri. "Implicative Verbs." *Language* 47(1971):340–58.

40 Katz, Jerrold J. *Semantic Theory.* Studies in Language. New York: Harper & Row, 1972.

41 Kufner, Herbert L. *The Grammatical Structures of English and German:A Contrastive Sketch.* Chicago: University of Chicago Press, 1963.

42 Kuhn, Thomas S. *The Structure of Scientific Revolutions.* Chicago: University of Chicago Press, 1962.

43 Labov, William. "The Place of Linguistic Research in American Society," 41–70 in *Linguistics in the 70's.* [Pre-publication edition]. Washington, D.C.: Center for Applied Linguistics, 1970.

44 ——— "The Study of Language in Its Social Context." *Studium Generale* 23(1970):30–87.

45 ———"Methodology," 412–97 in William O. Dingwall,ed., *A Survey of Linguistic Science.* College Park, Maryland: Linguistics Program, University of Maryland, 1971.

46 Lado, Robert. *Linguistics Across Cultures.* Ann Arbor: University of Michigan Press, 1957.

47 Lakoff, Robin. "Language in Context." *Language* 48(1972):907–27.

48 Lampach, Stanley. *The Grammars of English and French.* [EDRS: ED 043 251.]

49 ———and André Martinet. *The Sounds of English and French.* [EDRS: ED 043 250.]

50 Langellier, Alice, Sylvia Narins Levy, and Holt Editorial Staff. *Chez les Français.* New York: Holt, Rinehart and Winston, 1969.

51 Lenneberg, Eric. "Developments in Biological Linguistics," 199–209 in Richard J. O'Brien,ed., *Report of the Twenty-Second Annual Round Table Meeting on Linguistics and Language Studies.* Washington, D.C.: Georgetown University Press, 1971.

52 Macaulay, Ronald K.S. "Aspect in English." *Dissertation Abstracts International* 32(1972):3979A (University of California at Los Angeles).

53 McCawley, James D. "Prelexical Syntax," 19–33 in Richard J. O'Brien,ed., *Report of the Twenty-Second Annual Round Table Meeting on Linguistics and Language Studies.* Washington, D.C.: Georgetown University Press, 1971.

54 McNeill, David. *The Acquisition of Language: The Study of Developmental Psycholinguistics.* New York: Harper & Row, 1970.

55 Menyuk, P. *The Acquisition and Development of Language.* Englewood Cliffs, New Jersey: Prentice-Hall, 1971.

56 Moulton, William G. *The Sounds of English and German.* Chicago: University of Chicago Press, 1962.

57 Nickel, Gerhard,ed. *Papers in Contrastive Linguistics.* London: Cambridge University Press, 1971.

58 Obrecht, Dean H. "Fundamentals of Language and Fundamentals of Teaching:The Necessity of Cross-breeding," 181–88 in Paul Pimsleur and Terence Quinn,eds., *The Psychology of Second Language Learning.* London: Cambridge University Press, 1971.

59 Oller, John W. "Contrastive Analysis, Difficulty, and Predictability," *Foreign Language Annals* 6(1972): 95–106.

60 Partee, Barbara Hall. "Linguistics Metatheory," 650–80 in William O. Dingwall,ed., *A Survey of Linguistic Science.* College Park, Maryland: Linguistics Program, University of Maryland, 1971.

61 Patel, P.G. "Review of Dan I. Slobin, *Psycholinguistics,*" *Language Sciences* 23(1972):36–39.

62 Politzer, Robert L. *Linguistics and Applied Linguistics: Aims and Methods.* Philadelphia: Center for Curriculum Development, 1972.

63 Quinn, Terence J. "Toward a Pedagogical Grammar of the French Tense System:A Linguistic Analysis of Some Current Teaching Materials and Guidelines for Their Improvement." *Dissertation Abstracts International* 32(1972):3569A (Ohio State).

64 Richards, Jack. "A Non-Contrastive Approach to Error Analysis." *English Language Teaching* 25(1971): 204–19.

65 ——— "Error Analysis and Second Language Strategies." *Language Sciences* 17(1971):12–22.

66 ———"Social Factors, Interlanguage, and Language Learning." *Language Learning* 22(1972): 159–88.

67 Rusiecki, Jan. "Review of Robert J. Di Pietro, *Language Structures in Contrast.*" *TESOL Quarterly* 6(1972):271–78.

68 Saporta, Sol. "Applied Linguistics and Generative Grammar," 81–92 in Albert Valdman,ed., *Trends in Language Teaching.* New York: McGraw-Hill, 1966.

69 Savignon, Sandra J. *Communicative Competence:An Experiment in Foreign-Language Teaching.* Philadelphia: Center for Curriculum Development, 1972.

70 Selinker, Larry. "The Application of Linguistics to Foreign Language Teaching:The State of the Art," 2–17 in Jean-Charles Seigneuret and David P. Benseler,eds., *Reports and Papers from the State Conference in Spokane, March 17–18 [1972].* Pullman,

Washington: Washington Association of Foreign Language Teachers, 1972. [EDRS: ED 065 015.]

71 Slobin, Dan I. *Psycholinguistics*. Glenview, Illinois: Scott Foresman, 1971.

72 ———"Developmental Psycholinguistics," 298–410 in William O. Dingwall,ed., *A Survey of Linguistic Science*. College Park, Maryland: Linguistics Program, University of Maryland, 1971.

73 Stockwell, Robert P., and J. Donald Bowen. *The Sounds of English and Spanish*. Chicago: University of Chicago Press, 1965.

74 ———and John W. Martin. *The Grammatical Structures of English and Spanish*. Chicago: University of Chicago Press, 1965.

75 Twaddell, Freeman. "A Focus Report:Linguistics and Foreign-Language Teaching." *Foreign Language Annals* 4(1970):194–99.

76 ———"Some Grammatical Ghosts." *Modern Language Journal* 56(1972):69–73.

77 Wardhaugh, Ronald. "The Contrastive Analysis Hypothesis." *TESOL Quarterly* 4(1970):123–30.

78 ———"Theories of Language Acquisition in Relation to Beginning Reading Instruction." *Language Learning* 21(1971):1–25.

79 ———"TESOL:Our Common Cause." *TESOL Quarterly* 6(1972):291–303.

80 Whitaker, Harry A. "Neurolinguistics,"136–251 in William O. Dingwall,ed., *A Survey of Linguistic Science*. College Park, Maryland: Linguistics Program, University of Maryland, 1971.

81 Whitman, Randal L., and Kenneth L. Jackson. "The Unpredictability of Contrastive Analysis." *Language Learning* 22(1972):29–42.

82 Wilkins, D.A. *Linguistics in Language Teaching*. Cambridge, Massachusetts: MIT Press, 1972.

83 ———*Modern Languages. The Linguistic and Situational Content of the Common Core in a Unit Credit System*. Strasbourg: The Council of Europe, 1972.

84 ———*Grammatical, Situational and Notional Syllabuses*. [Paper presented at the Third International Congress of Applied Linguistics, Copenhagen, 21–26 August 1972.]

85 Williams, Frederick,ed. *Language and Poverty: Perspectives on a Theme*. Chicago: Markham, 1970.

Responsibilities

11

Quality and relevance in teacher education

Introduction

A substantial rethinking of purposes and goals in foreign language education is long overdue. The symptoms are more visible each day. Perhaps the most significant indication of the urgency of the need for change is the downward trend in foreign language enrollments. Meyerson and Scebold (24) indicate that in spite of the increase in population in the public secondary schools between 1968 and 1970 (approximately 863,000 pupils) foreign language enrollment decreased by 181,000 pupils. Many foreign language teachers are quick to impute the dwindling enrollments to the diminution of college entrance and degree requirements. These teachers would be deluding themselves, however, if they failed to recognize that the enrollment decline is merely the "tip of the iceberg." Probably a more accurate assessment of the situation is that many students are, and have been, disenchanted with foreign language learning. They are tired of dull dialogues and meaningless drills for nebulous goals. They are doubting the worth of risking respectable academic averages in exchange for two or three years of a subject matter for which they have no "foreseeable" use. They resent being taught by instructors who possess less than adequate proficiency in the language they teach and who also lack teaching skill. Today's students resent "being taught." They rebel against the implantation of knowledge. They yearn to be partners in the learning process. Today's educational consumers are reluctant to accept learning solely as an exhibition of academic prowess—a trophy to be

William E.
De Lorenzo
University of Maryland

Student disenchantment

William E. De Lorenzo (Ph.D., The Ohio State University) is Assistant Professor of Foreign Language Education, The University of Maryland, College Park Campus. He has taught Spanish at elementary, secondary, and college levels and has directed methods workshops in Indiana, Maryland, New Jersey, and Ohio. He is the author of "Rationale, Description, and Feasibility of a Partially Programmed Foreign Language Methods Course" in *Foreign Language Annals* and is the co-author of a section of the reports of Working Committee I, which will appear in the 1974 *Northeast Conference Reports*. He has served as Membership Chairman and Vice-President in Charge of Programs for the New Jersey Foreign Language Teachers Association. Currently, he is a member of the ACTFL Executive Council and is serving as Chairman of the Annual Conference Committee. His Professional affiliations include ACTFL, AATSP, MFLTA, and AAUP.

displayed on the mantel, a diploma to be hung on the wall. Like all wise   *Usable knowledge*
consumers, they are seeking an equitable exchange for their time and
effort. They want knowledge and skills that may be utilized as they
attempt to find their places in society. In short, our goals in foreign
language education must continue to change. As indicated in the
earlier chapters of this volume, the change is slow and often difficult,
but it is nevertheless real. These changes in turn must be reflected in the
area of teacher preparation. Jarvis (21) observes that "our activity is no
longer 'comfortable,' and the future direction of our discomfort is
intimately related to teacher-education goals" (p. 198).

The thrust toward change is not the unique responsibility of *foreign*   *Responsibility for change*
language educators. Jarvis (21) implies that the role of the teacher-
education profession in general is that of a principal change agent. He
observes that teacher education "must adapt to its environment—an
environment in which themes of 'survival crisis,' 'future shock', and
humanism merge in an utterly consuming vortex of uncertainty"
(p. 198). This advice implies that foreign language teacher preparation
must become diversified. We must become less myopic in our goals,
approaches, and philosophy. We can no longer ignore the implications
of innovative developments in other disciplines. If we are to respond to
the needs of a pluralistic society, we must broaden our perspective in
teacher preparation by developing new approaches to foreign language teacher education.

If foreign language education is to be a part of the future American
educational scene, it must meet its responsibilities by reevaluating the
quality and relevance of current teacher education.

The ensuing discussion deals with the nature of quality and relevance, their importance, and the obstacles that thwart rapid progress
toward achieving and maintaining them.

Esteem for the profession

Perhaps one of the most frequently quoted and, unfortunately, most
incriminating comments about the teaching profession is "Those who
can, do; those who can't, teach." These words have precipitated many
a verbal battle between members of the profession and citizens we serve.
This lack of esteem is manifested in many forms and emanates from   *Lack of public esteem*
persons in many walks of life, including members of the profession. We
are confronted by the *indignant* parent who, when Johnny is being
"wronged," does not hesitate to remind us of the source of our financial
support. We are *patronized* by the sincere, well-meaning physician who

often has established separate (usually lower) professional service fees for teachers. We are faced with the *indifference* of fellow educators who race the students to the exits at the close of the school day. Finally, we are confronted with the implication that our status is less than a professional one (Powers, et al., 27).

A news article in a December 1972 issue of the *Washington Post* (Prince and Williams, 28) was uncomfortably reminiscent of Toffler's (32) description of the industrial era school. The story began its assessment of the present teacher surplus problems with the following sentence: "The American education *industry*, which spends more than $50 billion a year and employs more than 2 million public school teachers, is now confronted with a serious surplus of *labor*" (Prince and Williams, 28, p. K1) [emphases added]. This terminology might well have been part of Toffler's (32) juxtapositions—masses of students (raw material), teachers (workers), school (factory) (p. 400). Unfortunately, news articles such as these perpetuate the very stigma that Toffler, Illich, Silberman, Holt, and others would rather discourage—that schools are merely an extension of the industrialized society. As such, the schools tend to emulate the rigid controls necessary to maintain production line efficiency—systematized seating, fixed-time schedules, lockstep instruction, teacher-centered (uni-directed) classes.

Less than professional

An assessment of our self-esteem

A profession's image is shaped by many factors. One significant factor that certainly affects the public's attitude toward the teaching profession in particular, is the esteem that the profession has for itself.

Many foreign language teachers have heard remarks like, "You speak the language so well, why aren't you a translator for the United Nations?" The implication of this inquiry—why is a talent like yours being wasted in a job like this?—is less disconcerting than the teacher's willingness to respond, "Oh, that requires a *special* talent and a very specialized training," or "I would if I could, but I can't, so I'm not." An analysis of this vignette reveals not only the lack of respect the public has for the profession, but the depressing absence of the language teacher's self-esteem. The mere use of such words as "special" and "specialized" to characterize this language-related profession implies a status of lesser talent and less specialized training for the teaching profession. It is precisely this type of defensive submission that perpetuates a negative image of the profession. The enemy comes from within. It is our own perception. We have not been able to view our own

Lack of self-esteem

359

profession as merely *different* from other language-related professions. We see ourselves as being less worthy of esteem than other status groups. We impugn our own profession by communicating our negative image to the public.

Our image needs a face-lifting. Twaddell (34) facetiously recommends a psychiatrist and a good press agent for the job. While the former may be nothing more than a clever characterization of our dilemma, the need for a press agent is not altogether unrealistic. We do suffer from a lack of publicity. If we are to seek wider recognition of the need for foreign language study, we, like our colleagues in other areas, must become adept at making visible our contribution to society. In addition to the psychiatrist and press agent, Twaddell might have also suggested an optometrist. A corrective prescription for our professional myopia would enable us to see beyond our area of foreign language education. We would finally be able to transform the art, science, and industrial education exhibits to foreign language expositions of student-made projects (games, films, tapes, maps, etc.); the gymnastics exhibition to a foreign language participation day (poetry declamation, skits, music, dances, etc.); the sports dinner to an international banquet; the PTA visitation night to the foreign language visitation night, day, or week. Lest our myopia be perpetuated, the reader is cautioned that all these events be directed to the real public we serve. Engaging in these projects for the exclusive consumption by colleagues will serve only to nullify any benefits to be gained from their main intent—positive *public* exposure of the foreign language profession. These activities do exist, but they occur only in limited instances. In her address to the 1973 Central States Conference on the Teaching of Foreign Languages, Warriner (35) reported that among other activities, her office has employed bumper stickers and posters to arouse public interest in foreign language study. The state slogan "Virginia is for lovers" was adapted to read, "Virginia is for lovers—*have an affair with a foreign language*." Enthusiastic teachers and students have elaborated on the idea and have introduced other versions of the slogan such as, "Virginia is for *Latin* lovers," and "Have a *romance* with a foreign language." Activities such as these are limited only by the foreign language profession's collective imagination and by the degree to which it desires to expend energies to insure that foreign language instruction is recognized as a legitimate component of the school's curriculum.

Improving image

Positive public exposure

Fanfare and positive public exposure alone are not adequate techniques for creating a positive professional image. Professional commitment is an intrinsic aspect of image-formation. The teaching profession is plagued by "insurance seekers." Andrews (3) has estimated that from 20 to 30 percent of newly prepared, degree-holding, certificated teachers do not begin to teach after graduation. He also estimates that more than 50 percent of those who begin to teach immediately become attrition statistics by the end of their fifth year of teaching. While some of the "committed" leave for reasons beyond their control, others (apparently not so committed) drop out for "better" occupations. The latter tend to exemplify a group that has utilized the profession, in Cheek's (9) words, as a "mattress curriculum." This, explains Cheek, is "something for students to fall back upon if other employment opportunities are in short supply" (p. 13). The problem appears to lie in our inability to identify the noncommitted early. The ability to screen out the "insurance seeker" would permit a redeployment of valuable resources for the purpose of improving the training of the truly committed professional.

"Insurance seekers"

Screening out noncommitted

Several teacher educators have developed and proposed models for improving the teacher-training process. Smith et al. (29) devote an entire publication to this vital reorganization of teacher education programs. Andrews (2) proposes an elaborate plan for preparing the teacher who is worthy of the title "Professional." His plan would parallel that of the medical profession (pre-intern experiences, study and clinical experience, internship, and residency). Unfortunately, these types of plans and models usually require a massive change in program structure as well as redeployment of finances and manpower. History has shown that no matter how vital the need nor how sound the plan, substantial changes in the teaching profession rarely occur rapidly. In these times of curricular and financial pruning, the proffering of such plans as an immediate response to the problems of assuring committed foreign language teachers would be as frustrating as it is financially unrealistic. The reader should not construe this hesitation as a plea to abandon efforts to overhaul teacher-preparation programs completely. On the contrary, the profession as a whole must develop, encourage, and support any plan that will enhance its professional training program. However, all too often critics of teacher-training programs advocate changes and innovations that are difficult to implement because of bureaucratic structure in many

Impracticality of proposed models

Change

Bureaucratic structure

of our educational institutions. Consequently, teacher trainers might do well to develop carefully and implement slowly small-scale changes that will ultimately become components of larger systems such as those envisioned by Andrews (2) and Smith et al. (29).

Professional commitment is difficult to detect in pre-service trainees, and unfortunately, this is precisely the stage at which the non-committed must be identified. A teacher trainer's subjective judgment of a prospective teacher's commitment, or lack of it, is risky business, even when such conclusions are based on keen intuition and extensive professional experience. Students and administrators alike are loath to accept such judgment as valid. In short, judgment without concrete evidence may be justifiably construed as invalid. How, then, can the "insurance seekers" be detected and subsequently discouraged? Those who at this point would suggest competency tests, interviews, etc. should take note that a distinction is made here between competency and commitment. Depending on the type of competency involved, one can easily demonstrate the former in spite of an absence of the latter and vice versa. Because of this difficulty, a valid procedure for judging commitment would seem to be by self-judgment. The student must decide for himself whether he wishes to continue in the profession. The teacher trainer's role then becomes one of providing experiences that will help the prospective teacher trainee to reach a conclusion on his own. These experiences must make the student aware (in the fullest sense of the word) of what it means to be a foreign language teacher. He must experience the role so vividly that any lack of commitment results in an overwhelming sense of hypocrisy. These experiences might include early exposure to the teaching field through tasks such as tutoring, structured classroom observation, and work as a teacher aide. Allen and Hawkes (1) suggest "shadowing." This activity entails intensive contact for two or three weeks with individuals who, for one reason or another, are excellent models for the profession. In cases where this activity is feasible, foreign language trainees might be asked to work with master teachers; local (school), county, state supervisors; and other pertinent staff. By making this a full-term academic assignment, the trainee could work with each "model" at various times during the term. These activities might be conducted through a strictly voluntary arrangement, an independent study assignment, or in a required service course. Where pertinent, academic credit would be given, the amount determined by the extent and scope of the experiences. Other experiences might include work with summer camps, community recreation centers, or church and other youth groups where a student

Detecting commitment

"Second-party" judgment

Self-judgment

Varied experiences

"Shadowing"

Arranging experiences

would have to enter into a "helping relationship" with young people. Until recently, practical, direct experiences have rarely occurred or have occurred too late to make much difference. The current emphasis on early experiences within many teacher education institutions, however, coupled with the felt need within the schools for para-professionals to assist within classrooms (particularly individualized programs) may yield as a by-product measurement of the potential teacher's commitment to the profession.

Controlling admission to teacher education programs

The question of commitment is intricately related to acceptance and retention policies in teacher training institutions. If the appropriate staff in a subject-matter teaching area (e.g., foreign language education) were allowed more say in these policies, perhaps more noncommitted and other poorly qualified students would be eliminated at an earlier stage. Unfortunately, a professional's *subjective* judgment of a prospective candidate's desire to teach is often rejected merely because it is subjective. Identifying competent and committed trainees is further complicated by the existence of several acceptance policies that appear to operate on campuses across the country. The most discouraging is the "open door" policy, in the view of some educators. Under this arrangement, any student who thinks that he might like to "try his hand" at teaching is admitted without question. Perhaps such measures were justified, at least on an emergency basis, during times of teacher shortage. However, in view of the present teacher job market, especially in foreign languages, this policy is anachronistic. Prince and Williams (28) report that "the 100,000 teachers who can't find jobs, according to the NEA are mostly those who specialized in English, *foreign languages* [emphasis added], home economics, social studies and business education. . . ." (p. K1). A more recent article in the Towson State College newspaper reported similar surpluses and, again, listed foreign languages among the surplus areas (Swecker, 31). There are, of course, those who believe that choice of career is a fundamental right of the individual rather than an institution, particularly when institutions are using the job market as a rationale for screening. There are also others who take odds with teacher surplus reports on the grounds that the need for teachers exists, if only the public schools were to meet minimum standards of quality in programs and staffing (Graybeal, 16). While this assessment may be accurate, it is more philosophical than realistic. No matter what we feel the profession *should*

Specific-area input

"Open-door policy"

Job market

Need for teachers

be doing, our priority is to respond to the reality of what is *presently* occurring. This is not to dismiss lightly the need to raise this philosophical question. Such matters must be settled by the profession as a whole. Our concern here is that reliable news releases, editorials, and institutional placement bureaus indicate that teaching positions in certain fields of study are scarce. In view of this situation, we must ask ourselves if an open enrollment policy is the appropriate response. Should not departmental screening committees, where they exist, have the *professional* prerogative to accept only those applicants who meet the qualifications set by that department? The imposition of an "open door" policy on the professional education college may well be a further indication of the low esteem for the profession and for its judgment.

Reality of situation

Another approach to acceptance into the teacher education program is one, which for lack of a generally accepted name, we shall refer to as the "personal-data-collection approach." Students who wish to declare their majors in Teacher Education must present certain information that, when evaluated by the appropriate personnel, indicates their degree of acceptability into the training program. Items that are typically collected for use as admission criteria are: (a) demonstration of an acceptable overall cumulative grade point average, (b) acceptable grades (based on the judgment of the specific area advisor) in content-area work, (c) several letters of support from various acquaintances in responsible positions, (d) a personal interview with the applicant to assess his or her understanding of and commitment to the profession. After all the data are collected and forwarded to the admissions officer, each individual criterion may be assigned a numerical rating ranging from 0 (very poor) to 100 (excellent). The ratings are averaged, and the results are subsequently reported to the area advisors for additional scrutiny. The advisors are afforded the opportunity to make further judgment on the acceptance or rejection of the applicant in question. The subject-area staff may wish to accept an applicant on the basis of favorable ratings in one or two of the above mentioned criteria (e.g., letters of support and personal interviews) rather than on a composite rating of all four items. Conceivably, an applicant's acceptance might depend on the relationship between the subject area's acceptance quota and his rank position on the composite list.

Personal data-collection approach

Obviously, the "personal-data-collection approach" is not a panacea. In spite of several drawbacks (its rigidly calculated point value system, questionable validity of letters of support, and subjective judgment of the interviewer), it does provide certain advantages over a blanket acceptance of any "interested body." With its features of personal con-

Limited input better than none

364

tact and varied input (G.P.A.; letters of support; first impressions of professional commitment, character, and personality), it is certainly more conducive to quality control measures than is a complete absence of screening procedures. Some teacher educators would dismiss this screening method as excessively time consuming in view of the great numbers of candidates the subject area is attracting. Such dismissal does not reconcile with Dickson's (12) assertion that "the teaching shortage in the United States has been met physically but not in terms of quality" (pp. 50–51). This observation can be interpreted as a viable justification for some method of screening applicants for the profession.

If the screening procedure described above is not feasible in a particular situation, the persons responsible for this task must devise systems that satisfy their own needs and may be generalizable to other institutions. An important implication here is the necessity to *share* these procedures with other members of the profession. This may be done through word of mouth or through the professional literature. The purpose of communication must become the betterment of the profession rather than self-aggrandizement. It is precisely this type of communication that will ultimately lead to viable solutions to problems.

Need to share

Post-admission monitoring for quality control

The foregoing comments assess problems of acceptance into programs. In the 1971 *Northeast Conference Reports* (27), Working Committee I advised the foreign language profession of its deficiency in admission and retention policies. In spite of the committee's report, the absence of a truly effective screening device is a reality the profession must still face. Teacher trainers are well aware that many students who are ultimately admitted into teacher education barely meet the minimum requirements for quality personnel (strong commitment; knowledge of subject matter; and in the case of foreign languages, acceptable proficiency in listening, speaking, reading, and writing the target language).

Screening

During the past several years, the teaching profession has witnessed an increasing amount of public reaction to its activities. Stinnet (30) cautions that "there are signs of a public revolt against the teaching profession" (p. 3). He cites, for example, the public's demand for assessment of performance. This demand obligates the profession to reassess its methods of granting credentials to its members. Con-

Increased public reaction

Monitoring progress

365

sequently, we must strive for a training program that carefully monitors progress toward established goals for those aspiring to be teachers. Because of institution-wide policies or inadequate screening procedures, many poor prospects are admitted to teacher education programs. Monitoring students' programs would insure that, at best, only those who meet the established criteria be granted certification—the license to teach in our nation's schools.

Precise definitions and understanding of competency to teach a foreign language (or any subject area) remain elusive to the profession. We can speak about it in the abstract, but the translation to the behavior of individual teachers becomes unwieldy. Thus, given our difficulty in describing competency in a useful and generalizable way, it is little wonder that there are in use multiple strategies for achieving the goal.

Competing designs

Considerable attention is currently being given to two competing designs. The first approach involves a system in which the prospective teacher is guided through a pre-determined sequence of professional "experiences" (i.e., content courses, teaching and learning theory, laboratory, and, possibly, clinical experiences and student teaching). Successful completion of the sequence (usually equated with passing grades of C or better) assures the student of certification. This strategy, Dickson (12) informs us, is known as "Experience-Based Teacher Education" (EBTE). The second strategy would also have students complete a series of experiences for the purpose of certification. However, the emphasis here would be placed on the student's ability to demonstrate competency by meeting predetermined performance criteria, rather than merely on the completion of a sequence of courses for a specified number of credits. This strategy would require that the profession establish appropriate performance objectives in order to evaluate the trainee's effectiveness in the actual classroom setting. In this type of program, teacher (trainee) competencies may be broadly constructed. The following exemplary statements of teacher competencies do not include criteria for successful demonstration of competence. They are presented here merely to illustrate the nature of this strategy as compared to the aforementioned EBTE approach. A supervisor of student teachers might look for the following competencies when observing a trainee:

Experience-based teacher education

Performance-based teacher education

1 Is sensitive to the needs and feelings of his students
2 Deals firmly, but fairly, with disruptive students
3 Seeks and subsequently utilizes students' suggestions in developing the course curriculum

366

4 Recognizes and adequately meets the need to respond to the diverse learning styles of his students

5 Works effectively with other members of the department

Thus, the prospective teacher would be certified on the basis of *demonstrating* attainment of these competencies and others like them rather than merely successfully completing a series of required courses. This strategy is identified as "Performance- (or Competency-) Based Teacher Education" (PBTE). Further discussion of this topic will appear in the 1974 *Northeast Conference Report of Working Committee I* (18).

EBTE, as described above, would appear to fall short of meeting the demand for an efficient method of assessing competency. Merely completing a state-mandated professional sequence (a series of specified course titles, credit hours, and student teaching) can no longer be the sole criterion for teacher certification. If the profession is to gain and maintain respectability, it may wish to endorse a system of training whereby not merely knowledge, but especially skill, in teaching is considered. Dickson (12) states that "an increasing number of people in the teaching profession are becoming unwilling to accept the assumption that simply because someone 'knows' something he can necessarily apply his knowledge" (p. 51). By requiring a trainee to demonstrate proof of attainment of competency in both subject matter and the teaching skill, the profession should be better able to control the quality of its members.
Efficiency of EBTE

Advocates of PBTE claim that this strategy is precisely the approach needed to meet the demands for a more accurate assessment of professional competency. Unless a prospective teacher is able to demonstrate that he has attained the competencies required to become a member of the teaching profession, he would be denied certification. Thus, a performance-based teacher education program would serve as an excellent strategy for quality control by denying certification to those students who would depend merely on *knowledge about* teaching (often less than adequate) rather than the ability to *perform* certain required skills. The profession's most crucial task in the development of this strategy is the *identification* of specific competencies.
Effective strategy of PBTE

Two key publications that are addressed to the design and implementation of performance-based teacher education programs in the area of foreign language education are Bela Banathy's "The Design of Foreign Language Teacher Education" (5) and Richard McArdle's "Training Language Teachers—A Systems Approach" (23). In the former, the author presents an explicit description of what Dickson (12)
Key models

367

explains as "the fundamental process of competency-based teacher education—a systems analysis approach" (p. 52). After a succinct explanation of the nature of a "system," Banathy discusses: formulation of performance objectives, analysis and characterization of learning tasks, designing the system, system integration, installation, change to improve, and application. Further elaboration of this design is presented in a more recent publication: *A Design for Foreign Language Curriculum* (Banathy and Lange, 6). McArdle's article differs from that of Banathy in that it presents a *specific* objective as it is dealt with in a systems approach to the foreign language methods course. The author presents a general and specific statement of the problem, an analysis of the problem, an assessment of the learner's entry behavior, the development of an instructional design, and a means of feedback and change within the design. Other pertinent descriptions of discrete program designs that might easily serve as integrated components of an overall systems approach are:

1 De Lorenzo's "Rationale, Description, and Feasibility of A Partially Programmed Foreign Language Methods Course" (11). This report deals with an attempt to program five foreign language teaching skills through the medium of the videotape recorder.

2 Hancock's "Guiding Teachers to Respond to Individual Differences in the Affective Domain" (17). The author presents a design for developing and implementing simulations on the topics of discipline, attitude, and motivation in the foreign language classroom.

3 Macías' "The Use of Simulation in Foreign Language Education in Activities—Specific Teaching Situations" (22). This study deals with simulated incidents in foreign language teaching that lead to alternative approaches to solving cognitive problems such as techniques of pattern drilling, dialogue presentation, questioning, etc.

4 Politzer's "Toward a Practice-Centered Program for the Training and Evaluation of Foreign Language Teachers" (26). The author has developed a series of micro-lessons that attempt to effect specific behavioral changes in pre- and in-service foreign language teachers. This idea was further developed later by Bartley and Politzer to include *specific languages*—English, (7), French, (25), and Spanish, (8).

5 Wolfe's "The Direct Experiences of Micro-Teaching and Team Teaching in Foreign Language Education" (36). This is a report

on the design and implementation of micro-teaching and team teaching (more appropriately described as *bit*-teaching) for training preservice teachers.

Each of these citatia involves performances (cognitive or affective) by the prospective or in-service teacher. A basic factor in PBTE is actual student performance to ascertain the degree to which the trainee has mastered a particular skill (teaching techniques, teacher-pupil interaction, problem solving, etc.). These projects should prove to be valuable sources to the teacher trainer in terms of types of skills to be developed and the manner in which skills acquisition may be evaluated.

The intent of this discussion is not to present PBTE as "yet another panacea" for the numerous problems that confront the profession. There are at least as many opponents to this strategy as there are advocates. I merely wish to emphasize the fact that the movement toward PBTE is quite alive, in spite of its pitfalls (Getz, 15). State Departments of Education appear to be increasingly interested in performance-based programs. The State of Maryland has placed an *indefinite* moratorium on approval of new certification programs. During this time, the question of state-wide adoption of PBTE is expected to be thoroughly reviewed and subsequently acted upon. State-sponsored all-day workshops on PBTE (one per month for six months) may be a good indicator of the direction the state intends to take in dealing with the question. *No panacea*

PBTE curriculum

Many states are well on their way toward developing PBTE programs. A recent publication of the New York State Education Department and Multi-State Consortium on Performance-Based Teacher Education (19) lists some of the states involved in Performance-Based programs: Washington, Oregon, Utah, Arizona, Texas, Minnesota, Vermont, New York, and Florida. This momentum toward state adoptions of PBTE makes it difficult to dismiss lightly this "controversial" trend. It must be evaluated in terms of what it means for foreign language education.

Commitment to professional growth and improvement

What are the goals of preservice training? Quite understandably, there is little agreement among responses to this inquiry. Goals appear to range from preparing a trainee who can "survive" his student teaching experience to preparing a "well seasoned" practitioner who is ready to handle *all* aspects of the teaching situation. *Lack of agreement*

A frequent complaint voiced by teachers in the field is that teacher

369

preparation institutions are not providing the neophyte with the type of training needed to meet the rapidly changing curriculum in the public schools. A disturbing insinuation here is that *four years* of education and often only *two years* of professional courses and limited, direct experiences should be sufficient for the production of a "finished" product. Andrews (4) has often stated that "no teacher is worth his salt until his fifth year of teaching." The implication is that during the beginning years, the neophyte is still in training. Jackson (20) advises us that "there is no specific time at which a person becomes a teacher" (p. 27). Concern for developing and maintaining teacher competence must extend beyond the teacher aspirant level and encompass those who are already in the profession. The nature of teacher education makes it a *perennial* task. Cloos (10) defines it as "the *continuing* [emphasis added] professional growth and development of educational personnel" (p. 247). In view of the rapid changes in the foreign language classroom, both new and experienced teachers are discovering the need to close the ever-widening gap between their preservice preparation and their present teaching situation. Feldman (13) sees in-service education as the vehicle for dealing with this dilemma. Cloos (10) cites a variety of agencies that seem to be responding to this challenge. It appears, according to Cloos' report, that the most successful programs are based *in-school*. That is, the course or training program is given in the actual schools where the teachers are employed. Teachers feel that such programs are well suited to their individual needs. This does not obviate the need for national (professional organizations), state (Departments of Education), and institutional (college and university participation. If anything, it is an inviting challenge for these agents to supply the impetus, finances, and talent that are needed to insure quality programs (Hancock and De Lorenzo, 18). Extensive teacher involvement in the planning and implementation of the program might well help to avoid problems (Turner, 33). When teachers assume the student role, they tend to behave accordingly. They often resent central planning, irrelevant topics, and encroachment on their personal time. The opportunity to allow "professionals" to be masters of their own education can only enhance the *self-esteem* the profession so urgently needs.

Are four years enough?

Perennial task

Need for in-service programs

Need for participant input

Teacher training programs: Models for innovative strategies

Toffler (32) warns us that in our rapid approach toward the future "one of our most critical sub-systems—education—is dangerously malfunctioning" (p. 398). This appears to be an equally fair assess-

Teacher education programs

370

ment when applied to the area of teacher preparation. The rapid changes in our dynamic society have prompted unprecedented changes in the nature of public education (e.g., individualized instruction, programmed instruction, humanized teaching, small- and large-group instruction, schools without walls, community-centered programs, and other such innovations). Efficient implementation and management of these innovative programs and concepts demand an equally dynamic and innovative supportive staff. Obviously this staff must receive appropriate and effective training in meeting the needs of innovative programs in the public schools. The question posed here is, "what type of practical training is the new teacher receiving to prepare him for these nontraditional programs?" Unfortunately, the most frequent response to this inquiry has been, "very little." All too often, the very nature of their training experience has rendered them obsolete before they begin to teach. Given traditional teacher preparation, is it any wonder that a prospective teacher, when afforded an opportunity to student teach in the school of his choice, invariably opts for one that operates in an equally traditional fashion (lockstep, 45- to 50-minute bell schedule, assigned seats, etc.). As a beginning teacher he becomes a force for maintaining the status quo.

Need for relevant training

Perpetuating obsolescence

Those who are responsible for designing and implementing professional courses and experiences for specific areas must be completely aware of the training needs of their clientele. This awareness may be achieved by keeping abreast of new developments in the public school curriculum and perusing professional literature from both within and *outside* the specific area (Freilich, 14).

Course instructors who are truly concerned with providing relevant training for prospective or in-service teachers must insure that their courses are exemplars of the very techniques and philosophy that they espouse. Teacher trainers would do well here to ask themselves:

Need for exemplary programs

1　How often do I allow my students to complete tasks independent of the structured classroom situation?
2　What percentage of my course syllabus is a direct result of student input?
3　How many opportunities do I allow my students to demonstrate an adequate mastery of information and teaching skills?
4　How often do I afford my students the opportunity to observe and participate in *real* teaching situations?
5　How frequently do I advise my trainees to seek out related courses in other disciplines or other departments (e.g., music, art, history, sociology, anthropology, linguistics, etc.)?

371

6 To what degree do I make an effort to become acquainted with my students on a personal basis outside the classroom situation?

The degree to which a teacher educator employs practices such as those mentioned above may determine the degree to which the prospective teacher will individualize learning in his own classes, involve students in curriculum planning, promote interdisciplinary studies, encourage students to realize their full potential in the academic setting, and take a personal interest in the aspirations (both immediate and long-range) of each individual in his class and utilize other such seemingly desirable approaches.

Teacher educators are often reminded of, but invariably ignore, the fact that students of teaching tend to teach as they were taught. When speaking about the need for teacher trainers to promote instructional innovations, Cheek (9) notes that "we must begin by recognizing that teachers employ in their own methods the styles and procedures which were influential in their [the teachers'] development" (p. 13). Therefore, it is totally logical to assume that until teacher trainers start "practicing what they preach," today's trainees will continue to take to tomorrow's schools, yesterday's ideas.

As they were taught

Summary

Achievement and maintenance of high quality, relevant teacher education are two of the foreign language teaching profession's most pressing problems. The preceding discussion has attempted to identify several responsibilities which the profession must assume in order to deal with these two problems. Succinctly stated they are: improving the esteem for the profession (both extra- and intra-profession), identifying professional commitment, controlling admission to teacher education programs, post-admission monitoring, commitment to professional growth and improvement, and developing exemplary teacher training programs.

Numerous related suggestions for meeting these responsibilities are proposed and are synthesized here for the reader's consideration.

1 Enhance the profession's public image by conducting: a language exposition which features student-made projects; a foreign language student-participation day which includes poetry declamation, skits, dances, music, etc.; an international banquet; a foreign language visitation night, day, or week, and other pertinent activities.

2 Encourage self-judgment concerning commitment by developing and implementing well-coordinated courses or tasks that require frequent, early exposure to the "real world" of teaching (supervised observations, tutoring, teacher aide, "shadowing"—close observation of selected teachers and administrators, work in summer camps, and community recreation centers.

3 Preserve high standards for entry into teacher education programs by careful pre-entrance screening (personal interviews, letters of support from previous instructors, employers, and other qualified persons, and a proficiency test [if available] in the content area).

4 Maintain consistent, acceptable quality in teacher training programs by developing and implementing a Performance- (Competency-) Based Teacher Education Program (PBTE).

5 Demonstrate a commitment to professional growth and improvement by supporting enthusiastically in-service programs that occur in teachers' "home" schools or teaching districts and involve extensive *participant* planning.

6 Demonstrate a sincere commitment to change and innovation by promoting professional teacher training programs which are exemplars of innovative strategies (flexible, individualized, humanized, performance-based, interdisciplinary, etc.).

References, Quality and relevance in teacher education

1 Allen, Dwight W., and Glenn W. Hawkes. "Reconstruction of Teacher Education and Professional Growth Programs or How the Third Little Pig Escaped The Wolf." *Phi Delta Kappan* 52(1970): 4–13.

2 Andrews, L.O. "A Curriculum to Produce Career Teachers for the 1980's." *Theory Into Practice* 6(1967):236–45.

3 ——— *Challenges and Needed Developments in Teacher Education.* M-STEP Monograph No.7. Baltimore: Multi-State Teacher Education Project, no date.

4 ——— Personal communication, 1970. [Class lectures.]

5 Banathy, Bela H. "The Design of Foreign Language Teacher Education." *The Modern Language Journal* 52(1968):490–500.

6 ——— and Dale L. Lange. *A Design for Foreign Language Curriculum.* Lexington, Massachusetts: D.C. Heath, 1972.

7 Bartley, Diana E., and Robert L. Politzer. *Practice-Centered Teacher Training: Standard English For Speakers of Nonstandard Dialects.* Philadelphia: The Center for Curriculum Development, 1972.

8 ——— and Robert L. Politzer. *Practice-Centered Teacher Training: Spanish.* Philadelphia: The Center For Curriculum Development, 1967.

9 Cheek, King V. "Challenge and Innovation in Teacher Education," 12–23 in Frank H. Klassen and John L. Collier,eds., *Innovation Now! International Perspectives on Innovation in Teacher Education.* Washington, D.C.: International Council on Education for Teaching, 1972.

10 Cloos, Robert I. "In-Service Programs in Foreign Languages at Elementary and Secondary Levels," 247–77 in Dale L. Lange,ed., *Pluralism in Foreign Language Education*. ACTFL Review of Foreign Language Education, Volume 3. Skokie, Illinois: National Textbook Company, 1972.

11 De Lorenzo, William E. "Rationale, Description, and Feasibility of A Partially Programmed Foreign Language Methods Course." *Foreign Language Annals*. [In press.]

12 Dickson, G.E. "Reform in Teacher Education Through Developing Performance- (Competency) Based Teacher Education Programs," 50–60 in Frank H. Klassen and John L. Collier,eds., *Innovation Now! International Perspectives on Innovation in Teacher Education*. Washington, D.C.: International Council In Education for Teaching, 1972.

13 Feldman, David M.,ed. "In-Service Training," 478–83 in Eberhard Reichmann,ed., *The Teaching of German: Problems and Methods*. Philadelphia: National Carl Schurz Association, 1970.

14 Freilich, Joan S. [Personal communication, 1973.] [Working Committee I report on self-service teacher training to appear in *Northeast Conference Reports*, 1974.]

15 Getz, Howard, et al. "From Traditional to Competency-Based Teacher Education." *Phi Delta Kappan* 54(1973):300–02.

16 Graybeal, William S. "Teacher Surplus and Teacher Shortage." *Phi Delta Kappan* 53(1971): 82–85.

17 Hancock, Charles R. "Guiding Teachers to Respond to Individual Differences in the Affective Domain." *Foreign Language Annals* 6(1972):225–31.

18 ———and William E. De Lorenzo. [Working Committee I report on pre-service teacher training to appear in *Northeast Conference Reports*, 1974.]

19 Houston, Robert W. *Strategies and Resources for Developing A Competency-Based Teacher Education Program*. New York: New York State Education Department and Multi-State Consortium on Performance-Based Teacher Education, 1972.

20 Jackson, Philip W. "Old Dogs and New Tricks: Observations on the Continuing Education of Teachers," 19–36 in Louis J. Rubin,ed., *Improving In-Service Education: Proposals and Procedures for Change*. Boston: Allyn and Bacon, 1972.

21 Jarvis, Gilbert A. "Teacher Education Goals: They're Tearing Up the Street Where I Was Born." *Foreign Language Annals* 6(1972):198–205.

22 Macías, Leo. *The Use of Simulation in Foreign Language Teacher Education in Activities—Specific Teaching Situations*. Columbus, Ohio: The Ohio State University, 1972. [Unpublished Doctoral Dissertation.]

23 McArdle, Richard J. "Training Language Teachers —A Systems Approach." *Foreign Language Annals* 4(1971):293–98.

24 Meyerson, Jeffrey, and C. Edward Scebold. "Foreign Language Offerings and Enrollments in Public Secondary Schools, Fall 1970." [EDRS, forthcoming.]

25 Politzer, Robert L. *Practice-Centered Teacher Training: French*. Philadelphia: The Center For Curriculum Development, 1967.

26 ——— "Toward a Practice-Centered Program for the Training and Evaluation of Foreign Language Teachers." *The Modern Language Journal* 50(1966): 251–55.

27 Powers, James R., et al. "Professional Responsibilities," 26–29 in James Dodge,ed., *Leadership for Continuing Development*. [Reports of the Working Committees of the Northeast Conference on the Teaching of Foreign Languages.] New York: Modern Language Association Materials Center, 1971.

28 Prince, Robert, and Robert Williams. "Teacher Surplus Rises To 100,000 a Year." *The Washington Post* (7 December 1972):K1,K7.

29 Smith, B. Othanel, Saul B. Cohen, and Arthur Pearl. *Teachers for the Real World*. Washington, D.C.: The American Association of Colleges for Teacher Education, 1969.

30 Stinnet, T.M. "Reordering Goals and Roles: An Introduction." *Phi Delta Kappan* 52(1970):1–3.

31 Swecker, Dale A. "Educational Job Market 'Gorged,' Teacher Surplus Seen by 1980." *Towerlight* (2 March 1973):1.

32 Toffler, Alvin. *Future Shock*. New York: Random House, 1970.

33 Turner, Harold E. "Improved In-Service: A Challenge for Supervisors." *Clearing House* 45(1970): 116–19.

34 Twaddell, W. Freeman. "Meditations About Us." *Bulletin of the Association of Departments of Foreign Languages* 4,i(1972):9–13.

35 Warriner, Helen P. *The Teacher as Quality Control: Program Options*. [Speech given at 1973 Central State Conference on the Teaching of Foreign Languages, Minneapolis, April 1973.]

36 Wolfe, David E. "The Direct Experiences of Microteaching and Team Teaching in FL Teacher Education." *Foreign Language Annals* 5(1971):226–34.

12

The future of professional associations

Introduction

The attributives that come to mind in describing our profession today tend toward the negative side of the thesaurus. We seem to be embattled, aggrieved, confused, more than a little paranoid. We are declining, unloved, and underemployed. In a profession whose normal state is a feeling of insecurity this represents an unwelcome extension of occupational hazard (Ryder, 8).

C. Edward Scebold

*Executive Secretary, American
Council on the Teaching of
Foreign Languages*

This statement clearly characterizes our current misgivings about ourselves and the state of our profession; indeed, it provides a commentary on contemporary society. The heretofore seldom used words *crisis* and *shock* have become commonplace, and the quiet acquiesence of former days has too often been replaced by panic when we see budgets reduced and programs eliminated as enrollments decrease.

Even a cursory examination of the history of foreign language education bears out the fact that the profession has faded or flourished in direct response to outside influences. Foreign language education has never quite succeeded in establishing itself as a vital component of school curricula, and it is still referred to as a "frill" by many who exert direct influence on the curricula of our schools and colleges. B. Frank Brown (4), Chairman, National Commission on the Reform of Secondary Education, in a letter to the ACTFL Executive Secretary dated 27 March 1973, stated, "One peculiar problem which we are having is that foreign language is an elitist subject and we should be interested in any innovative programs which involve the general population." Such is the image conveyed by the foreign language teaching profession to our colleagues in education and to the public in general.

Foreign Languages in the total curriculum

How others see us

C. Edward Scebold (M.A., University of Nebraska) is Executive Secretary of the American Council on the Teaching of Foreign Languages. Prior to assuming this position he taught Spanish on both the junior high school and university levels. He has also served as Consultant in Foreign Languages in the Nebraska State Department of Education. His professional affiliations include AATF, AATSP, the New York State Association of Foreign Language Teachers, and the Association for Supervision and Curriculum Development.

The future of professional associations/Scebold

Professional education associations have been challenged, as have other areas of the educational establishment, in the past decade. The National Education Association (NEA) quite suddenly found itself involved in teacher negotiations. The once nebulous distinction between teacher and administrator in professional circles has been clarified and the battle lines have been drawn. Similarly, groups such as the Modern Language Association of America (MLA) and the American Historical Association have faced the challenge of dissidents among their memberships who have demanded that associations take a stand on matters such as the Vietnam War, minority problems, and other social action concerns that have not in the past evoked such intense feeling.

Changing role of professional associations

Regardless of what else may be said of these "stirrings" and the new awareness of the world outside education, it is not difficult to discern that the ranks of the membership in professional associations are demanding that the passive role assumed during past decades be replaced by a new, vigorously active role that promotes the discipline through improving teaching and through creating in more overt ways a positive public image.

In a brochure describing the services of the American Association of Teachers of Spanish and Portuguese (AATSP), the following statement of purpose appears:

Your national professional organization—

Traditional role of professional associations

> Was founded in 1917 in New York for the purpose of fostering the study of the Spanish language and literature throughout the United States by the promotion of friendly relations among its members, by the publication of articles, by the presentation and discussion of papers at annual meetings, and by such other means as may tend to promote the efficiency of its members (10).

The brochure enumerates other services of the association, including: *Hispania*, the official publication of the association, bronze and silver medals of the association (awards for outstanding students in Spanish), placement bureau (for AATSP members only), Sociedad Honoraria Hispánica (for secondary schools), National Spanish Contest (for secondary schools), Officina Nacional de Correspondencia Escolar, and consulting on pedagogical matters.

The statement and services of the association are significant, not for their unique quality, but because they represent the general nature of what foreign language professional associations have considered to be their role, whether identified as local, state, regional, or national in scope.

In considering the role they felt the American Council on the Teaching of Foreign Languages (ACTFL) should serve, The Puget Sound Coordinators (Washington State) made several recommendations regarding "Where ACTFL Is and Where It Must Go:"

A view of the role for ACTFL

The foreign language profession needs and must have a very strong national organization. This is really the only way to solve some of the problems that have surrounded us in recent years. A strong organization means members—many more than we now have, and we simply must make it attractive enough to all concerned so that it will be unthinkable for any foreign language teacher to resist joining.

In addition to the functions which any professional organization carries out, there are special needs which must also be attended to. In the case of foreign language the special need during recent years has been to change attitudes toward language study within the educational community as well as within the general public. Unless we can pull ourselves higher up on the priority scale, we shall always be subject to the cyclical aberrations that have been our lot.

ACTFL must become far more responsive to national currents and anticipate them rather than reacting defensively after they have gathered strength. For example, all projects should have been subordinated to the effort to promote language study during recent times of low acceptance. Public relations activities should have been at their highest peak to combat the trends brought on by such events as the Vietnam war—or the reaction to it—the recurrent tendency of our nation to isolate ourselves from the rest of the world, and the general disillusionment with our involvement with "foreigners." Our organization must be prepared to drop everything when it is clearly necessary in order to concentrate on building the kind of emotional support system which the profession must have (Crosbie, 5).

It is significant that these thought-provoking comments conclude with this sentence: "We are willing to help."

If, indeed, there are those involved in foreign language education who share such feelings and motivation, why has so little been accomplished by the profession? Why are foreign languages in such a precarious position? Why does the profession continue to rise and fall with the whims of public opinion and government funding priorities?

Belief in the concept of a strong national foreign language association

History of national efforts

dates to 1916 when the National Federation of Modern Language Teachers Associations (NFMLTA) was founded. Yet, in that dream lay only the frustration of attempting to provide a forum for numerous regional and national organizations, each with its own distinct membership or constituency, its own range of services, and its own sense of personal identity. Somehow, the evasive sense of a "profession" of teachers with common interests and concerns never managed to emerge and create a cohesive community of language teachers, then estimated to approach a potential 100,000 members/subscribers. At present, the only remaining vestige of this once bright hope is a single project—the publication of *The Modern Language Journal*, to which there are currently approximately 8,700 subscribers.

In creating ACTFL, the founders sought to avoid the pitfalls that had beset NFMLTA. First, ACTFL is an individual membership organization rather than a federation of individual membership organizations and regional conferences. State associations, the Constituents of ACTFL, serve as the grass-roots contact with the membership, and the Affiliate Assembly provides a forum for the regional and national groups. ACTFL has the advantage of a full-time headquarters staff; and association business is conducted by the Executive Secretary, Treasurer, and an Executive Council which functions as the Board of Directors. At present, headquarters staff totals seven, excluding the Treasurer; several MLA offices also provide supporting services to ACTFL.

Nature of ACTFL

Through this structure ACTFL has been able to provide its membership with innovative programs unlike those provided by any of its predecessors. The list of activities has included:

Innovative programs of ACTFL

1 An Annual Meeting offering a vast variety of activities and presentations
2 Pre-conference Workshops in conjunction with the Annual Meeting (often including Proceedings of the Workshops)
3 State workshops in cooperation with the ACTFL Constituent organizations
4 A complete and growing Annual Bibliography on pedagogy
5 An annual edition of the *Review of Foreign Language Education* Series, which provides information on the latest in research as well as practical information on programs in action
6 Occasional publications of importance, through cooperation with the MLA Publications Center, such as the Michigan Oral Language Series
7 Complete information services, Focus Reports, and additional

publications, such as the *Leadership in Foreign Language Education Series*, in cooperation with the ERIC Clearinghouse on Languages and Linguistics

8 A bulletin, *Accent on ACTFL*, published four times each year, which provides practical information for the teacher in the classroom, as well as association news

9 An experimental study abroad program for high school students, innovative in concept and structure, accompanied by careful evaluation and reporting procedures

Other special projects of significance have been organized or co-sponsored by ACTFL during its first six years:

Special projects of ACTFL

1 *Early Childhood Bilingual Education*, by Vera P. John and Vivian M. Horner, with the cooperation and assistance of the Ford Foundation and MLA

2 Periodic surveys of public secondary school enrollments in foreign languages, under contract with the U.S. Office of Education and in cooperation with MLA

3 Seminars for state supervisors of foreign languages, under contract with the U.S. Office of Education and in cooperation with MLA

4 A national survey of innovative foreign language programs at the secondary level, in cooperation with the Far West Laboratory for Educational Research and Development, to be published in the fall of 1973 as *Options and Perspectives: A Sourcebook of Innovative Foreign Language Programs in Action, K-12* by MLA.

These projects have been provided in addition to the usual range of services offered by other foreign language associations (or have altered the concept significantly), such as a national meeting, an official journal, and information services. Still, certain services can be uniquely provided by the particular language associations.

As one examines the list of services provided by ACTFL, one finds it difficult to imagine that after six years of existence, the membership and subscriptions total only approximately 10,000. (Foreign and domestic membership is 8,384; foreign and domestic subscriptions are 1,541.) Recognition of the proliferation of groups, even within one language area, somewhat eases this disappointment. Within the American Association of Teachers of French (AATF), for example, there are local chapters, state chapters, regional chapters, and the national organization. The several other AAT groups have similar structures. Thus, the problem, insofar as it involves a group of individuals with a wide variety of specialized interests teaching at differ-

Approximate membership

Proliferation of groups

379

ent grade levels, is vastly more complicated than in most other curriculum areas because of the existence of a large number of autonomous, well-established state, regional, and national associations among which members of the profession divide their allegiance and support. A college instructor of French in the state of Connecticut, for example, might be expected to participate in the state and national activities of the American Association of Teachers of French (in time or under certain conditions also the Association des Professeurs Franco-Américains or the Société des Professeurs Français en Amérique), the Connecticut Council of Language Teachers, the New England Foreign Language Association, the Modern Language Association of America, the Northeast Modern Language Association, and the American Council on the Teaching of Foreign Languages. His department will very likely belong to the Association of Departments of Foreign Languages, and if he has interest in linguistics or in teaching English to French speakers, he might also want to join the Linguistic Society of America and the Teachers of English to Speakers of Other Languages—all of these organizations collecting dues, disseminating publications, and holding annual (and sometimes local chapter) meetings. Finally, he may choose to participate in the annual Northeast Conference on the Teaching of Foreign Languages, which is not an individual membership organization. Not all—very likely not any—French teachers in a given state belong to even half of the available associations, and probably a good many language teachers throughout the country do not belong to any association at all. With the exception of ACTFL, none of the individual membership organizations provides a national perspective that encompasses *all* languages at *all* levels of education. Language teachers today, therefore, tend to think of themselves as a part of the "profession" of teachers of a specific language, at a particular grade level, or within a particular state or region or district, but not as a part of a foreign language "profession" that has national identity and thus significant aggregate influence that can shape public opinion.

Where teachers identify

This pattern results in layer upon layer of organizational structure and, inevitably, the duplication of activities. Of even greater importance, it leads to parochialism and jealousy between groups because of the competition for members and the competition of simultaneous activities. Finally, this splintering and fragmentation renders impossible any professional control of crucial areas such as teacher education and certification programs. Consequently, the day when ACTFL, or any other national organization, will be in a position to "represent" truly the interests of the profession on a national scale seems

Duplication of effort

Parochialism and jealousy

Lack of "clout"

remote indeed. And so we proceed, willy-nilly, without common purpose, doing and undoing, seldom fully aware of the needs of the total foreign language community.

From the very inception of ACTFL, many associated with other national foreign language groups considered ACTFL a threat to their particular turf. Written communications exist between members and officers of these groups in which the concern is expressed that ACTFL might undermine their efforts. Members would be drawn away, services would be assumed, and so forth. Their worst fears have not materialized. As ACTFL has established itself, membership has grown in each of the three largest AAT groups—American Association of Teachers of French (AATF), American Association of Teachers of German (AATG), and American Association of Teachers of Spanish and Portuguese (AATSP). Yet, despite the continued growth of these groups, personal and professional animosities have continued to flourish; for the most part, tensions have lessened only because of the passage of time. As late as 1971 joint planning was undertaken on the national level by the five largest AAT groups—AATF, AATG, American Association of Teachers of Italian (AATI), American Association of Teachers of Slavic and East European Languages (AATSEEL), and AATSP—exclusive of ACTFL when, in fact, the nature of the activities being planned coincided directly with the purposes for which ACTFL had been created four years earlier.

Protecting turf

Growth of AATs

In March 1971 representatives of these five groups met in Chicago to plan new joint national efforts. As a result of this meeting, the National Committee for the Support of Foreign Languages was formed, consisting of the editors of the journals of each association represented at the meeting. Representatives of companies publishing foreign language materials were also involved at the early stages.

An AAT effort

At this same time ACTFL was planning a meeting of representatives of the ACTFL Affiliate organizations for the fall of 1971. As planning for the meeting and the invitation of participants proceeded, ACTFL was requested to provide a separate meeting with the members of the five AAT groups, tentatively called the Joint Committee of AATs. ACTFL complied with the request, and a special meeting was held on 30 September 1971 with the Joint Committee of AATs and representatives of ACTFL; on 1–2 October 1971 the meeting expanded to include the Executive Secretaries (or similar officials) of all ACTFL Affiliate organizations originally invited.

The following statement was agreed upon by those attending the

381

30 September meeting (AATF, AATG, AATI, AATSEEL, AATSP, and ACTFL):

Meeting Of The Joint Committee of AATs
and the Representatives of ACTFL
30 September 1971

It is the sense of the meeting between the Joint Committee of AATs and the Representatives of ACTFL that there will be continued and increased cooperation and coordination between the AATs and ACTFL for the benefit of foreign language teaching. *A call for cooperation* Specifically it was agreed to:

1 Invite ACTFL to participate in the National Committee for the Support of Foreign Language Study
2 Explore cooperation in planning of national meetings as to the dates and locations
3 Explore consultations in regard to the themes and programs of ACTFL meetings
4 Explore possible cooperation in the publications program
5 Explore cooperation in the evaluation of overseas programs

It is specifically agreed that the Joint Committee of AATs and the representatives of ACTFL will meet on 30 December 1971 in Chicago at which time the progress of the above points will be discussed (Scebold, 9).

It was, therefore, through steps taken by ACTFL that ACTFL's participation in the National Committee for the Support of Foreign Language Study began and ultimately, in September 1972, that The Joint National Committee for Languages (TJNCL) emerged and *The Joint National* included ACTFL as an integral part of its structure. The "manifesto" *Committee for Languages* drawn up at the September meeting outlined the structure:

The National Officers of AATF, AATG, AATI, AATSEEL, AATSP, and ACTFL, mindful of the importance of foreign languages in our society and of the pressing need for close collaboration between the various language associations, hereby announce the establishment of a permanent joint committee which shall meet at least twice a year, composed of a maximum of three representatives of each association, who shall be: the President, the Executive Secretary (or Secretary-Treasurer), and one other to be designated by the association. ACTFL, because of its structure, shall have the option of appointing two delegates to represent other language groups.

The Joint National Committee shall have as its main purpose the implementation of a continuing movement in favor of learning foreign languages in the United States, as well as the sponsorship of special projects to improve and enhance the teaching of these languages (2).

Growing out of this new structure, two Task Forces have been appointed to launch special pilot projects at both the state and national levels to accomplish the objectives of the Committee and provide workable ideas for implementation on a national basis, should funding become available for such a program.

The present membership of the Committee includes those groups that were responsible for the "manifesto" and two additional representatives, one person representing both the American Classical League and the American Philological Association and one person representing Teachers of English to Speakers of Other Languages.

The reorganization of the Joint Committee of AATs into The Joint National Committee for Languages was accompanied during 1972 by an MLA-initiated project to begin planning for the national foreign language needs of the country during the next decade. Responding to a need expressed by a number of active leaders of the foreign language teaching profession, a steering committee was appointed by the MLA Executive Council; during the 1972–73 school year that committee, supported by funds from the U.S. Office of Education, met on four occasions at MLA Headquarters and drafted the outline of "A National Foreign Language Program for the 1970's" (1). The com- *A master plan for the profession* mittee, which included members of diverse organizational and institutional components of the profession and which worked in conjunction with the American Council on the Teaching of Foreign Languages, conceived the program not as a self-contained project to be directed by the MLA or by ACTFL, but as a master plan for a concerted effort on the part of all interested persons, organizations, and institutions. The program as such is therefore not the property of the MLA or of any single organization, for the tasks outlined in it demand the participation and good will of all the available human and institutional resources.

As a result of four meetings over nine months, a draft document was prepared outlining a national program of action concerned with a revitalized language effort; the burden for carrying out this multi- level, many-faceted program must be shared by all individuals, *Shared effort needed* associations, and institutions concerned with the need for a revitalized language effort.

In the section of the document entitled "An Outline for Action" suggestions are made as to the kinds of programs that individuals, institutions, and professional associations must begin to develop, with possible foundation support of some programs. The "program" as such is simply a means for unifying—and providing visibility for—a national effort on the part of the entire profession. The areas discussed are:

Public awareness
Professional awareness and coordination
The classroom
Beyond the classroom
Bilingual education
The less commonly taught languages
Quality control and national standards

In July 1973, the draft document has been forwarded to the National Endowment for the Humanities (NEH), and it has been circulated among members of The Joint National Committee for Languages. Based on the interest expressed by NEH, specific proposals will be prepared and submitted to NEH for consideration for funding. Funding will also be sought from private foundations and from the U.S. Office of Education, should the final budget for 1973–74 provide funds through the Institute for International Studies. (Approval of U.S. Office of Education budgets is, at this time, still pending in Congress.)

Following discussion of the MLA-proposed Program at the 11–12 May 1973 meeting of TJNCL, the Committee unanimously approved a motion stating that a declaration of intention will be communicated to MLA indicating that the Committee plans to submit to the NEH a project proposal in line with the general ideas presented in the foreign language program document.

The apparent emergence of a new spirit of cooperation can be viewed optimistically. However, TJNCL is not constituted to be an action-oriented body. And action is what is needed. More must be done to influence *both* the leaders and the rank and file of the various organizations. Ways must be found to begin national cooperation on action-oriented programs, programs that transcend the boundaries of parochial concerns and individual identity. Only in this way will we begin to make of these groups some kind of unified profession.

Spirit of cooperation versus action

A resolution adopted at the 1–3 May 1973 meeting of the Pacific Northwest Conference on Foreign Languages reemphasizes the concern for cooperation at the national level in dealing with the problems and challenges which face the profession. The resolution begins:

> The Pacific Northwest Conference on Foreign Languages (PNCFL) welcomes the evidence of increased communication between national professional foreign language teacher organizations. The PNCFL is, however, convinced that the time has come to move from talk to action; the PNCFL maintains that *now* is the time to implement a unified professional structure.
>
> The goals of a unified professional structure would include, but not be limited to, the following concepts:
> 1 Vigorous public promotion of foreign language study
> 2 Sensitivity to varying local needs and joint cooperation in meeting these needs
> 3 Resolute opposition to all attempts to weaken education by groups and individuals who attack foreign language programs, for whatever reason
> 4 Articulation of the operations of the various foreign language organizations, specifically in the following areas:
>   a Joint annual meetings
>   b Cooperative professional publications
>   c Establishments of regional multi-level job information centers
>   d Coordinated collection of dues (Reinert, 7)

The resolution concludes by outlining areas in which PNCFL resolves to initiate action and urging that "the national organizations concerned with foreign language teaching. . .move with all deliberate speed to implement the goals outlined above."

Both the ACTFL and AATG Executive Secretaries attended the meeting and reported on the discussions leading up to the resolution adopted by PNCFL. Subsequently they expressed strong support of *Support for resolution* the sentiment reflected in the resolution, during the 11–12 May 1973 meeting of TJNCL. Although no action was taken on the resolution, the Committee expressed its interest in discussing and evaluating the ideas presented.

As these attempts at joint national efforts begin, another chapter is being written about the relationship of the National Federation of Modern Language Teachers Associations and ACTFL. Lengthy discussions and communications between the organizers of ACTFL and the officers of NFMLTA ensued during the months of planning for the creation of ACTFL in 1966–67. In essence, MLA was urging that NFMLTA join MLA to co-found ACTFL and establish *The Modern Language Journal* as the official journal of the newly created association. These discussions and negotiations broke down in early 1967; as a result, *Foreign Language Annals* was created as the official ACTFL journal, and discussions with NFMLTA ceased.

During recent months discussions into the possible merger of NFMLTA and ACTFL have resumed. At present, a proposal outlining possible merger, drafted by the 1973 President of NFMLTA and approved by the ACTFL Executive Council, is being circulated among the member organizations of NFMLTA. Final disposition of the matter is yet to be determined. Should the proposed merger become a reality, certain modifications in the ACTFL structure would be undertaken, and *The Modern Language Journal* and *Foreign Language Annals* would be merged into a single journal beginning in January 1975. The outcome is awaited—anxiously. *Forthcoming merger?*

As these efforts to "unify" the profession at the national level continue, efforts are being made to consolidate other activities. For the first time, AATF and AATSP will meet with ACTFL in Denver, November 1974, for a joint annual meeting. Of greatest interest is the potential that exists for a regular pattern of joint meetings by the national associations every two or three years. Through such cooperation, already limited travel funds could be stretched, and a greater awareness of problems and concerns—across languages—could be created. *Cooperative progress*

Discussion of the possibility of initiating a national newsletter, supported by TJNCL, to be sent to every foreign language teacher in the country, continues. Following the presentation of this idea to TJNCL by the Executive Secretary of AATG, steps are being taken to determine the possibility of formulating a mailing list of all foreign language teachers at all levels. Final action on the proposal will be taken during the fall of 1973. *A national newsletter?*

In addition to the projects proposed in "A National Foreign Language Program for the 1970s," numerous possibilities for cooperation at the national level have, from time to time, been proposed and discussed, particularly as they relate to the AATs. One idea of particularly great potential is that of expansion, to language groups other than German, of two projects of The National Carl Schurz Association. The first is the publication of *Rundschau*, a monthly newsprint review, published September through May. The purpose of the publication is ". . .to provide for the student of German language in *Expanding projects* the United States, a report of activities in German-speaking areas as seen from an American point of view." *Rundschau* is distributed to all members of NCSA and members of the National Federation of Students of German as the official publication of the organization.

The National Federation of Students of German (NFSG) is the second project that has been suggested for duplication by the AATs. NFSG was established in 1970 to create regional federations of German clubs at the high school level by fostering student leadership on the national level and by coordinating national student meetings. Current membership totals approximately 15,000.

These projects have had significant impact on the study of German and could have similar impact on other language areas. Exploration should also continue into the possibility of joint publication activities that would reach into areas other than the national newsletter proposed by TJNCL. Cooperation in the preparation and publication of bibliographies on literature and materials and the cross-development of the committee structures of the various organizations must also be explored, in the interests of economy and of better communication among professional groups at the national level.

Benefits of cooperation

An area of greater consequence is the relationship between national associations and teacher training agencies. As an example, during the summer of 1973 ACTFL co-sponsored with the University of Minnesota a program of In-service Cultural Classroom Materials Work-Ins abroad for teachers of French, German, and Spanish. Based on two years of experimentation on a pilot basis at the University of Minnesota, these work-ins draw from the highly successful emphasis on bringing teachers together, under the guidance of specialists in foreign language education, to develop instructional materials that suit their own students and school situations. The objectives of the project were:

Associations and teacher education

University of Minnesota work-ins

1   To help teachers become aware of aspects of the foreign culture that appeal to students
2   To help teachers gain background in the contemporary life of the country whose language they are teaching
3   To provide opportunities for teachers to gather culturally authentic materials they can adapt for enrichment of classroom language study
4   To allow teachers freedom (but give enough guidance) to develop whatever kinds of instructional materials best suit their own students and school situation

Guidelines are now being developed by ACTFL to allow for the

387

extension of this kind of cooperation to other institutions, based upon the desire of the Executive Council of ACTFL to provide support and greater visibility for projects that are truly innovative and take a practical approach to meeting the needs of teachers in the classroom.

Similar cooperation with the educational regional laboratories must also be pursued. During 1971 ACTFL worked closely with the Far West Laboratory for Educational Research and Development in adapting a unit on Deriving Objectives for use with foreign language educators. The materials were subsequently used in a pilot workshop in Texas during the fall of 1971 and later for a Pre-conference workshop in Chicago in November of that same year. Equally significant potential awaits exploration, both with the continuing projects of the Far West Laboratory and other regional laboratories that have, in recent years, provided significant leadership in developing new approaches and materials for teacher training.

Associations and the educational regional laboratories

As these possibilities are explored, a national assessment of professional needs and a division of labor in developing programs and initiating research activities that address the problems must be undertaken. At present our leading graduate teacher-training institutions are caught up in the same forces that lead to parochialism and jealousy between professional groups because of competition for students. Steps must be taken that will make it possible for the directors of these programs to assess cooperatively the areas of competence and expertise of the staff of each program and the areas of research that, consequently, ought logically to be undertaken by candidates in each program. The alternative is the present manner of operation in which each institution tries to attract any and all qualified candidates and research is undertaken in areas outside the areas of specialization of the college or university staff.

Graduate programs

This planning by those involved in graduate teacher education should be linked to some form of national foreign language planning so that research and training can be related to our national foreign language needs and priorities over the coming decades. To date, this planning has not been undertaken.

In a document that is currently being prepared for distribution to selected U.S. Congressmen and persons in agencies of the Federal Government, it is suggested:

That Congress and the Administration support and encourage the funding of a major nationwide survey, the purpose of which

388

would be to determine the specific national needs for linguistic and cultural skills. Such a survey should draw information and data from all sectors of the economy and from the majority of U.S. companies engaged in international trade. The survey ought to be conducted jointly by the U.S. Office of Education, the U.S. Department of Commerce, and the major organizations representing the country's foreign language teachers, i.e., the American Council on the Teaching of Foreign Languages and the Modern Language Association of America (Hempel, 6).

Such a survey relates directly to the needs of the profession; however, what is suggested here in the way of national language planning must also touch directly on our needs in relation to the preparation of teachers, the vital link between students and the skilled graduate who has been trained to function in those positions in government, business, and industry that require knowledge of a second language and culture.

Teacher education

Only through comparable national cooperation and planning will we, as a profession, be in the position to develop sound performance-based criteria for graduation and certification.

Finally, as we confront these difficult and far-reaching problems, we must institute a joint effort to reach the undergraduate programs, that maze of institutions that graduate from one to 51 language teachers each semester, some well prepared and others only poorly qualified to face the challenge of the classroom. In addition to continuing to improve the language and culture skills of teachers, we must place greater emphasis on preparing them to deal with change. In short, they must have the professional competency, the flexibility and the adaptability—as reflected in their attitudes and self-confidence—to face change without being threatened.

So much for what might be. The fact remains that little has been accomplished by professional associations, alone or in combination with teacher education institutions, that has had any direct influence on public opinion and the growth of language teaching or that has directly affected the status of language instruction in relation to the total school curriculum.

Will ACTFL, an alternative to ACTFL, or a confederation of the present foreign language associations ever wield enough influence to have significant impact on school curriculum or on the public's awareness of the importance of language study? Is the possibility illusory? It is with cautious optimism, that we say, yes, there is reason for hope.

The significant questions for an association

The conditions that militate against the emergence of a strong national force for foreign languages are as simple as they are complex. *There is no profession.* There are, instead, many groups of language teachers whose loyalties are splintered and whose interests are specialized. Professional commitment is divided among all of these loyalties and interests; the result is total fragmentation.

Essence of the problem

A review of the developments within the profession since 1970 does, however, lead one to a certain degree of optimism. Our pseudo-profession seems to have matured during this trying period. The signs of this maturity are numerous; our responses to new realities are numerous as well as diverse. The fact is significant that many foreign language educators have shown the stamina, the resourcefulness, and the ingenuity to create the exceptions to what we see reflected by the national figures and trends. They provide the headlines that report doubled enrollments, declining attrition rates, new teacher-training sequences, and the preparation of public relations campaigns for foreign languages. Moreover, if we look carefully, we find that the same problems apply to social studies, mathematics, or music.

If we hope to consolidate these gains, we must begin to identify the concerns that tend to bind us together in a crisis. Once we recognize what it is that we share, we can begin to create a profession, in the true sense of the word.

Summary

1 Throughout this chapter, phrases such as "parochialism and jealousy" and "splintering and fragmentation" have been used to characterize our current dilemma. Our literature is replete with claims that the study of a foreign language should be required as a necessary part of a liberal education because: "Study of FLs guarantees against provincialism and parochialism which threaten a nation isolated from its neighbors" (Alter, 3, p. 13). Or:

> The decisive factor is that the very process of learning and assimilating a second language breaks up the conditioned patterns of the original language, undermines routine responses, teaches how to acquire new reflexes in meeting new structures. Encountering a second language, to a surprising extent, is similar to living in a period of accelerated transition: One must discard old habits and discover new ones in what at first appears as a chaotic mass of signs. Of course a second

language is no panacea and will not transform groping youth into infallible analysts of social change. But better perhaps than other disciplines, expressed in, and hence bound by, the language of the past, it can supply the youth with the flexibility and adaptability required for their bout with modern life (p. 19).

2 It is paradoxical that we as a profession seem unable to exemplify the broad-mindedness that the subject we teach is supposed to engender in our students. In the last analysis, our cautious optimism will be justified only if we succeed in applying this same breadth and flexibility to our professional interaction. The achievement of this kind of breadth is the ultimate criterion for judging the effectiveness of any collective professional activity. A professional association will succeed, therefore, only if it can provide the leadership and services that help the classroom teacher make foreign language learning the kind of experience we have claimed it to be.

References, The future of professional associations

1 *A National Foreign Language Program for the 1970's.* [Draft document prepared by the Steering Committee, MLA Foreign Language Program—1970's, 1973.] [Mimeo.]

2 "AAT's, ACTFL Launch Cooperative Plans As Joint National Committee." *Accent on ACTFL* 3,ii(1972):3–4.

3 Alter, Maria P. *A Modern Case For German.* Philadelphia: The American Association of Teachers of German, 1970.

4 Brown, B. Frank. [Personal Communication, 1973.]

5 Crosbie, Keith. [Personal Communication, 1972.]

6 Hempel, Valdemar. [Personal Communication, 1973.]

7 Reinert, Harry. [Personal Communication, 1973.]

8 Ryder, Frank. *Image.* [Paper prepared for Steering Committee, MLA Foreign Language Program—1970's, 1972.] [Mimeo.]

9 Scebold, C. Edward. "Report of the ACTFL Executive Secretary." *Foreign Language Annals* 5(1971):285.

10 *Todos a una.* The American Association of Teachers of Spanish and Portuguese. [Brochure.] [No date.]

Index to Persons Cited

Index to Persons Cited

Index to Persons Cited

Index to Persons Cited

Index to Topics and Institutions Cited

Index to Topics and Institutions Cited

Index to Topics and Institutions Cited

Index to Topics and Institutions Cited